Theories of the Democratic State

Theories of the Democratic State

John S. Dryzek
and
Patrick Dunleavy

First published 2009 by
PALGRAVE MACMILLAN

Palgrave Macmillan in the UK is an imprint of Macmillan Publishers Limited, registered in England, company number 785998, of Houndmills, Basingstoke, Hampshire RG21 6XS.

Palgrave Macmillan in the US is a division of St Martin's Press LLC, 175 Fifth Avenue, New York, NY 10010.

Palgrave Macmillan is the global academic imprint of the above companies and has companies and representatives throughout the world.

Palgrave® and Macmillan® are registered trademarks in the United States, the United Kingdom, Europe and other countries.

ISBN 978-0-230-54286-0 hardback

ISBN 978-0-230-54287-7   ISBN 978-0-230-36645-9 (eBook)
DOI 10.1007/978-0-230-36645-9

This book is printed on paper suitable for recycling and made from fully managed and sustained forest sources. Logging, pulping and manufacturing processes are expected to conform to the environmental regulations of the country of origin.

A catalogue record for this book is available from the British Library.

A catalog record for this book is available from the Library of Congress.

10 9 8 7 6 5 4 3 2 1
18 17 16 15 14 13 12 11 10 09

Contents

List of Figures and Tables

Figures

Tables

Preface

Political science arguments necessarily entail comparing alternative interpretations and reaching relational judgements. As Charles Darwin famously observed in a very different context: 'How odd it is that anyone should not see that all observation should be for or against some view if it is to be of any service' (quoted in Dunleavy 2003: 227). Yet for people used to the relatively homogenous viewpoints of the physical sciences, or even the hegemonic mainstream view found in economics, this diversity of approaches has always appeared frustrating. The physical science paradigm has been one of 'rapid discovery with high consensus behind the research front' according to the sociologist Randall Collins (1994), and yet this pattern has not extended to most social sciences. Collins believes that this reflects the lack of a technology that reliably produces streams of new results, which in his view is a 'fundamental disability' for the social sciences. We take a different stance in this book, celebrating the debates between theories of the state as a key motor for both political and intellectual progress. We seek to show first how important (if still limited) advances in understanding emerged out of the intense twentieth century intellectual conflicts around the state; and second, how current twenty-first century debates map out a space of possible future changes in how democracy works, at the level of both the nation state and the world as a whole.

For better or for worse the politics of almost the whole world is now organized into and by states. Understanding how they operate, at least under conditions of liberal democracy, provides a particular kind of introduction to political science – focusing on the kind of explanations that political scientists can give about the operations of the state, and the kinds of evaluations and prescriptions they offer in association with explanatory frameworks. Competing theories of the state structure underpin much of the most significant empirical work in modern political science, and we will try to give a real flavour of that work. Of course, there is now an important (if fragmented) school of thought that sees the modern state itself as an institutional form in decline because 'glocalization' pressures are fuelling the migration of authority away from the sovereign state, both upward (globalization) and downward (localization). But even this school of thought takes the state as its starting point. We shall have plenty to say about phenomena such as globalization and networked governance that do not necessarily coincide with national boundaries.

Intense competition and conflict between rival theories of the state is pervasive. Throughout almost all the twentieth century these theories were closely linked with broader ideological wars (and sometimes real wars) between liberal democrats, communists and fascists. Many of the key points at issue in these rancorous conflicts focused on the possibilities and limits of democratic control of politics, and how far the state can ever function autonomously from and perhaps remould the social forces that seek to influence it. For more than a century before the fall of Soviet communism in 1991, these ideological conflicts left a trail of human misery and destruction in their wake. But analyses that saw the 'end of history' and liberal democracy's victory in the Cold War turned out to be premature. New types of conflicts quickly erupted, billed by some as a 'clash of civilizations', by others as the fragmentation of all 'grand narratives', and by still others as a consequence of globalization and reactions against it. Authoritarian models of state organization that initially seemed on the back foot re-emerged with renewed confidence in Russia and in an economically resurgent China.

Primarily we cover the liberal democratic state in this book. Occasionally we glance at other sorts of states, notably illiberal democracies where elected governments rule with few restraints on their power and do not respect human rights, as well as outright autocracies. The concept of liberal democracy itself is deeply contested in ways that we explore. But it is sufficiently distinctive for the identification of qualifying countries to be mostly uncontroversial. In these places significant constitutional and legal protection are assigned to rights to life, reasonably free speech, and the ability for people to secure their own property and form their own life-plans. Political mobilization and (mostly) free discussion are acceptable, extending to substantial criticism of governments and rulers. Elections are held in which leaders can be replaced without destabilizing the political system, at least in principle if not always in practice.

Yet quite how the liberal democratic states *do* work, in practice rather than on paper, turns out to be a very contentious matter. There are many different patterns of state organization and equally divergent patterns of political mobilization and control by citizens. How the liberal democratic state *should* work is equally contentious. These two questions (*does* and *should*) refer respectively to explanatory and normative theories of the state. Though conceptually distinct, in practice explanatory and normative theories are intertwined. For example, market liberal theorists (discussed at length in Chapter 5) typically explain the state in terms of the rational actions of self-interested individuals and groups. Their normative theory concerns in large measure how best to curb the harmful effects of such behaviour, and how to channel it in ways that actually benefit society as a whole. Each normative theory generally has an explanatory theory that goes along with it. So although we cover both sorts of theory, we do not separate them out into different chapters.

The structure of the book is organized chiefly in four parts, with introductory and concluding chapters. Chapter 1 discusses some significant arguments about how to identify and define the liberal democratic state and gives a synopsis of its rise to contemporary significance. Part I presents four chapters on the classical theories of the state, established in a period from the nineteenth century to the 1950s, from which more contemporary theories and critiques jump off in new directions. These four classical theories – pluralism, elite theory, Marxism, and market liberalism – once constituted the universe of theories of the state. Yet in recent decades each of the four has encountered major crises. Pluralism was shaken by the political turmoil of the late 1960s, and elite theory seemed to decay in the face of a variety of political forces. Marxism was dealt a heavy blow by the fall of the Berlin Wall in 1989 and the subsequent demise of the Soviet Union. Market liberalism's spectacular rise in the 1980s (especially under Ronald Reagan in the United States and Margaret Thatcher in the UK) has been followed by a slow but steady fall from grace. This accelerated in the context of the global financial crisis that began in the United States in 2007–2008 and spread quickly across other developed nations. Yet these classical theories have all managed an afterlife, and pluralism in particular has made a strong comeback to remain the central position in contemporary debates – if in a very modified form.

Part II begins our survey of contemporary positions by showing how pluralism has recovered, though sometimes at the cost of looking quite different from how it had appeared in the past. Chapter 6 examines the transformation of pluralism into a variety of theories that come to grips with new realities: the dominant power of business in existing pluralist systems as identified by neo-pluralists, the organization of groups into large coalitions, the development of governance networks that cut across formal political boundaries, and the existence of states that actively organize particular groups into government (while organizing other groups out). Pluralist authors insist that elections are still meaningful and perhaps central mechanisms for the transmission of public opinion to the state. Accordingly Chapter 7 examines the role of voters, parties, and elected legislatures in liberal democracies, especially in the light of challenges that call into question the competence of voters and impugn the meaningfulness of elections and legislative politics. We also pay attention to the consequences of different kinds of voting systems.

Assertions and denials of many different kinds of social identities are now central to contemporary politics, and how to manage identity politics provides additional challenges to pluralists. Chapter 8 looks especially at nationalisms that try to define the identity that should be associated with the state itself. It also addresses the destructive politics of identity that can accompany ethnic, religious, and national conflict within deeply divided societies – and what might be done about it.

Part III moves on to examine the most salient contemporary critiques of the liberal democratic state. Chapter 9 highlights the limited degree of democracy found in actually existing states, and looks at how pluralist theorists themselves have sought to deepen democracy through civic education, 'stakeholder grants' that give all citizens a financial stake in their society, or participatory and deliberative institutional innovations. Chapter 10 focuses on feminist critiques of a liberal state that still embodies male domination. Feminist theory offers both a substantial analysis of gender-biased political dynamics and some far-reaching reform proposals. Environmental theory, examined in Chapter 11, exposes and attacks the complicity of the liberal democratic state in ecological destruction and the political barriers to halting ecological degradation or tackling global collective action problems. Like feminism, environmentalism generates both a critique of the state and extensive proposals for its reform. Many substantial disagreements remain about the specific reforms required, and the range of solutions canvassed range from state centralization under ecological guidance to a decentralized ecological democracy.

Contemporary conservatives believe that environmentalists and feminists, as well as social democrats and liberal individualists have all had too much influence in the contemporary state, and with corrosive effects. Traditional conservatives (examined at the start of Chapter 12) seek to push-back rationalist reforms and to re-assert instead the values of community, tradition and religion, making democratic government more moralistic. Recently more radical and activist neo-conservatives in the US have tried a different approach. They are not afraid to turn both their own society and the wider world upside down in pursuit of ethical principles that would reverse the moral decay of the contemporary era.

Part IV looks beyond the state itself to wider arrangements, first considering (in Chapter 13) post-modern accounts of the world in which the state is embedded. Post-structuralists in particular try to demonstrate the way that power pervades society, of which the institutions of the state are just a part. Some post-modernists favour a radical pluralist politics of identity, of a kind that would reach far beyond the state. In Chapter 14 we move beyond the state in a different sense, considering the influences upon it of forces from the international system. Theorists of globalization stress the degree to which the state is being supplanted by international and global political and economic forces and institutions. However, the degree to which such processes actually diminish the role of states remains contentious. Finally, Chapter 15 presents a summary of the current state of play and considers some future prospects that may be dimly and fuzzily perceived in the coming years.

Throughout the book we ask some common questions of all the theories we cover. Especially with the classical theories, and with the later single chapters on critiques of liberal democracy, we examine the origins of the theory, and the historical forces and developments that engendered it. The core presuppositions of theories of the state involve assumptions about human nature, about the content of politics, or about what are the fundamental building blocks of political life (which might for example be individuals, groups, social classes, nations, or sexes). We examine how each theory pictures the relationships between society and politics, especially the influence of social and economic forces upon the state, and the way that state and society alike are constituted by common causes (such as ideologies, or economic changes). Third, most theories of the state have a great deal to say about the structure and operation of government itself and how policy making takes place. Finally, each theory generates an agenda of prescriptions concerning what should be done to the structure of government, the content of public policy, and the relationship of the state to society and other entities (such as ecosystems, or other states).

While these common questions inform the internal structure of most chapters, we often depart from the list of headings above for a number of reasons. Not all of the chapters present a complete and stand-alone theory of the state. The aspects of contemporary pluralism covered in Part II have origins that are fully covered in Chapter 2 on classical pluralism. Some theories (notably environmentalism, feminism, and neo-conservatism) do not have much in the way of detailed explanation of how government and policy making work – instead they offer mainly a critique of current state organization and practice. Some chapter topics, notably globalization, are composed mostly of challenges to existing theories. Others (for example, democratic renewal) are constituted almost entirely by a normative agenda. So we implement our main sequence of topics (origins and assumptions, society–politics relations, government and policy making, agendas and political change) in full for the classical models and wherever relevant in the later chapters. Wherever the material will bear it we revert to this main template, but not in a mechanical way.

Asking readers to look synoptically at theories of the state, to compare them and to consider how they have interacted and intertwined as they developed is not an easy task. So it will make sense for most readers to approach the chapters in the sequence set out here, which we hope presents a controlled release of information that allows readers to build up and master the material in accessible chunks and a rough historical sequence. But for (post)modern non-linear readers, those who want to 'hack it and see' by jumping straight into middle or later chapters, we provide a full index that can guide you to explanations of any unfamiliar concepts you encounter.

All books have their origins in other books, because scholarly work is necessarily a collective activity. This one has some specific origins in one particular book, *Theories of the State* by Patrick Dunleavy and Brendan O'Leary (published by Macmillan in 1987), for which in some ways it is a self-conscious attempt to provide a successor. The world has changed a great deal in the intervening two decades and every chapter in this new book has been written entirely afresh from scratch. Yet Patrick Dunleavy would like to take this opportunity to acknowledge his intellectual debt to Brendan O'Leary: their collaboration on the earlier book has continued to influence his thinking. The authors would also like to thank Brendan for generously commenting on and suggesting improvements to a number of chapters here.

JOHN S. DRYZEK
PATRICK DUNLEAVY

Chapter 1

The State and Liberal Democratic Politics

For the first time in human history a majority of people worldwide now lives in more or less liberal democratic states. This achievement rests in turn on the idea of the state itself – a form of government that is now near-universal. Originating in Europe in the seventeenth century, the modern state form was invented in response to some otherwise intractable and murderous political problems stemming from religious conflicts. From there, aided by the expansion of European imperialism and migration, the idea of the state spread worldwide, providing a framework for organizing government that progressively eroded or displaced most rivals – chiefly informal or tribal systems, feudal regimes, empires and more short-lived competitors such as communes, city-states and leagues of cities (Spruyt 1994). Yet the age of state dominance may have peaked. Some observers identify a new globalized international order that shifts key decisions beyond the reach of individual states. Others see these developments as minor adjustments to a world-system essentially still run by states.

We shall have much to say on these issues in the chapters that follow, but first we need to define the concept of the state itself. The second section of this chapter will show conceptually how states can develop both top-down from the activities of competing leaders and bottom-up from nations and other social formations. In the third section we move from theory to history to see how the contemporary world system of states came into being. Fourth we sketch how the evolution of the modern state is closely bound up with liberal democracy, which can be defined as elected government constrained by constitutional order.

Defining the State

States are among the most important political form and actors in today's world. As Edelman (1964: 1) puts it, 'The state benefits and it threatens. Now it is "us" and often it is "them". It is an abstraction, but in its name men [and women] are jailed, or made rich on oil depletion allowances and defense contracts, or killed in wars.'

1

The idea of 'the state' rests on the notion that there should be a single, unified source of political authority for a territory, drawing upon the undivided loyalties of its population, operating in a well-organized and permanent way, and directed towards the interests of the whole society. There is now substantial agreement among different analysts on seven *defining characteristics* of the state, and on five *associated characteristics*, shown in summary form in Table 1.1 (p. 4).

If a governmental system lacks one of the seven defining characteristics in the left- hand column, then it is not really a state. These features in more detail are:

1 *The state is a set of organized governing institutions which are formally connected to each other and have some cohesiveness.* 'Institutions' here are morally compelling and enduring social arrangements, varying from simple conventions (such as 'being honest' or 'promising') through to formal organizations (such as government bureaucracies) and complex bodies of rules (such as legal systems). To make a state, such institutions must work together to the degree that it makes sense to describe what they do in 'unitary' terms, as though the ensemble behaves as a single actor. Of course, states only look like this at some level of abstraction, for example, when we say that 'Sweden has developed a strong system of social welfare'. Looking more closely we will always see different actors and elements within any state, each pursuing different objectives, sometimes in conflict with one another. Some theories of the state stress its unitary aspects and the forces that compel its parts to act in unison, while others stress internal conflicts and diversity across these component organizations and institutions.

2 *A state must operate in a particular territory, where a substantial population lives as a distinct society.* There cannot be a state without a territory. The population in the territory must be organized so as to form a reasonably distinct society – for example, they must interact more with each other than with 'outsiders', and show some common bonds (involving language, culture, or economy). However, some states govern divided societies in which one group or more rejects these bonds, and whose members may have identifications and interactions that extend into other territories.

3 *The role of state institutions is to reach collectively binding decisions, and to ensure that decisions are obeyed by those living in the territory claimed by the state.* Governing is what any state must do (or try to do). In order to make effective decisions, the governing apparatus must have a considerable toolkit at its disposal in terms

of 'detectors', ways of generating information about what is happening within its territory, and 'effectors', ways of getting things done (Hood and Margetts 2007) .

4 *The state '(successfully) claims the monopoly of the legitimate use of physical force within a given territory'.* This is the classic definition of the state given by the sociologist Max Weber in his 1919 lecture on 'Politics as a Vocation'. The monopoly can be enforced through police and/or military forces against those who challenge it, be they individual criminals, organized crime syndicates, vigilantes, private armies, invaders, mobs, or insurgents.

5 *The state must claim 'sovereignty' (that is, unconstrained power over all other social institutions).* Sovereignty means that the state is the highest source of authority in the territory, the final locus of decisions, with few limits on its scope of internal control. That the state *claims* sovereignty does not however mean that all states will necessarily secure it absolutely – as civil wars and the coercion of relatively weak by relatively strong states attest.

6 *The existence of state institutions helps define a 'public' realm, a part of social life different from the 'private' sphere of concern only to the individuals or organizations involved.* The public realm includes not only strictly governmental activities but all political activities aimed at influencing state institutions and changing or stabilizing how the society operates.

7 *The state must be able to define 'citizens', those who are members of its society; and it must be able to control entry to and exit from its territory by citizens and others.* It was the French Republic's state that invented modern systems for comprehensively documenting a whole population in 1802, thus creating the basis for controlling all movements into and from its territory. Only recently has a 'closed boundary' partition of the whole of the global landmass between states precluded the once relatively free movements of people around the world.

These seven features define what we mean by a state, although particular states may have difficulty in securing all of them absolutely. For example, a powerful neighbouring state may undermine feature five, and large-scale illegal migration may compromise feature seven.

The characteristics shown in the right-hand column of Table 1.1 are also generally sought and achieved by states, although in principle a state could still exist (with great difficulty) if it did not secure any of them.

Table 1.1   *The defining features and associated characteristics of the state*

Defining features	Associated characteristics
The state is:	The state
– a unified set of institutions	– claims to advance common interests
– controlling a given territory and distinct society	– is accepted as legitimate by significant groups
– making and enforcing collectively binding decisions	– has a developed bureaucracy and tax system
– monopolizing the legitimate use of force	– operates with a constitution and legal system
– seeking sovereignty	– is recognized as a state by other states
– operating in a distinct public realm	
– deciding citizenship and controlling entry	

8 *Any contemporary state must claim to be advancing the common interests of its society.* States are not 'natural' – they are always artificial, political creations, constructed around and sustained by ideological or ethical justifications for their existence. Common justifications include the shared history or experiences of a people living within a territory, or a single ethnicity, or a set of durable moral and constitutional principles.

9 *The state should be accepted as legitimate by significant groups or elements in its society.* To survive for long any state must create substantial support bases somewhere. This 'somewhere' might be a particular social class, ethnic group, business leadership, the military, or religious establishment. Not every state will be supported by the majority of the people in its territory. Indeed, many states have endured for long periods where a minority group governs a cowed or coerced majority. Only in democratic states are there institutions for changing state leaders in response to mass opinion.

In the eighteenth century, the Scottish philosopher David Hume was the first to stress the significance of the above points:

'[N]othing appears more surprising ... than the easiness with which the many are governed by the few; and the implicit submission, with which men [and women] resign their own sentiments and passions to those of their rulers. When we enquire by what means this wonder is effected, we shall find that as FORCE is always on the side of the governed, the governors have nothing to support them but opinion. It is therefore on opinion only that government is founded, and this maxim extends to the most despotic and most military governments, as well as to the most free and popular' (Hume 1974: 32).

10 *Modern states are run in large part by bureaucracies – formal, hierarchical organizations financed by budgets. The operations of government are funded from general taxation, which any successful state must be able to collect effectively.* Unlike private business, states do not finance their activities by sales and profits. They must be able to requisition a flow of resources and to sustain that flow in predictable ways. Rudolf Goldscheid (1917) famously described the budget as 'the skeleton of the state, stripped of all misleading ideologies'.

11 *Modern states regulate social activities using a system of laws, and a constitution to control the activities of government institutions themselves.* Normally a constitution is codified into a single written document that can be changed only with difficulty. But even where this is not the case (as in the UK), a constitution can nevertheless be clearly identified and widely recognized as a set of rules to be respected – until and unless the current state should be overturned in favour of new arrangements.

12 *A regime should be recognized as 'a state' by other states.* Recognition of a sovereignty claim by other countries confers rights under international law that help to stabilize a state – chiefly a presumption of non-interference by other states.

With a list of characteristics as long and as demanding as this one, we might expect that relatively few government units could meet *all* of them at once. In fact, in today's world around 190 states successfully pass most of these criteria simultaneously – confirming the importance and success of the state form as a mode of organizing governance. Almost all of the world's land area is governed or claimed by a state. Bits of territory that are not clearly controlled by any state are often centres of crisis and instability, as well as misery for their inhabitants – think for example of the Gaza Strip, or Somalia.

The widespread coverage of the state form notwithstanding, states may find it difficult to achieve any or all of these twelve characteristics. State-building has often been a long, arduous and incomplete process. Consider for example the case of Southern Italy, which has formed part of the Italian state in something like its current shape since the late nineteenth century. The mafia is a long-established set of institutions (at least as old as the Italian state) that organizes or controls a great deal of political, social and economic life in southern Italy through mostly criminal enterprises (Gambetta 1993). The mafia undermines the Italian state's claims to sovereignty, limits the applicability of the legal system, saps the state's capacity to collect taxes, undermines the state's bureaucracies through systematic corruption of public officials, and challenges the state's monopoly on the organized use of force. Many other contemporary states face challenges to their continued maintenance, especially efforts by disaffected minorities to secede to form a territory and state of their own. But the existence of contested, failing and failed states should not disguise the pervasiveness of the state form.

Despite this pervasiveness, it is important to note that the concept of the state itself remains controversial and disputed. Modern political science is a discipline shaped largely in the United States. In the late nineteenth century its US founders were heavily influenced by European philosophy and legal thinking and regarded the study of 'the state' as the focus that would define their discipline. Many of them were reformers influenced by the kind of efficient centralized state they believed existed in Germany. Woodrow Wilson (1887), political scientist and later President of the United States, famously proclaimed that this kind of state could be introduced to the United States, where it would 'breathe free American air'.

Outside the political science profession, the attractions of a centralized state have always been very limited in the highly decentralized US political system. And with the onset of World War I, the German associations of the centralized state were easily stigmatized as an enemy form. So US political scientists from the 1920s onwards focused not on the state as a whole but on government institutions treated separately: federalism; the Presidency; Congress; and the Supreme Court. In the 1930s and 1940s, centrally planned and dictatorial Nazi, fascist and Communist states in Europe and the Soviet Union, sought to organize all social, economic and political life. The Italian dictator Benito Mussolini argued in a 1932 article *The Doctrine of Fascism*: 'For the Fascist, everything is in the state, and nothing human or spiritual exists, much less has value, outside the state'. American pluralism (discussed in Chapter 2) condemned such extremes, to the degree of refusing to recognize any overarching concept of the state.

The behavioral revolution in US political science in the 1950s shifted the focus of the discipline from institutions to individuals, be they voters, activists, politicians, or bureaucrats. Inasmuch as the ensemble of institutions and practices remained in view, it was characterized as 'the political system' (Easton 1953), not 'the state.' The political system concept could be applied to any sort of politics: within an extended family or small community, within a private organization, or in international interaction. The national government of the United States was treated as just one kind of political system, whose 'outputs' could be explained largely in terms of the relative weight of the 'inputs' it received from American society. In other Anglo-Saxon countries, notably the UK, Canada, Australia and New Zealand, political scientists followed the American lead in focusing on the political system and eschewing talk of the state.

The concept of the state returned very noisily to US political science in the 1980s (Evans, Rueschemeyer and Skocpol 1985). Its supporters argued that 'outputs' could not be explained just in terms of 'inputs' from society: that public officials had their own interests that influenced outputs; and that these interests of officials were not necessarily beholden to any group in society (be it a labour union, business federation, or interest group). Some members of this new generation of scholars embarked on studies that could speak of 'the state' in unitary terms – as sometimes acting as though it were a coherent, integrated actor – although they remained attuned to differences and conflicts among different state actors (such as departments of government, or elected legislators). But whether treated in relatively integrated or relatively fragmented fashion, the concept of the state was brought firmly back into the mainstream of US political science. From there it filtered back into the thinking of political analysts in other countries. The revival of Marxist theory in Western Europe in the late 1960s and 1970s had earlier reinforced a focus on the state. The fading of behavioralism and systems theory in the US and elsewhere in the late twentieth century meant the state had one fewer intellectual challenger.

Ironically, the general re-acceptance of 'the state' concept in political science coincided with the first recognitions that perhaps in an increasingly globalized world the state's role in structuring systems of governance was diminishing. In addition, the state's conceptual linkage to the nation became problematic in an era when nations multiplied and were often contested in their definition and identity, which did not always coincide with the territory of a state.

Theories of State Formation

States today are often treated as sovereign entities. *Sovereignty* means that the government of any particular territory should be organized exclusively by a state, and that no other external power has the authority to intervene in the affairs of this state acting on its own territory in relation to its own population. Sovereignty in this sense has never been absolute, because (powerful) states have found all kinds of reasons to intervene in the affairs of other (weaker) states. And the particular attributes and obligations that accompany sovereignty can change with time (Reus-Smit 1999). Nevertheless, sovereignty has served as a strong presumption, whose violation needs some justification.

Yet this is a very recent situation, and it is worth examining how it developed. While today the sovereign state may seem commonplace, most human societies throughout history have not been governed by states, still less anything like the modern state (Finer 1997). The sovereignty-claiming state as we know it is a European invention, first established as a general principle by the Treaty of Westphalia in 1648. The Treaty crystallized a peace settlement designed to end chronic wars of religion between Catholics and various strains of Protestantism. The Treaty confirmed that the principle established in the 1555 Treaty of Augsburg that the religion of the Prince (ruler) was to be the religion of the state and its whole population, and that no other state could intervene to change this choice, though Westphalia also specified no state could change the religion it had in 1624. The Treaty did not mean that organized violence inspired by religious difference came to an end in Europe, but merely that a set of presumptions was established to curb this violence. International relations scholars date the emergence of the modern states system to the Treaty of Westphalia. To appreciate the distinctiveness of this seventeenth century solution, we first consider two theoretical perspectives on state formation and then look at how states have developed in light of these perspectives. One perspective is framed top-down in terms of the behaviour of rulers and competition between states, while the other focuses on the bottom-up emergence of states from nations.

The top-down perspective on state formation

The top-down view emphasizes the behaviour and skill of ruling political elites (in the past often generals, monarchs or aristocrats) as the key determinant of a state's survival and growth in the context of competition with other states or proto-states. Random advantages for new states might include resources such as a healthy temperate climate or fertile land; or geography – for instance, being in protected niches like the periphery of well-populated continents (Portugal or Korea), or better still offshore islands protected by sea (Japan or the UK), or just a long way from potential enemies (the United States and Australia). Random disadvantages might include a population divided on religious, ideological, or ethnic grounds, which may need unifying in support of the state, be it through conversion, coercion, expulsion, or genocide – or more peaceful settlement.

The sequence shown in Figure 1.1 starts from the observation that periodic incursions and invasions by nomads and outside tribes or societies were a constant feature of ancient civilizations. Mancur Olson (1993) argued that a key choice was made by each of these waves of 'bandits', whether to loot and move on, or alternatively to settle down. In this view once 'stationary bandits' could hold off other incursions they quickly acquired interests over and above short-term pillaging, instead beginning to build up their society's economic capacity and long-run capacity to deliver revenues. Charles Tilly (1985) points out that war-making and state-making went hand-in-hand. They share some common features with organized crime when it comes to combining protection of a territory with exploitation of its population. A

Figure 1.1 *One top-down view of states' survival and development*

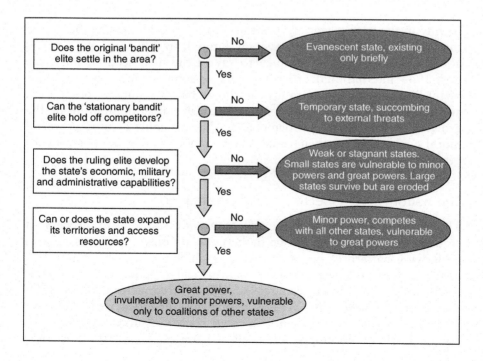

successful elite will develop the economy, military capabilities, and administrative competences so as to acquire comparative advantages over competitors in their immediate environment. States that fail in these respects will be vulnerable to conquest, unless they have a geographically protected niche (as did Japan after its rulers turned their backs on all outside contacts in the seventeenth century). Large and relatively stagnant empire states, such as China from the late fifteenth century onwards, could make similar choices (the Ming dynasty renounced all naval developments) and survive even in an obsolescent form through their sheer scale compared to their neighbours.

Even when a state could develop a comparative advantage in its immediate locale, unless it could expand to a critical mass in relation to its local threat environment it would remain a minor power, vulnerable to nearby great powers. From the fifteenth century to 1815 Europe was plagued by 'lengthy coalition wars', in which minor powers were repeatedly forced to choose sides in great power conflicts in order to survive (Kennedy 1989). By contrast, some states successfully built a comparative advantage and expanded their territory via monarchical marriages, land conquests, expansion into a lightly-populated hinterland, or by acquiring a seaborne empire. These countries could become 'great powers' able to see off any single enemy, and thus vulnerable only to a coalition of other hostile great powers mobilizing against them.

Only in the very recent era has the 'realpolitik' dynamic embodied in the top-down view been increasingly limited, by two strong influences about which we will have much to say in the next section. First, the post-1945 international order now places some strong (but not complete) limits on the unrestrained, no-holds barred military competition and economic rivalry between states. Second, public opinion inside the growing number of liberal democracies has arguably created powerful moral constraints on their ruling elites' actions and behaviour toward other states.

The bottom-up perspective on state formation

The bottom-up view sees the emergence of states as a process of securing a progressively better fit between political structures and an underlying pattern of human societies, each shaped by a common language, culture, religion, ethnicity or historical experience. In this view the behaviour, skills and resources of ruling elites might make some difference in the short term. Yet in the long run, the efficacy of a cohesive state rests on its mobilization of a single society, if necessary in a contest against external oppressors such as empires. This bottom-up view is epitomized by those who see nations as the obvious and most secure basis for states, such that 'the state' is shorthand for 'nation state', and not saying the 'nation' part underlines its taken-for-granted character. In this light, nations are the building blocks of the entire world order, the sole rightful possessors of territories (and adjoining seas) and of all the resources that lie within their boundaries. This sort of view backed President Woodrow Wilson's enthusiasm for national self-determination as the key principle for reconstruction of Europe after World War I. At an extreme, this principle implies that the whole land surface of the world (or at least that which can be occupied by humanity) can be assigned to particular nations by giving each one a state.

This kind of view is supported by all the nationalists who in recent centuries have demanded a state to go with their nation, be it Turkey, Serbia, Ireland, Scotland, Germany, Italy, Colombia, or Vietnam. When competing definitions of the nation lay claim to the same territory, the outcome is decided by force of arms, with civil war and genocide often live possibilities.

Figure 1.2 shows the bottom-up view of how the main forms of territorial political organization relate to the societies that they govern. The most important contrast here is between states and empires. The modern form of nation state emerged in its earliest form in very late medieval England and France, seeking governance of a relatively homogenous society in a single power centre. By contrast, in both

Figure 1.2   *The bottom-up view of the broad inter-relationship between nation states, empires and other political forms*

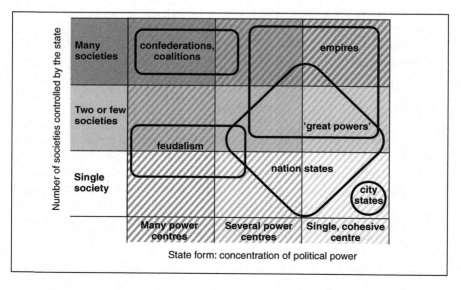

ancient and modern empires a main, metropolitan power centre ruled over many component societies – as in the Roman Empire, its Byzantine successor, the Moghul Empire in what is now India and Pakistan, the Ottoman Empire in the Middle East and Southeast Europe, and the Austro-Hungarian Habsburg Empire in Central Europe. Some empires, like those of Alexander the Great or Genghis Khan, spanned huge numbers of societies but collapsed quickly into smaller regimes once the military campaigns that built them lapsed. Other empires lasted much longer, including those that persisted into the twentieth century, and it is only when they failed that nation states sometimes emerged falteringly from their wreckage. This persistence of empire notwithstanding, the bottom-up view still holds that achieving a close fit between one society and a state apparatus configured to fit the same territory and population is what assigns superior political mobilization potential and legitimacy to the nation state.

In much of feudal Europe, and in India before British conquest, there were multiple overlapping political jurisdictions within the same territories and a strong political fragmentation between multiple proto-states (see Figure 1.2). Here the emergence of states entailed a lengthy and violent period of political reorganization, including massive centralization under strong monarchs. Modern nation states are very different from the city-states of ancient Greece, late-medieval Italy and Switzerland, where sovereignty was vested in a single government founded on a very cohesive micro-society. City-states can be dynamic players but their small size makes them vulnerable. Sometimes they have coped by linking up in confederations (as in the Hanseatic League of medieval Northern Europe), at other times by existing in niches or interstices between empires and great powers, or at still others by using their superior mercantile and economic power so as to make the military and economic costs of invading them prohibitive.

The History of State Formation

In the wider history of the state's emergence as the dominant political form on the planet both top-down and bottom-up perspectives have some applicability. Until late medieval times in Europe, familial, monarchical, and religious forms of political authority were mixed and overlapping. Lines of political authority and obligation often extended across geographical boundaries. Empires and kingdoms arose to govern large territories, and sought to impose central political authority over the territory they controlled, developing laws for the regulation of property and economic transactions, although never laws to control the authority of the powerful. In the occasional rare case (such as the ancient Roman Republic) a constitution regulated the distribution of power among aristocratic office-holders. More generally, in ancient and medieval empires and kingdoms there was no clear separation of political and governmental authority from family, aristocratic and religious sources of power. The focus of power in a king or emperor generally meant that no distinction was possible between office-holders and their offices.

In the feudal system of medieval Europe there were many levels of rulers, ranging from a weak 'emperor' in Germany, through kings, powerful nobles such as counts or dukes, to several levels of partly autonomous nobles. Multiple centres of power within the same territory were common; lords and monarchs had continually to negotiate their relative powers, and often disputes between them could not be decided even temporarily without recourse to force of arms. These different layers and levels of power were bound together in complex, interlocking patterns of obligation. In addition the Catholic Church claimed political as well as spiritual authority, and parliaments that were assemblies of various categories of the wealthy and powerful began to make claims to a share of power.

From the sixteenth to the eighteenth centuries centralizing, absolutist monarchies arose in many areas of Europe, each seeking to consolidate control over their respective territories. These rulers reduced the independent power of the barons and nobility, setting up elaborate royal courts to absorb aristocratic energies in conspicuous consumption and inter-personal court politics. They created central tax powers and bureaucracies, raised professional standing armies and put in place extended legal systems. In many countries these monarchs also squeezed the inherited power of parliaments, and sought to assert themselves over the influence of organized religion – especially in countries where the Protestant Reformation took hold, where rulers could establish state churches free from the power of the Vatican. At the dawn of the modern era it seemed that the most successful form of the modern state was going to be absolute monarchy – a far cry from today's liberal democratic norm. Some powerful monarchies built huge empires spanning diverse territories, such as the Spanish empire in Latin America. The Habsburg Empire covered much of Central Europe and the Balkans, governing disparate peoples with many languages. The Habsburgs successfully presented themselves as defending Christian Europe against the Turks of the Ottoman Empire. Their example illustrates a crucial dynamic in state building: if one's neighbour is a powerful state or empire, the best way to organize against it is to develop a powerful centralized state of one's own.

States could be further centralized and strengthened as a result of successful revolutions, especially those accompanied by effective nationalism. The French revolution is exemplary in this respect. Attempting to match British power, the French monarchy impoverished itself in the late eighteenth century by supporting the American colonies' revolution against British rule. Louis XVI sought to raise further revenues by squeezing the French landed classes, causing them to withdraw their support for the monarchy (Skocpol 1979). This rift between the landed upper classes and the monarchy created the initial space for revolution.

But revolutionary France faced exactly the same external pressures, and the new regime's responses involved further state centralization, now unconstrained by the weight of traditions, customs and religion. Republican France and then the Napoleonic regime demonstrated the power of a ruthlessly modernized state, capable of fielding mass armies and raising finance in pursuit of territorial expansion. Both regimes deployed a populist, mobilizing ideology that turned war from a remote affair waged by aristocratic levies into something like a patriotic crusade, absorbing the concerted energies of a whole society. This state-building transformation allowed France to repeatedly defeat apparently overwhelming great power coalitions constructed against her (until Napoleon met his Waterloo in 1815 and was defeated by Britain and Prussia). The Napoleonic example was not lost on the rest of continental Europe. In the mid nineteenth century centralized nation-states were eventually built in Italy and Germany by one unit among numerous smaller governments successfully extending its control (Piedmont in Italy, Prussia in Germany).

The American Revolution produced the first state designed with reference to a particular set of political principles, which today we can recognize as liberal democratic. The US Constitution of 1789 established a separation and sharing of power between a legislature that made laws, a presidency that executed and administered the laws and a judiciary that made sure both the other institutions of government and the population at large respected the laws. The Bill of Rights subsequently added to the US constitution codified the liberal rights that citizens had against their own government, and, more positively, to constitute for themselves a free realm of public debate.

From the seventeenth to the twentieth century the history of the state was entwined with the history of empires. The Portuguese and Spanish empires in Latin America collapsed amid revolutionary warfare that produced consolidated nation-states. But the late nineteenth century saw continued European colonial expansion in Africa and Asia. Japan embarked on a state-building modernization process that in the twentieth century enabled it to use massive military force to acquire an empire in East Asia.

The twentieth century saw conglomerate empires progressively disintegrate. The Habsburg and Ottoman empires failed to survive World War I and monarchs styled as emperors in Germany and Russia were also overthrown. However, the Soviet Union under Communist Party control rapidly rebuilt the fabric of the Russian imperial territories after a brief civil war. The Japanese and Italian empires were destroyed by military defeat in World War II. While never fully governed by any foreign empire, China had suffered repeated incursions by Western powers and the conquest of much of its territory by imperial Japan between 1931 and 1945. In 1949 the unification of almost all China under a communist regime led by Mao Zedong seemed to usher in its governance by a modern state.

For logistical and financial reasons the enormous French and British empires did not long survive the 1939–45 war. Their systems (and those of smaller European powers such as the Dutch) were profoundly schizophrenic. To their home (or metropolitan) populations these countries appeared as nation-states and liberal democracies, but externally they governed huge overseas empires in authoritarian fashion (Subrahmanyam, 2004). In September 1939 the writer George Orwell noted caustically that the two liberal democracies about to go to war with Nazi Germany between them controlled the lives of 600 million black and Asian people who had no votes or say in how they were governed. The defenders of these so-called 'liberal' empires (then and since) argued that rule by the British and French empires in Africa and Asia was a form of 'enlightened despotism' maintaining order and nurturing these countries towards self-government. But as George Santayana (1922: 468) remarked:

> [W]hen a people exercises control over other peoples its government becomes ponderous even at home; its elaborate imperial machinery cannot be stopped, and can hardly be mended; the imperial people become the slave of its commitment.

In the post-war period the claims of 'national self-determination' in Africa, Asia and the Middle East easily trumped the enfeebled liberal imperialist claims to be (very slowly) tutoring subject peoples towards democracy. Even the stubborn domestic ideological support for the British and French empires rapidly eroded. Two smaller shells of earlier European empires, Spain and Portugal, faced the same tension between being a nation-state and maintaining despotic colonial rule, but they solved it by maintaining dictatorships at home into the mid 1970s, whereupon they adopted liberal democracy and discarded the last outposts of empire.

The last empire turned out to be that of the Soviet Union (though it never admitted the 'empire' title). Its political and ideological grip was extended after 1945 via subordinate Communist regimes in Eastern and Central Europe. In 1956 and 1968 the Soviets showed their willingness to use military force to crush dissent in Hungary and Czechoslovakia respectively. The Soviet empire lost the countries it had acquired in 1945 in a few months in 1989, and in 1991 the Soviet Union itself (roughly coinciding with the territory of the older Russian empire of the Tsars) disintegrated into its component republics.

In all these cases of imperial collapse, the territories and peoples formerly governed by empires organized themselves into recognizably modern sorts of states – though not necessarily with great success. In the inter-war period the states of east-Central Europe formed after 1918 could not withstand the expansion of Nazi Germany, and in World War II they could not resist their 'liberation' by Stalin's Soviet Union. More recently, in post-colonial Africa many states have dissolved into civil war and anarchy, often repeatedly. These setbacks notwithstanding, it is almost universally assumed, even by protagonists in civil wars, that something like the modern nation-state form is the proper way to organize the government of any territory and people. By the end of World War II the Westphalian model was made both universal and standard by the establishment of the United Nations, even if it was not until the 1990s that the last vestiges of the European powers' empires and the Soviet bloc system of control of other states were in practice removed.

Yet it would be a mistake to assume that a system of states was now universally accepted. From time to time 'rogue' states behave outside the Westphalian limits. In 1991 the Iraqi dictator Saddam Hussein simply invaded and tried to annex his neighbour Kuwait, from which he was subsequently expelled, with a huge cost in Iraqi casualties, by a US-lead military coalition, acting under a clear UN mandate. A decade later the United States organized and assisted an overthrow of the Taliban regime in Afghanistan (which was implicated in supporting terrorists who carried out the 9/11 attacks in New York and Washington). In 2003 the United States and United Kingdom invaded Iraq with no UN mandate, creating a regime dependent on US military support for many years for its survival.

Thus one contemporary challenge to the system of states may be US hegemony, reviving some characteristics of imperialism, however much imperial ambitions are denied by US leaders. With a population of 300 million people set to grow to 500 million by 2050, with unprecedented economic wealth and controlling more than half of all military spending on the planet, the United States occupies a 'great power' position that is less constrained than that of any predecessor. Some neo-conservative thinkers believe the United States should exploit this historically unique position to order the world unilaterally to its own liking, instead of being constrained to accept the Westphalian doctrine of non-interference within other states (see Chapter 12).

A second challenge to the modern assumption that government should be organized exclusively by states is created by globalization processes, potentially displacing power upwards to supra-governmental organizations and sideways into transnational networks. States choose to give up some aspects of their sovereignty when they join international organizations such as the European Union, the World Trade Organization, or the International Criminal Court. The past presumption has been that even when states make such moves, they do so voluntarily and retain the ability to withdraw if they choose. Globalization theorists argue that the enmeshing of states within many different encompassing international and trans-national processes is now so extensive that this presumption no longer holds (see Chapter 14).

The most venerable tradition of anti-state thinking is however anarchism. While in popular language anarchism is often associated with destruction and nihilism, anarchism can also mean almost exactly the opposite: peaceful cooperation in the absence of any hierarchical authority – including state authority. Anarchy means, quite literally, no state. In anarchic social systems, there is no political specialization (so no division between voters and representatives, or leaders and followers), and no concentration of force (Taylor 1982: 9). There are actually many examples of anarchies; indeed, most of human history has involved small groups of hunter-gatherers living in anarchical societies. Peasant agricultural communities have also sometimes operated on this basis. Instead of coercion, such societies rely on mechanisms of social control such as ostracism of people who violate social norms, fear of violence and conditional cooperation – that is, making one's voluntary contribution to the public good conditional on others in one's society also contributing (Axelrod 1984).

Scholars of international relations (e.g. Bull 1977) have sometimes described the international system as an 'anarchical society' because historically it has achieved a large measure of cooperation without much in the way of central institutions at the system level. International law is very weak compared to its domestic counterpart, and there are few ways for international institutions to force compliance with their decisions. Of course the international system does sometimes degenerate into war – but most of the time it does not.

Anarchism is also a tradition in political thinking, beginning in the nineteenth century with the French philosopher Pierre-Joseph Proudhon, and developed later in that century by the Russian Peter Kropotkin. This tradition formed a rival to Marxism, and Marxist revolutionaries have seen anarchists as enemies who needed to be defeated. There have been a number of anarchist revolutions: the Paris Commune in 1871, the Ukraine in 1917 (soon swept aside by the rival Bolshevik Marxist revolutionaries), and Spain in the 1930s. All these attempts were soon crushed, illustrating what is perhaps the biggest problem faced by anarchists: hierarchical states are so much better at organizing military force than are anarchies. Thus no anarchists have ever had the chance to organize a large-scale, modern society. The real legacy of anarchism may be in its demonstration that voluntary cooperation is a way to organize the resolution of many problems in human societies – even if the anarchist programme cannot show how to organize large scale and complex societies in their entirety. This demonstration is echoed in contemporary work on resource management. Ostrom (1990), though not an anarchist, argues that communities of resource users can sometimes govern their own affairs and regulate access to a resource such as a fishery or water for irrigation without any help from any formal government. We will discuss such cases further in Chapter 11. Anarchist ideas about spontaneous cooperation also find echoes in some of the new forms of cooperative governance we will discuss in Chapter 6 (though practitioners and analysts of these new forms do not acknowledge anarchist antecedents).

Liberal Democracy

We now take a closer look at the emergence and condition of the currently most important state form – liberal democracy. Two sets of principles long stood in tension with each other, liberalism's limited state with a carefully demarcated constitutional order, and democracy's majority rule and free elections, with removal of privilege and inequality. It was only in the nineteenth century that it seemed democracy did not have to be the enemy of liberalism. Today, we can define a liberal democracy as a political system where:

> - Periodic elections determine how the legislature is constituted and who shall hold the executive power of government. There should be free and fair competition among candidates and political parties. This is the 'democracy' part of the concept.
> - Fundamental civil liberties are protected by law and constitutional safeguards, while legal enactments and rules are equally and impartially enforced by an independent judiciary and legal system. This is the 'liberal' part of the concept.
> - The constitution specifies the powers of particular public offices and branches of government and the relations between them.

Both the 'liberal' and the 'democracy' aspects have to be present for liberal democracy to exist. Elected government without the protection of civil liberties can be tyrannical – for example, by allowing a larger ethnic group to suppress the political freedoms of smaller ethnic groupings, as happened in many Southern states of the United States for a century after the formal abolition of slavery. Having an impartial legal system and protection of rights, without free elections can create a relatively open society and allow a capitalist economy to flourish, as in contemporary Singapore. But without elections through which people can change the composition of their government without fear of government action against them, such a society is not democratic.

This ease of definition is not to suggest, however, that liberal democracies are without tensions and problems. Indeed, the rest of this book is about the questions and conflicts that remain. As a prelude to this analysis, we examine how liberal democracy reached global ascendancy. Then we outline variations in the way liberal democracies arrange representation, and the ways they organize social and economic life.

The development of liberal democracy

For most of their history, the two principles of liberalism and democracy were thought to point in different directions. Of the two principles, **democracy** is the older. It began in ancient Athens with the reforms of Cleisthenes in 508–507 BCE (Grofman 1993), which created what we might now call direct democracy. Key decisions were made by an assembly that all the citizens were entitled to attend. But the Athenian citizenry or *demos* actually constituted only around 15 per cent of the city state's total population – because women, slaves, men without property and 'metics' who lacked the necessary ancestry were all excluded. Office holders were not elected, but instead selected by lot, to serve for a limited period. Such random selection still persists today in the way that juries are chosen for court cases, and it has recently been revived in practices associated with deliberative democracy (see Chapter 9).

Elections were also held in various assemblies that shared power in a complex fashion within the Roman Republic (509–27 BCE). Membership in each of the assemblies was restricted – most severely in the Senate, normally the most powerful of the assemblies. Rome was an aristocratic republic rather than a democracy. With the demise of the Roman Republic amid civil war and the victory of Octavian (Augustus Caesar), election to office on the part of even a small subset of the citizens went into abeyance in Europe for over a thousand years. In medieval times elections did appear in that otherwise most authoritarian of institutions, the Catholic Church, when monasteries would sometimes elect their abbot and convents their mother superior. The College of Cardinals also used a demanding unanimity voting system to choose the Pope.

For many centuries, no political thinker would describe himself or herself as a democrat – with the very occasional exception, such as the Leveller faction in the parliamentary army in the English civil war in the 1640s, which was soon brutally repressed. When in the aftermath of the conflict Thomas Hobbes wanted to belittle his opponents who supported the cause of Parliament against the king, he described them as 'democratical gentlemen' pursuing treason and instigating civil war (Hobbes 1969). If ever heard at all in political discourse, 'democracy' was a term of abuse:

> As it entered the eighteenth century, democracy was still very much a pariah word. Only the most insouciant and incorrigible dissidents . . . could take their political stand upon it, even clandestinely or amongst intimates. Anyone who chose to do so placed themselves far beyond the borders of political life, at the outer limits of the intellectual lives of virtually all their contemporaries. (Dunn 2005: 71)

Matters only began to change at the end of the eighteenth century, with the French and American revolutions. In the early 1790s the radical Jacobin faction of the French revolutionaries, notably Maximilien Robespierre, began to use 'democracy' in a positive fashion to denote the unmediated (and as it turned out unrestricted) implementation of the 'will' of the people. The revolutionary Babeuf declared in 1790, shortly before his execution:

> If the People are the Sovereign, they should exercise as much sovereignty as they absolutely can themselves . . . To accomplish what you have to do and can do yourself, use representation on the fewest possible occasions and be nearly always your own representative. (Quoted in Dunn 2005: 230)

But the excesses of the revolutionary radicals, involving the execution of many real and imagined opponents, helped reinforce democracy's bad name, and with the overthrow of the Jacobins and the rapid transformation of revolutionary France into Napoleon Bonaparte's empire, modern democracy at first looked no more stable than its ancient predecessors.

The key innovation that the French revolutionaries did not adopt but which eventually enabled democracy to become feasible in large modern societies was the idea of *representation*. In 1792 in *The Rights of Man*, the radical English theorist and activist Thomas Paine proposed 'ingrafting representation upon democracy'. Over the next century representative democracy became the dominant form in both theory and practice. Robert Dahl (1989: 28–30) considers this development central to what he calls 'the second transformation of democracy' (the first having been the invention of democracy in Ancient Greece).

On the other side of the Atlantic, a state was devised that initially featured plenty of representation but not a great deal of democracy. The American revolution produced what is now recognized as the world's oldest liberal democratic state, but its founders certainly did not think they were designing a democracy. James Madison, whose influence on the US Constitution was felt most strongly, insisted that the Constitution would establish a republic but not a democracy. To Madison, democracy was a byword for chaos and instability resulting from unchecked citizen control. In *The Federalist 10* (published in 1787) he wrote: '[D]emocracies have ever been spectacles of turbulence and contention; have ever been found incompatible with personal security or the rights of property, and have in general been as short in their lives as they have been violent in their deaths'. The US constitution did institute elections on a national scale for the House of Representatives alone, and state legislatures were also elected. However, the franchise was restricted to male property holders and slaves, black slavery itself persisted until 1865. Women and poor men were excluded from the vote. Moreover, the checks and balances specified in the constitution were designed to guard against an excess of democracy. Senators were originally appointed by state legislatures rather than directly elected by the people, as were the members of each state's Electoral College that chose the President. An unelected Supreme Court was given power to assess and overrule Acts of Congress as unconstitutional.

Only in the early nineteenth century did democracy cease to be a negative term in American political discourse. Accompanying the populist, anti-elitist approach to politics that Andrew Jackson rode to the Presidency in 1828 was a contrast drawn between 'the democracy' (the ordinary people) and 'the plutocracy' (the very rich and powerful) (Hanson 1989: 78–9). This usage still retained democracy's anti-elitist connotations. Only very gradually thereafter were these radical associations diminished. With time the US republic became more democratic. In the nineteenth century states gradually opened the choice of Electoral College members to popular vote, so that today they are ciphers for each state's winning majority of voters. The direct election of senators was made nationally uniform by constitutional amendment in 1913. Democratization was further advanced by full suffrage for women in 1920, the gradual abolition of property qualifications for the vote, and the abolition in the 1960s of tests designed to exclude African Americans from the franchise in Southern states in particular. However, ingenious mechanisms to restrict African-American voting in the South could still be found in the twenty-first century. These mechanisms arguably proved decisive in ensuring that Florida delivered a (contested) majority of votes to George W. Bush in 2000, thus handing him the Presidency.

Progress in other countries now considered the trailblazers of liberal democracy was no faster. In Britain, Parliament in the seventeenth century still had to struggle for its survival against a monarch (Charles I) asserting his divine right to govern unchecked. As of 2008 the UK Parliament's upper chamber, the House of Lords, remains completely unelected, although its powers have shrunk greatly with time. The House of Commons was long elected on the basis of an extremely narrow franchise. Voting rights were first extended to a large group of male citizens holding substantial property in the Great Reform Act of 1832, but the last 40 per cent of adult males only gained the vote in 1918. Equal votes for women in the UK came in 1928. But of course in the whole British empire, spanning at this time a quarter of the world's land mass, only the (white) metropolitan population and those in (white) self-governing dominions had the vote. And when the last major UK colony, Hong Kong, was handed over to China in 1992, its citizens still did not have full democratic rights. In Switzerland, often regarded as one of the world's model democracies, women gained the vote only in 1972, while in Australia aborigines' standing as citizens on a par with other Australians was confirmed only in 1967.

In the long period while democracy was in the doldrums, **liberalism** was in very gradual ascendant. The core ideas of liberalism are that government must be regulated by a constitution, and that all full members of society have rights that protect them against each other and against arbitrary government. Key rights are private property, freedom of contract, freedom of thought (especially in matters of religion), freedom of expression and of association, and rights to due process in the legal system. The ascent of liberalism began in 1215 when Magna Carta was signed by King John of England and his barons. Magna Carta limited the powers of the king and established some rudimentary civil rights – though these rights did not extend very far beyond the privileged classes. In 1649 King Charles I was tried and executed for the crime of waging war on his own people – a key event in the rise of liberalism, because it confirmed that there are rules which even kings had to follow. The political convulsions of seventeenth century Britain culminated in the 'Glorious Revolution' of 1688 to1689 ('glorious' to the winners and their successors). King James II was overthrown on suspicion of wanting to return England to Catholicism, and replaced by a constitutional monarchy in which political power was shifted away from the monarch and toward the legislature. The freedom of religion, under law (except of course for Catholics) was established in 1689. The revolution's key intellectual defender was John Locke, widely regarded as the main founder of liberal political philosophy. In Britain and elsewhere, the subsequent rise of liberalism went hand-in-hand with the rise of capitalism, for a political philosophy that stressed individual rights (especially private property rights) helped loosen the inherited legacy of feudal social obligations that restricted the flow of labour and capital.

It is quite possible for a state to be liberal without being especially democratic. A highly centralized regime might well choose to grant all kinds of individual rights – for instance, to facilitate economic growth that would benefit the regime. In practice, early liberal governments featured a highly restricted voting franchise, and a distribution of power that was quite oligarchical, conducing to rule by the aristocratic or wealthy few. Well into the nineteenth century, with the French revolution's lessons in mind, liberal political philosophers still feared that democracy would lead to mob rule and wholesale violation of the individual rights necessary for the functioning of liberal society. In 1859 John Stuart Mill wrote darkly of 'the tyranny of the majority'. In many respects Mill was among the most progressive and democratic of nineteenth century liberals. He favoured the emancipation of women and democratic elections, but proposed devices such as weighted voting in order to restrict the power of the masses. And when it came to the British Empire, he had no qualms in asserting that 'despotism is a legitimate mode of government in dealing with barbarians, provided the end be their improvement' (ironically in Chapter 1 of his book *On Liberty*).

The gradual expansion of the franchise generally showed that the fears of Mill and other nineteenth century liberals were groundless (except when majorities and minorities were permanently defined on an ethnic or religious basis). At most, the newly enfranchised poor used their vote to support social democratic parties that proposed moderate redistribution of income and wealth. But liberal hostility to democracy persisted to the end of the twentieth century. The political scientist William Riker (1982a) wrote approvingly of 'liberalism *against* populism' and praised the many 'defects' of representative politics that prevented any unmediated implementation of the popular will. In 1975 Crozier, Huntington and Watanuki in a famous report to the Trilateral Commission spoke of a crisis of democracy in which too many groups were making too many demands on the state, threatening overload and collapse. For the United States, Milton and Rose Friedman (1984) proposed the centralization of power in a strong presidency to stop people organizing into groups to demand that resources be redistributed in their direction by government, which the Friedmans thought was ruining the market economy. Some of Milton Friedman's students found a laboratory for liberal authoritarianism under the notorious military dictatorship of General Pinochet in Chile in the late 1970s and 1980s. Pinochet's government implemented rights only to protect private property, freedom of contract, and unrestricted private markets, while vigorously suppressing civil and political rights.

In short, the combined liberal democratic idea that all citizens of a state should jointly and equally determine its affairs via voting in elections, and should have equal civil and political rights including legal and constitutional protections, remains a novel and precarious accomplishment. From 1900 to the 1960s liberal democracies never numbered more than 24 countries at any one time, and for long periods in the twentieth century the number of liberal democracies dropped below 10. A low point was reached in 1942, with almost all of Europe (except for the UK, Ireland, Sweden and Switzerland) controlled by dictatorships.

The victory of the western democracies in World War II, followed by de-colonization of European empires in the 1950s and 1960s, increased the number of liberal democracies. However, liberal democracy generally did not flourish in the former colonies, with the important exception of India. Liberal democracy as a universal model did not really take off until the mid 1970s, when Spain, Portugal and Greece removed their dictatorships. In the 1980s and 1990s most Latin American countries did the same, while from around 1987 South Korea and Taiwan also began to move beyond military and authoritarian control. After the fall of the Berlin Wall in 1989 and subsequent collapse of the Soviet Union, most of the states in central and Eastern Europe moved toward liberal democracy (though with some authoritarian resistance). In 1994 South Africa abandoned its racist apartheid regime in favour of an exemplary liberal constitution and popular elections.

As we write this book liberal democracy is the dominant state form in Europe, North and South America, Australasia, the South Pacific, India, Japan, Korea, Taiwan, South Africa, plus a few outposts elsewhere. Other parts of the world such as Southeast Asia have witnessed some gradual movement in a democratic direction, amid many setbacks. Even China, while strongly resisting liberal democracy, has recognized the need to create consultative forums in government, and has undertaken experiments at the local level that allowed a measure of citizen participation. While not allowing any competition for the Communist Party or much in the way of civil and political rights, China has moved to establish the private property rights that help define liberalism, and provided some spaces for limited political and intellectual debate.

Quite where to draw the line between functioning liberal democracies and other sorts of states can be controversial. A number of countries, notably Russia after the election of President Vladimir Putin in 2000, combine apparently competitive elections with strong central control over what opposition is allowed, and very imperfect protections of human rights. Russian security forces, provoked by terrorist attacks, have ignored human rights in internal colonies such as Chechnya. Russia under Putin was actually what Carothers (2002: 12–13) calls a 'dominant power system', ruled by elites that manipulate the political system so that they cannot be defeated in elections. Under President Yeltsin in the 1990s, Russia was in Zakaria's (2003) terms an 'illiberal democracy', featuring competitive elections, but with no constraints on what election winners can do. Yeltsin himself preferred to rule by decree. Illiberal democracies have no constitutional constraints on the power of rulers, little accountability between elections and little respect for human rights. Illiberal democracy therefore resembles 'competitive authoritarianism' (Levitsky and Way 2002). Examples can be found in other post-Soviet countries, in Iran, the Palestinian Authority, in Latin America and in Africa. Looking at the world in 2006 through American eyes, the non-governmental organization Freedom House classified 89 countries as 'free' (i.e., liberal democratic), 58 as 'partially free' and 45 as 'not free' (www.freedomhouse.org/uploads/pdf/charts 2006.pdf).

For some observers, Islam's preoccupations with authoritarian or theocratic government since the religion's founding period (around 660 CE), the Islamic world appear the most problematic area for liberal democracy. But even here it should be noted that a majority of the world's 1.4 billion Moslems now lives in democratic countries – notably in India, Indonesia, Turkey and the more controversial case of Iran, where electoral democracy is compromised by the power of a theocratic religious establishment. (Bangladesh has been mostly democratic in terms of elections and civilian rule, but has proved susceptible to dynastic politics and occasional suspension of elections, while Pakistan has experienced only brief interludes of competitive elections amid successive military coups.) It is actually the Arab part of the Islamic world that is most resistant to democracy. As we write, competitive elections in the Arab world occur only in Lebanon and the Palestinian Authority (which is not yet a state according to our earlier definition). Sub-Saharan Africa is also a problematic region for liberal democracy, with the exception of South Africa (though even South Africa lacks an opposition party with any chance of winning national

 ⌐ns). While liberal democratic constitutions sometimes appear on
paper, and competitive elections sometimes occur in African states, dictatorship or civil war are generally not very far away.

Within the world system, liberal democracies have a key advantage
over other states in that they seem almost never go to war with one
another (Russett 1993). Thus with the spread of liberal democracy war
between states ought to decline. This is the essence of the 'democratic
peace' thesis, first proposed by the philosopher Immanuel Kant over 200
years ago (though Kant spoke of 'republics' rather than 'democracies').
Quite why this should be the case is a matter of some dispute among
international relations scholars. Certainly the costs of making war are
high for leaders and voters in liberal democracies. The voting population
can easily punish leaders if they launch into a war that proves miscon-
ceived and costly. And democratic leaders have to justify the war
morally to their electorate to begin with, while dictators do not.

Yet these internal political constraints on democratic leaders have not
stopped liberal democracies gratuitously initiating wars against non-
democracies. Consider for example the invasion of Iraq by US and
British forces in 2003, ostensibly undertaken to remove 'weapons of
mass destruction' that proved not to exist. Liberal democracies have
also initiated war or escalated conflicts with other democracies that are
not liberal. Think for example of Israeli military actions against
Lebanon and Palestinian-controlled Gaza in 2006, or the bombing
campaign against Serbia in 1999 over Kosovo, undertaken by NATO,
an alliance of liberal democracies. Most liberal democracies have
existed only in the late twentieth century, and they have generally been
in strategic alliance with the dominant Western powers that are themselves liberal democracies. So it is perhaps no surprise that wars
between liberal democracies have been rare. The much more recent
spread of liberal democracy well beyond the West means that the
democratic peace thesis will face tougher tests, though so far it is
holding up reasonably well.

Institutional variations among liberal democracies

The institutional arrangements of liberal democratic states vary consid-
erably along four dimensions:

(1) *Electoral systems.* Different voting systems produce very different
    sorts of popular control in a democracy. Governments can be
    elected with the support of as few as 35 per cent of voters in some
    systems or of a very strong majority in others. The former outcome
    is possible under the simplest and crudest voting system, *plurality*

rule (sometimes called first-past-the-post) used in the United States, United Kingdom, and British-influenced countries. Here candidates stand in particular areas (such as congressional districts in the United States, or constituencies in the United Kingdom), where voters, in that area, elect a single winner based on the largest number of votes. If there are multiple candidates this winning number can fall well short of 50 per cent. There is no mechanism for ensuring that the overall distribution of seats in the legislature reflects the pattern of votes in the country as a whole. In a famous proposition originated by Maurice Duverger (1955), plurality rule is expected to produce two-party systems. Duverger's 'law' was once advanced as the closest thing that political science has to a universal scientific law (see Riker 1982b). But this claimed association now holds perfectly only in the United States. Everywhere else, even in the UK, the number of significant political parties in plurality systems is at least three, sometimes more. In India, the world's largest liberal democracy, plurality voting now yields a very diverse multi-party system.

The main alternative kind of voting system is *proportional representation (PR)* where parties' seats in the legislature more or less match their shares of the votes in the electorate. Proportional representation usually produces a larger number of parties, and means that most governments are coalitions of several parties. Most liberal democracies (even sub-national units in the UK) now use some kind of PR, which comes in varied forms. They mostly rely on electing several legislators in larger constituencies, so that parties secure seats in the legislature in proportion to their total votes in the electorate as a whole.

There are also a number of hybrid systems. France uses run-off ballots among the top candidates from a multi-party election. Italy has used different PR and non-PR systems designed to give extra parliamentary seats to the most successful party or coalition and thus ensure a working government majority, as opposed to very close results that make governments unstable. Turkey and Russia use PR systems but with parties required to win a very high minimum national vote share (7 or 10 per cent) before they can take seats in the legislature. This measure is designed to guard against party fragmentation and protect large parties' vote shares, but it does so only at the cost of considerable (and in Russia massive) disproportionality. We will pay closer attention to electoral systems in Chapter 7.

(2) *Executive and legislature.* In a liberal democracy the legislature must be elected. But in full *presidential systems* (such as the US) a

president is directly elected by popular vote to serve as both head of the executive branch and head of government, while the legislature is elected separately. The US Congress is almost unique in not being controlled at all by the executive. In pure *parliamentary systems* (such as the UK, Australia, Germany, and many others), ministers are appointed from the legislature, usually from the largest party or coalition. The Prime Minister is normally the leader of the largest party in parliament, and can head the government only as long as he or she retains majority support therein. In hybrid systems (some Latin America countries, France and South Korea) there is both a directly elected president with executive powers, *and* a government of ministers headed by a premier appointed from and responsible to the elected legislature.

(3) *Centralization and decentralization.* In the few remaining *unitary states* (such as Japan, Israel and New Zealand) a central government dominates revenue-raising and spending and its powers dwarf those of local or municipal governments. At the other end of the spectrum are *federal states* where there is both a national government and regional (or state-level, or provincial) governments (as in the US, Canada, Australia, Germany, and Spain). Their relative powers are carefully specified in the constitution. The trend in Western Europe has been strongly in the direction of more quasi-federal and decentralized internal arrangements. Even the United Kingdom has moved in the direction of asymmetric federalism, as elected governments in Scotland, Wales, Northern Ireland and London (but not England) share power with the Westminster government that runs UK policy-making. Similarly, previously centralized Bonapartist countries (like France, Italy and Spain) have moved towards multi-tiered governance systems. In the European Union a unique form of quasi-federalism has developed between the member states (which are no longer termed 'nation states') and the EU's powerful central institutions (the European Council, European Commission, European Parliament, and European Court of Justice).

(4) *The role of the legal system.* In all liberal democracies judges must be independent of politicians' control. But in some countries featuring *parliamentary sovereignty* (such as Britain and New Zealand) there was no supreme court capable of striking down decisions made by the legislature, although the UK has now moved in that direction. In other systems (especially presidential and hybrid ones) a *constitutional court* has the power to declare both legislation and executive decisions unconstitutional. The American Supreme Court represents judicial review of government in its

strongest form. The United States is unique in the degree to which many major political issues end up as legal issues, thus reinforcing the 'liberal' as opposed to the 'democratic' aspect of its political system. A much weaker constitutional court exists in France. In the European Union the European Court of Justice has begun to act as a constitutional court, while a separate European Court of Human Rights helps protect civil liberties in member countries.

Changing functions of liberal democratic states

A final dimension of variation among states, and among liberal democratic states in particular, concerns what exactly states do, their functions and how they relate to the social and economic systems of the societies they govern. Here the conflicts between the liberal push to define state powers narrowly and the democratic push to use political power to address social inequalities remains strongest, and most clearly shapes the state's core priorities.

The early modern state operated in an insecure external environment and in the days before capitalist market economies. It had three core priorities: to maintain order internally (prevent civil conflict); to compete externally with other states; and to raise the revenues necessary for these first two activities (Skocpol 1979). These can be termed the order, security and revenue imperatives. Revenue was generally raised from taxation – which was often resisted by those from whom it was sought. A state unable to collect taxation could encounter deep trouble, especially in the face of enhanced external threats. If a state cares *only* about maximizing the revenues it raises then it is what Levi (1988) calls a 'predatory state' that may even undertake the impoverishment of its own society to fill its own coffers. Recent examples are not hard to find, especially in Africa, of dictators who have amassed massive personal wealth even as average incomes in their societies declined. But most states that want to maximize revenue will find that impoverishment is not a good idea, for two reasons. The first is the violent resistance it can provoke. The second is that there is a more effective way to increase revenue in the long run.

With time and the development of capitalism, state officials found that there was a less painful way to secure additional revenues. By promoting economic growth in the capitalist market economy, total revenues from taxation could increase even as rates of taxation remained constant. Thus grew what can be called the economic priority of government, or what Marxists would call the 'accumulation' imperative (see Chapter 4). Capitalist economies developed at different times in different countries, beginning in the seventeenth century with what is now the Netherlands, followed by Britain. Today, this economic imperative has become the foremost priority of most states – or at least those prosperous states that have escaped the threat of invasion by other states, or severe civil conflict. A prosperous capitalist economy requires a range of rights instrumental to the protection of private property – which was a major boost in creating liberal states, for liberalism is defined by its stress on a range of rights. Given that the core interests of business and the state now coalesced around the promotion of the conditions for economic growth, corporate leaders could enter into government from which they had been excluded when the state was dominated by absolute monarchy, landed aristocracy, and the church. Thus did the state become the *capitalist* state.

Capitalist market economies are however a mixed blessing for the state. They can generate wealth, but they are also subject to boom and bust cycles, and the associated political instability can threaten internal order. Karl Marx and his successors on the socialist and communist left long believed that this instability would necessarily culminate in a social revolution by the working class (see Chapter 4). Developed capitalist states mostly managed to avoid this fate by cushioning the blows felt by those at the lower end of the income and employment security scales. This key change was accomplished through welfare state programmes such as unemployment insurance, social security and pensions. Marxists had a name for this too, terming it the 'legitimation' function (Offe 1984), because the welfare state helped to legitimate the capitalist political economy in the eyes of the social groups that otherwise stood to suffer most from its associated instabilities. The development of welfare states meant that democratic socialist parties and union leaders, the main political representatives of the organized working class, could be accommodated within a democratic state, because their interests now coincided with one of its core priorities. The political and social stabilization thus achieved made the welfare state critical in immunizing liberal democracies against Marxist revolution, and so preserving capitalism. So the welfare state is still a kind of capitalist state.

The modern liberal state therefore has five key functions, summarized in Table 1.2, which may often stand in tension with one another. The conflict between the economic growth and welfare priorities is stressed by market liberals, who see the taxation necessary to finance the welfare state as a major drag on economic growth, and welfare itself as constituting a disincentive to the hard work on which a dynamic growing economy relies (see Chapter 5). In subsequent chapters we will explore possible additions to this set of core imperatives.

The trend for liberal democratic states to add functions and extend their reach into more areas of social life has always been controversial.

Table 1.2 *The evolving core priorities of the state*

Period	Key functions (cumulative)
Early modern state	Providing external security Maintaining internal order Raising revenue
Capitalist state	Promoting economic growth
Welfare state	Legitimating the political economy and societal arrangements as a whole through providing income security and social provisions (health care, education, etc.)

The late nineteenth century liberal democratic capitalist states in Europe and North America mostly limited themselves to external defence, maintaining internal law and order, collecting taxation, underpinning markets with a legal system, and undertaking limited public works. But they also turned a blind eye to extremes of poverty and social inequality. The rise of the welfare state meant that government got involved in a range of social programmes, developed most comprehensively in the Scandinavian countries where around 60 per cent of GDP is now allocated by governments, as opposed to around half this level in the US or Japan. Governments also came to play increasingly large roles in funding and operating public education systems – seen as an economic necessity even by most market liberals.

The path to the mixed capitalist-welfare state was followed most smoothly in western Europe. Especially between 1945 and 1976 the state in many countries grew steadily larger in terms of budgets and personnel. Military arms races associated with the Cold War also played a part in the growth of government in the US, alongside a growth in welfare and educational spending, and increasing regulation of the market economy. A counter-attack strongly influenced by market liberal ideology and responding to a perceived crisis of excessive demands upon the state, saw some shedding of functions and personnel by governments in developed Western states during the 1980s and 1990s. But outside the most advanced industrial economies, welfare provision still remains patchy or poor. Many states (including long-lived liberal democracies like India) still have poorly developed capitalist economies, and weak to non-existent welfare systems for the mass of their populations.

Conclusion

The state remains central to modern political processes. Laws or regulations may be remade to ban or restrict activities; state budgets may be enlarged and resources requisitioned in taxes; existing public facilities may be closed or government subsidies redirected to other groups and interests; or wars or crises may erupt. But state processes equally lie at the heart of positive changes to promote economic development, to create hope for people to escape from or alleviate poverty, and to oversee general improvements in living standards. The state's involvement in virtually all political processes accounts for the frequently high intensity of the conflicts associated with it. There are many ways in which a different majority at the ballot box, a change in the relative influence of interest groups, the arrival in power of a new political leadership, or a shifting balance of influence in international relations may reconfigure the state and so change people's conditions and life prospects.

Part I

The Classical Theories

For much of the twentieth century the configuration of theories of the state was much simpler than it is today. Four classical theories competed for the attention of scholars, students, activists and political leaders. Though all four theories have since run into problems, they still set the basic terms of reference for all theories of the state, and the liberal democratic state in particular. And all still gain some support, however qualified that support might be, and however much it might have shrunk over time. Even when a particular theory seems to be in the doldrums, its supporters can still hope for a comeback. Thus an understanding of these four classical theories – pluralism, elite theory, Marxism and market liberalism – is essential for anyone who wishes to understand how liberal democratic states work, as well as come to grips with the nuances of contemporary accounts of how states can, do, and should operate.

Pluralism as analysed in Chapter 2 stresses the multiple influences within and upon policy making, and in particular the role played by diverse organized interest groups, though it does not ignore other influences, such as that of ordinary voters in elections. Relevant groups might include labour unions, business associations and organizations campaigning for social justice, environmental, religious or conservative values. Pluralists explain policy making and the operations of the state in terms of the interaction of multiple forces. They also believe this diversity is a good way to organize government and policy, and so support mechanisms for dispersing power.

Elite theorists as addressed in Chapter 3 believe that all this talk of pluralist multiplicity is a sham: that in reality the state and society are controlled by a single, unified elite. In the first half of the twentieth century most elite theorists defended elite dominance. In the mid twentieth century elite theory was adopted by radical critics of the liberal democratic state, who sought to expose and criticize the role of elites, especially economic elites.

Marxists, discussed in Chapter 4, believe that in the end politics reduces to economics, so that the dominant economic class is also the dominant political class. Thus in capitalist economic systems, it is the owners and controllers of business who will exercise control; and ultimately the state will be structured and operated so as to serve their interests. Only with the overthrow of capitalism could this situation be changed.

Market liberals as examined in Chapter 5 also stress economics – but in a very different way. While Marxists emphasize economic classes, market liberals emphasize individuals. Market liberals believe that individuals interacting in markets produce generally good results, but individuals interacting in governments (whether as voters, politicians, bureaucrats or lobbyists) produce collectively bad results. Thus the prescription is for the role of markets to be maximized, while that of government should be reduced to its minimum necessary functions.

Chapter 2

Pluralism

Pluralism is a belief in many (plural) ways of life, many approaches to knowledge and many centres of power in society, committed to moderate, non-rancorous competition. These conditions are thought by pluralists to be best achieved, and ultimately perhaps only achievable, under liberal democracy. Intellectually, pluralism is opposed to all forms of 'monism' in political and social thought – those belief systems which appeal to a single philosophical idea or over-arching value, a single theory of history or evolutionary path, a single culture or way of life, a single religion or sacred book, or a single centre of government.

As a *normative* theory, pluralism stresses the beneficial consequences of social and cultural diversity, of having many different institutions, values, groups and ways of life. It also advocates constitutional ways of accommodating different perspectives on public policy issues. As an *explanatory* theory of politics, pluralism shows how policy gets made in interactions across diverse actors and institutions. Liberal democracies are described as 'polyarchies' with multiple centres of power, so governed by the many, not the few. This effect is achieved primarily by the interest group process; competitive elections that can only be won by organizing coalitions of minority views; and representative government. It is possible to believe in explanatory pluralism while denying normative pluralism, and vice versa. However, in practice explanatory and normative pluralism mesh together in the theories of prominent authors.

In the 1950s pluralism became the dominant American political science approach to analyzing liberal democracy, though it has a European history too. We examine here pluralism's diverse origins, its basic assumptions, its account of the social sources of interests, its view of government; and the reasons for some eventual challenges to it.

Origins and Core Assumptions: The Roots of Pluralism

Pluralism has philosophical origins in liberal views opposed to rule by a single person (such as an absolute monarch or dictator), or a single faction, such as a dominant religion. Thus pluralism draws on core liberal ideas arguing for limited, constitutional government, especially:

- *Individual rights* such as freedom of speech, association and private property. The British philosopher John Locke, writing in the late seventeenth century, developed a pivotal justification for these rights. He thought that excessive infringements of rights by a ruler could justify rebellion. His nineteenth century successor, John Stuart Mill, argued for the primacy of civil rights in all social arrangements. In his view rights are inalienable human attributes – they are not capable of being given away or taken away from people.
- *Balanced institutional arrangements* originally designed to undermine absolute monarchy by splitting up legislative, executive and judicial powers and assigning them to different institutions. The term 'separation of powers' was coined in 1748 by the French commentator Baron Montesquieu, writing mainly about British constitutional arrangements, dominated by a bi-cameral Parliament. Montesquieu's interpretation of Britain was not quite accurate, for this was a period when British monarchs controlled the executive and had perfected the art of creating majorities by buying votes in an overwhelmingly aristocratic Parliament. And while the British judiciary was genuinely separate, it was hardly neutral or incorrupt. None the less Britain had a more inclusive and competitive power structure than most European states at this time.
- *Decentralized or federal systems of government*, of the sort first established by the constitution of the United States in 1789. In the mid 1830s another French commentator, Alexis de Tocqueville, toured the United States and in his influential *Democracy in America* lauded the 'absence of central administration. The national majority does not pretend to do everything' (1945: 281).

All these proposals for countervailing distributions of power were anathema to the centralizing impulse of the absolute monarchies that dominated Europe from the sixteenth to the eighteenth centuries, against which liberal ideas struggled. For liberals, civil rights would give individuals and companies (newly established as important legal entities in their own right) a way to resist unwarranted government demands. The separation of powers would give the different branches of government specified authority in relation to the other branches. And federalism would position the powers of different levels of government against one another. The overall ensemble of provisions, as in James Madison's design for the American republic adopted in 1789, would guard against any one 'faction' acting tyrannically. These arrangements would also constrain the operations of democracy, so that even a large majority of voters could not oppress minorities.

By the middle of the nineteenth century this general liberal position was well articulated, even if it was still to be completely implemented anywhere. It was only in the late nineteenth century that a distinctive pluralist position could be separated from liberalism as a whole. Its subsequent rise to dominance in political science was influenced by three main streams of thought, which we discuss in turn: philosophical and political pluralism; the sociology of modern industrial society; and the scientific development of political science.

Philosophical and political pluralism in the early twentieth century

From the late nineteenth century through to the inter-war period there were intense conflicts between three competing primary philosophical ideals – the individual, the state and groups or voluntary associations (see Figure 2.1). Classical liberalism posited the primacy of individual flourishing and development as the rationale for all human life, justifying individual rights against the state. There were disputes within liberalism about the role of firms and corporations, which in industrial societies had greatly increased in their size, political power, and significance.

Pluralists highlighted groups and voluntary associations in an effort to transcend the state versus individual (absolutism versus liberalism) conflicts which had been waxing and waning since the seventeenth century. A range of thinkers in the US and Britain began to stress that the

Figure 2.1   *Competing philosophical ideals in the period from 1880 to 1939*

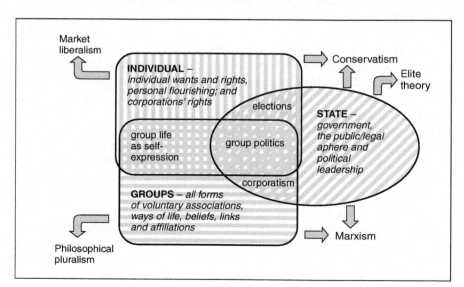

life of an isolated individual is culturally rootless and impoverished compared with that of someone whose life is rooted in their community, strongly shaped by their class, ethnicity, religion or political affiliation. In the United States, the arrival of massive numbers of immigrants and the vast expansion of industrial cities sparked fears among liberals that the established democratic culture would be swamped by the newly arrived 'masses'. In fact, nothing of the kind took place, for the incomers had strong cultural traditions of their own which they preserved and adapted in American conditions, while assimilating into the politics and economics of the US. Yet US pluralists did not rest their arguments on the multiplicity of cultures, but rather in the diversity of experience – and eventually diversity of economic interest. The philosopher John Dewey (1917: 288) noted that 'the theory of the melting pot always gave me rather a pang', because of the loss of diversity it implied.

In early twentieth century Europe the focus of pluralist thought was on historically voluntary associations like the churches, community organizations and charities. Some conservative pluralists (consistent with the social thought of the Catholic Church) stressed the importance of voluntary and intermediate organizations as bridging between business and labour, bringing business into social responsibility while integrating organized labour into moderate politics instead of radical militancy. Left-leaning pluralist thinkers grappled with the emerging community life of the newly enlarged industrial cities and assigned a central role to the increasingly powerful trade unions, which organized self-help welfare, housing and health, and to mass political parties, with their youth and women's organizations.

In some European countries, such as in Scandinavia and the UK, pluralism sat uneasily alongside social democratic ideas about welfare state provision as the twentieth century developed. Inadequate voluntary efforts to provide health insurance or protection in old age for the poor were rejected by social democrats in favour of fully government-run, national, universal provision. But in France and Germany governments were more often assigned an integrating and supporting role in welfare provision, underpinning (rather than completely replacing) the efforts of voluntary, regional and local bodies. After 1945 these ideas contributed to a centre-left version of corporatism – a kind of restricted interest politics encompassing trade union federations and business associations negotiating directly with government.

American advocates emphasized relatively unbounded pluralism, with any group seen as capable of carving out some political influence. In contrast, European pluralists proposed a more organized and government-influenced system, and wondered how welfare state programmes (and perhaps public ownership of key problem industries, like coal-mining) might mitigate the conflicts between business and labour. Both European and American pluralists saw elections and representative government as key facilitators of group influence.

The different strands and emphases of philosophical pluralism came together and acquired much wider and deeper cultural resonance in the United States and Britain around World War II. Nazi Germany's defeat gave way to the onset of the Cold War with the Soviet Union under Stalin and China under Mao Zedong. Pluralists stigmatized the common monist character of Nazi, fascist and communist regimes under the concept of 'totalitarianism'. Hannah Arendt (1951) saw its essential feature as the 'atomization of society', where every interme-diate association (family, friendship, religion, trade union, business association, profession, university and the media) was either destroyed or taken over by the state. In a vision also given vivid expression by George Orwell in his novel *1984*, Arendt argued that totalitarian states' penetration and governance of all aspects of society, their unceasing and pervasive propaganda, and systematic use of terror were closely and necessarily connected. Such states sought to create a mass of iso-lated individuals, absolutely loyal to the state, personified in a single dominant leader (Hitler, Stalin or Mao). Each person would be unshel-tered by any form of independent social organization against complete state surveillance and direction. Another pluralist philosopher, Karl Popper, summed up the conflict between pluralism and totalitarianism as one between *The Open Society and its Enemies* (1966). The core message (in the words of Isaiah Berlin) was that any argument for 'enlightened despotism' leads inevitably to state monism and hence is 'one of the most powerful and dangerous arguments in the entire his-tory of human thought' (Lezard 2007).

Philosophical pluralists believe diversity is basic to all phenomena. As Hannah Arendt (1978: 183) writes:

> Everything which exists in a plurality of things is not simply what it is, in its identity, but it is also different from other things; this being different belongs to its very nature. When we try to get hold of it in thought, wanting to define it, we must take this otherness or differ-ence into account. When we say what a thing is, we also say what it is not.

In the West, this pluralism can now seem common sense:

> There are respects . . . in which we are all pluralists. At the core of pluralism is a recognition that there are a multiplicity of persons

and groups that are, on the one hand, identifiably related to one another and, on the other hand, can be usefully distinguished from other persons and groups ... Thus understood, I can think of no one who is not, here and now and however regretfully, a pluralist. (Flathman 2005: 1)

Flathman's observation may apply to contemporary Western democracies, but plenty of ideologies have exhorted individuals and groups to subordinate their identity to some common whole. Fascists, communists, ethnic nationalists and religious fundamentalists have all seen the world in such terms.

Post-1945 philosophical pluralism therefore embraced with renewed vigour the arguments of John Stuart Mill in his classic book *On Liberty* (1859), that both individual liberty and diversity of opinions are necessary for humans to flourish and for societies to progress. Only in encountering and disagreeing with people with different ideas and experiences could individuals come to know and develop their own interests and opinions. Pluralism would help create reflective and capable individuals. Isaiah Berlin in 1950 developed the notion of 'value pluralism', in which different fundamental systems of goods and bads are recognized as competing for acceptance, their relationships being incapable of being uniformly resolved. Thus pluralism was a necessary, integral and permanent aspect of the human condition. Popper (1966) argued that in the 'open society' only very limited 'piecemeal social engineering' should be planned or contemplated, for more radical solutions to social ills would always go wrong. Faced with failure, their instigators would be tempted by a slippery slope of ever-growing coercion to make their schemes work.

The sociology of modern industrial and urban society

A second key impetus for pluralism came with the need for liberalism to confront the realities of industrial civilization, especially in the major conurbations and cities in which the late nineteenth century concentrated huge numbers of people. Some versions of pluralism were nostalgic for Jefferson's liberal vision of self-governing agrarian communities. But the implication of the sociological literature on industrialization was that there was no going back. In the US the inter-war years were particularly important in the social scientific documentation of the rich tapestry of urban life. The Chicago School of Sociology led by R.G. Burgess traced the rich variety of communal life in cities and the never-ending competition of different social groups for 'territory'. People of similar origins, race, nationality, language and religion grouped together in neighbourhoods with their own distinctive customs and social life, and used urban housing markets and cycles of development to work out an always changing accommodation of different groups (Dunleavy 1982). Burgess and his colleague Park believed in a kind of 'survival of the fittest' dynamic, so that often neighbourhoods were forcibly wrested from one ethnic group or social use and then rapidly switched character, expelling laggards at considerable social cost.

Where elite theorists saw only undifferentiated and powerless 'masses', the American urban sociologists traced the flourishing of ethnic variety. And where earlier liberals had feared the consequences of immigrant groups' cultures surviving and coming to dominate American society, the new focus saw 'cross-cutting cleavages' of ethnicity and social class as forces for stability. In his 1920 textbook Ross argued:

> A society . . . ridden by a dozen oppositions along lines running in every direction may actually be in less danger of being torn with violence or falling to pieces than one split along just one line. Each new cleavage contributes to narrow the cross clefts, so that one might say that society is sewn together by its inner conflicts. (Ross 1920: 164–5)

In Europe pluralist thought tried to dispel the gloomy generalizations of theorists of mass society by looking at the robust community life found in working class areas as much as in middle-class suburbs or upper-class enclaves.

Post-1945 European social policy was dominated by the newly enlarged welfare state, whose advocacy became the most distinctive European element of pluralist thought. In 1950 the British sociologist T.H. Marshall wrote a classic of 'welfare pluralism', arguing for an ineluctable modernization process in which the rights of citizens in liberal democracies developed into social democracy through three phases:

- *Legal and civil rights*, involving property and inheritance, rights to form companies and enterprises, and legal protections against arbitrary state interference and requisition. At first restricted to privileged groups, the logic of legal implementation would mean that these rights became progressively generalized to everyone, opening the way to achieve
- *Political rights*, with freedom of speech and association (for example, in trade unions), the extension of the franchise and the advent of liberal democracy; leading inevitably to

- *Effective economic and social rights*, especially protection against poverty caused by unemployment, provision for people to live decently in old-age and effective insurance against the worst contingencies of ill-health.

The development of political science

On the face of it, the political system designed in the US Constitution might seem very hospitable to pluralist analysis. The men of property who wrote the Constitution believed that the separation of powers, federalism, a strong set of individual rights against government, and a complex and indirect system of representation, all protected against the centralization of power and oppression of minorities. They also helped ensure a multiplicity of centres of power of the kind that pluralists favoured.

Yet, oddly enough, in the late nineteenth and early twentieth century, the new academic discipline of political science in America was anything but pluralist. It was instead defined professionally by its focus on an ideal of a modernizing and integrating state. When they looked at US arrangements, early political scientists such as Francis Lieber, John Burgess, and Woodrow Wilson saw not a paragon of effective government, but instead a shambles of corruption (especially in cities dominated by party machines), patronage, amateurism, parochialism, sectionalism (with the South especially protecting its interests), and inefficiency. They looked to undemocratic Germany as the model of an efficient modern constitutional state, with a centralized bureaucracy implementing clear policy decisions (Gunnell 1995: 21–2). They believed that the modern dynamic industrial economy of the United States now required a modern dynamic and unitary state. As Frank Goodnow (1904) put it in the first presidential address to the new American Political Science Association, the discipline was to help in the 'realization of state will'. These US political scientists were not exactly elite theorists, because they recognized the importance of a supportive and active national community. And they had no wish to import German monarchy, aristocracy or authoritarianism, instead believing that an efficient administrative state could be combined with American freedoms and democracy. Their national state would be accompanied by a virtuous national citizenry that would transcend local and regional identifications. We noted in Chapter 1 that Woodrow Wilson (1887) believed this kind of state could 'breathe free American air'. The task of political science was to advance the cause of the centralized state. The early political scientists' reform agenda did find some political allies, notably in the Progressive Movement which flourished from the 1890s to 1920s seeking to modernize American politics, clean up corruption, and open up government to public scrutiny. But in the end the reformers proved no match for the durable complex features of the American system they opposed.

These early centralizing statists in the political science profession could recognize multiplicity in the influences acting upon the US federal state, but they called it 'fragmentation', seeing it as a problem to be overcome, and certainly not a 'pluralism' to be valued. Although the US constitution was supposed to provide a cure for 'the mischiefs of faction' in checks and balances, these arrangements could not prevent the acute and long-lived factional conflict between North and South leading to civil war in the 1860s. Professional political scientists believed lingering parochialism and sectionalism could only be overcome by a strong, centralized federal state, which was eventually glimpsed in World War I.

In the early twentieth century a number of US theorists began to speak of pluralism in more positive terms. Foremost among them were Mary Parker Follett (1918) and Harold Laski (1917) – Laski was actually British but spent a few years in the United States, where his criticisms of the US political and social systems achieved widespread resonance. They emphasized the variety of ways in which individuals could experience the world, and so the variety of legitimate political positions it was possible to take. Democratic politics therefore involved debate across these different sorts of positions. Follett and Laski offered a normative theory of pluralist politics, though they were not specific on its details.

Since its nineteenth century founding, US political science has always featured movements trying to render it more scientific. In the 1940s the advent of new methods, such as large-scale sample surveys and statistics, boosted the scientific disposition. Surveys in particular could measure observable phenomena and express with quantitative data propositions that had hitherto been based on impressionistic generalizations.

Survey research and election studies were joined to the influential account of democracy developed by the Austrian émigré Joseph Schumpeter (1943), whose realist and cynical approach to liberal democracy also made him a bridging figure between pluralism and modern elite theory. Political scientists influenced by Schumpeter (e.g. Berelson 1952) attacked what they imagined to be the 'classical' picture of democracy given by philosophers, in which 'the will of the people' could be expressed in public policy through informed voting (though no political philosophers actually subscribed to this view). Schumpeter had a low opinion of ordinary people, believing that the typical citizen became 'infantile' when called upon to exercise political judgment. Yet harried from continental Europe by the onset of Nazism, first to the UK and then to America, Schumpeter nevertheless thought that the two-party systems of his host countries were worth defending. In his view they alone resisted the rise of fascism in the 1930s and 1940s because their electoral arrangements froze out extremist parties and required that voters either endorse the incumbent government or a single main opposition party alternative. Voters in his view did not have any well-formed political opinions, so there was really no such thing as 'public opinion'. As Robert Dahl (1956: 131) later noted:

> [E]lections . . . are quite ineffective as indicators of majority prefer-
> ences . . . A good deal of traditional democratic theory leads us to
> expect more from national elections than they can possibly provide.
> We expect elections to reveal the 'will' or the preferences of a
> majority on a set of issues. This is one thing elections rarely do,
> except in an almost trivial fashion.

Schumpeter argued that it is only political elites (politicians and parties) that generate ideas. Government inherently rests with these elites, but they must be plural and forced to compete for popular endorsement in order to guard against dictatorship. All that ordinary citizens are required to do is thus to choose periodically between alternative teams of leaders provided by different parties.

Schumpeter's view of the limited capabilities of ordinary citizens was apparently confirmed by studies of voting behaviour. The first mass surveys seemed to show an electorate in the US and later in the UK and Europe where people had minimal levels of political information, had little interest in politics and voted on habitual lines based on party identification in the US and on social class in the UK. In 1967 the political scientist Peter Pulzer wrote that 'class is the basis of politics in Britain – all else is embellishment and detail'. These findings were taken up and rationalized in what came to be known as 'empirical democratic theory' (Berelson 1952) in which Schumpeter's minimal view of elections played centre stage. It seemed that greater electoral participation could only bring into political life groups of even less well-informed voters, so that widespread public apathy contributed to political stability.

As Anglo-American political science eulogized the simple plurality rule voting systems of the World War II victors and explained why minimally informed voters could none the less suffice to maintain elite competition, political science attention also shifted from elections toward the interest group process. In the 1920s George Catlin (1927) had introduced an explanatory theory of American politics in which competition among groups was seen as the driving force in producing public policy. The centrality of groups in the American political process was earlier stressed by Arthur Bentley (1908: 208) who argued: 'When the groups are adequately stated, everything is stated. When I say everything, I mean everything'. His 1908 book on *The Political Process* was rediscovered as a key pluralist text in the post-war period by David Truman (1951). Truman's insistence on documenting only observable political conflicts influenced all subsequent pluralist writers.

Pluralists believed that the fundamental building block of political life is the interest group (and not, for example, the individual or the state itself). The term 'interest group' was cemented into political discourse by Truman (1951). Groups for Truman are based on the common interest of their members – especially material economic interest. This stress on interests differentiated mid twentieth century pluralists from their predecessors, who stressed diversity in experience instead. Professional associations, chambers of commerce, labour unions, student unions and organizations of retired, disabled or unemployed people are all examples of associations based on material self-interest. Advocacy groups for the environment, human rights, animal welfare, international justice and so forth are less easily reduced to material interests. But whatever the kind of shared interest, pluralists believed that groups promote human flourishing. Groups provide a training ground where ordinary people can hone political skills and acquire an understanding of how democratic politics necessitates bargaining and compromise.

Aside from the simple existence of groups, pluralists stressed two other key features. The first was rough equality across groups: no category of people is systematically blocked from either forming a group or competing on equal terms with other groups. The second was the idea of 'latent groups': any category of people who share an interest *could* form a group, even if they have not yet done so. Awareness of latent groups induces a measure of responsiveness to them on the part of policy makers.

The interest group process operates continuously between elections and creates a complex interplay of influences in which pluralists argued that every social group can find some place and some leverage over elected politicians when it comes to issues that matter to them. Pluralist political scientists argued that a 'civic culture' where ordinary people believe in their capacity to influence officials while not being too enthusiastic about politics for its own sake is the key safeguard of democracy (Almond and Verba 1963). By the 1960s this culture was supposedly much better developed in the US and UK than in countries like France that had succumbed to Nazi invasion; or Germany, Italy and Japan, where democratic regimes were painstakingly rebuilt in the 1950s.Thus the voluntary associations and groups highlighted as important by philosophical pluralism and linked to modernization and industrial/urban civilization by sociologists also turned out to be politically decisive, supplementing imperfect electoral mechanisms for linking people to politics.

Society and Politics

The 1950s and 1960s were the heyday of pluralist influence in political science. Despite their supposed behavioralist objectivity, many mid twentieth century American political scientists often ran together their explanatory and normative models, at least when it came to US politics. As Seymour Martin Lipset (1960: 403) put it, there was no need for theorists to look for the good society, because the United States was 'the good society in operation'. Critics portrayed this school of thought as simply rationalizing US and European liberal democracy, as part of the Cold War ideological battle with the communist bloc.

   Robert Dahl introduced the concept of 'polyarchy' to describe a political system conferring control of policy by the many, in order to characterize the *imperfect* extent to which liberal democratic ideals were realized in America, Europe and other countries with representative governments. He recognized explicitly that apart from the vote 'with few exceptions, the . . . resources [for influencing politicians and the policy process] are unequally distributed' (Dahl 1961: 228). 'If you examine carefully any policy decision, you will always discover, I believe, that only a quite tiny proportion of the electorate is actively bringing its influence to bear upon politicians' (Dahl 1956: 130).

   Yet he also claimed that: 'Virtually no one, and certainly no group of more than a few individuals, is entirely lacking in some influence resources'. And while he more dispassionately recognized the US political system as an 'American hybrid' (rather than any perfect or best attainable form of liberal democracy) he still wrote:

> I defined the 'normal' American political process as one in which there is a high probability that an active and legitimate group in the population can make itself heard effectively at some crucial stage in the process of decision. To be 'heard' covers a wide range of activities. (Dahl 1956: 145)

Yet Dahl was also well aware that his definition had get-out clauses built into it, remarking:

> In the South, Negroes were not until recently an active group. Evidently, Communists are not now a legitimate group. As compared with what one would expect from the normal system, Negroes were relatively defenseless in the past, just as the Communists are now. (Dahl 1956: 138)

Written in the wake of the visceral campaign led by Senator Joe McCarthy against alleged communist influence in American government and the media, this is at best a laconic understatement. But, in the end, McCarthy's influence proved short-lived and his bullying methods and cavalier attitude to evidence led to his marginalization from political influence. The anti-communist hysteria of the early Cold War period abated somewhat and in the 1960s the apparently shattered non-Marxist American left regrouped.

Key pluralist propositions about US politics advanced by Dahl and others were:

- The resources for political influence are widely distributed and the underlying political consensus supports the legitimacy of diverse viewpoints.
- Any category of people who share an interest *can* form a group, even if they have not yet done so. Awareness of these 'latent groups' guarantees some consideration of their interests by policy makers and politicians.
- There are multiple channels of access, with opportunities for interest groups shut out of one way into political influence to find other ways in. Groups can lobby members of Congress, make campaign contributions to elected officials, participate in public hearings, seek meetings with administrators in bureaucratic agencies, use the media to reach the attention of publics and politicians, and take action through the courts if they can argue that government is either acting in unconstitutional fashion or if an administrative decision is inconsistent with a relevant law. Strikes and demonstrations were also a possibility, though pluralists tended to stress orderly and non-coercive influence.
- By combining their votes, finance and supporting activities together a wide range of groups can secure a reasonably effective political voice, including coverage by the media.
- There is no single dominant type of political resource that is

instantly convertible into a currency of power. Money does not
buy everything, when it comes to politics.

* Although there are elites who run activities in each sphere of social
  life (politics, the legal system, the media, business corporations,
  cultural systems), these elites are separate from each other and
  their interests often diverge. For instance, although politicians and
  media journalists often have a symbiotic relationship, their interests also diverge over scandals and scoops about abuses of power
  or even about freedom of information.

Competitive elections with party policies ranging across a whole spectrum of policies provide the foundation for enlarging the number and
range of groups who are influential, and a deep pool of opinion that
can be mobilized against any group that seems to have excessive political influence. Pluralists debunked claims of overwhelming business
influence by showing that most corporations were politically inactive
most of the time, and that business trade associations often failed to
intervene politically on issues where they had interests at stake (Bauer
et al. 1963; Grant and Marsh 1977). And in a series of community
power studies of American cities pluralists claimed to show empirically
that at this level there was no single 'power elite' (see notably Dahl
1961). Instead a broadly based political system existed in which elected
politicians made the key decisions, always with a keen eye to their
political consequences, needing to involve other social and economic
interests in most major projects and always concerned to minimize
organized opposition. Pluralists also stressed the creative role played by
politicians in assembling coalitions of different interests, persuading
them to work together, and formulating a policy programme that they
could all accept.

The weight that each group can exert is a function of factors such as
its financial resources, professional expertise, the charisma of its leadership, the number of its supporters, its capacity to affect election results
and its ability to inflict damage through withdrawing its cooperation
with government. A generalization of the pluralist view said that its
effectiveness (E) is a function of the group's size (S) which affects how
many votes it controls; its rate of mobilization (M), which affects how
many of them pay attention to the group's leadership; the extent to
which its members are willing to undertake costs, reflecting in turn the
intensity of its members' preferences (I); and finally the extent to which
the group is pivotal (P), so that its position makes a difference to politicians' chances of winning or losing (Dunleavy 1991: 23).

In Europe and Commonwealth countries (like Canada, Australia and
New Zealand) the American emphasis on the primacy of interest

groups was taken up with enthusiasm by some scholars. But in other countries (such as France) the evidence suggested that interest groups and voluntary associations were weakly developed in terms of their political impacts. Instead, political parties and elected politicians were much more important. Efforts to detect a 'community power structure' in European cities matching the decentralized and multi-centred networks that pluralists claimed to have uncovered in the US also foundered (Dunleavy 1980: Ch. 2). Instead elected mayors or councils and their political parties (plus trade unions) seemed to be the key actors, with politicians relying on state revenues and capabilities in shaping urban policies. At least in the UK, most economic and social elites of this time were simply very distant and removed from the political process. Elsewhere (such as France and Italy) local 'notables' clearly remained important in city and regional politics, but in close knit structures more suggestive of elite theory than of pluralism.

Government and Policy Making

Pluralist political scientists have studied processes of government and policy making in legislatures, executives and public administration. The US Congress was portrayed as a world where legislators were constantly striving to protect their constituencies' interests, bringing home 'pork barrel' benefits to boost groups' support (Mayhew 1974). With weakly organized parties (voting together no more than 65 per cent of the time) Congress was dominated by its committees, each composed mainly of Representatives or Senators with strong constituency interests in the committee's jurisdiction, often with strong links to relevant interest groups and to the relevant federal agencies – the so-called 'iron triangle' of influences. So the House and Senate Agriculture committees would be composed of members from farm states, cultivating links with agribusiness and the federal Department of Agriculture.

Political scientists were generally less active in studying the inherently less observable internal politics of executive government. Accounts of top-level decision-making stressed the US President's need to build legislative coalitions and the subordination of the US's growing post-war military establishment to civilian direction and control. The Cuban missile crisis of 1962 became the best documented case study of executive policy making where diverse perspectives were brought to bear in productive fashion (Allison 1972).

In the study of bureaucracies pluralist scholars argued that while officials and departments contribute to the pluralist mix of influences on public policy, they do not exercise decisive or autonomous authority in doing so. Instead public policy was seen as the resultant of the forces applied to government, pulling it in different directions. So for example when it comes to health care policy, the American Medical Association, health insurance companies, major hospitals, patients' groups and unions representing workers in the health care system all push for their own interests. The policy result will be some compromise, sensitive to the relative weight of the different interests. The content of this compromise might well shift over time as the relative power of groups waxed and waned, and as they manoeuvred with and against one another. For 'hyper-pluralists' the government machine functioned as no more than a weather vane, assessing the group influence behind different policy alternatives and then reflecting it faithfully, but not positively shaping policy. This was a society-centred view of politics.

Yet the heyday of American pluralism from the 1940s to the 1960s also saw a diffuse recognition that federal bureaucracies were now such large organizations in their own right, and controlled areas of discretionary policy so often removed from the immediate concerns of interest groups, that to see them as inactive ciphers was not plausible. The growth of the post-war US state produced many attempts to reform government through centralized planning and goal-oriented policy analysis. Popular rationalist techniques included cost-benefit analysis from economics, systems analysis from engineering, decision analysis from game theory, management by objectives and programme budgeting (which involved allocating public expenditures according to how they could most efficiently contribute to realizing the explicit goals of government, the 'bangs per buck' criterion).

Pluralist theorists such as Charles Lindblom (1959) ridiculed such a 'rational-comprehensive' approach to public policy as essentially impossible, imposing an unfeasible burden of calculation on policy makers. The organization theorist Herbert Simon stressed that decision-makers must necessarily operate in a 'boundedly rational' manner, conducting only a limited search for 'satisfactory' solutions, rather than the comprehensive search across all options for a perfect maximizing solution envisaged by classical economic models. Aaron Wildavsky (1964) took aim at the rationalizers' budgeting techniques, arguing that the federal government's annual budget was inescapably formulated through a set of informal practices and rules of thumb. This process always used the previous year's budget allocations as a baseline, rather than starting from scratch with a presumption of zero and then justifying the whole of a department's or a programme's budget. That is, the budgetary process was incremental.

A general theory of incrementalism as a paradigm of pluralist decision-making was developed by Lindblom (1959; see also Dahl and Lindblom 1953), who tried to move away from treating the policy making process itself as a 'black box', and to show exactly why politicians and government officials are responsive to the influence of different groups. He argued that decision-makers normally suffer from a shortage of relevant information, not just data but also causal models about how policy takes effect. Thus they must take shortcuts and operate in Simon's 'satisficing' manner, seeking solutions that are acceptable or 'good enough', rather than optimal. Making collective decisions when there are incompatible preferences among interests in society is very difficult. The best way to navigate these incompatibilities is through some form of accommodation, a process Lindblom termed 'partisan mutual adjustment'. Decision makers look for policies where 'the adverse consequences of any one decision for other decisions in the set [of all policy decisions] are to a degree and in some cases frequently avoided, reduced, counterbalanced or outweighed' (Braybrooke and Lindblom 1963: 154). Together these constraints mean that the decision-making process operates as 'disjointed incrementalism', or in more colloquial language, 'muddling through'. The best defence against making mistakes and suffering losses of political support is to change from the status quo in many small and reversible steps, filtering out the most controversial options and progressing those with least disagreement. Here Lindblom echoed philosophical pluralists' views, such as Popper's claim that in an 'open society' only 'piecemeal social engineering' can ever be attempted.

The implicit conservatism of the pluralist stance was highlighted by many critics, who argued that disjointed incrementalism makes sense as a strategy only if the societal status quo is already accepted as tolerable by most or all interests and groups. In fact pluralists were not as conservative as the summary above implies, since they believed that the creative competition of politicians for votes will lead them to identify and appeal to under-represented interests, in some circumstances promoting substantial social change. In Truman's (1951) view President Roosevelt's New Deal programme in the depression-hit 1930s was a good example of how political entrepreneurs in a democracy can mobilize the support of what seemed to be weak but were still electorally numerous minority groups, re-weighting and aggregating their demands and finding new policy solutions so as to allow inequalities to be addressed in radically new ways. The post-war expansion of welfare states, especially in Western Europe, was also seen as testifying to the overall responsiveness and inclusiveness of polyarchies.

In European and other non-American contexts pluralist empirical studies of the policy-making process were thin on the ground, but by the 1960s US models were influential elsewhere. The theory of incrementalism seemed especially applicable because budgetary systems in

Europe often explicitly allowed for the up-rating of an unanalysed 'base budget' for inflation, with explicit attention focusing only on new budget items. European studies focusing on social policy often ascribed stronger influence to elections and party politics and less influence to interest groups in shaping welfare state policies than did American analyses.

Crisis and Change in Pluralist Thought

Pluralism was shaken to the core by political events of the late 1960s, and further weakened by changing intellectual currents. While still defended by the political science mainstream, pluralism was on the defensive. Four developments contributed to this radical change.

(i)   Political changes that revealed successful alternatives to US and British style political systems.
(ii)   The rise of public choice theory and an associated 'market liberal' challenge from the political right.
(iii) American pluralism's failure to engage sufficiently with the changing size and capabilities of the US federal government and of the political salience of big corporations.
(iv)   The impact of unprecedented civil unrest in the US and Europe in the late 1960s and early 1970s. This was the killer blow.

We briefly review each of these changes in turn.

Political changes.

The intellectual impacts of World War II diminished with time, and the seeming need to rally around the US and UK political systems (as somehow the natural order of things for liberal democracies) faded. Germany, Italy and Japan all established successful liberal democracies. And west European nations with proportional representation systems and strong welfare states increasingly seemed as stable as the Anglo-American pattern of two-party competition.

Pluralism was bolstered by the retreat of monist ideas throughout the world, but this very retreat showed that the world could not be understood in terms of a simple, Manichean 'pluralism versus monism' struggle. The threat of fascism faded away, making the 1930s and 1940s increasingly appear as an atypical 'dark age' that would not return. France and West Germany bound themselves and their smaller neighbours closely together in the European Economic Community (EEC), resolved to make European wars impossible. Monism lingered in the Soviet Union, though countries in the Soviet orbit often strained to escape it. China entered a new totalitarian terror phase in 1967 with Mao Zedong's 'Cultural Revolution', but this had little appeal in the West.

The rise of public choice arguments

The US economist Mancur Olson (1965) challenged the idea that people with a common material interest could easily or naturally organize to advance that interest in politics, a proposition that seemed so obvious to the pluralists that they had not analysed it in detail. Olson pointed out that even if individuals share an interest, then in any reasonably large group a rational individual should realize that his or her contribution can make virtually no difference to the success of the group under two conditions – when the group membership is so numerous that it will win anyway; and if the group is so small that it can not win. In these circumstances any rational actor should 'free ride' on the efforts of others, meaning that they will only contribute in the rare event that the group's success or failure is so finely balanced that it depends in some visible way on their individual participation. The problem is that all individuals should feel the same way, so that most of the time none of them should rationally put any effort into the group. To overcome this problem, Olson suggested that groups must rely on either coercion of their members, such as physically threatening or boycotting someone who refuses to join a trade union; or providing 'selective incentives', benefits going only to those who join the group, such as legal insurance if you join a trade union or glossy magazines and recreational opportunities for those who join environmental groups.

This 'logic of collective action' model was devastating for pluralists in several ways. It implied that whether groups exist or not depends primarily on things that have nothing to do with how strongly their members feel about issues, but only on the almost random availability of private benefits (or costs) that can be allocated to members. Those groups that can organize coercion or selective incentives will be political active, while those where members cannot easily be coerced or given private benefits must remain chronically unorganized. The analysis also implied that smaller groups are always easier to organize than large ones, so (for instance) business associations with a few big firms will always be better organized than trade unions that need the active support of hundreds or thousands of members in order to be effective. In Chapter 5 we will discuss in detail how market liberals (including Mancur Olson) eventually constructed a powerful condemnation of the influence of interest groups in politics, which led in the 1980s to an assault on some interest groups (especially trade unions) by governments in the United States and United Kingdom.

Olson's argument may be compelling in theory. The evidence is more equivocal. Surveys find precious few people who admit to free riding or assign much significance to selective incentives in deciding whether or not to join groups. Market liberals can reply that people offer ethical replies to surveys while acting on base calculations in private. But in behavioural economics there is consistent evidence suggesting that around 40 per cent of people will always join collective endeavours at first, even in experimental situations designed to make such cooperation irrational.

A cooperative instinct seems to be hard-wired into many peoples' mental architecture and there is no reason to think that they suffer because of it. Robert Axelrod (1984) showed that in playing repeated prisoners' dilemma games (with an incentive to be non-cooperative whatever the other person does, but with joint gains if both players cooperate), it is best to adopt a strategy called 'tit for tat'. The essential idea here is that you cooperate with the other player but only if they cooperate with you. But if the other play does not cooperate, you punish them by subsequently not cooperating. Tit for tat works because so long as they cooperate, both players make substantial gains. They quickly learn that while non-cooperation may produce one immediate high payoff, cooperation produces sustained gains over time.

The post-war growth of the state and the increasing importance of multi-national corporations

Pluralism's faith in groups and voluntary associations looked increasingly anachronistic in an era of big government and global corporations, both undertaking massive projects with long planning horizons and mobilizing vast resources. There was no 'incrementalist' way of planning to get men to the moon, as the United States did in 1969. Nor was there any strong group process, nor even clear Congressional politics, centrally directing the US's massive nuclear arms build-up. Instead the scientists, military planners and civilian contractors set an ever-changing technological agenda that dragged Congress along in its wake. Giant US and multi-national corporations made carefully planned investments and showed they could manage consumer demand (Galbraith, 1969). Media and advertising penetrated and linked the corporate and political worlds by commanding the dominant means of communication. Pluralism risked seeming an old-fashioned doctrine, studying only the things that fitted its historical roots, but incapable of grappling with modern realities of central control. This challenge led key American pluralists (Dahl and

Lindblom and Galbraith) and a range of European theorists (Scharpf, Giddens and Luhmann) to re-think their core ideas. These changes eventually created 'neo-pluralism', which we will discuss in Chapter 6.

Extensive civic unrest in the US and Europe

Political unrest undermined pluralism's intellectual credibility, and was a key trigger for its eventual transition to neo-pluralism. The civil rights movement began in the southern states of America in the late 1950s with protests against racial segregation in schools, universities, employment, restaurants and public transport and the forcible exclusion of African-American voters from politics. These protests were not met with the easy inclusion and recognition of their legitimacy that pluralist theory predicted, but instead by a fierce backlash from white supremacists, indifference from the two main political parties anxious about losing votes, and organized repression by southern state governments and their police forces. As early as 1956 President Eisenhower reluctantly sent in federal troops to protect African-American students attending universities and high schools that courts had ordered should be desegregated. But violent resistance to civil rights protestors continued into the mid 1960s, including the murders of some activists. A peaceful campaign of civil disobedience, led by Martin Luther King (assassinated in 1968) became a national movement involving many black churches and community groups (Chong 1991). A more radical and militant 'black power' movement advocated violence against the white power structure and riots affected many large cities.

At the same time, America's involvement in the Vietnam War created intense unrest among students. The various streams of protest came together in a counter-culture that rejected conventional politics and materialist lifestyles. The counter-culture engaged civil rights and anti-war activists, radical environmentalists, feminists and opponents of nuclear weapons and US imperialism. This heady ideological mix set the scene for several decades of radical politics. The protestors successfully used the media to break through from the political margins and reach a mass audience. Student protests broke out in many universities and in 1968 the national convention of the Democratic Party in Chicago became the focus of intense protests and demonstrations, brutally suppressed before a national TV audience by the city's police force under orders from Mayor Daley.

These developments gave the lie to pluralism's idea of an underlying consensus on the rules of the game, and easy appeasement of group demands. Large and active groups assaulted the system, and were met by violent defence of the established order.

In Europe, student protests against Vietnam and against the limiting curriculum and old-fashioned governance of universities started to flare in 1967. Another heady mix of left-wing radicalism, anti-racism, feminism, environmentalism, counter-culturalism and pacifism erupted in France, Germany, Italy and Scandinavia. Protests in Berlin and in Paris in May 1968 became watersheds. The Paris 'events' developed into a general strike by workers against the government of the French Fifth Republic, which for some weeks faltered, until President Charles de Gaulle managed to restore control. The impacts on elections and party politics were small at first but they built progressively over the next two decades, as the radicals embarked on a 'long march through the institutions' (some eventually becoming government ministers). Far-left terrorist groups emerged for a few years in West Germany and Italy. The idea of a pluralist consensus on the rules of the game was always tenuous in France and Italy, whose large communist parties followed a pro-Soviet line. The widespread rejection of orthodox democratic politics as limited and elite-run, and protestors' demands for deeper and more inclusive democracy, sparked enormous changes in European politics.

Especially in the United States, the crisis of confidence in pluralism in the early 1970s stemmed from pluralists' past errors in mixing normative and explanatory arguments, and so idealizing the status quo (Connolly 1969). Their ostensible claims to be undertaking 'positive' scientific analysis of political behaviour were exposed as ideologically motivated defences of the status quo. Consistent with a Cold War mentality, they covered up their polities' limits and deficiencies behind myths of universal political inclusion. They romanticized the operations of representative institutions in quaint portrayals of 'community power' structures and micro-level interest group processes drawn from a bygone era. No group of critics made these charges with more vigour than the radical elite theorists, to whose views we turn in the next chapter. But pluralism was not yet spent, and in Chapter 6 we show how it made a comeback.

Chapter 3

Elite Theory

An enduring critique of liberal democracy originated at the end of the nineteenth century in two newly unified and very imperfectly democratized European states; Germany and Italy. This critique contrasted the inherent concentration of power in any political system within a small, leadership group, *the elite*, with the powerless situation of the bulk of citizens, *the mass*. Elite theorists argued that whatever the ostensible form of government, an elite minority must always rule. They scorned both liberal claims about democratization under capitalism and Marxist beliefs that after a social revolution the working class majority could effectively govern.

An even older tradition of normative elitism argued that elite domination is both natural and desirable. This position can be cultural as well as political, contrasting the vulgar masses with a refined elite. At the end of the nineteenth century many anti-modern intellectuals recoiled from the consequences of large-scale industrialization, technology, urbanization and democracy. The original elite theorists formed part of this anti-democratic reaction.

Crossing the Atlantic in the 1920s and 1930s, in the United States elite theory progressively metamorphosed into a more professional, sociological approach. The more recent social science version of elite theory is essentially empirical and descriptive in that it sets out how social and political processes actually work. Most of the new generation of American elite theorists used their findings not to celebrate elite domination, but to criticize the imperfections of representative government and popular control. They offered a radical but non-Marxist critique of pluralist orthodoxy, and this is the form in which much elite theory is found to this day.

We begin this chapter by examining the historic origins and core assumptions of the main types of elite theory. Then we look at how elite theory depicts the relationship between society and politics. Next we consider elite theory's account of government and policy-making, emphasizing leadership, bureaucracy and technocracy.

The Origins of Elite Theory

European foundations

Three key authors originated the earliest elite theory – Gaetano Mosca and Vilfedo Pareto in Italy and Robert Michels, who moved from Germany to Italy. Pareto and Mosca observed a new Italian liberal democracy in the late nineteenth and early twentieth centuries that featured corruption, clientelism, domination by industrialists and landed magnates, and rancorous conflict between social classes. They argued that society, irrespective of its formal system of government, always divides into two major groups:

- an elite (in Mosca's terminology, a 'ruling class') controlling economic, social and political power through its expertise, ownership of wealth and property, social status, intelligence, and economic and political guile; and
- a mass of all other citizens, disorganized and excluded from effective influence on public policy.

These conditions are inevitable in their view, because the masses could not possibly acquire the competence to be effective participants in politics (except as followers of some charismatic leader). In contrast to the pluralist interpretation of society organized into many diverse groups, Mosca (and later Pareto) portrayed the mass as an undifferentiated amalgam, disorganized and unpredictable in its behaviour. This analysis responded to fears of mass demonstrations, general strikes and crowd violence in the growing industrial cities of Europe.

Mosca often wrote of ordinary citizens in frankly contemptuous style, characterizing the mass as preoccupied with immediate needs and wants: 'Their first, their natural, their most spontaneous desire is to be governed as little as possible, or to make as few sacrifices as possible for the state' (Mosca 1939: 411). He saw a need to 'place restraints on the [press and media] corruption of minds that are, and will forever remain, minds of children' (Mosca 1939: 492). And he remarked disparagingly: 'Even in the lower classes every individual in the long run gets a loaf of bread and a mate, though the bread be more or less dark and hard-earned and the mate more or less unattractive or undesirable' (Mosca 1939: 30).

The economist Vilfredo Pareto in his thirties espoused left-wing, but non-Marxist, causes so much so that he was forced to leave Italy and work as an academic in Switzerland to escape police attention. In 1900 Pareto had a sudden change of heart, switching to right-wing and anti-democratic elitism – igniting a feud with Mosca over who originated its key doctrines, such as the circulation of elites (which we discuss later). In *The Mind and Society*, Pareto (1916) argued that most people most of the time are governed by irrational emotions, prone to swings of hysteria, panic and enthusiasm. Competent elites could learn to manipulate the public's emotions, as illustrated by irrational trends in consumer demand and fake democratic party politics controlled by party leaders.

Both Mosca and Pareto believed in the constant rising of exceptional individuals into ruling positions. They favoured vigorous and open circulation of elites and interpreted many political problems as resulting from the ossification of existing elites in power, blocking the rise of new elites. Any such blockage would lead the rising elites to turn instead to anti-system or revolutionary politics, jeopardizing the social order. Yet Mosca and Pareto dismissed the utopianism of Marxist doctrines, which looked to create genuine majority rule by the working class through revolution. Mosca linked his anti-Marxism to the claim that a socialist transformation could only work if essentially human characteristics, such as love of family and kinship ties, were extinguished:

> The rulers of a collectivist state pile economic power on political power and so, controlling the lots of all individuals and all families, have a thousand ways of distributing rewards and punishments. It would be strange indeed if they did not take advantage of such a strategic position to give their children a start in life . . . In order to abolish privileges of birth entirely, it would be necessary to go one step farther, to abolish the family, recognize a vagrant Venus [that is, foster sexual promiscuity] and drop humanity to the level of the lowest animalism. In the *Republic* Plato proposed abolishing the family as an almost necessary consequence of the abolition of private property. (Mosca 1939: 418)

Elite theorists predicted that even if a revolution succeeded, it would simply install a different elite in power, leaving the mass powerless as before.

The establishment of a tightly controlled communist regime in the Soviet Union following revolution in 1917 was taken by the elite theorists as further proof of the inevitability of elite rule. The elite theorists correctly predicted the actions of the communist leadership, which quickly extinguished opponents and press freedom. The communists' alleged 'dictatorship of the proletariat' was in fact a dictatorship of the party hierarchy. The pessimistic message here was later summed up in George Orwell's fable, *Animal Farm*, where the farm animals revolt and expel their brutal farm owner. But in many small steps the pigs who led the original revolt emerge as the new owners of all the animals, every bit as bad and exploitative as the original human owner. (Orwell himself was a democratic socialist and certainly no elite theorist.)

The third key elite theorist of this era, Robert Michels, developed an anti-Marxist position in more detail. Born in Germany, Michels was originally a radical socialist, following the syndicalist doctrines of Georg Sorel, a French socialist who advocated spontaneous strikes and crowd violence as the key routes to revolution. By 1911 Michels had changed his mind. His book *Political Parties* argued that all parties, including those espousing democracy, are inevitably oligarchic in their internal organization, controlled by a small leadership clique. The book focused on the German Social Democratic Party (SPD). Influenced by the theories about bureaucracy of his German contemporary and friend, the sociologist Max Weber, Michels linked large-scale, mass organizations run by bureaucracies to elite domination. His famous iron law of oligarchy was that 'he who says organization says oligarchy'. So parties like the SPD claiming to serve the working class and represent ordinary voters in fact served mainly the interests of their own leadership. Faced with a choice between radical activism and organizational survival, Michels believed the party would always choose the latter.

In 1910 Michels moved to Italy, aided by a supportive reference from Weber, and met with Pareto and Mosca. Michels opposed World War I. The fact that virtually all the European social democratic parties endorsed their own country's position in the war in a patriotic fervour, instead of opposing the slaughter of the working classes in the trenches, solidified Michels' cynicism. Italy's unnecessary entry into the war in 1915, and subsequent military disaster, confirmed the elite theorists' scorn for party leaders in liberal democracies.

By the 1920s Michels was supporting fascism and its cult of a single dominant leader as personified in Italy by Benito Mussolini. Michels accepted a prominent university post from Mussolini. He was attracted by the fascist idea that the masses of ordinary people can be mobilized for social change behind a leader and a party committed to national glory. Michels's *First Lectures* (1927) argued for the importance of a charismatic and exceptional leader to engage the masses in huge projects, which alone could overcome the conservative, oligarchic character of large-scale modern organizations. (The Nazi regime in Germany installed in 1933 was exceptionally effective in these terms.)

Mosca too had backed Mussolini's seizure of power in 1923. However, he did oppose Mussolini's 1926 abolition of parliamentary control over the government, and in his later years he stressed the importance of maintaining legality, implicitly criticizing Mussolini's lawless regime. Pareto accepted appointment as a senator by

Mussolini in 1923, ten months before his death. His defenders argue that this was only an honour and that he would soon have repudiated the crude abuses of the fascist regime. But fascist ideologues cited Pareto's political and sociological work (not his economics) to justify their regime.

In philosophy, thinkers from a very wide range of different positions were either attracted to fascism or called in support by its exponents (see Figure 3.1). In the late nineteenth century Friedrich Nietzsche stressed the importance of exceptional actors in advancing the progress of culture and civilization against the dead-hand of customary and religious beliefs. His disdain for the masses found many echoes amongst intellectuals. 'The radical elitism of Nietzsche was felt as "the earthquake of the epoch" by many of [this] generation' (Lassman and Spiers, 1994: xii). This inheritance is clear in the work of the Spanish intellectual, Ortega y Gasset, who was ideologically close to the Spanish fascism of Franco. His book *The Revolt of the Masses* condemned the failure of ordinary citizens to defer to intellectual and knowledge elites. The German philosopher Martin Heidegger (1977) was driven by an anti-technological sentiment to embrace Nazi ideals, which he thought might enable a kind of humanity not enslaved by technology.

Figure 3.1   *The development of elite theory*

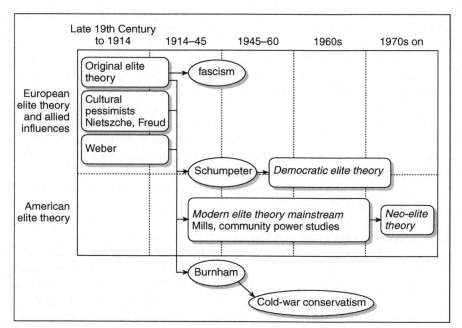

Sigmund Freud's pioneering work in psychoanalysis was also pessimistic about mass capabilities, revealing the often deeply hidden drivers of behaviour, exposing conventional social organization as a thin veneer concealing barbaric impulses. In his 1931 essay *Civilization and its Discontents* Freud anticipated wartime excesses to come (p. 58):

> Men are not gentle creatures who want to be loved and who at the most can defend themselves if they are attacked; they are, on the contrary, creatures amongst whose instinctual endowments is to be reckoned a powerful share of aggressiveness. As a result, their neighbour is for them not only a potential helper or sexual object but also someone who tempts them to satisfy their aggressiveness on him, to exploit his capacity for work without compensation, to use him sexually without his consent, to seize his possession, to humiliate him, to cause him pain, to torture him and to kill him . . . When the mental counter forces which ordinarily inhibit aggression are out of action, [aggression] manifests itself spontaneously and reveals man as a savage beast to whom consideration towards his own kind is something alien.

More ambiguous support for elitism came from the great sociologist Max Weber, influenced by both Marx and Nietzsche: 'Weber was deeply affected by the peculiarly German intellectual traditions of idealism, romanticism and conservative cultural despair' (Langenbacher 2001:1). Weber identified three types of leadership:

- *Traditional rule* by a leader vested with aristocratic, monarchical or established religious legitimacy, whose rule is accepted as 'natural' by those subject to it.
- *Rational/legal authority* resting on the efficacy of management structures in producing results and operating in line with legal requirements. In the modern era the dominant form of rational/legal authority is bureaucracy in government administration.
- *Charismatic leadership* by a religious or political figure whose followers vest him or her with extraordinary perceptions and visionary capabilities.

Weber saw the modernization of all aspects of life under advanced capitalism as systematically eroding traditional rule, replacing it with systems of rational/legal authority. But he also feared that such systems are inherently unsustainable in several ways. Universal bureaucratization would leave people unsatisfied and so receptive to dangerous charismatic leaders offering new faiths to replace lost moral and religious certainties. Weber was equally fearful of government bureaucracies monopolizing the information and expertise for directing the state, without any effective political counterweight. He saw such uncontrolled bureaucratic machines leading the European powers to sleepwalk into all-out war in 1914, following a logic only of army mobilization manuals and railway timetables (Germany wanted to declare war only on Russia, but had to attack France as well because the only bureaucratic plan was for war on both fronts).

Yet Weber was also deeply critical of 'professional politicians', underpinning his diffident view of liberal democracy as an imperfect but inescapable necessity. In 1917 he wrote: 'Whether one loves or hates the whole parliamentary business, it is not to be got rid of' (Weber 1994: 166). He doubted that the party system and elections could generate politicians capable and powerful enough to command government bureaucracies. Weber condemned the negative, oppositional parliaments of Germany under Kaiser Wilhelm before 1914. He tried (but failed) to get the post-war Weimar republic in Germany to adopt a powerful directly elected president, believing that parliaments elected under proportional representation would yield only weak leaders. Yet, whatever the defects of representative government:

> the creation of orderly, *responsible* political leadership by parliamentary leaders . . . weakens as far as possible, the impact of purely emotional influences both from 'above' [tyrannical takeovers] and from 'below' [street-based unrest and mob rule] . . . [O]nly the orderly leadership of the masses by responsible politicians is at all capable of breaking unregulated rule by the street and leadership by chance demagogues. (Weber 1994: 125)

Although Weber himself never used the concept of elite, he influenced the post-1945 emergence of 'democratic elite theory' shown in Figure 3.1. This school seeks a reconciliation between elite theory and representative government, on the basis that even if elite rule is inevitable, *competitive* elite rule can still be responsive to popular preferences. Another influence here was Joseph Schumpeter, whose attempted reconstruction of democratic theory around competing party elites we discussed in Chapter 2. In the post-war period the hallmarks of all forms of democratic elite theory were an emphasis upon the inherent limitations of democratic control in large, modern states; a down-playing of citizens' knowledge and competencies; and a stress on the detailed arrangements for (a strictly limited process of) party competition and selection of leaders (see below). Usually this position also entailed a preference for simple 'two party' politics and against proportional representation.

Elite theory in the United States

The fascist connections of the three founders of elite theory meant that after the defeat of fascism in World War II they had no successors. Elite theory then moved to the United States. The political scientist Harold Lasswell (1936: 13) connected elites to the very definition of political science: 'The study of politics is the study of influence and the influential. . . . The influential are those who get the most of what there is to get. . . . Those who get the most are *elite*; the rest are *mass*.'

James Burnham linked elites to the structure of a capitalist economy dominated by large corporations rather than small entrepreneurs. In his 1941 book *The Managerial Revolution* Burnham drew on Mosca and Pareto and stressed the rise of 'organization man' (and they were almost always men at this time), claiming that a new class of managers and directors of giant corporations would collectively dominate the economy and government and so run society. Denounced by C. Wright Mills as 'a Marx for the managers', Burnham copied elite theory's founding fathers by moving right in his views, becoming a Cold War conservative.

But very soon elite theory became associated with the radical left in the United States. US sociologists linked an account of the power of elites not with a justification of elite rule, but rather with a radical critique of that rule. This critique reached its zenith in the 1950s and 1960s in the work of C. Wright Mills and a series of 'community power' studies. The early European elite theorists did not specify exactly where ruling elites came from – their existence was simply asserted as inevitable. By contrast, American elite theorists devoted great attention to where in society elites were likely to spring from and what they actually did. Mills remarked dismissively of Mosca in particular:

> It is not my thesis that for all epochs of human history and in all nations, a creative minority, a ruling class, an omnipotent elite shape all historical events. Such statements, upon careful examination, usually turn out to be mere tautologies, and even when they are not, they are so entirely general as to be useless in the attempt to understand the history of the present. (Mills 1956: 20)

Mills focused only on the United States and was relentlessly empirical. Most of his text is taken up with description, and theory is relegated to brief incidental comments amid the piling up of evidence. He drew in eclectic fashion on both earlier European thinkers and on homespun American populists (espousing the virtues of the 'small man'). Mills offered a radical critique not only of the corporate rich, but also of their salaried upper middle class allies, the hierarchies of labour unions, elected politicians and their aides, and the military. His key concept was that of the 'power elite' (discussed below) and the concept travelled to Europe and elsewhere.

Later theorists stressed the 'non-decisions', by means of which many issues are consciously kept off the formal political agenda to suit the elite's interests, Bachrach and Baratz (1963). They also revived arguments harking back to Marxist theorists (such as the Italian Antonio Gramsci) that ruling elites can often stop important issues from reaching the political agenda by controlling society's ideology, such that nobody can even think of raising such issues. Lukes (1974) called this the 'third face of power'. Domhoff (1978a) identified an 'ideology process' whereby this was accomplished through control of the mass media and education. So policy making on key issues is often low-visibility and low-conflict, with supposedly competing party elites in fact colluding to stop voters having any effective choice about what should happen. All this was very hard to study empirically, because it highlighted the importance of what was *not* happening, and so could not be observed. Eventually the idea of power as the capacity to keep issues off the agenda was outflanked intellectually by post-modern, 'de-centred' views of power, which we will discuss in Chapter 13.

The 1960s events that shook pluralism also affected elite theory. Claims of limits on political access and on the dispersion of power were largely vindicated by the revolt of excluded social groups. But in the late 1960s and 1970s political practices in most liberal democracies became somewhat more diverse and inclusive. The elite theorists' critique was subsequently absorbed and largely neutralized by neo-pluralist theory, which we discuss in Chapter 6. It became a commonplace response to elite theory to say that *of course* there were elites in any sphere of life in any society, but that what was key was to show in detail whether they were democratically constrained or controlled, and whether different kinds of elites, operating in different spheres of society, behaved in separate or integrated ways. For its critics, the sociological thrust of post-war American elite theory led to a style of 'generalizing empirically about the most readily measurable, if often quite trivial, characteristics and correlates of elite status. This led to a "conceptual swamp" in which "elite" had no agreed meaning and clearly perceived theoretical utility' (Higley 1984: 143).

Society and Politics

For elite theorists of all persuasions, there are two dominant themes in the inter-relationship of society and the political process. The first is the circulation of elites, a perennially important aspect of any society, whether liberal democratic or not. The second is specific to liberal democracies, concerning the role of 'professional politicians', and how this relates to political parties and associated interest groups.

The circulation of elites

An elite may often look static at the collective level – 'to endless years the same' in its overall composition. Yet its personnel are ever-changing, as established older members age and die and new people arrive. Both Mosca and Pareto identified this process as central to explaining why societies are stable or unstable. For Mosca the root of many problems is an ineradicable human drive for the present genera-tion of social and economic leaders to want to secure positions of power for their offspring, who may not be well suited for such roles. The forces of heredity and established inequalities of wealth constantly tend to make elites ossify and degrade, shown in Figure 3.2 as flow 6.

If elites are secure and unthreatened by any counter-elites, a degree of ossification may go undetected. Yet in modern societies, as Figure 3.2 shows, an insurgent or counter-elite will often exist, as the most tal-ented and energetic members of the mass look for ways to acquire influence and resources (flow 1). For instance, in the early twentieth century the labour movement and socialist parties constituted an insur-gent counter-elite, with leadership from self-educated workers and dis-sident intellectuals. The ruling elites seek to undermine the influence of a counter-elite in various ways. One is by co-opting, bribing or other-wise bringing over to their side some of the most threatening and/or tal-ented leaders of the counter-elite (flow 2). Alternatively the incumbent elites may encourage the most active elements of the mass and counter-elites to leave their society altogether (flows 3 and 3a), by fostering emigration (pervasive in late nineteenth century Europe and in imperial countries with a far-flung empire) or by forcibly exiling potential rebels.

Pareto stressed that ruling elites become vulnerable when they lose the will to disrupt and suppress the processes operating within the mass that create and sustain counter-elites (flow 4 in Figure 3.2):

> When an elite declines we can generally observe two signs which manifest themselves simultaneously:
> 1   The declining elite becomes softer, milder, more humane and less apt to defend its own power.
> 2. On the other hand it does not lose its rapacity and greed for the goods of others, but rather tends as much as possible to increase

Figure 3.2 *Pareto's theory of elite circulation*

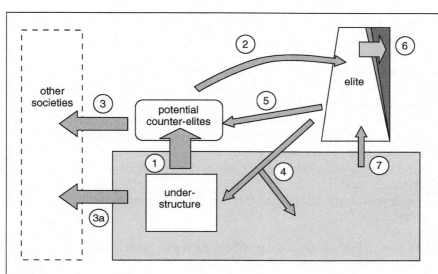

Main circulation flows:

1 Upwards flow of people from within the mass (mainly in the 'under-structure' areas) into the potential counter-elites.

2 Absorption of individual members of the potential counter-elites into the elite, at various levels.

3 Outwards movements of potential counter-elites' members into other societies, mainly due to

    forcible exile; or

    permanent emigration.

3a Emigration also has stabilizing impacts at mass level in inhibiting the recruitment of talented individuals into potential counter-elites.

4 Use of guile, ideology and symbolic politics by the elite to

    (a) prevent counter-elites from emerging (and hence targeted at the 'under-structure' areas) and

    (b) to keep the mass as a whole generally disorganized,

both supplemented by the less visible use of force.

5 Direct and observable repression of counter-elites by the elite (for instance, imprisonment, executions, 'disappearances', intimidation).

6 Movement of elite members into ineffectualness, mainly due to

    (a) the lottery of inheritance (capable people have less capable children); or

    (b) a loss of elite morale and ruthlessness.

7 Upwards social mobility allowing individual members of the mass to enter the lower ranks of the elite (via entrepreneurship, job promotion, marriage, etc.).

its unlawful appropriations and to indulge in major usurpations of the national patrimony.

Thus, on the one hand it makes the yoke heavier, and on the other it has less strength to maintain it. (Pareto 1991: 58)

As subtler ways of disrupting threats to its position weaken, a ruling elite in crisis must resort to crude repression (flow 5). Mosca and Pareto followed the Italian renaissance theorist, Niccolò Machievelli, who argued that state leaders did not and should not hesitate to use violence, terror, deceit and guile to preserve their position, irrespective of conventional morality. Yet in liberal democratic conditions, and under media scrutiny, the costs of overtly repressing opposition are greatly increased.

This leaves a great deal hanging on the relative importance of three processes:

- As some children of elite members prove to be hopeless successors (flow 6), the elites must look outside their own ranks for replacement personnel.
- Potential counter-elite leaders must be absorbed into established elite structures (flow 2).
- People from the top of the mass must be recruited into the bottom rungs of the elite, through upward social mobility, inter-marriage, and promotions within firms and state organizations (flow 7).

In liberal democracies electoral competition and party systems were seen by the early elite theorists as critical for elite renewal.

The central role of political parties

Until the late nineteenth century parties had mainly operated as small cadres of national political elites in parliament, sustained by a network of established regional and local elites (in Europe often aristocrats or the local wealthy). These 'notables' delivered the votes of people in their areas, in return for influence with national elites and an opportunity to create clientelist networks of patronage (controlling titles, government jobs, publicly funded services and economic concessions). This traditional and informally organized pattern of political mobilization could not survive the growth of electioneering in both the US and European democracies, as the right to vote was extended more widely. Patronage did not die out completely but it was displaced by new bureaucracies specializing in political tasks. In the United States, 'machine politics' in the big cities integrated millions of new immigrants with the vote into American society. In Europe the trade unions moved into politics, creating an organized labour movement active in elections in support of socialist parties. Conservative and liberal parties created their own mass organizations in response.

Parties broadened their activities in many ways. 'The political parties created democracy and modern democracy is unthinkable save in terms of the political parties' (Schattschneider 1942: 1). Elections became mass mobilizing events, involving canvassing for votes, posters, leafleting, large rallies and speeches. These labour-intensive activities required large numbers of volunteer workers and activists to sustain them, and bureaucratic knowledge about how to organize them effectively. In large countries party memberships spiralled into the millions, and parties set up conferences, committees, newspapers, youth wings, women's organizations, social organizations, reading clubs, bookshops, cultural organizations, trade unions and professional associations. Local and regional governments, long run in non-partisan or disguised-partisan ways, became more explicitly party-politicized. Policy also ceased to be defined by legislators freely debating in parliaments. Instead carefully constructed pledges were collated and integrated together into policy platforms. 'The parties have their experts on every question, just as the bureaucracy has its officials with particular responsibilities' (Weber 1994: 171). Especially in European cities, socialist parties tried to convince voters that their policies could deliver real improvements in living standards.

The rise of mass parties required some re-thinking about elite composition. 'Throughout history', Weber (1994: 21) noted, 'it has been the attainment of economic power which has led any given class to believe it is a candidate for political leadership'. But now 'the only persons with the training needed for political leadership are those who have been selected in political struggle' (Weber 1994: 219). Party politics seemed a relatively closed process, shutting off the vast majority of citizens from influence: 'The ordinary voter, courted by the parties but not a member of their organisation, has no active role at all, and notice is only taken of his person during elections or in public advertisements formulated for his benefit at other times' (Weber 1994: 211). Power accumulated in the hands of professional politicians, a new class of actors whose rise to prominence sparked many resentments from those they displaced.

One of the earliest studies of parties was by the Russian historian Moisy Ostrogorski, whose *Democracy and the Party System in the United States* (1910) highlighted the enormous discretionary power exercised by party officials in American party machines. Until just prior to the general election:

> not much has been seen of the people, although it has been talked of a good deal; everybody quoted its authority, acted in its name, took pledges on its behalf, but this everybody was made up almost exclusively of the class of professional politicians. Hitherto the contact between the party organization and the electorate has been very slight. (Ostrogorski 1910: Ch. 9)

Ostrogorski disliked both the oligarchical tendencies in US machine parties in the late nineteenth century, and the aristocratic predominance in British parties, so much so that he called for parties to be outlawed. Yet Ostrogorski's work founded the more democratic strand of elite theory. Unlike Mosca and Pareto, he refused to see the problems of party politics as fundamental to the whole political system: 'The mishaps and failures which we have only too often witnessed cannot be attributed to democratic government as such. Through this very experience, so full of sadness, democracy has vindicated itself again and again' (Ostrogorski 1910: Ch.17).

The threats posed by organized parties to democracy crystallized across Europe in the 1920s and 1930s. Fascist and Communist parties developed propaganda machines and battalions of uniformed, street-fighting thugs, intended to intimidate opponents and break up their meetings. In post-World War I Germany both left and right staged attempted putsches against the Weimar republic, and in Italy and Germany fanatical, leader-worshipping party organizations eventually took over and integrated themselves into state structures. In the Soviet Union the Communist Party became a vehicle for a massive personality cult focusing on Stalin. As a revolutionary organization that allowed no competitors, the Communist Party did not have to bother with competitive elections (though it did allow elections in which only Communists could stand).

After 1945 political parties became progressively smaller and less inclusive. The highly drilled massed battalions of the Nazi Nuremburg rallies or the Red Square parades in Moscow were now a potent image of what democracy was not. Communication technologies changed. First radio and then TV became critical in elections campaigns. As advertising and use of the media increased in sophistication, the importance of rallies and the activities of party workers declined. And the development of opinion polls into reasonably accurate guides to voting intentions meant that advisors to political leaders could study and understand the dynamics of public opinion and calculate the chances of different policies succeeding, without relying on their party organizations.

Mass mobilized parties gave way to 'catch-all' parties. These were still run in top-down manner by national political elites, especially in Europe (less so in the United States). Leaders constructed their own campaign teams of speechwriters and policy experts, press, TV and advertising gurus – paying little heed to the views of their legislators or party functionaries. Party bureaucracies withered, memberships declined, and party social activities became ever less relevant. Only periodic political embarrassments created by mishandled party conferences or conventions, or occasional rebellions by disillusioned party factions, punctuated this transition to a mode of operation focused exclusively on winning elections through media activities. In the US the spread of primary elections as the main way to choose candidates further weakened party organizations. The press and television were more important than party caucuses in determining who parties ended up with as presidential or legislative candidates, and media-savvy politicians played to this audience.

Michels' 'iron law of oligarchy' could be applied to both mass parties and their catch-all successors. Democratic elite theorists argued that the marginalization of internal party democracy and consultation processes did not matter much, so long as competition between parties still gave voters the decisive hand. They agreed with pluralists that internal party oligarchy did not actually demonstrate that the state itself was dominated by a single elite – only that each political party in a two-party or multi-party system would be dominated by an elite.

Catch-all parties are expensive to operate, especially in the US where campaign costs have mushroomed, increasing the influence of corporations and other wealthy donors. In the eyes of elite theorists, this wealth buys political power by recruiting capable individuals to serve the interests of the ruling class, and by financing the campaigns of politicians and the operations of political parties. In the United States and elsewhere, many large corporate donors give to both or all main political parties. Corruption of politics by money can sometimes be curbed by campaign finance legislation, but the wealthy always find a way around restrictions. So in the United States, the response to limits on individual contributions was the creation of political action committees (PACs), often associated with corporations or unions.

Financial elites can hire the best lobbyists to make sure that legislation and regulation are to their liking, and they control privately-owned media. Elite theorists (for example, Domhoff, 1978a) described additional aspects of the social system that help to secure the power of elites and to undermine the importance of the party barriers that supposedly divide them. These include the common social background of business and political leaders; the social clubs and networks to which they all belonged; the consequently easy access to political power enjoyed by corporate leaders and their lobbyists; and the revolving door between top business and governmental positions.

Government and Policy Making

Elite theory's view of government and policy making emphasizes three defining features of contemporary societies that go almost unmentioned in traditional pluralism: bureaucracy; technology; and large scale. C. Wright Mills in particular analyzed the changed circumstances of the top state elite, as well as more prosaic public policy-making operating at the 'middle levels of power'.

The power elite

Bureaucracy (literally 'rule by bureaus') was first identified and named in Germany in the early nineteenth century, when the formalization of decision-making and reliance on written records was first seen as breeding a new concentration of power. At the turn of the twentieth century Max Weber offered a thorough account of bureaucracy's routinization of tasks, codification of easily-retrievable records, impersonal allocation of offices on merit, and close structuring of social life by rules and regulations – all of which we now associate with the organizations of modern society. Bureaucratization affects business and state organizations alike, concentrating control in hierarchies with established standard operating procedures, to which their staff adhere. In the economic sphere Weber argued that only innovative and assertive entrepreneurs can resist the extreme stabilization of organizational processes that results, periodically shaking up markets with new inventions. Within the liberal democratic state, only effective value guidance from the class of professional politicians could ever hope to counteract the inertia of bureaucracy. However, as we noted earlier, Weber also thought that charismatic leaders can sometimes shake up government bureaucracies.

C. Wright Mills saw the transformation of the scale, bureaucratic character and technologies of government in the post-1945 United States as the critical issues of his day: 'The political directorate, the corporate rich, and the ascendant military have come together as the power elite, and the expanded and centralized hierarchies which they head have encroached upon the old balances and have now relegated them to the middle levels of power' (Mills 1956: 296)

The massive Manhattan project that developed the atomic bomb triggered what Mills called 'the militarization of science'. The subsequent H-bomb and missile programmes established a 'military ascendancy in the world of science' (Mills 1956: 217). By the early 1950s the United States had renounced its historical isolationism and bestrode the Western world as a military colossus, locked in an apparent death-match with the Soviet Union's authoritarian Communism. The huge expansion of US forces in wartime and its maintenance afterwards created what Lasswell (1941) had foreseen as 'a garrison state'.

These changes forged an alliance between the US's largest corporations (Mills's 'corporate rich') and the military ('the warlords'), dramatized in President Eisenhower's farewell address to the American people in 1960 warning of the dangers of a powerful 'military-industrial complex'. Defence spending sustained the research and development efforts of growing numbers of scientists and technologists. And although postwar consumer spending quickly rebalanced the US economy from its military orientation in the war years, significant defence programmes remained. Foreign policy prioritized a national interest defined in economic as well as security terms, especially when it came to securing raw material supplies (Krasner 1978).

Mills deplored the lack of an impartial civil service and the dominance of Washington policy-making (then as now) by political appointees of the President. These nominees were either law, media or political professionals involved in the winning candidate's campaigns. After their period of government service many of these people would resume their business careers, able to take further advantage of their contacts in government.

This power elite of political executives, the corporate rich and the military hierarchy operated across all the 'history-making' major issues of economic and foreign policy-making. In Mills's view they did not bother to resolve or even consider lower-level issues :

> What was Caesar's power at its peak compared with power of the changing inner circle of Soviet Russia or of America's temporary administrations? The men of either circle can cause great cities to be wiped out in a single night, and in a few weeks turn continents into thermonuclear wastelands. That the facilities of power are enormously enlarged and decisively centralized means that decisions of small groups are now more consequential. (Mills 1956: 23)

The power elite concept also pointed to the enormous ideological effort deployed to justify the transformation of American society that postwar militarization entailed:

> In the last thirty years, there have been signs of a status merger among the economic, political and military elite. [T]hey have begun to seek, as powerful men [and women] have always sought, to buttress their power with the mantle of authoritative status. (Mills 1956: 91)

These themes resonate in subsequent decades. Authors such as Noam Chomsky describe US power in the twenty-first century in similar terms.

The middle levels of power

Mills condemned the pluralist theory of his day for its blinkered focus on interest group process, its ideological celebration of an ineffectual diversity, its want of hard-edged empirical observations, and its unproven 'theory of balance':

> You elaborate the number of groups involved, in a kind of bewildering, Whitmanesque enthusiasm for variety . . . You do not try to clarify this hodge-podge by classifying these groups, occupations, strata, organizations according to their political relevance or even whether they are organized politically at all. You do not try to see how they may be connected with one another into a structure of power, for by virtue of his [or her] perspective, the romantic conservative [pluralist] focuses upon a scatter of milieux rather than upon their connections. (Mills 1956: 244)

Mills did not deny the existence of a vigorous political process involving Congress, party politics and state and regional governments in post-war America. But he saw them as merely a political side show, like Hollywood celebrities who create a constantly absorbing spectacle. This was not always so – in earlier epochs such as the civil war period, there were real political conflicts that had engaged regional and local politicians and citizens in deciding history-making events (see Figure 3.3(a)). But not any longer.

   The key danger Mills saw in the separation of the elite from the middle levels of power is the enormous scope for discretionary decisions conferred on the power elite, to decide issues in its own interest and to keep decisions secret, without having to account to elected representatives, let alone citizens at large. The middle levels of power are for Mills a cushioning layer that absorbs popular views and influence; they do not transmit public opinion (Figure 3.3(b)). The power elite stands above criticism partly because it develops an insulating 'prestige' and cultivates myths about where power really lies. Collusion by the elite ensures that its behaviour is hidden from public view. For example, the elite can persuade media corporations that publicizing embarrassing foreign policy or intelligence failures is against the 'national interest'. The more complex power structure of earlier American history was now lost for good.

Figure 3.3   *Mills's picture of how modern US society differed from past patterns*

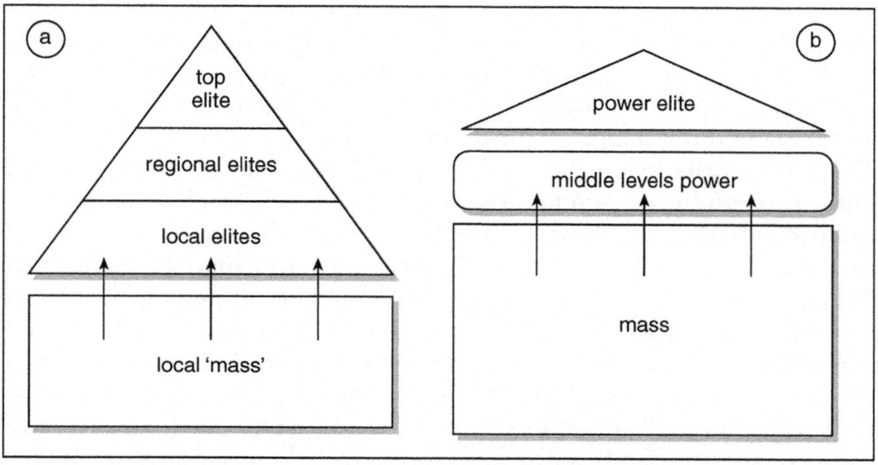

Later elite theorists by and large followed Mills's core components. For Domhoff (1978a) the US power elite has pretty much the same membership as it did for Mills. However, Domhoff also treats the power elite as 'the leadership group or operating arm of the ruling class', arguing that members of this privileged class may choose not to become involved in public affairs (1978a: 13). Domhoff's power elite (like that of Mills) excludes 'labour leaders', 'middle America politicians' and 'leaders of minority group organizations' (1978a: 15). His analysis stresses a broader range of elite influence, based on money's role as a primary social good in many different spheres of social life. So wealthy individuals and corporations can hire the best lawyers and initiate the most favourable cases to make sure that legal knowledge is skewed to serve their interests, such that the legal system works for them. For Domhoff, the state is very much the instrument of the ruling elite, and systematically serves its interests.

Community power studies

Elite theorists did not confine their attention solely to US national politics. Drawing on his own case work in Illinois, Mills saw the 'local society' of American small cities and towns as a domain where small businesses, local leaders and diverse community groups were politically active and processed the most tractable and immediately vital issues. Metropolitan politics (in New York or Los Angeles) had a different dynamic, driven by a social and economic elite of wealthy families (sometimes numbered as 'the 400'). Their periodic ambitions to define *the* public society of the nation had actually failed repeatedly in Mills' view, disrupted by new elites, economic turbulence and populist resistance. But local elite life was a marginal area of 'conspicuous consumption'. For all its economic significance in encouraging economic production, local American upper class affairs remained a sphere of social life without major political implications.

Other elite theory sociologists, notably Floyd Hunter (1958), carried out a succession of 'community power studies' in American cities that reached different conclusions. In city after city the sociologists argued that the diverse political leadership structures anticipated by pluralists did not exist. They used a reputational method, systematically interviewing people across the community's main organizations about who was influential. The lists thus drawn up were then pruned to identify a top 50 or top 20 of elite power-holders. Power at the city level seemed to be concentrated in a mini-version of the national elite, usually composed of locally significant businesses (especially property developers), and politicians dependent on business for campaign contributions and investment in their cities. It was chiefly in this form that elite theory spread back from the US to post World War II Europe. In the 1980s analysts stressed the domination of city politics by 'growth coalitions' bringing together property and investment interests with mayors elected by working class and middle class, white and African-American constituencies (Logan and Molotch 1987).

It would be easy to portray the pluralism versus elitism debate about American national politics as a disciplinary clash between pluralist political science (described in Chapter 2) and elite theory sociology (epitomized by Mills and Hunter). But this would not be quite right. The top-selling introductory textbook on US politics in multiple editions since the 1960s has been *The Irony of Democracy* by political scientists Thomas Dye and Harmon Ziegler, which took a determinedly elite theory perspective. However, for all their realist cynicism Dye and Ziegler steered clear of any suggestions that the US political system merited radical reform. Another popular textbook on US politics, Michael Parenti's *Democracy for the Few*, had no such hesitation – but never sold in the same numbers.

Conclusions

The early European elite theorists were anti-socialist, anti-communist, anti-democratic, anti-egalitarian, and in the end they supported the rise of fascism with its stress on the mobilization of the masses in search of charismatic leadership.

The more empirical American elitist theory authors who followed in the middle of the twentieth century were subtle leftist critics of the distribution of power in the US political system. Their implicit agenda involved the redistribution of wealth and power to make American society more equal and more truly democratic. Quite how this redistribution ought to be achieved was generally left unstated. For European radicals, it is easy to look back at C. Wright Mills and Floyd Hunter and wonder why they did not advocate socialism – as their European contemporaries (and even some American successors) surely did. The answer may have a lot to do with the character of US politics in the late 1940s and 1950s. This was the era of anti-communist witch-hunts led by Senator Joseph McCarthy, a time when social science was being rebranded as 'behavioral science' so as not to be confused with socialism. Speaking of the political science of that era (in which he was a major figure), David Easton (1991: 209–10) recalls that the discipline's emphasis on basic science as opposed to social problems served the discipline particularly well amid the dangers of McCarthyism. In this light, elite theorists such as Mills and Hunter were courageous in daring to raise critical questions about US politics.

In the pluralism versus elite theory debates of the 1950s and 1960s, neither side really had an explanatory theory as to *why* the state was pluralist, or *why* it was dominated by elites – in contrast to the earlier European elite theorists, who could ground their explanatory theories in the psychology of elites and masses, or accounts of how large organizations worked. For all post-war elite theorists, it was easy to *assume* that a ruling class or power elite exists, and interpret politics and the state in this light, but much harder to *demonstrate* the existence of an elite to pluralist sceptics. Pluralists argued that even very large inequalities in society do not mean there exists a cohesive elite, for members of the alleged elite often seem preoccupied with their own internal rivalries. Proving, or for that matter disproving, elite theory claims is actually very hard. Clearly public policies sometimes involve redistribution of resources to the poorer members of society. Elite theorists can always say that any such redistribution does not represent any real political influence on the part of ordinary people, merely a way of stabilizing society in the interests of the elite.

American pluralists and elite theorists never claimed to be discussing any political system beyond the United States; they were concerned with *how* power was distributed in the United States, but not *why* it had to be that way. The legacies of this debate remain with us to this day. We will see in subsequent chapters how both sides have been transformed in recent decades, and how both made themselves felt beyond US borders. Conspicuously missing in American social science, but very important everywhere else, was a third classical theory of the state, Marxism, to which we now turn.

Chapter 4

Marxism

When Karl Marx died in London in March 1883 he was a stateless intellectual without a will. His funeral was attended by just 11 mourners and attracted few press mentions. These may seem unpromising origins for a theorist to achieve global significance. But Marxism became a worldwide belief system, professed by Communist regimes, which 80 years after Marx's death governed a third of all human beings. Marxism also influenced many on the left in Western countries who bitterly rejected Communist regimes as totalitarian and anti-democratic, a gross perversion of all that Marx intended in the struggle for equal freedom for everyone when he urged: 'Workers of the world unite! You have nothing to lose but your chains'. Marx himself once declared 'I am not a Marxist', rejecting the simplified versions of his ideas propounded by disciples.

Marx was a complex and nuanced figure, whose wide-ranging influence reflects his genuine insights and originality. Initially a nationalist radical, then a liberal humanist, Marx became a radical socialist and creator of intellectual systems. He left a corpus of work that sought to interpret much of history, all of politics and all of economics through a lens of class struggle and a theory of how all human societies develop and change. He died largely friendless because of his incessant and intense feuding with virtually all other thinkers in the socialist movement of his day, often over personal issues or small points of doctrine. Yet his ideas have undergone periodic revival, and from the 1950s until the 1980s, re-workings of Marx's ideas by western intellectuals influenced the development of many academic disciplines, especially economics, sociology, cultural and literary studies, history and political philosophy.

Marxism offers a comprehensive explanatory theory of the development of human societies. Within its grand historical sweep, the focus is on how capitalism came into being, how capitalism works, and how it will eventually exit the world stage. To Marxists, the basic fact of the state in this era is its capitalist context, which means it must serve the interests of the dominant class within that economic system, or serve the system itself. This theory of the state begins with the work of Marx himself in the middle of the nineteenth century. Since then, Marxist theorists have taken the theory of the capitalist state in a number of different directions.

Communist parties inspired by Marxist ideals have carried out successful revolutions in countries such as Russia, China, Yugoslavia, Cuba and Vietnam; and such parties have been installed in power in other countries (including most of Eastern Europe at the end of World War II). These parties were then faced with the problem of how to organize a non-capitalist economy. In most cases they adopted a form of centrally planned economic production that could organize heavy industry, but not produce goods that consumers actually wanted.

With the fall of the Berlin Wall in 1989, the demise of the Soviet Union in 1991, and the adoption by the Chinese Communist Party of a capitalist economic system open to foreign investment in the late twentieth century, Marxism looked to be in terminal decline. This implosion suggests that Marxism rested on the now forlorn hope that an alternative economic system to capitalism is possible. But Marxism as an explanatory theory of the capitalist state is not necessarily affected by the failure of Marxism (strictly speaking, Marxism-Leninism) as a political programme. At any rate, the Marxist theory of the state is one of the classical views that set the scene for contemporary theories of the state, and so a knowledge of this theory is essential, even for those who do not wish to delve into the truly arcane complexities of recent Marxist state theory. We look first at the origins and development of the Marxist approach, then at its view of how society relates to political activity, followed by its account of how the state operates.

Origins and Core Ideas

Marx grounded his advocacy of revolutionary change in a comprehensive analysis of human history, which he saw as a science that paralleled in significance Darwin's account of evolution in the natural world. When it comes to society, Marx (1963: 15) stated in *The Eighteenth Brumaire of Louis Bonaparte* that 'Men make their own history, but they do not make it just as they please; they do not make it under circumstances chosen by themselves, but under circumstances already existing, given and transmitted from the past'. To his followers, this scientific aspect meant that Marxism was certain knowledge and not an ideology. As his co-author Engels said at Marx's graveside in 1883: 'This was a man of science'. Underpinning the Marxist claim to be a science was the idea of a dialectic in human history, which we will explain shortly, and an associated materialist logic of all human social development. Marx's theory of revolutions provided practical guidance on how to achieve radical social change. Vladimir Lenin, leader of the Russian Revolution in 1917, then introduced two significant changes in Marxist theory, placing the Communist Party leadership at the centre of revolutions, and affirming (correctly) that revolutions would occur first in non-industrialized, rural societies. These alterations also meant creating not a short term dictatorship of the proletariat (roughly, the working class) of the sort Marx had anticipated, but rather an extended dictatorship of the Communist Party.

Understanding the dialectic

In his youth in Germany (before being exiled to London) Marx was influenced by the philosophy of Georg Hegel (later also the inspiration for Francis Fukuyama's liberal capitalist 'end of history'; see Chapter 9). Hegel stressed the power of ideas in moving history, and in this sense was an 'idealist'. Marx, in contrast, became a 'materialist', seeing history as moved only by material economic forces, not ideas. However, Marx retained two key elements of Hegel's thought. First, he accepted that there was an ineluctable pattern of progressive development towards perfection in human history. Second, he rejected any gradualist model of this progress, believing that advances could only result from a fundamental clash between two opposing social forces – in Hegel's terms, an accepted 'thesis' eventually conflicting with its opposite, or 'antithesis'. From this clash would emerge a new 'synthesis' combining the best of the thesis and antithesis. This process of progressive development based on overcoming clashes was what Hegel meant by the dialectic.

For Hegel, thesis and antithesis were bodies of ideas. For Marx, thesis and antithesis were to be found in the economy and its associated power structures. The thesis was the developmental impulse of the dominant mode of production, the antithesis the resistance that eventually strained at the boundaries of the mode of production. So the feudal mode of production that had long characterized Europe featured classes of serfs and peasants who were subservient to aristocratic landlords. The success of this mode of production eventually produced surplus resources in the hands of landlords, which was the impetus for the development of commerce and industry in a market economy to supply goods to the landlords. Commerce and industry in turn created a new class of capitalists who eventually wanted to escape the restrictions of the feudal system, and to trade freely – their actions constituted the antithesis of feudalism. The English civil war of the 1640s, the French revolution of 1789, and the American civil war of the 1860s could then all be understood as capitalist revolutions, or what Marx himself would call bourgeois revolutions, in which the shackles of feudalism (or in the American case, slavery) were thrown off and the emerging capitalist class asserted its political power against the old landed aristocracy. Society as a whole then moved from feudalism to the higher plane or synthesis of capitalism.

For Marx, matters certainly did not stop there, for capitalism too had a thesis and antithesis. The thesis came with capitalism's drive to create new products, more efficient production methods, new markets and greater profits. The antithesis arose in the forces of instability and opposition that dynamic capitalism generated. Once capitalism was instituted as the dominant economic system or mode of production, capitalists would seek ever more efficient ways of making profits. This led to the creation of factories concentrated in urban centres, with masses of propertyless industrial workers (in Marx's terms, the prole-tariat) subjected to ever more dehumanizing forms of labour, and so becoming alienated from their work and what they produced. Workers would be exploited ever more efficiently by capitalists in order to pro-duce more profit. Marx spoke of the expropriation of 'surplus value' from workers by capitalists. Workers were only paid a fraction of the full exchange value of their labour power.

As production was increasingly mechanized, so Marx believed that the rate of profit would be squeezed by the cost of capital and the lack of demand for products from poorly paid workers (who were also con-sumers). Falling profits would force the bourgeoisie into ever harsher methods of exploiting workers; but this would do nothing to arrest profits' decline, because it would also reduce demand for products. Periodically there must be tremendous crises of the economic system, recessions and depressions where workers would be laid off, factories lie idle and social unrest would mount. These forces would eventually lead to the growth of revolutionary consciousness among the workers, who would rise up to seize political power and overthrow the capitalist system. (Later, Lenin added resistance by colonized peoples of imperi-alist powers to the mix.)

The final 'synthesis' for Marx could only occur with a successful workers' revolution (see Figure 4.1) There would need to be a disci-plined workers' party to take advantage of these conditions and orga-nize the revolution – and Marx himself was involved in organizing such parties internationally. There was no such revolution in Marx's own lifetime, and as a 'scientist' he was reluctant to predict what might then follow. But clearly he looked forward to a free and prosperous society, where economic exploitation of the workers was a thing of the past, and the technological advances made under capitalism could finally be put to good use in benefiting everyone, putting an end to scarcity and alienated labour.

Figure 4.1 *The dialectic under capitalism*

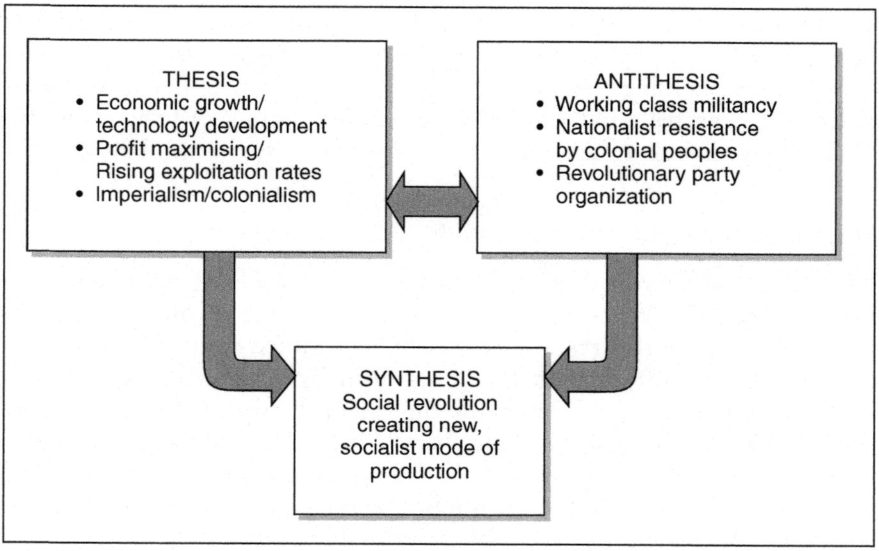

```
┌─────────────────────────────────────────────────────────────┐
│  ┌──────────────────────────┐   ┌──────────────────────────┐ │
│  │ THESIS                   │   │ ANTITHESIS               │ │
│  │ • Economic growth/       │   │ • Working class militancy│ │
│  │   technology development │◄─►│ • Nationalist resistance │ │
│  │ • Profit maximising/     │   │   by colonial peoples    │ │
│  │   Rising exploitation    │   │ • Revolutionary party    │ │
│  │   rates                  │   │   organization           │ │
│  │ • Imperialism/colonialism│   │                          │ │
│  └──────────────────────────┘   └──────────────────────────┘ │
│          │                                 │                  │
│          ▼                                 ▼                  │
│            ┌──────────────────────┐                          │
│            │ SYNTHESIS            │                          │
│            │ Social revolution    │                          │
│            │ creating new,        │                          │
│            │ socialist mode of    │                          │
│            │ production           │                          │
│            └──────────────────────┘                          │
└─────────────────────────────────────────────────────────────┘
```

Revolution and social crisis

In *The Eighteenth Brumaire of Louis Bonaparte*, Marx (1963: 121) compared revolutionary activism with a mole that periodically erupts in a molehill on a seemingly smooth lawn. 'And when it [the Revolution] has accomplished the second half of its preliminary work, Europe will leap up from its seat and exult: "Well burrowed, old mole"'. But Marx appreciated only too well the many factors that regularly prevented workers from rebelling against capitalist control, and the demands and risks that revolution placed upon the working class. Revolution may be accompanied by, and in the short term even perpetuate, what Przeworski (1985) terms the 'valley of transition', a reduction in production levels and living standards sustained for years while recovery from the crisis takes place, back to the previous trend rate of capitalist development. Revolution, in other words, requires huge sacrifices of life chances and living standards by workers.

And the experience of living through a revolution will necessarily be a complex one, with the final outcome unclear. Revolutionary socialist leaders might make mistakes, their initial allies might desert them and switch sides, state authorities might be able to repress initial uprisings, or fight back even after early losses, as happened in the savage response to attempted revolutions of 1848 in several European countries, the Paris Commune of 1871 and in Russia in 1905. While the dialectic suggests that history moves ever onward and upward, short term regressions downward are possible and painful, be they 'busts' in the boom-and-bust cycles of capitalism, or attempted revolutions that are defeated. Social crises come in different kinds. Some are positive from a Marxist viewpoint by helping to radicalize the working class. Others are potentially very negative – like the 1979 Iranian revolution, overthrowing the Shah only to install a theocratic government by religious mullahs.

The dictatorship of the proletariat

Marx thought there would need to be a disciplined workers' party to take advantage of crisis conditions and organize the revolution, though his own efforts in this respect produced very mixed results. The revolution was to be stabilized in the short term by what Marx mentioned (but did not describe in depth) as the 'dictatorship of the proletariat' over potentially counter-revolutionary forces. Admitting dictatorship into the revolutionary process proved to have profound consequences. Vladimir Ilych Lenin, leader of the Bolshevik party that carried out the Russian Revolution in 1917, took dictatorship several steps further. He believed that effective revolution required a highly disciplined, ideologically uniform and hard-line Communist party under coordinated leadership. Lenin did not believe the working class left to its own devices could ever develop the consciousness necessary for revolution. In 1904, 13 years before the Russian revolution, Leon Trotsky (then a critic of the Bolsheviks) wrote in *Our Political Tasks*:

> Lenin's method leads to this: the party organization at first substitutes itself for the party as a whole. Then the central committee substitutes itself for the party organization, and finally a single dictator substitutes himself for the central committee.

Trotsky would have done well to remember his own words, for this is exactly what happened after the revolution, and Trotsky himself was eventually on the receiving end. Under Joseph Stalin, who succeeded Lenin as General Secretary of the Communist Party in 1924, the dictatorial aspects of the Soviet state intensified in a 'cult of personality' surrounding Stalin.

Imperialism and revolutionary dictatorship

Marx expected that revolutionary change would begin in the most advanced industrial nations of his day (Britain, France, Germany and perhaps the US), fuelled by prolonged economic crises and the descent of increasing number of workers into worsening poverty. In fact, no developed capitalist society has ever experienced a communist revolution. Faced with the practical need to justify a revolution in largely agrarian Russia, Lenin took from Trotsky the idea that the two key modern revolutions that Marx foresaw (bourgeois and socialist) could be compressed or telescoped together. Taking advantage of the chaos of the initial bourgeois revolution against feudalism, a Communist vanguard party could push almost immediately for workers' control. In October 1917, Lenin (with Trotsky at his side) put theory into practice and pushed through a Bolshevik coup d'état (immediately proclaimed as Russia's 'socialist revolution'), just 9 months after the Tsarist regime had been overthrown in a liberal revolution. Later in China, Mao Zedong took the theory still further away from Marx in asserting that the poor peasants could carry out the revolution – a class that Marx himself had scorned as belonging to a past feudal era. Between 1927 and 1949 Mao's Chinese Communist Party led peasant armies in a prolonged and eventually victorious revolutionary war.

Lenin's theory of imperialism legitimated initiating communist revolutions in 'backward' countries. Capitalism had gone global, exploiting labour and sources of raw materials across the globe in undeveloped countries, as well as often forcibly opening up new markets there. Some of the profits generated could then be used to make life better for the workers in the developed capitalist countries, so quenching their revolutionary fire. Thus the initial spark for revolution would *have* to come from workers in undeveloped countries.

The consequence was that Communist parties in practice came to power in societies where their preferred support base, the industrial proletariat, was a small minority of the population and where the task of building an industrial economy was necessarily a very prolonged enterprise. Faced with an economy and a society debilitated by war, revolution and civil war, and confronting a host of external enemies, the Soviet Communists set about organizing the economy through centralized control – which required the creation of a massive state bureaucracy. This seemed to be the only alternative to re-establishing capitalism as a way to develop the economy. Beginning in the 1920s, Stalin's regime attempted to convert the Soviet Union from an agricultural to an industrial economy in short order. This plan involved the forced incorporation of the peasantry into collective farms, with confiscation of agricultural production to sell on international markets, so as to obtain finance for industrialization. In the countryside hundreds of thousands of people starved, even as agricultural products were exported.

The economic change was brutally effective in producing heavy industry, which in turn enabled the Soviet Union to manufacture the weaponry to withstand and eventually defeat Nazi attack in 1941–1945. But the political repression of Communism had no redeeming features. From 1917 onwards in the quasi-religious ideological systems of state-communist regimes, Marx, Engels, Lenin and (in China) Mao became 'saints' or ideological prophets, their pictures carried at enormous May Day parades and their icons in every school textbook. In the universities of Communist countries their writings were treated as authoritative, scientific texts, to be pored over and cited as gospel, but always interpreted in line with current party orthodoxy. The alleged 'dictatorship of the proletariat' in the Soviet Union became, as Trotsky had foreseen in 1906, the dictatorship in practice of Communist party elites and of the state bureaucracy, run by Stalin's iron hand. Trotsky himself was murdered in exile on Stalin's orders in 1940. Nor did the model stop at the borders of the Soviet Union. It was imposed by the USSR on most of Eastern Europe after 1945, and adopted as orthodoxy by communist parties throughout the world. In the Soviet Union and its satellites totalitarian dictatorship lasted until the mid 1970s and in China until the early 1980s – after which they progressively became more normal authoritarian regimes, maintaining a political dictatorship, but no longer seeking to organize all aspects of social and economic life.

Reformist Marxism

Before the Soviet Union's global imposition of Marxist-Leninist orthodoxy upon communist parties began in the 1920s, there were also strands of Marxism that adopted a more reformist approach to the state in capitalist societies. These strands too could be traced back to Marx himself, who in 1852 in an article in the *New York Tribune* stated that if achieved in Britain, universal adult suffrage could lead to 'the political supremacy of the working class' without any need for violent revolution. And in an 1872 speech to a socialist conference in the Hague Marx acknowledged:

> Someday the worker must seize political power in order to build up the new organization of labour; he must overthrow the old politics which sustain the old institutions, if he is not to lose Heaven on Earth, like the old Christians who neglected and despised politics. But we have not asserted that the ways to achieve that goal are everywhere the same. You know that the institutions, mores, and traditions of various countries must be taken into consideration, and we do not deny that there are countries – such as America, England, and if I were more familiar with your institutions, I would

perhaps also add Holland – where the workers can attain their goal by peaceful means.

After Marx died, Engels also eventually conceded that the electoral arena was one place where the real interests of the working class could be pursued – though he also believed that struggle should continue on other fronts, such as workers directly confronting capitalists in strikes and protests.

In Germany at the beginning of the twentieth century Karl Kautsky and Eduard Bernstein of the Social Democratic Party (SPD) became the leading figures in what Lenin disparaged as 'revisionist' Marxism. Kautsky declared that the SPD was 'a revolutionary party but not a *revolution-making* party'. For many social democrats, then and since, the ultimate end was the same as for Marx: a classless society of free, equal, and prosperous people, where capitalism was no more.

Communist orthodoxy as enforced after 1917 had no time for this reformism, attacking liberal democracy as a sham. At the height of Stalin's control of the Soviet Union and the Communist International, Western social democracy was routinely denounced as 'social fascism', no different in kind from Naziism – a level of unreality now hard to fathom. In the post-1945 period Communist regimes denounced Western welfare states as simply the highest (most sophisticated) form of 'state monopoly capitalism'.

Social democratic parties of course contained many people whose ultimate aims were less radical than any Marxists, who accepted capitalism but wanted to pursue social justice only as far as the liberal democratic state would allow. Over the course of the twentieth century this less radical version of social democracy gradually displaced the more radical anti-capitalist variety, though many internal party battles were fought along the way. The SPD finally eradicated Marxism from its platform only in 1959 at its Bad Godesberg conference. As late as the 1980s the British Labour Party had to purge its ranks of the 'Militant' faction of Marxists. Finally even communist parties in the west belatedly tried to shed their baggage of revolutionary theory. The Italian Communist party, which polled up to a third of votes in free democratic elections in 1974, later adopted a reformist 'Eurocommunism'. Along with its Spanish and French counterparts it embraced electoral politics and promotion of the welfare state, and sought alliances with other parties to advance progressive reforms. Eurocommunist parties faded in the 1980s.

Another strand of Western non-revolutionary Marxist had no obvious agenda for political change at all. Some Marxist academics have developed analyses and critiques of the capitalist state, but fall short of saying what exactly might be done with it. These authors might support radical causes in their own personal politics, but they have little or nothing to say when it comes to how the state and economy as a whole might be changed for the better.

Society and Politics

While we have surveyed the concepts that provide the basic vocabulary of Marxist analysis, when it comes to understanding the social basis of politics, the fundamental concept is class, and the most important process is struggle between classes. In this section we examine why bitter class struggle should be pervasive according to Marxists – and why in practice it often seems so subdued or even absent.

Class conflict and class struggle

Marxists believe class antagonisms and struggles always define the core substance of politics. As Marx and Engels put it in the *Communist Manifesto*, 'The history of all hitherto existing society is the history of class struggles'. The main social classes depend on the economic system, and are defined in terms of their relationship to the dominant mode of production. So in feudal society, the two main classes are the landed aristocracy and the peasantry. In capitalist society, the main classes are the bourgeoisie or capitalists who own the means of production, and the proletariat or workers employed by them. Other classes may be present: for example, a middle class of managers and small business operators, and a 'lumpenproletariat' underclass of unemployable people. But these other classes have much smaller roles to play, especially when it comes to their relationship with the state. The main classes are seen as cohesive (or potentially cohesive) blocks in an antagonistic relationship with each other. Class is never a matter of degree, always an absolute; classes do not shade into one another. The state is then needed mainly to manage this antagonistic relationship.

This picture of cohesive classes in essentially conflicting relationships with each other is very different from the pluralist picture of a multiplicity of groups defined on many different bases competing for influence (discussed in Chapter 2). It is also strikingly different from the kind of market liberal emphasis on competing individuals that we will examine in the next chapter. For Marxists, the consciousness of individuals is created by their position in a social class. There is no essential human nature (as there is for liberals of all kinds), because who humans are at any time is determined by their class position. However, often members of subordinate classes may suffer from 'false consciousness', being under the influence of the ideology promulgated by the ruling class, and so yet to realize their own real class position. Another exemption from the idea that consciousness is determined by class location is granted to people like Marx himself, intellectuals who can stand outside their class position and observe the larger picture of how the world works and how history is moving.

Since Marx's day, developed capitalist societies have seen a massive shift of their job base from manufacturing to services, such that today Marx's manufacturing proletariat is actually a small minority of the working population. Moreover, Marx's expectation of an increasing polarization of social conditions between classes has not been borne out. The creation of European welfare states in the twentieth century provided a comprehensive 'safety net' of benefits that insure workers and managers alike against unemployment, illness and old age. Inequalities of income, wealth, life chances and health remain, and have sharply worsened since the 1980s, and the consequences are felt acutely by the 45 million Americans without any form of health insurance. But none of this has translated into mass immiserization and class polarization as anticipated by Marx.

Three other important changes have led large numbers of workers into identifying with 'capital' interests. First, workers who own their own houses benefit whenever house prices accelerate faster than overall inflation. Second, many people in western countries have invested heavily in acquiring 'educational capital' for themselves. Third, from the 1950s to the 1970s, the growth of occupational pensions tied their recipients into a dependency on rising stock markets. Since the 1980s the scope of occupational pensions has declined in the US, UK and Australia, but remains high in Japan, South Korea and much of Europe.

Marxist authors have struggled to cope with these changes in class structure. Industrial workers who are foremen, self-employed contractors, or employees in defence industries may all resist trade unionism and be hostile to socialism. Marxists analyse the permanently unemployed underclass as in Marx's own terms a 'lumpenproletariat' with no interest in class struggle and incapable of mobilization. They also now recognize the importance of cross-class identifications based on race, religion, ethnicities and country or region of origin. These lines of cleavage can be manipulated by employers and governments so as to fragment workers into rival groups, unable to take effective collective action. For example, poor whites in western societies can feel privileged compared to racial or ethnic minorities. Marxists once expected that racial, ethnic and religious divisions would decline in significance with industrial modernization and eventually die out. Marxists have had to come to terms with their persistence and apparently constant renewal. In some countries sectoral conflicts between public sector employees and private sector workers have persuaded private sector workers to identify with right-wing, low tax parties (Dunleavy 1986).

By the 1990s it was apparent that these trends were so pervasive as to require a fundamental rethink of how to identify classes and class boundaries. One response accepts the traditional Marxist approach of sticking to identifying the working class within individual capitalist societies, but abandons the equally traditional vision of the proletariat as manual workers. Workers are defined instead as anyone who takes orders, who has no control over their work tasks and who can be exploited unless organized. This 'large working class' still accounts for around three-fifths of the American or British workforce.

The second response concedes that advanced industrial societies have only limited internal class conflicts. An immense, property-less and miserable proletariat still exists, but now on a globalized and not a national basis:

> The revolutionary imagination of the twentieth century took as its social reference point the proletarian collectivity forged from the working class that emerged from the Second Industrial Revolution, out of the great industrial plants of Petrograd and Turin, Berlin and Glasgow, Detroit and Billaincourt, Gdansk and Sao Paulo. But we live today amid the ruins of this working class collectivity, which was systematically dismantled in the great neo-liberal offensive and capitalist restructuring of the past generation. Today's working class is concentrated in new places – for example, in the factory complexes of the Pearl River delta in southern China – and in new kinds of workplaces – hypermarkets and call centres, for instance. But these novelties do not mean that capital is any less dependent on its labour, even if that labour may not lead to any identifiable physical product. (Callinicos 2006: 251)

This second response extends Lenin's analysis of imperialism, placing class struggle on a global stage.

Immanual Wallerstein (2005) points out that the whole world is now fully owned by settled states and hence that the presumptively open 'frontier' zones that fuelled European and American imperialism of the nineteenth and early twentieth centuries are gone for good and cannot return. There is no longer any part of Nature that can be simply and brutally pillaged for profit, no safety-valve area where dissatisfied workers can be dispatched to seek their fortunes, nor compliant coun-

tries where pollution and other problems can be simply dumped by corporations. Wallerstein argues further that, de-ruralization of the
world's huge agricultural populations, especially in India, China and
Latin America, is also proceeding fast. So that the 'reserve army' of
labour that has allowed capitalists to press wages downwards for
decades is being drained. Finally Wallerstein thinks that the long-
delayed spread of liberal democracy and human rights to now encompass the large majority of the world's population will progressively
push up wages and end the current ruthless exploitation of the South's
workers. Together these trends will force a rebalancing of the world's
economic and political power in favour of the global proletariat.

Ideologies and consciousness

Marxists distinguish between a class *in* itself, defined by its relationship
to the means of production in the economic system, and a class *for*
itself that has attained a correct consciousness of its own position and
what should be done about it. This distinction enables Marxists to
explain why the proletariat so often fails to live up to the task assigned
to it in the Marxist theory of history.

In the 1920s the Italian Marxist Antonio Gramsci developed the concept of 'hegemony' to explain why workers in capitalist societies so
often are not rebellious. Capitalists can promote a hegemonic set of
ideas, accepted by all significant classes in society. These ideas are dis-
seminated by education systems, churches, newspapers, radio and television. This taken-for-granted set of beliefs, attitudes and values defines
the boundaries of legitimate thought, debates and political conflict.
Everyone becomes convinced that there is no alternative to the way
things are. So social democratic parties may call for a limited redistribution of income – but not for an end to an unjust economic system.
Even democracy is complicit, by giving workers the illusion that they
have a real say. For Moore (1957: 87–8), a 'democratic republic is the
optimum political shell for capitalism'. Marxists concur with elite theorists that elections, the competition of interest groups and legislative
debate are a sideshow.

Liberalism professes a commitment to human rights that are universally applicable to and enjoyed by all members of society. Marxist theorists point out that in practice this is not true. Private property rights
work in favour of those with large amounts of property and against
those with little or no property. The right to free expression may be
enjoyed very easily by wealthy media proprietors and the journalists
they hire. Such a right is less easily enjoyed by radical critics of the capitalist system, who will often find themselves investigated by the police,

shunned by employers and harassed by the criminal justice system for their political views. Freedom of association is rarely a problem for the wealthy, but workers may find laws passed to restrict where, when and how they can assemble and organize.

Government and Policy Making

Marxists insist that government policy making should never be ana-lyzed in isolation from the dialectical processes and class conflicts that are basic to economic and so to political life. They examine the state and its workings in holistic fashion, in terms of how the state is gener-ated by, and then regulates, class struggle. Among Marxists there are three main accounts of the state in capitalist society. The first treats the state as an instrument of the ruling capitalist class. A second account points out that the state can sometimes be an arbiter of class conflict. The third emphasizes the necessary functions that the state must per-form for the maintenance and stability of the capitalist system. We examine these views in turn.

The State as instrument of capitalist control

Marx himself originally conceptualized the state in capitalist societies as an instrument directly controlled by the ruling class. As Marx and Engels put it in the *Communist Manifesto*: 'The executive of the modern state is but a committee for managing the common affairs of the whole bourgeoisie'. Thus the state is staffed by personnel closely connected with and controlled by the capitalist class. There are tight social and political connections between the owners and managers of large corporations and leaders of government, be they elected officials or senior bureaucrats. Today, proponents of this instrumental view agree with elite theory's observation that in the USA business leaders move directly into governmental office (see Chapter 3). In Europe the links run more indirectly through parties, political donations and social networks. As Lenin put it, the liberal democratic state is 'tied by a thousand threads' to capitalist interests and to courses of action that advance economic growth and enforce capitalist domination.

In this light, the central purpose of policy-makers is 'the containment of pressure from below' (Miliband 1969), to repress workers, divert voters' attention from oppression and inequality, and deflect political unrest onto harmless diversionary issues. However, because firms and corporations compete against each other, and because they often look only to their short-term profits, especially in over-exploiting their workers, the state may sometimes intervene in ways that stabilize capitalism for the long-term but are nonetheless opposed by specific capitalists. For instance, in specific periods the creation of a limited welfare state and a somewhat more even-handed regulation of labour markets by government may be needed to head off social unrest. But no long-term, systematic or large-scale divergence between the state and bourgeois interests is feasible in the instrumental view. In particular, once the pressure of potential social unrest slackens, the instrumentalist view implies that capitalist interests will ruthlessly seek to curtail redistributive state activities. They will once again want to roll back welfare state benefits, eliminate social regulation of capitalist processes, and let social inequalities expand unchecked. These trends can be observed in the renewed social inequalities of countries such as the United States, United Kingdom and Australia since the 1980s.

The state as arbiter between classes

Marx and especially Engels also envisaged that sometimes the state could act as *an arbiter between social classes*, at times when class struggle was evenly balanced. Periods of this kind had occurred in the struggle between the rising bourgeoisie and the aristocrats and monarchs of the 'feudal' mode of production from the sixteenth to the eighteenth centuries in Europe. In capitalist society, the bourgeoisie and the working class might at times be similarly balanced. This analysis gives the controllers of state power far more choice over their strategy, and allows for some capitalist states to adopt radically different approaches from others.

In *The Eighteenth Brumaire of Louis Napoleon* Marx applied this analysis to explain France's lapse into dictatorship under Napoleon III 1852. Napoleon III claimed to reconcile the interests of workers, capitalists and agricultural land-owners. The development of fascism and Naziism in the 1920s and 1930s could also be interpreted as radically nationalist forces being able to take control of the state as a result of a stalled conflict between the bourgeoisie and proletariat. Similarly, the persistence of dictatorships in Spain, Portugal and Greece into the 1970s, and the frequent resort to military coups in Latin American and Asian countries until the late 1980s, all suggest that capitalism has no 'natural' push towards liberal democracy. Instead military or bureaucratic or political interests can periodically take advantage of a balancing of capitalist and non-capitalist forces to seize control of the state. Arbiter state regimes may subvert liberal democracy, or they may arise during a prolonged transition towards liberal democracy, especially in the now numerous 'semi-democracies'. Regimes as dissimilar as modern

Russia and Singapore also show that arbiter state arrangements are by no means temporary phenomena, but can instead stretch over decades.

Some Marxists argued that the arbiter state has become extensive even in established liberal democracies (Poulantzas 1978). For instance, when the French Fourth Republic in the late 1950s became locked in vicious decolonization conflicts that it could neither win nor resolve to abandon, first in Vietnam and then in Algeria, it was forced to accept what was almost a coup d'état by General Charles de Gaulle. He took power as President, legitimated himself via referenda, and changed the French constitution from a parliamentary to an executive-dominated system, with a directly elected and powerful president. In other countries, such as the USA and UK, where competition between parties to control state power is apparently more resilient, political control under arbiter state arrangements takes the form of a ruling consensus spanning across the main party competitors. Party leaders ostensibly compete for popular support, but in practice the same pro-capitalist policies are implemented whoever wins elections.

In 'corporatist' political systems such as Austria, Germany and the Scandinavian countries, policy gets made by agreement between peak executive branch officials, business leaders and union leaders. These agreements may or may not be submitted to parliament for a rubber stamp. On a Marxist account, this kind of formal corporatism is just another way to co-opt labour union leaders and prevent the workers disrupting capitalism. Part of the corporatist bargain is that union leaders discipline their members, and stop them striking. In return unions get guarantees when it comes to wage rates, social insurance, and other material benefits – but Marxists believe that the bargain is always heavily skewed in favour of business.

The state as arbiter balances class forces, but for Marxists it is never substantively neutral. It manages class conflict, but it does not so equitably. The arbiter state insists first on maintaining social order. Military and semi-democratic regimes often imprison, execute or 'disappear' left-wing dissenters, and crush trade union militancy. They can even occasionally take populist action against capitalist interests, such as imposing controls on foreign exchange markets and movements of capital, or mandating price freezes in inflationary crises. But once the crisis is past these measures are quickly abandoned.

The functional state

A third Marxist view sees the state as performing key necessary functions for the capitalist economic system, some of which (like the maintenance of order) may even look like they are in everyone's interests.

This view begins in Marx's more 'scientific' work on economics in *Das Kapital*. On this account it matters little who actually manages the state apparatus, for the state is compelled to implement pretty much the same public policies, irrespective of whether it is run by a dictator, a right-wing pro-capitalist party, or even a social democratic party notionally representing the workers. The presence or absence of social influences and networks connecting capitalists, politicians and bureaucrats (of the sort stressed in the instrumentalist Marxist and elitist accounts of the state) are irrelevant. Everything depends instead on the state's structural position in relation to the capitalist economy (Poulantzas 1969).

Foremost among the tasks the state must perform is the creation of social and economic conditions conducive to capitalist enterprise (such as securing private property rights, enforcing laws of contract and maintaining a predictable money supply). This is the 'accumulation' imperative of the state – the need to promote the accumulation of capital, which is in turn achieved by promoting of economic growth (O'Connor 1984). According to Block (1977), the state may actually have a greater interest in the wellbeing of capitalist economic growth than do capitalists themselves. Politicians and government managers will be hurt very quickly by an economic downturn: politicians lose credibility and votes, and government bureaucrats lose revenues. Conversely, if the economy is flourishing, the lot of politicians in power and government bureaucracies will be much happier. Thus there is a permanent incentive for governments to deliver and provide the policies that are as conducive as possible to sustaining business investment and the confidence of financial markets. Individual corporations may happily support decisions that are bad for capitalism as a whole (for example, if they can secure government contracts for themselves that are inefficient and involve raising taxes).

In this light, capitalism without the state is barely conceivable. Unregulated competition would easily descend into chaos. We could imagine an economy in which there was completely unregulated competition between corporations. For instance, in the dystopian novel *Jennifer Government* even police action to catch murderers depends on corporations or the victim's families raising money to finance police investigations, meaning that law enforcement favours the wealthy. Private property could be secured only by force controlled (at great expense) by each individual property owner; and organized crime would have a competitive advantage (as in the 'mafia capitalism' of Russia in the 1990s). A social system where private property is secure, laws of contract are enforced, and a basic infrastructure is provided is advantageous to all capitalists. But there is what economists call a 'collective action problem' in creating this sort of social system: each individual capitalist corporation would rationally put its own immediate interest in profit first, and seek to avoid contributing to the 'public good' of securing the capitalist order itself. This is the same problem we discussed in Chapter 2, where it gets in the way of individuals who share a material interest forming, joining and contributing to an interest group to advance that interest. For capitalists taken as a whole, the state exists as an answer to this collective action problem. Once the state is in place, politicians and bureaucrats have an added interest in ensuring that capitalism flourishes – because state revenues themselves, and so the financial self-interest of politicians and government managers, come to depend on that flourishing. In addition to providing the basic legal and physical infrastructure, the state needs to stabilize capitalism by maintaining social order (through police, courts and prisons).

In analyzing the ebb and flow of government policies, Marxists insist that we should always look at the big picture, especially concerning how the various processes of class domination and the structure of the state in relation to the economy combine to produce particular patterns of government action. The pluralist strategy of focusing on one small decision may be quite misleading – if (for example) that decision can be interpreted as a concession to mollify a potentially troublesome section of the working class. To take an example; in 1973 a British Conservative government got into a serious conflict with striking coal miners (who worked for the government-owned National Coal Board and were crucial to power generation in the UK). As coal stocks began to run low the Prime Minister put the country onto an emergency economic footing, and in early 1974 called a general election to determine who ruled the country, the miner's union or the government. In fact voters were equivocal about who was responsible for the crisis and returned a minority Labour (social democratic) government, which promptly settled the strike with a generous financial settlement. Pluralists might see this outcome as proof of the political power of the miners' union. But in 1985 the power of the mine workers and their union was broken by a different Conservative government under Margaret Thatcher, carefully prepared with new anti-union legislation, used to encourage a break-away 'moderate' miners union, and having extensively diversified power supplies away from coal. A few years later what was left of the coal industry was privatized, and by the mid 1990s the UK coal industry ceased to exist. Completely deprived of their economic rationale, the mining towns and villages whose strong community spirit sustained the militant coal strike of 1973–74 sometimes degenerated into centres of crime and drug-taking. So while the first conflict apparently showed the state responding via liberal democratic processes to foster workers' interests, within a single generation the miners' militancy was completely crushed and their industry destroyed.

Such instances of overt conflict dramatize the ways in which an apparently independent state apparatus acts against a potentially rebellious working class. But a far more pervasive and important means of state action is to convince workers, the poor, disaffected youth and disgruntled ethnic minorities that the political-economic system operates in their interests too. The latter is called by Marxists the 'legitimation' imperative, because it involved making the capitalist political economy appear legitimate in the eyes of those who actually suffer most from it. It operates in two main ways. The first is through actually providing material resources to cushion the working class from economic recession and other instabilities generated by the capitalist economy. The development of the welfare state can be interpreted in these terms (Offe 1984): workers are insured by government against unemployment, poverty, old age, sickness and injury. The second way that legitimacy is secured is through the many state functions that create and sustain ideology: ensuring that the ideas that favour the capitalist class are also accepted by all other classes.

In the days when he was still influenced by Marxism and before he became a liberal, the German social theorist Jürgen Habermas (1976) spoke of a 'legitimation crisis' in which the capitalist state failed to manage the competing demands upon it. The basic demand was the 'accumulation' imperative stemming from the structural position of the state in relation to the economy. The legitimation imperative pointed the state in very different directions, in terms of its need to appear responsive to the citizenry, and provide income security through social welfare. This sort of analysis was developed further by Offe (1984), who pointed to a systematic crisis in the welfare state, torn between 'commodification' and 'decommodification'. Decommodification is by definition the use of interventionist social policies to curb the instability of capitalism. Such policies may stabilize the political and economic systems, but the income security they create undermines incentives to work, and so interrupts the supply of willing labour to businesses. There is a striking parallel here to the analysis of market liberals, discussed in Chapter 5. Market liberals believe the solution is obvious: to roll back the welfare state. For Offe that solution is not available, inasmuch as the welfare state is required to stabilize capitalism. He believed that a more likely resolution was a strengthening of corporatist arrangements that managed the contradictions of the welfare state though an alliance between government executives, business and trade union leadership – though this outcome would systematically favour business rather than labour, and threaten legitimacy because it bypassed elected governments. Quite where all this would lead was left open by Offe, who limited himself to the identification of 'crisis tendencies'. Offe was wrong about corporatism, which has done much better than its alternatives in delivering an egalitarian distribution of income, especially in its Scandinavian and north European heartlands. Corporatism has come under threat mainly from the right rather than the left, excoriated by market liberals for its tendency to prop up the welfare state and restrict competitive capitalism.

The arcane debates among the three different schools of Marxists about the state's relationship to society and, in particular, the capitalist economic system and the capitalist class, intensified from the 1960s through to the 1980s. The Marxist theorists of this era certainly did much better than their predecessors in analyzing state structures in sophisticated fashion. Often impenetrable to outsiders, these theoretical debates reached a climax of complexity in the work of Jessop (1990), for whom the state could be many different things at different times in different places. By the 1990s the collapse of Soviet communism saw most Marxist intellectuals in the West either ceasing to produce much new work or moving on from classical Marxist concerns into postmodern modes of political reasoning (see Chapter 13). Marxism lives on chiefly as 'critique', highlighting the biases of the capitalist state, the persistence and worsening of social inequalities, and the continuing importance of social tensions and class conflict underneath the surface of liberal democratic politics.

Conclusions

Marxism offers a comprehensive explanatory theory of the development of human societies. Within its grand historical sweep, the focus is on how capitalism came into being, how capitalism works and how it will eventually exit the world stage. With the demise of Soviet communism, the Chinese Communist Party's embrace of private markets, and capitalism now apparently established internationally as the universal form of production, Marxism no longer offers any claim to define an alternative fundamental way of structuring society. Marxist analysis has also dried up. Marxist theorists may still support strikes and anti-globalization protests, but they no longer try to say what exactly might be done differently or how the democratic state itself might be changed for the better. Marxism can still however be deployed to critique the limits of capitalism and liberal democracy. The concept of dialectic is tipped by some theorists as the most enduring legacy of the huge intellectual outpouring on Marxist themes (Rees 1998). Stripped of its utopian and futurological elements, Marxism might be read as constantly alerting liberal thinkers to the ineradicable nature of conflicts over the acquisition of economic control and the distribution of resources.

Some Marxists still hope the 'old mole' of revolution has not gone to sleep or ceased to work away, albeit in surprising ways. Lin (2006) points out the oddness of assuming that China's Communist government is a non-socialist regime, when it has moved around 400 million people out of rural poverty and into more or less adequate urban/industrial conditions in the space of a little over a decade. China may also realistically hope to shift perhaps another 300 million people out of poverty in the course of the next decade – in all perhaps one-seventh of all humanity in less than a quarter of a century. This process has of course entailed huge transition costs, appalling social dislocations, adverse living conditions, massive environmental degradation, and numerous injustices and violations of human rights, all managed within the Communist Party's political monopoly. But Lin argues that this is none the less a progressive transformation that holds true to a socialist platform and has been a mainly peaceful achievement. Against social change of this pace and scale, the English industrial revolution (affecting a population of 4 to 5 million), the development of the United States over a much long period, and the more recent industrializations of Japan and South Korea all pale in comparison. So the cycle of Marxist theorizing, currently in a downswing, could yet turn up again, as Griffiths (2006: 7) optimistically hopes: 'These are good times for Karl Marx . . . Freed at last from the burden of legitimizing dozens of cruel and useless monolithic regimes Marx himself can look forward to a brighter and more interesting future.' The global financial convulsions of the late 2000s could give Marxists renewed hope that their diagnosis of the inherently crisis-prone character of the capitalist political economy has life in it yet.

Chapter 5

Market Liberalism

Market liberalism seeks to reform government in the belief that capitalism is the optimal system for discovering and using knowledge, for securing prosperity, and for promoting economic and political freedom. Clearly then it flatly opposes Marxism, but its adherents also criticize pluralism and any theory of the state that allows a positive role for government planning.

Market liberals stand on the political right, but reject both the moderate reformism tolerated by many mainstream conservatives and traditional conservatism's defence of an established (often aristocratic) social order. As Hayek (1960) put it:

> While the conservative inclines to defend a particular established hierarchy and wishes authority to protect the status of those whom he values, the [market] liberal feels that no respect for established values can justify the resort to privilege or monopoly or any other coercive power of the state in order to shelter such people against the forces of economic change.

Unlike true conservatives of the kind we discuss in Chapter 12, most market liberals are happy to deduce what is optimal for organizing society from some first principles, as opposed to the test of experience. Their ideal society may bear little resemblance to any existing society

Until the 1970s, market liberals claimed only that less government was desirable. From then on, they started to believe that government itself could be re-engineered along market liberal lines. By then 'rational choice theory' had developed deductive arguments that could be drawn up to specify better forms of government. Thus emboldened, market liberalism achieved a peak of worldwide influence in the 1980s and early 1990s, in Anglo-American governments in particular. In the United Kingdom, it was known as the 'new right' or sometimes 'Thatcherism' (after Prime Minister Margaret Thatcher who dominated British politics throughout the 1980s). In Australia, it was called 'economic rationalism'; and in many places 'neo-liberalism'. The approach was adopted in some post-communist states after 1989 as 'shock therapy' for their economies (notably Russia and Poland). In the hands of international financial institutions it informed the 'Washington Consensus', whose policies were imposed on struggling debtor states. Market liberalism has subsequently receded from this high point of influence, having failed to restructure government or 'roll back the state' as intended. Yet the ideas remain important, even as they mutate into less extreme or distinctive proposals.

Origins and Core Assumptions

Markets have existed for thousands of years, but they were long despised by monarchs, aristocrats and religious leaders alike as the domain of ill-educated and grasping merchant classes. Hence, from ancient times through to the dawn of the modern era, markets were often hedged with restrictions about who could produce what, who could consume, who was allowed to labour for monetary income, and who was allowed to trade. Even within markets, powerful interests such as medieval guilds sought to limit competition and regulate technologies. With the rise of capitalism and financial markets in the seventeenth and eighteenth centuries markets began to shatter these restrictions. The idea that markets are always the best way to organize society's economic life received eloquent expression in the Scottish political economist Adam Smith's *The Wealth of Nations*, published in 1776. He argued that an 'invisible hand' converted the self-interested decisions of manufacturers, traders, consumers and workers into outcomes that maximized collective wellbeing. As Smith put it: 'It is not from the benevolence of the butcher, the brewer, or the baker that we expect our dinner, but from their regard to their own interest.'

Hayek, Friedman, and the classical liberal heritage

Since Smith's day the idea that markets generally maximize social welfare has been a cornerstone of the mainstream (Western) discipline of economics, although most economists also recognise market failures. This philosophy resonated with the interests of merchants and manufacturers in emerging capitalist economies. In nineteenth century liberalism the market became the site of economic liberty intertwined with political liberty, and private property rights were valued as much as rights to speak and associate. Governments in liberal capitalist states came to see one of their main tasks as facilitating the growth of commerce and industry, at first because their own finances could benefit from growth (see Chapter 1). In this era market liberals had no explanatory theory of how the state actually worked to match their

economic theory of how the market worked. They had only a normative theory about what the state should do: practice minimal interference with property rights or commerce, an approach called laissez faire.

Yet in the late nineteenth century, governments began to take on
more domestic policy functions. They regulated markets to preserve
competition, they developed social policy by providing public education, pensions and sickness pay and health care, they regulated housing
and working hours and conditions. These trends accelerated in the
wake of World War I, with the launch of public housing programmes
in west European countries. In many liberal democracies the Great
Depression of the 1930s was initially met by market liberals with, des-
perate re-assertion of the virtues of free market economics, accompanied by austerity measures that restricted public spending. Most
governments followed what turned out to be very bad advice, often
making matters still worse with disastrous restrictions on imports that
market liberals opposed.

The countries which seemed to best combat the Great Depression
were those where the state eventually asserted control over the
economy through planning, public employment, and increased government spending. In their different ways the United States under
Roosevelt's 'New Deal', Nazi Germany with a government-sponsored
military build-up, and the state-planned economy of the Soviet Union
all followed this path, to the horror of the by now dwindling band of
market liberals.

Intellectual justification for interventionist government policies to
combat economic recession by borrowing and spending money was
provided by the British economist John Maynard Keynes in his key
1936 book, *The General Theory of Employment, Interest, and Money*.
Before Keynes, most governments accepted the economists' orthodoxy
that budgets should be balanced and government spending cut in recessions. After Keynes the orthodoxy became instead that governments
should run (temporary) deficits to counteract recessions, to spend their
way out of a slump. The post-World War II boom created global consensus around the new prescriptions, so that in 1971 even conservative
US President Richard Nixon could declare: 'We're all Keynesians now.'

World War II was another blow for market liberals as all the main
protagonists adopted government planning of industrial production for
the war effort, along with expanded social programmes and rationing
to ensure that their citizens received a minimum of food, shelter and
clothing in difficult times. The war stimulated technological innovations that often had civilian applications. This effective central planning
of production and the distribution of basic goods suggested that the
prescriptions of socialists for a planned economy might be feasible.

After 1945 even conservative parties accepted a much more interventionist economic role for the state. Across Europe, key industries were brought into state ownership (nationalized). Government spending on social welfare expanded dramatically during and after the war, partly as a matter of social solidarity in the face of shared threats, partly as a response to the enhanced risks associated with the war (Dryzek and Goodin 1986). Market liberalism was exiled to the margins of politics in Europe, and accorded lip service but ignored in practice in the United States.

With exquisitely bad timing, the seeds of fightback were being sown by the Austrian émigré and British economics professor Friedrich A. von Hayek in his 1944 book *The Road to Serfdom*. For Hayek the overarching value of personal freedom is guaranteed by stable, general and impartial laws, implemented predictably by government officials, and policed by neutral judges and courts. On this basis citizens can make life-plans, develop their talents, choose occupations and launch businesses. From economic freedom alone would come prosperity and human flourishing.

Hayek detested social welfare programmes and state provision of services (such as public housing or health care) because they meant government officials deciding at their own discretion who should receive how much of the benefit in question, and who should pay for it. Citizens would become powerless supplicants, dependent upon bureaucrats and politicians for key decisions affecting their lives, such as whether they secured medical treatment or not. Power would be transferred from ordinary people to the state apparatus.

If laws and regulations affecting the economy could be changed at the whim of bureaucrats, politicians or changing majorities of voters, then private businesses would lack a predictable environment for long-term investment decisions. Rather than risk seeing profits being sequestered in taxes, or wiped out by future government actions, businesses and investors will make only safe, non-innovative commitments. The result is slower economic growth, and eventual economic sclerosis. Thus all government regulation, subsidy and interference has to be resisted.

Economic theory before Hayek had generally assumed that individuals were rational and knowledgeable in their transactions. Hayek, however, stressed limits to human knowledge and capability that applied to private economic actors and government officials alike. He argued that markets were much better than governments when it came to aggregating limited, partial and fleeting fragments of knowledge. Each actor knows a bit about their immediate environment, which is all they need to be able to operate effectively. Markets in Hayek's view provide the best environment for generating and disseminating knowledge, with strong incentives for people to make key innovations and investments. By contrast, he argued that state-directed economic policies require the centralization and processing of information and knowledge on a scale beyond human cognitive capacities.

This sort of market advocacy was subsequently developed by Milton Friedman and the 'Chicago School' of economists (Friedman and Friedman 1962; for a popular version, see Friedman and Friedman 1979). Friedman made his reputation as an anti-Keynesian monetary economist, who thought that governments should manage the economy only by maintaining close control of the money supply. Friedman argued that the Great Depression had been the fault of mistakes in government policy, such as restricting free trade, and not of any inherent flaws in the market system. One of the foundations for the revival of market liberalism's intellectual fortunes beginning in the 1970s was Friedman's prescription for control of inflation, which after price rises in the wake of the 1974 OPEC oil price shock became a major economic priority of most governments. Following Hayek, Friedman linked economic and political freedom, arguing that economic freedom of the sort secured in a capitalist economy was a necessary condition for political freedoms. (But not a sufficient condition – even Friedman had to accept that there are many political dictatorships in market economies.)

Ironically, the image of the state found in Hayek and the early Friedman mirrors that of their Marxist and socialist opponents. This generation of market liberals treated the state as a coordinated and centrally-directed entity and (like Marxists) made no attempt to explain the internal operations of government. Their millennial forebodings, ignored and marginalized in Hayek's case for a quarter of a century, suddenly seemed plausible in the 1970s. With the election of Margaret Thatcher as Prime Minister of the United Kingdom in 1979 and Ronald Reagan as President of the United States a year later, a new, decade-long golden age of market liberal influence began. In his First Inaugural Address in 1981, Reagan proclaimed that: 'Government is not the solution to our problem. Government is the problem.'

These market liberal governments faced a paradox. If Hayek is right about the impossibility of effective government management of complex political-economic systems, then that impossibility applies no less to managers trying to reform government itself along market liberal lines. As American humorist P.J. O'Rourke put it: 'The Republicans are the party that says government doesn't work and then get elected and prove it.' This paradox was solved by abandonment of Hayek's worldview in favour of a more analytically confident form of market liberalism.

The rise of public choice

By the late 1970s a flock of market liberal theorists had built a comprehensive explanatory theory of the state, based on assumptions about human capabilities very different to those of Hayek. They took basic microeconomic assumptions about self-interested and 'maximizing' human behaviour and applied them to politics, creating what came to be known as 'rational choice theory' or 'public choice'. Now, it is possible to deploy microeconomic assumptions without ending up as a market liberal, as the politically agnostic forms of rational choice theory that have flourished in US political science since the 1970s make clear. There are even some Marxist rational choice theorists. But most public choice analysts who took a political stand did so on behalf of market liberalism. Key luminaries here include James Buchanan, Gordon Tullock, Geoffrey Brennan, William Niskanen, William Mitchell and Mancur Olson.

Proposals emerging in this new wave included privatization of state owned enterprises, competitive bidding for private contractors to supply government services, and de-regulation of the economy. Big, hierarchical public service systems should give way to more competitive arrangements designed to establish individual consumers' control over services like education, health care and social insurance. These ideas were picked up by the Thatcher and Reagan governments. And market liberalism also flourished in New Zealand after 1984, and in the state government of Victoria (Australia) in the 1990s. Similar recipes were imposed on states in developing countries and post-communist states by international financial institutions, in an extreme form that developed governments (even those in the United States and United Kingdom) would never have accepted for themselves.

The basic assumption of rational choice forms of market liberalism is that the world can be analyzed as if it is populated entirely by homo economicus individuals. Homo economicus is a rational egoist who calculates what is in his or her best material interests and chooses a course of action accordingly. (Many feminists would deny that there is any 'her' in this assumption, see Chapter 10). This perspective actually harks back to economic theory as it existed before Hayek. The Nobel laureate James Buchanan (1991: 217) claimed that presuming the primacy of self-interest is both free from 'romantic and illusory notions' about political behaviour and 'surely more consistent with the political reality'. Yet the concept of 'interest' can be broadened, encompassing whatever it is that particular people see as benefiting them. In concrete analyses of particular institutions and actors, we can specify exactly what it is that rational egoists maximize.

Roughly speaking, consumers maximize their utility (or wellbeing). Private producers maximize profits or sales/market share. Interest groups (or firms operating in government-regulated markets) try to obtain from government a 'rent' or unearned benefit, either financed via general taxation or achieved by manipulating regulatory rules. Politicians maximize the probability of being re-elected, because that is instrumental to their income, prestige, and whatever else they want to accomplish. Senior bureaucrats want to expand the budget of their bureau, because organizational growth is instrumental to their salaries and personal career advancement (Niskanen 1971). Politicians, interest groups and bureaucrats may all claim to be serving the public interest, but that is just cheap talk that justifies their actions and cloaks their real motives. For rational choice market liberals the state no less than other social institutions is staffed by rational egoists. 'What kind of a society isn't structured on greed?' asked Milton Friedman. 'The problem of social organization is how to set up an arrangement under which greed will do the least harm.'

Hence the basic problem of the state is how to convert private interest into some form of public benefit. According to most economists this is not a problem in the market, where (given a few assumptions) Adam Smith's 'invisible hand' can be relied upon to maximize social welfare. But in politics the problem is substantial. It is magnified by the fact that if market liberals' assumptions about human motivation apply comprehensively, then there is nobody in government who could possibly put into effect market liberal prescriptions. To do so would mean acting in the public interest, not in the private self-interest of the political leader or public official in question. So there has to be some slippage in the assumption about individual motivation, if there is to be any hope of implementing market liberal reforms.

Focusing on individuals leads market liberals to deny primacy to other social actors, whether groups (as in pluralism), elites (as in elite theory), social classes (as in Marxism), or society as a whole (as in traditional conservatism). As Margaret Thatcher famously put it (in a 1987 interview in *Woman's Own* magazine), 'There is no such thing as society.' Market liberals can recognize that groups and other organizations exist, and indeed analyze them. But they assume that organizations or interest groups, indeed any form of collectivity, can only be understood in terms of the individuals who compose them, and the rules under which these individuals interact. So to speak of 'the working class' or 'business' is just a loose kind of shorthand for individuals A, B, C, etc who happen to share some characteristic, but who do not act as a unit. Instead they act only if their individual interest pushes them to realize a net benefit, a return that is better than the costs they incur in acting.

In genuinely free situations, individuals only enter into a transaction when its material benefits for them will be greater than its material costs. While competition in markets is central, market liberals recognize that rational egoists may sometimes decide to constitute themselves into hierarchies – for example, the management of a corporation. But hierarchical firms present no problem, so long as they compete against each other in free markets. Market liberalism also allows that individuals may sometimes find it expedient to cooperate rather than compete, though all cooperative relationships are a matter of strategic calculation.

The market liberal stress on material exchange as basic to all human relationships means denying the relevance of citizenship. A citizen is somebody who acts in public-spirited fashion. Public choice theorists and politicians are much more likely to speak of 'customers' or 'clients' of government rather than 'citizens'. For example, one of us while living in Victoria in Australia received many circulars from government agencies, all beginning 'Dear Customer'.

Thus for rational choice market liberals the social world is a machine for the production of goods and services that satisfy human wants. The machine itself can be understood completely by looking at its component parts (individuals and organizations) and how they interact. Of course the machine may be working badly – and that is especially true when it comes to government. Rational choice market liberals believe the machine can be re-engineered – just like Marxists do, though in an opposite direction. (In Chapter 12 we discuss a genuinely conservative view, which treats the state in organic terms, incapable of being understood by reduction to its components.)

On the outer fringes of market liberalism are 'anarcho-capitalist' thinkers who deny that any state is necessary. Rothbard (1970: 2) argued that all existing government functions (including national defence, civil protection and judicial services) could

> be supplied by people or firms who (a) gained their revenue voluntarily rather than by coercion, and (b) did not – as the State does – arrogate to themselves a compulsory monopoly of police or judicial protection . . . Defense firms would have to be as freely competitive and as noncoercive against noninvaders as are all other suppliers of goods and services on the free market. Defense services, like all other services, would be marketable and marketable only.

The vast majority of market liberals do not go this far. Instead they recognize that a state is necessary. Its legitimate roles are:

- defining and protecting private property rights;
- establishing and enforcing laws of contract;
- preventing overt coercion of individuals by others;
- issuing and controlling money;
- regulating monopolies that cannot be avoided (but some market liberals believe the evil effects of regulation will always exceed those of the monopoly they are designed to correct);
- providing some minimum basic infrastructure (although many market liberals believe that this can be done privately);
- protecting people who are unable to take care of their own interests;
- organizing national defence; and
- collecting sufficient funds to finance these activities.

Beyond these basic functions, governments may sometimes have to provide 'public goods' such as urban streets (private toll roads can carry traffic longer distances), but market liberals interpret this need as narrowly as possible (Friedman and Friedman 1979: 22).

Society and Politics

Market liberals may accept democracy, but they believe any sort of politics is full of deficiencies and problems, compared with virtuous markets. Whereas Hayekians merely lamented what could go wrong, rational choice analysts provided a detailed critique of democracy. Rent-seeking, the paradoxes of electoral politics, and log-rolling play key parts in this account of how rational social actors enter politics to bad effect, and we now visit each of these.

Rent-seeking

Market liberals believe that pluralists are living in a dream-world in their positive evaluation of interest groups. The attraction that causes interest groups to buzz around government like bees around a honey pot can only be a private benefit that can be restricted to group members. This private benefit is a 'rent', an economic term meaning an unearned profit, gained by rigging competition. For example, when a speculator 'corners the market', by hoarding a scarce resource and then makes super-normal profits selling in the conditions of artificial scarcity, he or she has created a rent. All rational actors should have an eye for such benefits.

Government provides many opportunities for such gains. Rather than compete in markets, corporations will try to get government to protect them from competition. Manufacturing industry will lobby government for tariffs on imports to protect them against more efficient foreign firms. Established companies seek expensive health, safety or environmental regulations that discriminate against new competitors. Defence, public service and information technology contractors seek exclusive deals with government that freeze out potential competitors. Firms can seek restricted licenses or franchises – for instance, to secure radio wavelengths for mobile phones. In North America and Europe, governments from the 1940s to 1980s would not allow new airlines to compete with established carriers. Farmers try to get government to subsidize their production. Labour unions pressure government to specify a minimum wage that advantages their members in work, but disadvantages the jobless still seeking work. Professional associations of doctors or lawyers urge government to impose restrictions on who can practice medicine and law.

Market liberals argue that even 'public interest lobbies' are really seeking to benefit only themselves. For example, a group that campaigns to ban smoking at work secures rent for non-smokers, increasing their promotion chances and benefits at the expense of smokers. Similarly, pro-environment groups that campaign for conservation really operate to protect the interests of those who already have access to resources (e.g. country cottages next to green spaces) against those who do not.

Interest groups, corporations and wealthy individuals seek influence and so rents through contributions to parties and candidates, mobilizing the votes of their members, publicity campaigns, legal action, and cultivating cooperative relationships with government officials (for example, by promises of jobs and consultancies for ex-members of government). Market liberals believe rent-seeking political action always undermines the economic efficiency of the free market. Consumers and businesses must pay the costs of restrictive regulations in higher prices for goods. Taxpayers are forced to subsidize a range of special interests. The cumulative effects of rent-seeking are destructive, continuously pushing up the state budget and cluttering the economy with restrictive regulations, all of which slows economic growth.

The smaller a group is as a proportion of citizens in society, the more extreme its demands for rents can be. This effect occurs because the costs of meeting the rents for a small group are dispersed across the great mass of taxpayers, with little imposition of costs on the group members themselves. Thus it makes sense for the small group to press for policies that are ineffective or which damage social welfare and economic growth, so long as they themselves reap concentrated benefits. Market liberals explain the subsidies going to agriculture in industrialized Western countries (such as Japan or the US) in these terms. By contrast, if a group is large enough to constitute a high proportion of the population as a whole, it is more likely to worry about the overall social and economic effects of the policies it seeks. But as Olson's (1965) analysis (discussed in Chapter 2) tells us, organizing such large groups is hard.

Log-rolling

Why do not majorities of voters or legislators simply reject propositions that create benefits for minorities while reducing social welfare? This could indeed happen if each self-serving proposal from a minority (for example, farmers making up 2 per cent of the population in the US or UK) were considered on its own. But in elections many issues are voted on at the same time. The programmes of parties or candidates similarly bundle together disparate issues to create manifestos. And inside legislatures, although most new laws refer to only one policy area, elected representatives and parliamentary parties often trade support, creating coalitions across multiple issues.

Log-rolling is the process whereby different small minority groups organize a broader coalition that can command a majority, with each component group promising to support the key proposal of the other groups in the coalition. This approach works best to the degree that different groups are not competing in the same policy area, but seek benefits in different policy areas. For instance, right-wing parties often draw support from farmers seeking agricultural subsidies, the defence forces seeking higher military budgets, police forces and 'law and order' interests wanting tough policies on crime, industrial interests seeking anti-trade union laws, and middle class home owners wanting higher property prices. A skilful politician should be able to come up with a budget package that gives something to each of this coalition's components. Such a coalition of minorities will try to ensure that there are other social groups not in the winning coalition who receive little or nothing. The victors' rents will be paid by all taxpayers, be they inside or outside the winning coalition.

Coalitions of minorities are however unstable and can also be broken by skilful politicians, possibly producing an alternation of successes for different coalitions, each of which adds to the accumulated pile of government obligations. Occasionally more public interested politicians may try to curb obviously excessive rents, but they will quickly encounter an adverse consequence of Olson's logic of collective action. Cutting rents will impose concentrated costs on minorities, who will mobilize politically to protect their benefits. In contrast, each member of the majority that benefits from rent-cutting will have an incentive to free-ride, leaving it to others to fight the good fight. Public-interested politicians will thus incur the opprobrium of intense minorities, while the apathetic majority fails to give them support.

In a 1982 book, *The Rise and Decline of Nations*, Olson argued that the longer a society is a stable liberal democracy, the more rent-seeking groups will be able to organize and reap benefits for themselves at the cost of overall economic growth. Hence long-lived democracies (such as the USA and the UK) will become 'sclerotic' and have much slower rates of growth than economies that have suffered political disruptions. This thesis was popular in the 1980s, when economic growth in Japan and Germany (societies refounded as liberal democracies only in 1946) was still high and the US was flagging. But Olson's argument has seemed less convincing since then with the stagnation of German and Japanese economies. Were he still alive Olson might reply that this stagnation is a result of the long passage of time since 1945 causing Germany and Japan to become sclerotic and overtaken by newly indus-trializing countries. Other market liberals suggest that in Germany and elsewhere in continental Europe the electoral system of proportional representation and the form of guaranteed interest representation known as 'corporatism' (which we discuss in Chapter 6) makes it espe-cially difficult for elected politicians to avoid appeasing multiple sec-tional interest groups.

Elections

Market liberals do not share pluralists' faith in elections as one way to signal the 'will of the people' to government. Elections are much worse than markets in giving people what they want. The problem, according to Buchanan and Tullock (1962), is that majority rule means that all those individuals who do not vote for winners – up to half the voters – receive nothing in return for the expenditure of their vote. Members of this losing multitude might wish to make trades with members of the winning majority in order to alleviate this situation. A political market would allow such trades to take place, and so make society as a whole better off. But majority rule debars any such outcome, instead giving the majority a free rein to impose costs on the losing side. In a market, one 'votes' freely with money only when you get something worthwhile in return. Under majority rule, those voting for a losing candidate or position get nothing in return for their vote. For Buchanan and Tullock, the remedy is an electoral system that works on the basis of something closer to unanimity than majority rule, for then almost all voters will have to be promised something in return for their vote.

Scepticism about democracy is reinforced by results from 'social choice theory' showing that no voting system, be it majority rule, unanimity, or proportional representation, can meet some apparently simple and desirable conditions simultaneously. According to the classic result of Kenneth Arrow (1963) it is – surprisingly – impossible to aggregate the preferences of individual voters in a way that satisfies the following five criteria:

- Unanimity: if any particular choice is unopposed, it should be part of the collective choice.
- Non-dictatorship: no one person should decide all policies.
- Transitivity: if society as a whole prefers policy A to policy B and B to policy C, then it should also prefer A to C.
- Unrestricted domain: individuals can have any preferences they like over the available policy alternatives.
- Independence of irrelevant alternatives: how society decides its preference between two alternatives X and Y should not be affected by the introduction of a third alternative Z.

To see how these conditions might not be met, consider an election about three issues (defence, welfare and education) that produces votes for left, centre and right parties shown in the first column of the Table 5.1 below. The next three columns show each party's preference ordering for spending the first £100 million of uncommitted tax receipts:

Table 5.1   *Voting preferences*

	Top priority	*Second priority*	*Third priority*
Left 35%	Welfare	Education	Defense
Centre 25%	Education	Defense	Welfare
Right 40%	Defense	Welfare	Education

We could now run a series of 'pairwise' votes to see how to allocate the £100 million. We get the following results:

- Defence (supported by Right and Centre) beats Welfare (65% to 35%)
- Education (supported by Centre and Left) beats Defence (60% to 40%)
- Welfare (supported by Right and Left) beats Education (75% to 25%)

This is a 'voting cycle', a situation where each group has transitive preferences, but society as a whole does not. Any choice can be outvoted by one of the other options in an endless cycle of votes. To avoid this situation, at least one of the five Arrow criteria must be violated. The last two are the easiest to relax. Any democracy must then in practice either restrict the preferences individuals are allowed to express, or limit the policy alternatives that can be advanced.

The political scientist William Riker built upon these sorts of results to argue that democracy is ultimately meaningless because of the arbitrary restrictions it must impose on either preferences or policy alternatives. There is no such thing as the will of the people – a doctrine he calls 'inconsistent and absurd' (Riker 1982a: 241). Skilled manipulators will seek ways to promote outcomes in their best interests – rigging agendas or the sequence of votes in legislatures; and introducing new issues to fragment opposing coalitions. Collective choice is therefore an arbitrary affair, highly vulnerable to the manipulations of skilled operators. By contrast, in markets there is no problem for people to get what they want.

A powerful twist to market liberal scepticism concerning elections and voting is provided by Brennan and Lomasky (1993). Their starting point is the standard observation in rational choice theory since Anthony Downs (1957) that the vote of one ordinary person in an election with large numbers of voters will almost never be decisive in affecting the overall outcome. Thus there is actually little point in individuals' voting for whatever is in their own material interest – because their vote will not affect the likelihood of that interest being met. Voters are hence free to vote based on their 'expressive' preferences that make them feel good. These preferences might be morally defensible – for example, when rich people vote for income support for poor families. But 'expressive' preferences can also be more destructive – for instance, voting for or against a candidate based on gender or racial prejudice. Citizens may, then, vote in ways inconsistent with their own material interests. The implication is again that the number of issues to be decided by elections should be kept as small as possible, and the number to be settled in markets as large as feasible.

Government and Policy Making

For market liberals, problems associated with rent seeking and arbitrariness and instability in collective choice also pervade government and policy making. First we discuss legislatures, before moving to bureaucracy and then the 'iron triangles' that unite organized interests, legislators, and bureaucrats.

Legislatures

The same problems of cycling and inconsistent collective preferences that plague elections can also be found within legislatures. Precisely because legislators spend most days together doing politics they will always be 'trading' off between at least two issues. A famous rational choice proof (called the McKelvey-Schofield theorem after its two authors) shows that when there are two or more issues under simultaneous consideration, a legislature can move in a series of majority votes from any point in the issue space to any other. Thus many different outcomes can be produced from a single set of legislators' preferences on the two issues. A competitive legislature should therefore be chaotic, changing policy inconsistently from one year (or one month) to the next.

In his book on *The Art of Political Manipulation* (1986) Riker argued from historical cases in the US that because of voting cycles, legislative politics is especially prone to arbitrariness and manipulation, and so collective irrationality. Clever politicians will try to craft political alternatives exactly so that a voting cycle between alternatives A, B and C occur. If there is a cycle, then the outcome depends solely on the order in which votes are taken. If a committee chair favours C, he or she should ensure that the first vote taken is between A and B, so that A knocks out B, but will be beaten by C in a subsequent vote.

This threat of incoherent policies and vulnerability to manipulation is counteracted in countries with parliamentary systems by strict party discipline that reduces the legislature to a rubber stamp for a government that controls a majority, as for example in the UK's House of Commons. In the United States Congress the threat of chaos has been counteracted chiefly by vesting strong powers in committees, each of which is controlled by the groups most actively rent-seeking in that policy area. Thus the Agriculture Committees are dominated by senators and representatives from farm states, and policy for federal lands is set by committees dominated by members from large western states with large federal land areas – and whose politics is dominated by interests seeking subsidized access to that land. The consequence may be political stability – but it is bought at the expense of exacerbated rent seeking.

In legislatures where coalitions of several parties are needed to form a majority (the normal case in Europe) Riker argued that 'minimum winning coalitions' should be the norm. A minimum winning coalition contains just enough parties to create a majority. This result has the effect of maximizing the number of losers left outside the winning coalition whose voters can be exploited in the generation of rents, so again legislative politics produces suboptimal results compared to markets.

Self-interested politicians can wreak further havoc in their efforts to serve their particular constituencies. Sometimes this will be a matter of 'pork-barrel' politics, exemplified by the US Congress's financial appropriations. Each member of Congress has an incentive to secure federal government spending for his or her own constituency – irrespective of whether that spending actually produces public benefits to outweigh the tax costs involved. Thus coalitions of legislators are formed to promote their own favoured projects; the result is a profusion of wasteful government spending on highways, bridges, dams, military bases, new government office buildings and so forth. The practice of 'earmarking' funds in pieces of legislation for particular constituencies is widespread, and senior members of Congress can become adept at this practice. Fiorina (1977) argues that many public policy programmes are deliberately created by Congress in ways that require the intercession of individual representatives or senators to secure benefits for constituents, causing constituents to be grateful to them and thus boosting their re-election prospects.

Of course, these sorts of problems occur mainly in legislatures of the US sort, found also in Brazil, Mexico, Ecuador and other Latin American countries. Where party discipline is more pronounced, as in most European or Westminster style parliamentary systems, legislators have much less (sometimes almost no) freedom to engage in pork-barrel politics, vote trading and earmarking. But equally these parliaments tend to do what the government of the day tells them to do.

Bureaucracies

Government officials make their living from public services. Especially in senior ranks, their welfare is often dependent on the level of budgets that their department or office receives. Market liberals assume that all bureaucrats try to maximize their budgets. More money means more promotion opportunities, a greater number of other officials that each tier in the hierarchy can supervise, and increases to the bureau's status and prestige. The guru here is William Niskanen, whose 1971 classic *Bureaucracy and Representative Government* offered a detailed economic theory (not backed up with any facts) about how bureaucrats will always over-supply outputs.

Any organization (whether a private firm or a government bureau) probably delivers some benefit to society in its initial operations. Take the first sheriff appointed in a previously lawless Western town. His (or her) arrival will immediately bring citizens considerable marginal benefits, far exceeding the cost of paying the salary. Adding more deputies (assuming the same salary is paid to each) may also additional deliver net benefits, until a point is reached where the gains to the town in terms of law-abidingness and protection of property equal the costs of paying the last deputy's wages. At this point a profit-maximizing sheriff's office operating in a market will stop hiring. Figure 5.1 shows this situation, displaying the marginal benefits and costs conferred by each member of the sheriff's staff for each additional unit of output for the bureau. Here the point of equilibrium is at *e*. The whole of the shaded area is the citizens' 'consumer surplus', an amount of welfare that society at large gains because the benefits from each staff member exceeded their costs.

But in the big bureaucracies of government, like defence or social security, the situation Niskanen sketched is shown in Figure 5.2. Here we have smoothed the marginal benefit and marginal cost curves out, but their intersection at point *e* still defines the welfare optimum – the point that economists believe will be achieved in a competitive industry. But a government bureaucracy will not stop there, because only the bureaucracy will know the shape of its own marginal benefit and marginal costs curves. When senior bureaucrats negotiate with the legisla-

Figure 5.1   *How the initial units of output of a bureau create social welfare for society, or consumer surplus*

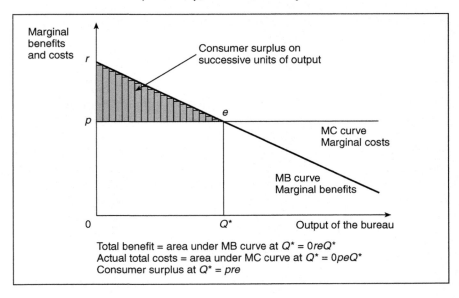

Total benefit = area under MB curve at $Q^* = 0reQ^*$
Actual total costs = area under MC curve at $Q^* = 0peQ^*$
Consumer surplus at $Q^* = pre$

ture or government ministers they will offer a whole suite of services in return for a bloc budget. Thus they will be able to exploit the existence of the consumer surplus area so as to push government outputs up beyond e. They will push towards point *f* – a limit where the bureau performs excess activity that has created an area of waste, exactly off-setting the consumer surplus. The bureau's activity in this oversupply range still has some value for citizens – but not enough to cover the costs involved. There is continual upward pressure on budgets from inside government.

For their part, politicians in power come to expect continuous requests from bureaucracies for budget increases. Indeed, if such requests are not forthcoming, they may suspect the agency of lacking dynamism. Politicians lack expertise and information about the activities of a bureau they are supposed to be supervising. Their incentives to monitor closely what officials are doing and how money is being spent are weak. Cutbacks will alienate vested interests benefiting from an agency's operations. Thus in the original Niskanen model, budget-maximizing bureaucrats are limited only by the requirement that their agency should not actively *reduce* the social welfare.

In his later work (1994), written after the post-war boom in government spending had tailed off in the US and other developed countries, Niskanen developed an alternative rent-seeking model. Bureaucracies

Figure 5.2   *How bureaucracies expand output so as to over-supply outputs*

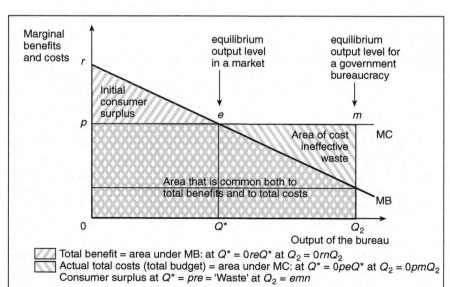

still monopolize information about their own benefits and costs, but now instead of trying to push up their whole budget so as to also inflate the small portion going to top officials, they try to charge the government more for their services than they actually cost to produce. The difference is a kind of rent that Niskanen calls the 'discretionary budget' – the monies that top officials can more or less spend as they wish. Bureaucratic rents will be spent on items such as pleasant office accommodation, travel to meetings or retreats in exotic places, personal assistants, generous pay and pension plans, and subsidies or gifts to outside interests who can organize a flowback of benefits to top officials. This rent-seeking model generates different predictions from the earlier over-supply model. The agency is not producing too much, just paid too much for doing what it does. Niskanen himself went on to head President Ronald Reagan's Council of Economic Advisors, indicating how far market liberalism achieved influence in the 1980s.

The most important manifestation of bureaucratic power is the continuous growth of the state at the expense of the market. In periods of crisis (like the two world wars) massive increases in state spending and tax levels occurred, that then became accepted and hard to reduce once the emergencies were over. Later wars maintained or boosted military spending. And in the United States, the open-ended 'war on terror' declared in 2001 by President George W. Bush had a similar though smaller effect on 'homeland security' spending. Over time, advanced societies may find that they must spend larger and larger proportions of national income on government services.

Iron triangles

Budget-maximizing bureaucrats can expect support from the private interests served by their agency, and from legislators who want to attract government spending to their own constituencies. In the United States, we have already noted that legislators want to sit on Congressional committees dealing with affairs that matter in their state or district. Hence in asking for bigger budgets, officials will often be pushing at an open door. Cosy three-way relationships can develop between the government department, its alleged oversight committee in the legislature, and rent-seeking private interests. In the USA and Japan these are called 'iron triangles' and they monopolize policy in ways that exert powerful upward pressure on government spending. Classic examples are the triangle that upholds agricultural subsidies and services and the US military-industrial complex. Budget-maximizing bureaucrats in the Pentagon have every incentive to procure expensive weapons systems from military contractors – giving contracts to companies that provide consultancy and employment opportunities for ex-Pentagon personnel. For market liberals, iron triangles waste public resources at the expense of taxpayers and economic efficiency (Friedman and Friedman 1984).

In parliamentary systems iron triangles ought not to exist because budgetary control is exercised by a minister rather than a legislative committee. However, if a minister is in office for a long time he or she will often 'go native' – because the only people paying close attention to his or her activities will be lobbyists for the clients of an agency. For example, for a health minister, these will be patients' groups, medical insurance companies, doctors' associations and health workers' unions. In many parliamentary systems ministers often serve for very short periods in a particular job. If they do not quickly master the job, they will be easily manipulated by the senior budget-maximizing bureaucrats in their ministry. And if they want to advance their own career by making a big splash with new projects and programmes, the price tag will be substantial.

Agendas and Political Change

The basic agenda of market liberals is clear enough: shrink government so that it performs no more than the essential functions described earlier. However, in a political environment populated by rent-seeking interests it is easier said than done. For example, when it comes to national defence, it ought to be most efficient to contract out to private firms the task of supplying weapons and other necessary materials. But once firms start producing weapons for the government, they have an interest in the expansion of military spending, in eliminating competitors for government contracts, and in 'gold-plating' weapons requirements to make them as expensive as possible. Moreover, voters and legislators in cities where arms factories and military laboratories are located will also want spending increased on sophisticated weapons. The jobs and career prospects of public officials charged with procuring arms from contractors will also come to depend on spending levels. Thus there will be massive political resistance to any attempt to curb spending. So market liberals had to develop a sophisticated and multi-pronged strategy for curbing and reforming government growth, moving beyond vague calls for cutbacks.

However, spending cuts do remain a key goal, given that bureaucracies maximize budgets and oversupply outputs. An incoming government committed to a market liberal ideology ought therefore to implement across-the-board cuts. The information to make effective targeted cuts is in the hands of bureaucrats who have every incentive not to divulge it. A strategy used by Thatcher and Reagan was to demand substantial phased reductions in personnel and budgets over 4 years, leaving the bureaucracy itself to organize where the axe fell. Ministers and government executives intervened chiefly to stop officials offering up 'sore thumb' policies as targets, that is deliberately trying to focus cutbacks on popular policies in hopes that interest group resistance would reverse them.

Tax cuts accompanying spending cuts transfer resources back to firms and citizens, signalling to rent seekers inside and outside government that the downshift in resources is permanent. At first sight it might seem logical that spending cuts and tax cuts should proceed together, for of course it is taxes that finance spending and market liberals abhor budget deficits that fuel inflation. However, the Reagan administration was persuaded by an economist Arthur Laffer that cutting taxes could proceed *without* first cutting spending. For if governments are overtaxing their economies then when tax rates are cut economic growth will increase. The resultant boost to the size of the economy should mean that total tax revenues actually increase. This Laffe Curve analysis became a cornerstone of 'supply side economics' pursued in the 1980s. Unfortunately the consequences for tax revenues were not as predicted, and so Reagan presided over an enormous increase in the federal budget deficit. The deficit was eventually reduced to zero under President Clinton in the late 1990s, only for President George W. Bush to follow the Reagan precedent of cutting taxes while in his case actually increasing spending, especially on defence, wars and homeland security. Another massive US budget deficit followed.

Privatizing (selling off) state owned enterprises and assets is one of the most widely adopted market liberal prescriptions, partly because it delivers short-run gains of great value, raising money to help finance tax cuts. After World War II many governments took on a range of functions involving the delivery of utilities and services and (sometimes) the production of goods. Market liberals argue that service delivery and manufacturing can always be performed better by private corporations operating under the discipline of the market. Beginning in the 1980s, governments sold telecommunications enterprises, transportation systems (railways, buses, subways and airlines), water companies, mail operations, mining and (in Europe) manufacturing (including heavy industries such as steel, shipbuilding and aircraft production). Most privatized 'network' services (such as electricity, gas, water and telecommunications) have remained closely regulated by government.

In countries such as the United States, where government owns a large proportion of the land area (state and national parks, national forests and rangelands), market liberals propose selling this land to the private sector. Private operators will then find the most profitable and so most efficient use for the land, be it tourism, conservation, recreation, mining, grazing or timber production (Anderson and Leal 2001). This agenda for public lands has not been successful: many private interests actually prefer the land to remain in government hands, so that they can enjoy subsidized access. For example, the US Forest Service builds logging roads at no expense to the timber corporations that use them. Market liberals have had more success in encouraging governments to sell other government-owned assets (such as wavelength bands in the radio spectrum) and franchises (such as the right to run a lottery or run a television station).

Deregulation was a right wing cause long before the heyday of market liberalism. Market liberals believe that businesses in contemporary liberal democracies have become enmeshed in complex systems of controls that add to costs and limit competition, by making it expensive for new firms to enter an industry. This is particularly the case if existing operations are exempt from regulations (for example, in US energy production, more stringent regulations apply to new power sources than to old ones). Regulations are often introduced for the sake of environmental protection, health, work safety and other social values. But market liberals believe there are less expensive ways of achieving the same goals that do not involve regulation. For example, when it comes to environmental pollution, a re-specification of property rights to establish a right to clean air would allow those suffering from pollution to sue polluters without any need for coercive regulators, though a government-funded court system would still be needed to process claims (Meiners and Yandle 1993).

If this approach does not work (because it is often too hard to trace the chain of cause and effect from particular pollutant to health damage), market liberals fall back on the idea of establishing a market in pollution rights. Polluters are then free to decide whether to cut back emissions or to buy rights to pollute. Government sets a limit on total allowable pollution but has no need for regulators to force polluting industries to adopt particular kinds of technology (Anderson and Leal 2001). Such markets in pollution rights have been adopted for sulphur dioxide emissions from power plants in the United States. And international markets in carbon credits are being established as a way to curb greenhouse gas emissions. This approach to pollution is one of the few market liberal schemes to have found favour across the political spectrum.

More generally, market liberals believe that relying on rational consumers making good decisions across competing products is much better than direct government regulation of products or service content. For example, this would apply to food safety – where purveyors of unsafe foods ought soon to go out of business, if the market works properly. In medical care, it would mean government not granting a monopoly to particular kinds of producers and treatments while excluding others (for example, unlicensed doctors and unconventional treatments). Deregulation was a key part of the programme of the Reagan administration in the United States in the 1980s. In 1981 an Executive Order of the President specified that all significant federal regulations henceforth would have to pass a cost-benefit analysis carried out by the Office of Management and Budget. The expectation was that this test would be hard to pass. Cost benefit analysis continued to be applied to regulation by the Clinton and G.W. Bush administrations (if with less marketizing zeal than in the Reagan era).

Yet while market liberals can turn a blind eye to the risks of markets working imperfectly or failing altogether, Western publics and politicians have proved far more risk-averse, preferring to keep direct regulations rather than trust to market solutions. Campaigns for de-regulation rarely seem to produce noticeable reduction in levels of regulation, still less the radical 'rolling back of the state' that market liberals foresaw in the 1980s.

Contracting-out the production of government services is one Niskanen's most enduring policy legacies. Recall that in his model an essential foundation of bureaucratic power was senior bureaucrats' control of information about the costs and benefits of their department's activities. The solution here is to separate the 'purchaser' role in the public sector from the 'provider' role. The latter should be contracted out, ideally to private companies. This approach to service delivery reached a high point in the Australian state of Victoria in the 1990s; Victoria became the 'contract state' (Alford and O'Neill 1999). Widely applied in areas like office cleaning or catering, contracting out has been extended into functions such as running prisons. It is less common in major public services such as health care or education, where public opposition has tended to be greater in many countries.

Overall market liberals' prescriptions have had substantial influence on policy making from the 1980s to the early 2000s, notably in the Anglo-American world, especially when it comes to deregulation, privatization, union-busting and tax cutting. These prescriptions subsequently informed a more consensual and less ideological style of managing the public sector, adopted by governments of both the left and right, called 'new public management' (Dunleavy *et al.* 2006). Its three core principles were:

- *disaggregation*, breaking up large government bureaucracies into smaller units;

- *competition*, forcing public services to perform competitively in order to attract customers and finance, rather than getting a budget as of right; and
- *incentivization*, shifting away from professionalism or a public service ethos toward pecuniary incentives to encourage personnel to perform better.

However, it proved hard to engineer substantial shrinkage in the size and scope of the state. Some very expensive government programmes were too salient with a broader public to be cut – for example, the National Health Service in the United Kingdom and Social Security in the United States. Many lesser government expenditures proved popular with their recipients who could organize politically to defend the programmes in question just as market liberals themselves had pointed out. Often such recipients were large and powerful businesses such as defence contractors or agribusiness corporations. Market liberal policies such as privatization and deregulation themselves create new sorts of interests, notably those who bid successfully for government contracts for service provision, who can then engage in rent seeking. Contracting-out creates new opportunities for corruption, as service providers can influence government officials who give out the contracts, either by direct bribery or offers of lucrative employment to those officials once they leave government. No government committed to market liberal principles has managed to maintain its zeal to see through the kind of wholesale transformation in the state that market liberals believe is necessary. And US Presidents Reagan and George W. Bush presided over the creation of massive budget deficits, exactly the kind of behaviour that consistent market liberals believe to be irresponsible government.

Constitutional Change. Mindful of the fragility of budget cuts, deregulation and privatization, some market liberals want to re-make the playing field of political life by changing the constitution. There is a subfield of market-oriented public choice analysis whose flagship journal is Constitutional Political Economy. For Friedman and Friedman (1979: 290–7) a package of constitutional amendments is needed:

- Balanced budgets, so that governments are not permitted to allow total spending to exceed total revenues in any financial year.
- A limit on total government spending, specified as a restrictive share of GDP.
- No import duties.
- No wage or price controls (policy tools much used in the 1970s but now fallen out of fashion).

- No licensing of occupations (even medicine or law) by government.
- Free trade: a presumption in favour of the free exchange of all goods and services.
- A flat rate income tax, instead of a complex system of income tax rates that vary with income levels with numerous exemptions and deductions. All income tax payers would pay at the same percentage rate, with deductions only for business expenses.
- Sound money: the money supply to grow at a fixed annual rate.
- Adjustment of government contracts for inflation – this is designed to stop government causing inflation in oreder to diminish the real value of bonds (debt) that it has issued.

Later, Friedman and Friedman (1984: 54) added for the US:

- Line item veto, allowing the President to veto particular expenditure items within the budget presented by Congress, which market liberals assume would be used to eliminate pork-barrel and earmarking. (This point is irrelevant in parliamentary systems where the executive already controls the budgetary process.)

Some theorists take market logic to an extreme in suggesting that we can have markets in constitutions (Vanberg and Buchanan 1996). Individuals can move between countries if they believe they can get a better constitution by so doing. Following market logic, this should mean that countries with bad constitutions would suffer from emigration of their most able people, as well as the flight of mobile capital to places where property rights are best protected.

Direct election of executives such as presidents, governors and mayors is seen by market liberals as a way to counteract the rent-seeking behaviour of legislatures. By creating a single constituency spanning the whole of a country (or state or locality) encompassing elections work against parochial rent-seeking. Presidential systems (and their counterparts at state and local level) instead create an office whose incumbent must deliver economic growth and prosperity for all as his or her first priority. Centralizing political and budgetary power in a single chief executive at each level of government can also help overcome the resistance of vested interests to attacks on their privileges and rents. According to the Friedmans (1984: 166): 'The President and Vice-President are the only federal officials elected by all the people. They are the only ones who have a political incentive, once elected, to put the general interest above sectional interests'.

For all Riker's decrying of 'populism', market liberals have often espoused a prescriptive model of politics where the mass of voters can be activated for reform by a heroic president, committed to curbing all the side-deals, iron triangles and special favours that contribute to a 'sclerotic' society. The hero once elected should operate in essentially dictatorial fashion, centralizing power, pushing radical solutions and breaking down the opposition of vested interests. Such an executive is rarely if ever available in the United States, because presidents are constrained by a host of constitutional checks and balances. However, this kind of executive was achievable in Chile in the late 1970s and 1980s under the military dictatorship of General Pinochet, who was closely advised in applying market liberal policies by Friedman's students.

In the United Kingdom, power is more easily centralized in the executive than in the United States, and a Prime Minister and cabinet can dominate both Parliament and the legal system. Prime Minister Margaret Thatcher followed this course following her election in 1979. She was completely committed to market liberal ideology, which in her hands became 'Thatcherism', and set about legislating to destroy the power of associations that stood in her way – in particular, labour unions. In addition, access to government was denied to lobbyists such as environmentalists and advocates for the poor (though toward the end of her years in office Thatcher suddenly discovered the validity of environmental concerns, and access for environmentalists opened as a result). Businesses were less easily excluded from the corridors of power. Thatcherism epitomized an 'actively exclusive' state committed to destroying the basis for political association in civil society (Dryzek 1996b). Thatcher's view that 'there is no such thing as society' confirmed that all that matters are individuals, ideally competing with each other in market relationships, with no social interests above the sum of individual interests. The Thatcher approach to associations, and especially the attack on labour unions, created an apparent peacetime alternative to war and revolution as a way of eliminating Olson's (1982) rent-seeking coalitions.

Yet a radical decentralization of the administration of public service and domestic government is also a market liberal commitment, one in obvious tension with the push for centralized control. The foundations here were laid by the economist Charles Tiebout. In 1956 he argued for maintaining multiple local governments (there are 89,000 municipalities in the US), each offering its own mix of taxes and services. This diversity allows citizen-consumers to 'vote with their feet' in choosing the mix that suits them best. People with similar preferences (say, for low taxes and low service provision) could cluster in particular areas, enabling everyone to get what they want from government. Competition between multiple municipal suppliers would create market pressures for increased efficiency.

Market liberals also like the fact that when public services are decentralized, they can no longer be used as agents of redistributing income from the rich to the poor. Where people's mobility is unrestricted, then any municipality or state or regional government that tried to promote redistribution would quickly go bankrupt. It would attract subsidy-seekers (who would flock to it in search of free rents) and immediately lose taxpayers (who could get the same services cheaper next door).

In the later new public management movement in the UK and Europe, the Tiebout thesis was adapted to apply not to whole local governments with tax-raising powers, but rather to 'micro-local agencies' (MLAs) funded by national government budgets, such as individual schools and hospitals. Instead of getting monies allocated to them as of right, these MLAs depend on competing for customers (e.g. school children or patients), attracting them by proving that their standards and outcomes are good ones.

Internationalizing a market agenda

Most market liberals treat the nation state as the key political unit, and in Europe uniformly oppose any shift of power to the European Union. Their US colleagues have often criticized the accretion of unaccountable power in the United Nations and other world governance bodies. Yet the internationalization of a market agenda has proven very successful. In Europe the EU's liberalization of markets has been more successful than similar national policies. And on the world stage the World Trade Organization has achieved substantial success in eliminating tariff barriers, reducing subsidies to agriculture and persuading countries to accept freer trade.

Beginning in the early 1980s, market liberalism became the orthodoxy of two key international financial institutions, the International Monetary Fund and the World Bank, backed by the US Treasury Department. Known as the 'Washington Consensus' (because all three organizations had their headquarters in the US capital) the consensus later extended to the World Trade Organization (based in Geneva). If a national government in financial trouble sought assistance from the IMF or World Bank then the government in question would have to abide by a set of conditions that involved free trade (no tariffs on imports or subsidy of exports), free investment for multinational corporations, deregulation and privatization. 'Third World' governments facing financial crisis were generally in no position to refuse, and had to swallow the medicine they often despised.

Critics pointed out that the developed Western governments controlling the IMF and World Bank were imposing on the developing countries a model that they had never followed themselves, and remained incapable of implementing at home. But once the Washington Consensus was established as orthodoxy, all actors in the international economy – including private banks and transnational corporations – came to perceive that the only way for governments to get the seal of approval from international institutions was to follow market liberal principles. Thus did market liberalism become ingrained in the international economy, not because it offers any objective economic truths, but because key actors believe that everyone else who matters believes it to be true (Hay and Rosamond 2002).

If a country sought to depart from Washington Consensus precepts, all these actors punished the transgressor through disinvestment, capital flight and speculation against the currency. For example, in 1997 the East Asian financial crisis led the government of Indonesia to seek financial help from the IMF. Indonesia accepted the package specified by the IMF, not because it believed they were the right policies for it to adopt, but because it knew it had to adopt them in order to secure the confidence of corporations, bankers, investors and accountants (Dalrymple 1998). That crisis also led to the discrediting of an alternative East Asian development model of cooperative capitalism, where large corporations and government negotiated the terms of economic development. What had been accepted (and often praised as high-performing) 'Confucian capitalism' suddenly became a discredited 'crony capitalism' – not because the model had actually failed, but because the perception of failure became embedded in international discourse about the crisis (Hall 2003).

Conclusions

Market liberalism's glory days of dominance in the theory and practice of Anglo-American states are now long gone. Financial meltdown in 2008 was widely blamed on the excesses of unregulated capitalism, and governments in the United States and United Kingdom responded by extending government control of private financial institutions. Such intervention was welcomed – not least by the leaders of troubled financial institutions themselves. In these countries the public sector share of GDP in 2008 was no lower than at the beginning of the market liberal era. The evidence of recent decades is that new threats and risks (terrorism, financial market collapses and climate change) constantly create new demands for state intervention. Yet market liberalism's influence lives on in developments like new public management – and in international economic institutions and trans-national economic discourse, about which we will have much more to say in Chapter 14 when we discuss globalization.

The protestations of its partisans notwithstanding, market liberalism offered only a partial and ideologically-charged theory of the state. It may be interpreted more usefully as offering a nightmare picture of what the state would be like if every political actor were a rational egoist pursuing material self-interest. In this light, the logical prescription ought to involve limiting the role of rational egoism in politics. However, this is not how market liberal theorists have seen matters. In believing their own assumptions and the theories that follow from them, market liberals have proposed policies calculated to make the assumption about rational egoism and rent-seeking become more applicable, rather than less true. Like other theories of the state when misapplied, market liberalism is adept at creating its own nightmare.

Part II

Pluralist Transformations

Though they had to cope with some major challenges and criticisms in the latter part of the twentieth century, pluralists eventually regrouped and continue to make significant contributions to our understanding of the liberal democratic state. In Part II we look at the contemporary condition of pluralism, and how it has coped with a number of challenges, including the power of business in a market economy, the development of new kinds of political organization, the seemingly problematic nature of elections and voting in large scale societies, and the continuing importance of identity politics. The first development examined in Chapter 6 is the development of neo-pluralism, which recognizes the dominant position of business corporations in politics, and considers how pluralism might be retrieved in the face of this challenge. Chapter 6 also examines several ways to include the variety of social forces in politics and the state, ranging from corporatism (state organization of interest representation) to governance networks that cut across sovereign power centres.

Chapter 7 turns to the central place that elections still hold in pluralist thinking, with an emphasis on responses to the argument that elections are decided by incompetent voters who together produce meaningless results. Chapter 7 also looks at different ways in which representatives can be elected, and how electoral politics is translated into legislative politics. Chapter 8 turns to the problems and opportunities presented for pluralism by identity politics, emphasizing the role of national identities that people feel deeply, to the extent they are prepared to kill or die for them. The boundaries of contemporary states have often been forged from such conflicts; but often boundaries remain contested, as particular minorities do not accept the legitimacy of the state as it is constituted. So Chapter 8 also looks at how contested identities can be managed, and violent conflicts avoided.

Chapter 6

From Neo-pluralism to Governance

The Development of Pluralism

In Chapter 2 we left pluralism shaken by the political events of the late 1960s and early 1970s. Pluralism then had to repel attacks from market liberals who saw groups as obstructions to the public interest, as well as cope with the lingering hostility of elite theory and Marxism. Some pluralists were eventually ready to ask some serious questions (of the sort they had hitherto ignored) about the unequal distribution of power across different sorts of groups. We begin this chapter with the consequent development of 'neo-pluralism', and then turn to how pluralism has since evolved in other ways that enable it to escape its once close ties to the mid twentieth century status quo in US politics.

The pathways turn out to be many and varied, with the result that the contemporary territory of pluralism is quite complex. Its adherents remain joined in the belief that the politics of the state is ultimately about the interaction of groups, and the assumption that groups (or at least groupings) are the basic building blocks of political life. However, some believe the real number of groupings that matter is small, others that it is large. Some point to profound inequality across groups (with business corporations dominant), others see rough equality in access and influence. Some stress essentially cooperative relations among groups and between groups and government officials; some stress conflictual relationships both within the state and across the boundary between state and civil society. Some believe that the ultimate locus of collective decisions can be found in the formal institutions of the state, others that it has devolved into more informal networks. We also need to be attuned to substantial variation across different kinds of states on all of these dimensions. At any rate, pluralism did make a comeback, to the degree that: 'Pluralism has become the common sense in Anglo-American political thought and there is, it seems, a palpable sense in which "we are all pluralists now"' (Wennan 2008: 158).

From pluralism to neo-pluralism

The most important figures in the development of neo-pluralism were two theorists who had long been central to pluralism, Robert Dahl and Charles Lindblom. The first move in their development involved an increasing emphasis on 'polyarchy' as a way to think about the closest approximation to democracy possible in the real world (Dahl 1971; Lindblom 1977). The pluralist emphasis on freedom to establish and join political associations that could then exercise influence on government was retained, along with a familiar range of individual rights and freedoms and competitive elections. Constitutional rules matter, but so do the more informal aspects of political interaction. Public policies and collective choices in general are generated by interactions involving large numbers of actors, be they interest groups, elected politicians, bureaucrats, or judges, none able to exercise anything like complete authority over the process and content of choice. All these elements are shared with earlier versions of pluralism. However, in contrast to earlier pluralist celebrations of balance across all kinds of actual and latent groups, neo-pluralists believe that *in*equality of influence is inevitable. This degree of inequality can vary, and can be criticized if it proves excessive.

The particular kind of imbalance of influence that preoccupied neo-pluralists was that between business corporations and everyone else. The view that 'business has far more clout than any other real or potential interests has become a commonplace in this much more cynical age' (van den Berg and Janoski 2005: 78). Partly the influence of business is a matter of the sheer wealth at its disposal, which business can use to hire the best lobbyists, best market research, most persuasive spin doctors and top lawyers. There are several further reasons that explain business dominance. The first can draw upon Olson's (1965) rational choice analysis of interest groups, which we discussed in previous chapters. Recall that Olson points out that rational individuals will generally try to take a 'free ride' on the efforts of others who share their interests, on the grounds that their own contribution is unlikely to be decisive when it comes to group success. Olson suggested that the resultant problem in organizing collective action is much easier to solve in small groups than in large ones, and in groups where some actors are large and have high stakes. In any industry, especially one dominated by a few large corporations, the number of corporate actors is small, so it should be quite easy for them to pursue collective action in a trade association. It is much harder to organize a trade union, which necessitates mobilizing very large numbers of individual workers if the union is to have any chance of political success in pushing its members' interests. Once organized, trade unions can offer what Olson calls 'selective incentives' to their members – such as insurance against sickness or unemployment, or social clubs, or access to legal advice. They may also have to rely on coercion to bring free-riders into line. In the nineteenth century, workers were concentrated in industrial cities where they could easily be organized by unions (Dunleavy 1991: Ch. 3). More recent deindustrialization has undermined the ability of unions to organize workers.

If collective action is hard for unions, it is on Olson's analysis much harder for groups campaigning on behalf of causes such as environmental conservation, animal rights, poverty alleviation, the rights of the homeless, international justice and so forth. For such groups cannot coerce members in the way that unions once could; and their ability to offer selective incentives is limited (though for example environmental groups can offer glossy magazines and adventure holidays to their members). Thus when campaigning groups come up against business corporations – as they frequently do – they are systematically disadvantaged. There are in effect 'two logics of collective action' (Offe and Wiesenthal 1980), one for business (especially straightforward when business can focus narrowly in its own profits), and one for everyone else.

Lindblom (1977: 170–88) develops an explanation of 'the privileged position of business' in polyarchy, based on the functions that business performs in any liberal capitalist system. Business runs the economy and has great discretion in deciding where, when, and in what to invest, and how production and distribution shall be organized. If businesses choose not to invest, the consequence is economic downturn. Government tax revenues will fall, causing fiscal strains in the state. Declining economic activity is unpopular with voters who will suffer from unemployment, job insecurity or income loss. Voters will punish incumbent governments. Thus business behaviour matters enormously to governments in the way that the behaviour of other interests and actors in society does not. As a result, when business talks, governments listen very attentively. Business leaders will always have privileged access to the corridors of power, and business interests will always be given great weight.

In fact, to gets its way, business will often not even need to lobby or pressure politicians and government bureaucrats. For government officials know that their policies must please actual and potential investors, bankers and financial institutions. So they will not need to be explicitly told or advised what to do by business. Any deviation from a business-friendly policy will be punished automatically and quickly by markets, in the form of disinvestment, capital flight and speculation against the currency. Such deviation might come in the form of high levels of taxation, regulation, or spending on social programmes that reduce the incentive to work. Even if such policies were supported by a large majority of voters, they would be vetoed by the reaction of markets. For Lindblom the market is a 'prison' that constrains what government can do. Pluralism has not disappeared, but as he points out, 'pluralism at most operates only in an unimprisoned zone of policy making' (1982: 335. Here, the argument of an erstwhile pluralist converges with that of the functional Marxist theorist of the state, as expressed by Fred Block (1977), who explains why the state responds to capitalist interests in exactly the same terms (see Chapter 4). Thus by the 1980s Pluralist theory had indeed come a long way from its 1950s celebration of US democracy.

Advocacy coalitions

Another variant of pluralism grew up in the United States subsequent to neo-pluralism and also sheds light on the privileged position of business. This is the 'advocacy coalition framework' developed by Paul Sabatier, Hank Jenkins-Smith, and their associates (Sabatier 1988). According to this framework, policy issues generally feature long-running conflicts of ideas and interests across a small number of groupings (usually two or three). Each grouping is an advocacy coalition, united by some core beliefs (defined as values, assumptions and perceptions). So for example when it comes to the issue of smoking, one coalition is composed of doctors associations, the health care industry, insurance companies, advocates for those suffering from smoking-related diseases, government departments of health, unions representing workers in bars and restaurants and anti-smoking legislators. On the other side is ranged the tobacco industry, tobacco growers and their employees, government revenue departments that raise taxes on cigarettes and other tobacco products, organizers of professional sports benefiting from tobacco company sponsorship (such as motor racing), advertising industry groups and bar and restaurant proprietors' associations. Each side will have sympathetic journalists and legislators. In this smoking case there are business groups on both sides of the issue, so the 'privileged position of business' does not determine the outcome. On other issues, such as pollution policy, we might expect business to be on one side only – the polluters. Traditionally this was true, and Sabatier (1993) analyzes the history of air pollution in the United States in these terms, as a 'clean air coalition' versus an 'economic feasibility coalition', with industry found only in the latter. But even here, the anti-pollution side has over time been joined by businesses with a monetary stake in clean air. Such businesses might include producers of pollution control equipment, service industry and high-technology companies wanting a healthy environment for their workers, real estate interests concerned about the effects of pollution on property prices, and producers of 'clean' energy wanting to gain competitive advantage against their dirtier competitors (for more on this case see Chapter 11). The advocacy coalition framework was developed in the United States; to date it has found limited applicability elsewhere.

For better or for worse, pluralism as a theory of the state was from the 1950s to the 1980s closely associated with one country in particular: the United States. However, once we situate the US in comparative perspective, it turns out that there are a number of different ways that groups in a plural society can relate to the state. Let us now examine this variety, and see what it means for the contemporary pluralist theory of the liberal democratic state.

Society and Politics

Among scholars of comparative politics, the United States is normally classified as the most pluralist of political systems (see for example Lehmbruch 1984). However, the United States actually exemplifies a particular kind of pluralist state, one that is passively inclusive. Its state is passive in the sense that it does not attempt to manage the pattern of interest representation in civil society. It is inclusive in that it provides a relatively large number of channels for groups and organizations to exercise political influence. These channels may involve the provision of money or personnel for election campaigns, lobbying legislators, consultation with administrative agencies or legal action. On the face of it, the state is quite accepting of different groups, so there is every incentive for those who share a political concern to organize as an interest group and make use of these channels in very conventional fashion. For those immersed in US politics this statement might seem wholly unremarkable – but as we will see shortly, matters are very different elsewhere. Of course, if the neo-pluralists are right, non-business groups will find themselves systematically disadvantaged whenever they run up against the economic interests of corporations.

Social movements

In addition to interest groups, another kind of political formation that can arise from civil society are social movements. 'Self-limiting social movements of reform are a dramatic success, in fact perhaps the greatest invention of twentieth century politics' (Soltan 1992: 4).

Movements are not necessarily the same as interest groups. They normally lack the kind of organizational coherence and leadership hierarchy that interest groups develop. Sometimes they will take an ideological stand against formal organization. Their action repertoire involves protests, events staged for the media, as well as plenty of discussion and dialogue among their adherents – and with outsiders. Often they raise novel concerns not traditionally encompassed by public policy. The 1960s saw a range of such movements, especially on behalf of civil rights, peace, environmentalism and feminism. In the United States, social movements were soon converted into interest groups. For environmentalism, this conversion took the form of groups such as the Sierra Club, Friends of the Earth, and National Wildlife Federation organizing headquarters in Washington, staffed with professionals adept at fundraising and moving within the capital's corridors of power. Feminists formed organizations such as the National Organization of Women. Most groups also hired lawyers to pursue their ends through the court system.

Like interest groups (discussed in Chapter 2), social movements face a collective action problem: how to overcome the incentives to individuals to 'free ride' on the efforts of others. Dennis Chong (1991) shows how the 1960s African-American civil rights movement overcame this problem. Many of the organizational foundations for the movement could be found in a dense network of black churches and youth groups. Martin Luther King, Jr. and other movement leaders placed black church and community leaders in a quandary. The latter sometimes feared to support the movement, fearing a white backlash. But they also feared that the movement might succeed without them. As more preachers and community leaders swung to the movement, so it became more rational for others to make the same jump.

Active inclusion

On one account, this conversion of social movements into interest groups pursuing conventional 'insider' politics is the natural order of things, part of the life cycle in which an initial disorganized radical effort has to give way to a more permanent and effective organizational structure (see for example Offe 1990). But matters actually work out very differently in different sorts of states. In 'actively inclusive' states, such as those in Scandinavia, social movements do not organize themselves. Instead, concerns that would in other countries motivate movements are identified and validated by the state, and representatives of those concerns are organized into the state. So for example in Norway, the arrival of the modern environmental era in the early 1970s was met with government funding of environmentalist organizations such as the Norwegian Society for the Conservation of Nature, and the representation of its leaders on key policy making committees (Dryzek *et al.* 2003: 22–7). Women's issues were treated similarly around the same time. The result is that in Norway there are no significant social movements or groups that lobby from the outside; all major concerns are fully integrated into the state, which organizes its own inputs. While activists in other countries often look on Norway with envy, this kind of actively inclusive state is not free from political problems. Organizations have tiny memberships in comparison with their counterparts elsewhere. The reason is that if groups are funded by government and have guaranteed participation in policy making, there is no need for them to recruit grassroots supporters. In addition, the cooperative relationship between groups and the state means that there few radical critiques of government and politics. Such critiques were the reason for the expansion of representation to begin with. But now they generally have to be imported from other societies.

Corporatism

The Nordic actively inclusive state is actually an extension of the 'corporatist' state form. Under traditional corporatism, federations of business corporations and labour unions are co-opted into the policy process. The most important policy decisions are made on the basis of agreement between business, labour and the leadership of the executive branch of government (Schmitter and Lehmbruch 1979). Legislatures are largely irrelevant, though sometimes they may be called upon to 'rubber stamp' corporatist agreements. Elections are not very important either, because key policy decision will be made in the same way by the same participants irrespective of who wins the election. Examples of corporatist systems can be found in Austria, Germany and other smaller western European countries. 'Corporatism without labour' characterizes Japan. In the smaller European countries, corporatism developed as a way for them to try to control their own destiny in the face of international market forces (Katzenstein 1985). In Germany, corporatism was initially a matter of business and labour pulling together with government in the post-war reconstruction.

When it comes to tripartite corporatism, Offe (1984) suggests that ultimately business still dominates. But this conclusion should not be taken at face value, especially in light of developments since the 1980s. Corporatist political systems tend to be accompanied by what Hall and Soskice (2001) call 'cooperative market economies' where large corporations cultivate cooperative relationships with government, with each other, and with their own workers. Cooperative market systems tend to produce goods and services that sell on the basis of high quality rather than low price. The dynamics are very different from the 'liberal market economies' found in the less corporatist Anglo-American countries, whose state has in recent decades featured some combination of passive inclusion with bouts of exclusionary market liberalism. In particular, in cooperative market economies there is less downward pressure on wages, working conditions, and welfare state provisions – and so more scope for labour unions to have an effective place at the policy making table. Market liberals would claim cooperative market economies are sclerotic and destined to fail under an epidemic of rent-seeking (see Chapter 5), so sooner or later they have to turn into liberal market economies to survive and prosper. But Hall and Soskice argue that cooperative market economies may be able to flourish in the international political economy just as much as liberal market economies.

The essence of the corporatist bargain is that labour agrees not to engage in strikes or otherwise disrupt the economic system, while business agrees to a package of welfare state provisions that redistribute income and security to ordinary working people. Market liberals strongly dislike corporatism because it restricts free competition in labour markets, and puts existing businesses in a good position to protect themselves against competition from other businesses. A post-Marxist sceptical take is advanced by Offe (1984), who sees corporatism as a means of disciplining labour, with the bargain necessarily favouring business. However, compared to their alternatives, corporatist systems turn out to perform quite well according to a variety of indicators – including greater equality in the relative well-being of different social classes. Compared to their more liberal counterparts, corporatist states feature lower levels of strikes and industrial disputes, greater income equality, and better economic growth performance at least up until the early 1990s – matters are not so clear since then (Freeman 1989; Pekkarin *et al.* 1992). Corporatist states also exhibit better environmental policy performance (Scruggs 1999).

Corporatism oncludes a 'passively exclusive' state: interests other than labour and business have no channels through which they can access the state and exert influence over policy. The state is 'passive' toward civil society because it does not intervene to try to destroy or undermine some groups (in the way that 'actively exclusive' states under market liberalism do – see Chapter 5). Rather, the state leaves them alone. Paradoxically, this passively exclusive orientation may actually contribute to political dynamism in civil society. The contrast with passive inclusion here is instructive. Under passive inclusion of the kind we see in the United States, social movements are generally converted into deradicalized interest groups. But in a passively exclusive corporatist system, this route is unavailable to them, so they are more likely to maintain the aspects of grassroots activism that define social movements. So in the 1970s and 1980s 'new social movements' flourished and persisted in passively exclusive Germany (Dryzek *et al.* 2003: 35–42)) and elsewhere.

New social movements are normally defined in terms of what Cohen (1985) describes as their self-limiting radicalism and concern with issues of identity as well as strategy. Self-limiting radicalism means that the movement does not seek any formal share of state power in contrast with earlier socialist movements. Identity means a preoccupation with debates over what the movement is and what it wants, rather than concentrating solely on achieving established goals. The demands of such movements are often non-economic and so not easily negotiated in the traditional currency of interest group politics. As Offe (1985) points out, they embody a 'selective radicalization of modern values' such as liberty and equality. In Germany and elsewhere, they included green, feminist, anti-nuclear and peace movements. The passively exclusive state inadvertently provided a space for such movements to flourish in an oppositional public sphere. This sphere developed its own counter-institutions – for example, networks of ecological research institutes with connections to green groups. In the late 1980s the German state became less exclusive and so members of movement groups began to percolate into government – culminating in the Green Party's participation in the federal governing coalition from 1998 to 2005. However, it made a big difference that the activists who came into government had a long experience in radical social movement politics, rather than in interest group lobbying. Germany experienced policy shifts that proved much more radical than elsewhere (for example, a decision to phase out nuclear power).

'Corporatism without labour' is central to the 'Confucian capitalism' that characterizes Japan and South Korea. However, pursuit of unanimous agreement in East Asia often means making sufficient concession to labour and other interests to avoid dissent. And small groups such as rice farmers in Japan can sometimes exert substantial influence.

At first sight corporatism looks dubious from the point of view of democracy, because elections are not especially important in determining who governs. However, under any pluralist theory of the state, elections are just one way in which the state is influenced by a variety of inputs from society at large. In tripartite corporatism, there appears to be little scope for social interests other than business and labour to have any influence in policy making – more bad news for democracy.

But closer inspection reveals that the lively oppositional public sphere that can coexist with the corporatist state does have a number of ways of influencing government policy, even while formally excluded. Fear of the costs of political instability can force government to make concessions to movement demands. The rhetoric of social movement spokespersons may lead to a reframing of issues that is accepted by key policy makers. And good arguments and ideas developed in the public sphere may be accepted by governmental actors. Sometimes the movement can induce pervasive cultural change that induces ordinary people to change their social behaviour – much of the success of environmentalism and feminism can be interpreted in this light (Tesh 1993).

So contemporary states do differ in the sorts of inclusions and exclusions they arrange, which has substantial consequences for how groups organize and how they can seek to make a difference. This is not a matter of groups flourishing in some kinds of states and languishing in others. Political group life can make a difference in all kinds of states, exclusive and inclusive, corporatist or more competitively pluralist. It just does so in different ways. The only kind of liberal democratic state that makes life really hard for (some) groups is the market liberal state described in the previous chapter.

Since the 1990s corporatism has been eroded by international financial markets seeking greater national 'competitiveness', the growth of powerful low-wage competitors in India, China, Brazil and elsewhere, and a political backlash against the 'sclerosis' allegedly associated with corporatism yet the slump of 2008 meant that the idea of a regulated and cooperative political economy did not look so bad, given the financial crises generated in more freewheeling market economies.

Policy Making: From Government to Governance

We turn now to developments in the organization of institutions and policy making in many societies that can be interpreted in light of contemporary pluralism. Our coverage emphasizes the degree to which models of collective decision in plural societies now feature *governance* rather than *government* (Rhodes 1997). Governance was once synonymous with government, but the more recent usage of the term involves something a bit different: the production of collective outcomes (in the context of public problems) that is not controlled by centralized authority. The decision-making power of public administrators or formal government diffuses outwards to be exercised also by interest groups, non-governmental organizations, private businesses, research

institutes, charities, professions and academics, while inside government agencies with different goals and missions are often themselves
balanced off against each other.

This kind of governance stems in part from the multiplication of
influential actors. In the United States, 'hyper-pluralists' have recorded
the very large numbers of stakeholders who seek to influence policy,
charting the accumulation of many small pushes and nudges in shaping
government decisions. Hyper-pluralists see political leaders and government departments essentially as 'brokers' who bring together and balance multiple conflicting pressures, and who must normally stay
relatively neutral to carry out their function (Laumann and Knoke
1987). In Europe and Australasia pluralists have stressed the 'hollowing
out' of government (Rhodes 1994), whose functions are often either
formally contracted out or informally undertaken by a mix of actors,
some in the public sector, some outside. In the European Union, there is
a stress on the principle of 'social partnership', involving formal, reg-
ular and pervasive consultation and coordination with trade unions,
professions, and businesses.

In this light, the simple days when authoritative governments could
steer many different aspects of society in a coherent overall direction
are gone. Prime ministers or presidents or party leaders can no longer
dominate across a range of different issues as (say) Franklin Roosevelt
did in the US in the 1930s and 1940s. Those who try to do so, as
Margaret Thatcher clearly did in Britain in the 1980s, eventually come
to grief because the different systems and sub-systems of society are
increasingly autonomous, and cannot be made to work according to a
single logic – such as that of Thatcher's market liberalism. The political
system, the economic system, the media system, the legal system, the
cultural system and other social systems have all developed their own
distinct dynamics, connecting with similar spheres in other countries
and in the international system as a whole to constitute highly complex
amalgams not easily controlled by central government. They interact to
constrain each other, but particular spheres of society often operate in
self-governing, self-regulating manner. Thus 'governance' denotes the
complex direction of an advanced post-industrial society within which
there is no longer any single dominant point of societal leverage (Pierre
and Peters 2000). Further, social change is driven in large part by international influences, examples and pressures. Clearly this kind of world
is much more complex than that portrayed by traditional corporatism
and the advocacy coalition framework – both of which see policy as
made by the interactions of a small number of key actors (cooperative
in the case of corporatism, adversarial in the advocacy coalition framework). Corporatism's golden age of effective tripartite concertation of

government, business and labour is perhaps over. With time, corporatist systems have softened their exclusive character and opened themselves to a wider range of influences on policy. The sharing of public decision making authority with private interests that features in corporatism has found renewed life in the governance idea.

Where, then, can power be located in the 'governance' model? Pluralist authors stress the importance of networks (or 'policy communities'). Networks can involve actors from different government departments, different levels of government, interest groups, the professions, the media, non-governmental organizations, businesses, consultancy firms – even from other countries (Slaughter 1997). Networked governance is pluralistic in the sense that it involves many different actors in the production of collective outcomes. But it differs substantially from the sort of pluralism that we introduced in Chapter 2 (and from neopluralism), because government does not simply register the relative weight of inputs and produce policy outputs accordingly. Theorists of networked governance assign far less significance to the formal moments of legislation and peak-level executive decision that pluralists once highlighted. Networked governance also differs from corporatism, because much of the action does not occur in peak-level negotiations between a small set of major players – it is more decentralized than that.

Networks are organized horizontally rather than hierarchically, which follows from the presumption that there is no sovereign power within a network. They can be problem-specific, with a membership that coalesces around a particular common problem – and disperses once the problem is no longer on the agenda. Even relatively persistent networks may change their membership as the specific content of the problems they face changes. Thus there is a degree of fluidity in institutional form. Networks can have a formal existence – but they may also have an existence that is almost entirely informal, with boundaries defined simply by the relative density of interactions among key players. The following examples illustrate the range of forms that governance and networks can take.

Collaborative problem solving

Pluralist systems often feature access to veto power that is more widespread than access to power that actually makes things happen (Lindblom 1977). So for example in the United States, it is relatively easy for environmentalists to bring lawsuits to stop environmentally destructive proposals – but much harder for them to secure policy commitments that would craft a path to a more sustainable society.

Collaborative problem solving is designed to move beyond the impasse that can result when many sides to an issue have the power to veto, and when the relevant governmental authorities lack the capacity to craft and implement effective solutions to problems. The idea is to bring in all the relevant actors with an interest in an issue and promote a constructive dialogue among them, oriented to the generation of mutually acceptable proposals. Participants suspend any adversarial relationships (of the sort prized by mid twentieth century pluralism) for the purposes of the dialogue. Innes and Booher (2003) describe cases from water policy in California – one of the most crucial policy issues in this arid state. The first case is the Sacramento Water Forum, made up of local government officials, businesses, farmers and environmentalists that in 1999 produced a plan for water management in Northern California. Later, a group called CALFED began to work state-wide on water issues, broadening participation to state and federal officials. Both groups worked on the basis of consensus, and the content of that consensus then had to be endorsed by local and state governments. This kind of approach to problem solving has been widely used in environmental and resource management policy in the United States. While these water policy examples show collaborative dialogue's results taken up by government, government can sometimes resist. Sagoff (1999) describes a forestry case from California where local environmentalists, loggers and local governments came to an agreement that moved beyond impasse on contentious issues of resource extraction and employment versus environmental conservation. However, the agreement was resisted not only by federal government land management agencies who saw it as usurpation of their prerogatives, but also by national environmental groups who did not want their local affiliates compromising the national struggle.

Financial networks

International finance and business are increasingly organized on a network basis, as money and information flow quickly and easily between different nodes in transnational networks. Financial institutions and corporations form complex webs that interact without any apex or command. Organizations such as corporations are themselves structured as networks. Castells (1996) describes the 'network society' in these terms. Control in the network society eludes government, but also private managers. Governmental and business institutions become enmeshed in networks that produce outcomes, such as investment decisions or changes in the relative value of currencies. The old binary distinction between government and market loses its force, for a network may contain parts of what used to be in the market and government alike. Financial network relationships are partly competitive, partly cooperative, so the old model of market competition also fails to capture what is going on.

Public-private partnerships

Public-private partnerships can be found in the delivery of many sorts of services (Rosenau 2000). For example, private corporations can be involved in running public prisons (especially in the United States); religious charities join with government to deliver social services to the poor; and private contractors provide logistical support (or even troops) for defence forces. At the international level, sustainable development was once a goal urged by activists upon governments. More recently, large corporations organized under the World Business Council for Sustainable Development have sought to involve themselves in both the development and implementation of policy. The World Summit on Sustainable Development in Johannesburg in 2002 saw hundreds of partnership agreements negotiated between businesses, non-governmental organizations and governments (Frantzius 2004). The basic idea was for corporations to provide finance and expertise, NGOs to supply political commitment, and Third World governments the receptivity to advice and innovation in (for example) setting up projects to promote public health and environmental quality.

Civil regulation

In the traditional model of regulation, a government agency imposes restrictions on the operation of a private industry or industries. In practice, there was rarely a command relationship: regulator and industry might develop a more cooperative relationship, and in some cases the regulated industry might even 'capture' its state regulator. Civil regulation reduces the dominant position of government in regulation still further, because many of the functions of the regulatory agency are performed by non-governmental organizations. Examples would include organic food certification, done by evaluators set up by organic producers themselves. International forest certification would be another example, where a regulatory scheme operates without government involvement to certify forest products as being produced in ecologically benign fashion (for example, no felling of old-growth ecosystems). The scheme is administered by a network of non-governmental organizations including the Rainforest Alliance and Worldwide Fund for Nature (Meidinger 2003). Braithwaite and Drahos (2000) describe a global web of business regulation involving governments, activists, and non-governmental organizations.

Paragovernmental activity

Civil regulation is one kind of activity where some of the traditional functions of government seem to have been usurped by non-governmental actors. The general category here can be called 'paragovernmental' (Jänicke 1996). Paragovernmental action comes in many different forms, which may feature cooperation, competition and confrontation mixed in varying proportions. Alternative dispute resolution brings the parties to a policy dispute together in order to arrive at an agreement. There are many cases where non-governmental activist organizations have initiated boycotts of corporations – on issues such as the employment of child workers in Third World sweatshops. Sometimes such campaigns have been successful in forcing companies to change their practices without any government involvement. Sometimes corporations have seen it as advantageous to enter into cooperative dialogue with their former adversaries with a view to getting approval for their practices and products. Paragovernmental activity can sometimes come to involve governments – if in complex ways. So for example the Shell Corporation in the mid-1990s found itself the target of NGO-orchestrated pressure because of its alleged complicity in political repression in the oil-producing region of Nigeria. Eventually Shell undertook a major corporate repositioning in response to this charge and others levelled against it (Frynas 2003). But the NGOs also targeted governments in developed states to put pressure both on corporations such as Shell that operated in Nigeria and directly on the Nigerian government to behave in less oppressive fashion, though the effects on the ground were unclear.

Multi-level governance

The huge size of some contemporary liberal democracies – 300 million people in the United States, a billion in India, and both growing – might seem to imply weaker accountability compared to local democracy or small states. The European Union (in 2009) spans 27 member states with 489 million people. As size increases, policy issues arise at many levels, not all the prerogative of national governments. In response, liberal democracies have evolved complex structures of multi-level governance, ranging from the local to the global.

In almost every liberal democracy, elected local governments have long governed services such as roads, primary and secondary education, local planning and environmental conservation. In Europe, some even deliver welfare state services funded by block grants from national government; in Scandinavia, these include health care and social security payments. Sometimes local governments raise their own revenues through property, sales or income taxes. Local and regional governments also provide sites for experimenting with policies that can be adopted more widely if successful.

Federal systems found in the United States, Canada, Germany and Australia feature a fixed constitutional division of powers between the national or federal tier and the component states, provinces or regional governments. Subnational governments in federal systems often have their own legislatures, executives and judicial systems. Some countries have a kind of asymmetric federalism in which particular regions dominated by an ethnic group different from the majority have their own regional government – while other regions have less autonomy. Examples would include Scotland, Wales and Northern Ireland in the United Kingdom, Catalonia and the Basque country in Spain, and Quebec in Canada. In Belgium and Switzerland, subnational regions are defined on a more symmetric basis, with each region (canton in Switzerland) dominated by a particular ethnic group. In India the structure of the federal system responds to the country's huge population and complex patchwork of linguistic, ethnic and cultural differences. The post-1945 development of many such states was marked by increasing federal-level spending and sophisticated arrangements to equalize resources across states and regions. Often federal governments would get involved in areas such as regional development and urban regeneration.

Some large European states long resisted decentralization. But even France, the United Kingdom and Italy have now moved in this direction. In France, national government control over local authorities (inherited from the days of Napoleon Bonaparte) was changed in the 1970s to introduce elected councils at the prefecture and regional levels. In Italy (with its own Bonapartist legacy) in the mid 1970s a political compromise between the right-wing Christian Democrats and the left-wing Communist party saw the creation of new regional governments, which have subsequently grown in importance. In Spain, following a centralized dictatorship under General Franco that suppressed regional identities and languages in the Basque country, Catalonia, and Galicia, and lasted until 1974, the advent of liberal democracy saw the component provinces re-emerge as strong regional governments.

The United Kingdom was long a centralized state resting on a long imperial history, an unwritten constitution, and a doctrine of the unconstrained sovereignty of the Westminster parliament. However, within the UK, Scotland gained a parliament running many domestic policies in 1999, and at the same time Wales secured a less powerful national assembly. A powerful elected mayor and regional assembly were established in London in 2000. Northern Ireland resumed devolved government in 2007. However, within the UK, the 43 million people of England outside London are still governed centrally from Westminster. One other very prominent exception to the decentralizing trend is Japan, whose 128 million people have no structure of regional government (except for an elected governor of greater Tokyo).

Multi-level governance can involve authority moving up from the national level as well as down. The European Union (EU) has developed into a unique kind of confederation of 27 states with its own directly-elected legislature (the European Parliament), government (the European Council, composed of ministers or heads of government from member states), bureaucracy (the European Commission) and supreme court (European Court of Justice). The Euro currency is used by 16 member states (with more expected to adopt it), and the European central bank is one of the four biggest in the world. Decisions on most issues are made on a 'qualified majority voting' basis, requiring a majority of around 72 per cent of votes in the European Council, though on some issues there is a unanimity requirement. The EU's policy style is therefore consensual rather than adversarial, 75 per cent of such votes are actually unanimous.

The EU's member states have delegated powers to the centre in Brussels to build a single European market (including labour market), to run economic regulation, to control the common currency, to negotiate international trade agreements, to reduce regional inequalities, to improve transport and cultural links, to pay farm subsidies (the most costly item in the EU budget) and to regulate environmental pollution and resource use (for example, North Sea fisheries). Yet the government in Brussels remains small, with fewer than 30,000 staff administering policies affecting 500 million people. And the EU budget accounts for less than 2 per cent of the European GDP. Some member states desire a more integrated federation, some a much looser form of inter-state collaboration. However, efforts to formalize an EU constitution failed in the face of referendum defeats on constitutional proposals in France, the Netherlands and Ireland. The number of people voting in local, regional and EU-wide elections is generally much lower than for national elections. Although trans-European party groupings exist (linking for example social democrats, or moderate conservatives), they have no profile with voters (Hix 2008).

Elsewhere in the world, free trade zones and regional groupings are much less well-developed. The North American Free Trade Areas links Canada, the United States and Mexico. Mercosur is a developing free trade block in south America. The Association of South-East Asian Nations and the African Union both remain undeveloped. At the global level the United Nations is relatively weak and economic institutions such as the World Trade Organization are somewhat stronger in their capacity to impose decisions on states. We will discussion international bodies further in Chapter 14.

For pluralists, multi-level governance is a positive development, in part because of the multiple and countervailing powers it can embody (though one does not have to be a pluralist to support multi-level governance). It is important not to assign tasks to the wrong level of government. For example, if a national government is asked to run regional policy then political constraints usually mean that it will try to equalize aid across regions. But it may then be hard to foster a concentrated pattern of economic development in one region, in the way that the region itself could do if it controlled its own economic policies. Thus nationally-run regional policies may create slower economic growth. In the European Union, the 'subsidiarity principle' specifies that every issue be handled at the lowest possible level in the EU's multi-tier structure. Issues should only move up the hierarchy (from local to regional to national to EU level) when they are clearly incapable of being addressed at a lower tier. Critics charge that this principle has not stopped a pervasive shift of power up to the EU level.

Evaluating governance

The rise of networked governance poses some major questions for the theory of the liberal democratic state: most notably, whether it is still really democratic, or indeed still a state in the traditional sense.

Is governance democratic? Electoral democracy means accountability of government to the voters; but if collective outcomes are not in the end being produced by the sovereign state, it is hard to see how such accountability can be arranged. Governance can involve outcomes being produced in many different locations; sometimes they just emerge, with no moment of final, authoritative decision. Networks can be very low-visibility compared to electoral and parliamentary politics. Sometimes the very informal character of networks means that it is hard to determine where decision making authority actually lies. But while electoral conceptions of democracy may fare poorly when it comes to governance, other conceptions of democracy can fare better. Networks can be more or less inclusive, more or less deliberative, more or less dominated by business. Thus democratic principles can be applied to the evaluation of networked governance (Sørensen and Torfing 2007). It makes little sense to either condemn or praise networked governance from a democratic point of view – it all depends on the specific context. Sometimes governance may open up an issue to more democratic control – as in our brief earlier example of Shell and Nigeria. At other times the development of governance may close off democratic control – as when a network of financial transactions manages to elude government regulation, or professional dominance excludes citizen influence.

Does governance involve dissolution of the state itself? Certainly it entails the further blurring of the boundaries between state, economy and civil society (though those boundaries have never been completely clear-cut). Some examples of collaborative problem-solving and paragovernmental activity can exclude governmental actors altogether – though often this is a mistake if government actors subsequently prove to have veto power over any agreed-upon outcomes (as in the Quincy forestry case discussed earlier). Some theorists insist that all governance really represents is a relatively flexible way for governments to operate that retains ultimate governmental control. For example, networks can be set up by, and ultimately be responsible to, particular government departments. Theorists of governance dispute among themselves whether governance represents movement beyond the state, or simply a transformation of the state (Pierre and Peters 2000). It is hard to know what would constitute conclusive evidence here, given that most governance networks include actors who are formally part of the state, or require the validation of the state for agreed-upon outcomes to take effect (though as our discussion of finance networks, civil regulation, and paragovernmentalism indicate, some do not). At a minimum, governance provides a new context for pluralism, understood as the effective participation of multiple differentiated actors in the production of collective outcomes. Beyond that, so much depends on the details of particular societies. For example, governance is likely to take a very different form in the liberal market economy of the United Kingdom with its 'hollowed out' state than in post-corporatist Germany, still operating as a coordinated market economy. Different again would be the expansive corporatist Nordic systems, which have long welcomed a variety of actors in cooperative policy making, and which treat networked governance as simply an extension of their state-dominated form.

Agendas and Political Change

The contemporary pluralist theory of the state is itself pluralistic in the sense of having several different versions, and so are the political agendas associated with it. There turns out to be very little in the way of a common political programme that neo-pluralists, corporatists, expansive corporatists, advocacy coalition analysts and governance theorists in all their variety could support. In the following discussion we pick out some proposals that could be endorsed by one or more of these groups. But these proposals are not additive and certainly constitute no common programme of the sort we could identify with the Marxists and market liberals covered in Chapters 4 and 5 respectively – or indeed the earlier generations of elitists and pluralists discussed in Chapters 2 and 3.

Curbing the privileged position of business

For neo-pluralists (and some critics of unbalanced corporatism) the main democratic problem in existing pluralist government is the privileged position of business. Yet on how to curb business privilege, neo-pluralists themselves have not been too forthcoming. Some possibilities are as follows.

First, business dominance stems in large part from the essential functions performed by the capitalist market economy. If that market context could somehow be changed, then perhaps business power might be restricted. In the past, central planners have tried to exert governmental control over business decisions. Such central planning of the economy reached a peak under communist regimes that operated the whole manufacturing side of the economy through government command. In mixed economies, as we saw earlier, states in the decades up to the 1970s also took whole industries under their ownership and control. Today, even that kind of mixed economy looks implausible – many such industries eventually proved a burden on government and were privatized or allowed to disappear. The only remaining possibility lies in the contrast we discussed between liberal market economies and cooperative market economies. In the latter, business accepts that unions and government have a legitimate say in business operations. So while business remains the key player, its dominance is not quite so clear-cut as in liberal market economies. And if this is true, then to the extent liberal market economies can be shifted in a more cooperative direction, the disproportionate power of private business might be reduced. Any such shift would involve major changes in the institutional structure of the state – and in the dispositions of corporate leaders and financiers. In liberal market economies thet can punish policies that look bad for business.

The global credit crisis that began in 2007 as a result of under-regulated housing loans in the United States and escalated in 2008 eventually prompted increased government regulation and control of large financial institutions, extending in some cases to governments taking over banks. But this dramatic re-regulation came only after a long period of de-regulation.

Business regulation can also be pushed up a level. In the European Union, 70 per cent of economic regulations have shifted up to the EU level. Critics argue that business now has a privileged position in EU policy making. Defenders respond that the EU's large scale is a match for the large scale of multi-national corporations that would otherwise escape regulation. So in 2007 the European Commission won a key anti-monopoly case against the Microsoft corporation, a case which none of the EU's member states could contemplate taking on its own.

Another way to work with business rather than against it would be for non-business groups to define their concerns in ways that are compatible with core business interests. For example, environmentalists can push the idea that 'pollution prevention pays' (because pollution indicates inefficient materials usage by industry). It is no coincidence that this kind of discourse gained ground most effectively in the 1980s onwards in countries with cooperative market economies. The idea of 'corporate social responsibility' adopted by many large businesses may also open some doors to activists trying to get corporations to change their ways.

Strengthening groups

Pluralists of all sorts believe a healthy society is one with a vigorous group life, and they worry about the kind of individualization of social life promoted by market liberalism (see Chapter 5). Pluralists ought to resist market liberal attempts to demonize and demolish groups. Further, they ought to advocate government policies that promote group life. Along these lines, Michael Walzer (1991, 1994) laments a society of 'dissociated individuals'. He believes that in the United States at least, 'it makes sense to call the state to the rescue of civil society' which would involving 'mobilizing, organizing, and, if necessary, subsidizing the right sort of groups' (1994: 125, 191). The groups in question would include labour unions, 'charter schools' run by parents and teachers, housing and workers' cooperatives, community project organizers, and religious and ethnic 'cultural associations' that also provide social services. (A cynic would say that Hezbollah in Lebanon and Hamas in Palestine are exactly like that.) Such groups would help produce good citizens, as opposed to the social isolates of market liberalism, who can only consume and produce, never support the state.

In a similar but more radical spirit, Hirst (1994) proposes a model of 'associative democracy' in which associations of citizens would take on many of the tasks currently undertaken by the state (such as education, health and community development). Hirst's agenda can be linked to the governance model we have discussed, but it is different in wanting to exclude governmental actors from participating in the administration of projects and programmes. For Hirst, the state's role would be limited to just enabling such associations to grow and flourish, and thereafter not intervening in their affairs.

Some analysts argue for a more actively inclusive state that would have as one of its prime tasks organizing channels to express the interests of poor and oppressed groups, who are normally at a disadvantage in pluralist interaction. This would involve extending the Nordic model of expansive corporatism discussed earlier. So Cohen and Rogers (1992) propose a model that (confusingly) also goes under the name of 'associative democracy', under which government would intervene in civil society to create the required associations, especially of the economically underprivileged. These associations would then be formally incorporated into the governmental process. But as we saw for the Nordic cases, this kind of active inclusion does not necessarily produce a vibrant civil society of countervailing powers – instead, group leaders can adopt a very moderate and compromised orientation. Iris Young (1989, 1990) proposes a still more radical equalization of political power by arguing that oppressed groups in society should have formal veto power over any policy decisions that affect them. 'Clear candidates for group representation in policy making in the United States are women, blacks, Native Americans, old people, poor people, disabled people, gay men and lesbians, Spanish-speaking Americans, young people and non-professional workers' (Young 1989: 265). Together these groups constitute the vast majority of the population. Nothing like this has ever been adopted – nor is it easy to see how it could be, given the scramble for 'oppressed' status that would occur once it became understood that massive power would (paradoxically) accrue to the oppressed. A politics of widespread veto power is also almost bound to be a politics of stalemate.

An alternative approach to the equalization of power would strengthen groups in civil society rather than seek to integrate them closely with the state. We have already seen the power that activists and social movements can wield in relation to corporations – in the case of Shell in the 1990s, inducing a corporate repositioning. Social movements can also make themselves felt as a counterweight to corporate influence on the state. Strengthening the power of civil society groups can be done as a matter of public policy: for example, through laws that protect political activism and association. Conversely, policies such as the application of anti-terrorist laws against environmental and animal rights groups may help destroy civil society activism. (In the United States, the FBI has identified the Earth Liberation Front as the number one domestic terrorism group, despite no person having been hurt as a result of an ELF action.)

Building and democratizing networks

Analysts of networked governments generally lack any comprehensive political agenda, but they do have some prescriptive ideas (Rhodes 2006: 432–3). The plea here is generally for better integration across those involved with an issue: in the United Kingdom, the relevant catch-phrases are 'joined-up government', partnership and a 'whole of government approach'. Such exhortation begins with the idea of getting all the government departments concerned with a common issue to work with, (rather than against) each other. A spectacular failure of the Central Intelligence Agency, Federal Bureau of Investigation, and Immigration and Naturalization Service to share information enabled the 9/11 attacks on the World Trade Center and Pentagon to happen in 2001. The subsequent establishment of a Department of Homeland Security was a conventional, hierarchical, non-networked approach. It responded to failure by pulling together 22 previously separate small agencies – but not the FBI or CIA.) 'Joining up' within government can then be followed by joining with relevant non-governmental actors. Currently, however, there is nothing remotely approaching a science of network design, beyond what Rhodes (2006: 433) calls 'an ephemeral mix of proverbs and injunctions'.

Network-building is not the only or perhaps even most important agenda associated with the governance approach, however. More important may be efforts to democratize networks. These have been very slow to take off, given the continuing association of democratic theory with the image of a sovereign state responsive to its voters. But if all legitimate authority in today's world has to be democratic, then networks too ought to be moved in a more democratic direction. As we have seen, networks can be exclusive and invisible: from the point of view of democracy the idea must be to render them more inclusive, more visible, and engaged by more competent actors. In the context of networked governance, models of democracy tied to the aggregation of votes fare very badly. Approaches to democracy that stress inclusion and open communication (see for example Young 2000) ought to be capable of providing much more in the way of democratic remedies for networked governance. Such guidance is much more like to be found in 'post-liberal' rather than liberal democratic theory (Sørensen and Torfing 2007), because networked governance sidelines electoral and parliamentary democracy. We return to some aspects of democratic renewal in networked governance in Chapter 9.

Conclusion

Pluralism today grapples with the realities of concentrated business power, corporatist partnerships, the influence of technical expertise in policy making, large and complex states and networked and multi-level governance. At the same time pluralism remains committed to dispersed power and representative government. Money must not be allowed to be the dominant good that controls the distribution of all other social goods – such as political power, health, favourable media coverage, electoral popularity, and achievement in education, sport or other areas of life (Walzer 1983). The complex landscape of contemporary pluralism now covers a variety of approaches to the theory of the state – some of which have left the 'pluralist' terminology behind. Others even seem to want to leave the state behind. However, the state often proves hard to shake off. It lies in the background of paragovernmental, civil and networked governance, which often feature an eventual return to the state – or they require state involvement in problem solving, regulation, and collaboration.

Classical pluralists and their successors saw competitive elections as vital to any polyarchic state. While many of the approaches surveyed in this chapter downplay elections, none of them believes elections are irrelevant. In the next chapter we take a close look at what has happened to elections – arguably the cornerstone of the *democratic* aspect of the liberal democratic state.

Chapter 7

Competitive Electoral Politics

There is much more to democracy than elections. Yet elections are central to the particular form of democracy that has come to characterize most liberal states. As President Franklin Roosevelt put it: 'The ultimate rulers of our democracy are not a president and senators and congressmen and government officials, but the voters of this country'. Many observers treat the presence of competitive elections as the minimal requirement for a state to be called democratic. However, the criteria of freedom and fairness normally applied to elections require civil liberties and unconstrained choice for voters, conditions that are often not met in practice. So the mere presence of periodic votes involving the broad population is insufficient to validate the democratic credentials of any state – as contemporary Russia, Singapore and many African countries like Kenya and Zimbabwe continue to demonstrate.

Pluralism is committed to meaningful elections. By contrast classical elite theorists see elections as mere legitimating devices for the continued rule of elites. Marxists too regard elections as a necessary sham, a cover for class rule and a state that must act according to the dictates of the capitalist economy. Market liberals have highlighted a range of problems in discerning anything meaningful from election results (see Chapter 4) – some of which we revisit in this chapter. Market liberals are concerned with getting the right political leadership in place, not with how this leadership gets there. They also highlight a range of problems in discerning anything meaningful from election results. Pluralists keep faith with elections as a crucial way of promoting the political competition that is required by polyarchy, and a means of securing group influence in politics (because groups can be active in election campaigns). No pluralists would believe that elections are fully decisive in determining who exercises effective political power and the content of public policies – but none would see elections as irrelevant. As we saw in Chapter 2, even the minimal pluralists who follow Schumpeter in seeing elections mainly as a periodic submission by competing elites to public opinion nonetheless assign elections an important role.

In this chapter we take a closer look at electoral politics, in terms of how citizens vote, how representatives get elected and what they do once elected. We look at the roles played by voters, parties and candidates, different voting systems, and different ways of representing public opinion. Next we examine the politics that occurs within elected legislatures – and how the latter affects the content of public policy.

Society and politics: voters, parties, systems

On a naïve view of the democratic ideal, elections are the means through which ordinary voters ensure that their preferences are enacted by government. This would require all voters to be knowledgeable about their own interests, to know how the positions of different candidates would affect those interests, and then to make a considered choice across candidates accordingly. In the 1950s, a number of US sociologists and political scientists carrying out studies of electoral behaviour imagined such a normative theory into being involving hyper-rational and hyper-informed voters. It was called the 'classical' theory of democracy by survey researchers from Berelson *et al.* (1954) to Beck (1986: 246), who set out to debunk the model demonstrating to the limited capacities of ordinary voters. This 'classical' theory of democracy never actually existed in democratic theory – and survey researchers never bothered to ask democratic theorists what they thought should be required of ordinary citizens and voters (Natchez 1985).

Rational choice theorists would also make assumptions something like this – though not as the foundation for some imaginary prescriptive theory, but rather in order to construct explanatory theory about how elections actually worked. With rational choice theory there is no need to determine empirically that the assumptions about the rationality of individual voters are true. Models may still be useful even if they rest on dubious assumptions about individuals – so long as they yield predictions that can be tested (in economics this position is associated with Friedman (1953)). Shortly we will take a look at some rational choice analyses of popular elections, but first we examine several decades of work on the capacities and dispositions of voters – and what they tell us about the influence that elections can have on government and public policy.

The limited competence of voters

The main and most familiar device for ascertaining the behaviour of voters is the opinion survey. A survey consists of a number of questions about (for example) the opinion of the individual on particular issues, his or her social characteristics and political identifications, dispositions towards particular candidates and parties, and likely political choices. The central debate in survey research studies of voting behaviour over the past 60 years concerns the competence of voters. For the most part, survey researchers have painted highly unflattering portraits of the mass public (Kinder and Sears 1983: 664–8). Most people care little about politics and do not bother to inform themselves about political issues; they have little political knowledge and few real opinions. If they do have opinions, sometimes they are a matter of intolerance and prejudice toward different others. Certainly they lack what Converse (1964) called 'belief systems' about politics.

So what does motivate voters, if not their considered opinions and beliefs? For the most part, the answer may be found in psychological or social forces that the individual voter does not fully comprehend. Psychologically, partisan identification acquired at an early age from one's parents might be important, and this became a staple of US voting studies (Campbell *et* al. 1960). Or a desire to conform to the opinions of those with whom one mixes might prove powerful (Noelle-Neumann 1984). Social characteristics such as religion, ethnicity, race and class might prove to determine how people vote, and these were highlighted in studies of voting in European countries (for example Butler and Stokes 1971). So working class people would normally vote for socialist parties, middle class people for more conservative parties. Disadvantaged ethnic minorities would often vote overwhelmingly for parties of the left – so in the United States, African-Americans mostly vote for Democrats.

Elite theorists took the findings of survey research about mass lack of interest in politics as confirming the idea that politics is mainly an elite activity. Theorists critical of elite dominance would see the problem here as one of elites keeping mass publics in the dark. In contrast, Dye and Zeigler (1987: 14–17) in their best-selling US politics textbook draw the conclusion that the 'irony of democracy' is that democratic values are held and cherished by elites – but not by masses, who are under the sway of ignorance and darkness. Yet pluralists, too, could draw comfort from opinion survey research. For mid twentieth century US pluralists, groups not individuals were the central reality of political life. Too much interest and participation in politics on the part of ordinary people would probably accompany only mass movements led by demagogues. If drawn into politics, ordinary people might well choose to support anti-system communist parties, or far-right fascist parties – of the sort that were available in Europe, and had indeed come to power in Germany and Italy to disastrous effect. Compared to such possibilities, in the 1950s mass apathy and low electoral turnout did not look so bad. Mass interest and mobilization might threaten the multiplicity of centres of political power prized by pluralists. For example, Dahl (1956) drew upon survey research findings to argue for an ordinary citizens' influence in politics that is restricted and indirect.

A novel twist on the incompetence of voters has recently been supplied by the economist Bryan Caplan (2007). He argues that the problem with voters is not their ignorance or unformed opinion. Rather, it is that most voters want bad things from politics; which democracy then delivers. So 'democracy fails *because* it does what voters want' (Caplan 2007: 3). Most voters want regulation rather than free markets, protection over free trade (because they dislike foreigners) and security of employment rather than increases in production. In a democracy, these prejudices drive out good economics, with the result that people are poorer than they could be. However, all this only looks problematic to an economist or a market liberal: it is quite easy to find non-economic values that justify everything that Caplan condemns.

Reconsidering the competence of voters

With time the unflattering image of the mass public originating in the mid twentieth century party reappraised, even by some survey researchers. Surveys were sometimes badly drafted, failing to recognize the depth and strength of voters' political cognitions because the elites who drew them up used poor language in their questions. In addition, it was eventually shown that voters are often quite capable of passing retrospective judgment on the performance of governments, turning against administrations that performed badly (Fiorina 1981).

The early emphasis upon how little voters know about political issues when interrogated by survey researchers eventually proved irrelevant. We can draw an analogy here between elections and economic markets. Consumers do not have the perfect information specified in formal models of markets, and many consumers may behave habitually, knowing little about better products or suppliers. Yet this does not stop economic markets responding to consumers, with huge potential gains to be made by a firm that comes up with a better product and huge penalties for firms who fall behind the curve. It only takes a small minority of well-informed consumers, plus a mass media that can make money from providing better information to them, to make markets responsive. The same is true in politics. Citizens do not need to read a complete handbook of political life before they participate, or even to have an especially sophisticated view of how government works, so long as they have some general political awareness of a few issues they care about. The electorate as a whole can then behave as a 'rational public'. Particular minorities of citizens who care about different issues then create 'public opinion' (Page and Shapiro 1992).

Two further developments reinforce this conclusion. First, in many established liberal democracies both party identification and social characteristics have become less relevant in determining how people vote. Declining numbers of citizens identify themselves with any party. Correspondingly, surveys show that voters are becoming more likely to vote on the basis of their issue opinions. As Rose and McAllister (1986) put it, 'voters begin to choose'. Political campaign management has become more sophisticated, reflecting the fact that fewer voters' support can be taken for granted by parties. Second, old worries about mobilized masses voting for extremist parties of the left or right became increasingly anachronistic. The liberal democracies that existed following World War II have proven very stable indeed – irrespective of the kind of voting system they deployed, or the number of political parties they featured. Isolated surges by far right parties appealing to racism and anti-foreigner sentiments have generally been both small and short-lived. Moreover, fascist and military dictatorships in countries such as Spain, Portugal, Greece, Argentina and Brazil in the 1970s and 1980s yielded to liberal democracy. Since 1989, most post-communist countries have made the transition to liberal democracy with competitive parties (with some backsliding, notably in Russia).

The final reason not to worry about most voter deficiencies revealed by survey research lies in the limitations of the survey instrument itself, which generally involves ambushing ordinary people with a battery of questions they have had no opportunity to think about. As we will see in Chapter 9, when ordinary people are given a chance to deliberate on issues they can prove remarkably competent.

Pleasing the median voter

Some simple analytics drawn from rational choice theory developed by Downs (1957) can be brought to bear to show that the electorate as a whole can behave somewhat like a 'rational public', forcing parties to converge on a central position that also maximizes social welfare. Downs starts by assuming that politics can be represented spatially, as in Figure 7.1, where there is a range of political positions spanning from left to right. He next assumes that each voter chooses whichever of two parties is closest to their own position on this left-right dimension. Figure 7.1 shows a highly simplified picture of an election. Let us suppose that there are just nine voters who are distributed along a political dimension from left-wing (radical) positions on the one hand, through moderate positions in the middle, to right wing (conservative) positions. Assume too that voters are evenly spaced along this dimension. Now suppose that two political parties are set up, one on the left and the other on the right. In Figure 7.1 the left party A initially adopts a position very close to voter 3, and the right party B is close to voter 8. What happens next? If individuals vote according to which party is closer to their own position, voters 1, 2, 3, 4 and 5 will choose party A and voters 6, 7, 8 and 9 will support party B. Party A wins by 5 votes to B's 4 votes.

If party B wants to avoid losing again it must move its policy positions toward the more centrist voters; and party A should respond by also moving to the centre. The parties will converge on the position of voter 5, who is the *median voter*, the person with as many people on their left as on their right. The median voter position is dominant in that it is unbeatable by any other alternative. The median voter will get what he or she wants far more of the time from the political system than voters who have more extreme positions. Figure 7.2 shows what happens if Party B gets to this position first.

This outcome arguably *maximizes the welfare* of voters as a whole. Figure 7.3 shows the winning party at voter 5's position, along with the distances from the winner's position to the positions of all the other voters. If we add up these distances, scoring 1 for each space, we get a score of 20 points in total distance between the winning party and voters as a whole. Suppose instead that the winning party for some reason was located at a more extreme position, such as the voter 8 position over on the right, a situation shown in Figure 7.4. Here if we add up the distance scores we get a score of 29, a position much worse in welfare terms. The median voter position does better than any other in minimizing the total distance between all voter positions and winning the party's position.

Figure 7.1   *Competition between two parties on a left–right dimension*

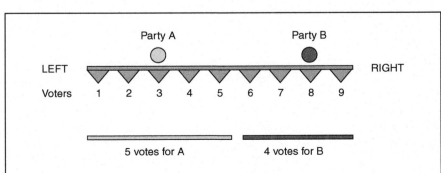

Figure 7.2   *In two-party competition, the parties converge on the median voter*

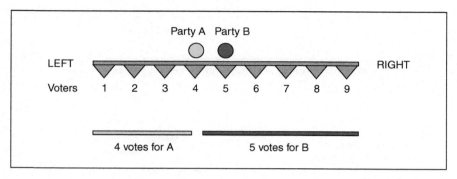

In real world political systems there are many more than 9 voters, who are not likely to spaced evenly, but rather cluster at various points on the spectrum. But the median voter argument still holds. In Figure 7.1 the median voter happens to be in the middle of the spectrum. But if for example voters cluster on the right of the spectrum, the incentives for parties to seek out the median voter position remain – though the median voter is now located toward the right.

Figure 7.3   *A governing party at the median voter position maximizes social welfare*

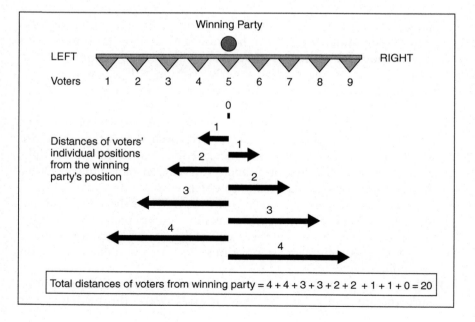

Figure 7.4 *A governing party located away from the median voter's position will be worse in welfare term for most voters*

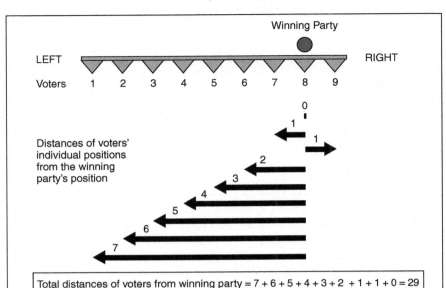

Total distances of voters from winning party = 7 + 6 + 5 + 4 + 3 + 2 + 1 + 1 + 0 = 29

In practice, elections may not work out as this highly simplified model suggests. The key problems are:

1 Parties may not be led by flexible vote-maximizing politicians who will say anything to get votes, but rather by ideological leaders who have made commitments that they will not or cannot change. Convergence on the median voter's position will not happen, but whichever party or candidate is closest to median voter will still win.

2 Voters and parties may not line up along a single dimension, but rather on two or three dimensions – research shows that there are rarely more than this. For instance, people may think in left-right terms but also in terms of ethnicity or religion or language. Other possible dimensions may relate to defence policy (hawks to doves), or environmental issues (green to brown). When there are multiple dimensions, electoral competition is more complex and its outcome less predictable. However there will still be a tendency for winners to adopt relatively centrist positions close to the median voter on each dimension.

3 If there are more than two political parties, there will be less pressure on any individual party to move toward the median voter

position. Even in a one-dimensional polity organized on left/right lines alone, when there are four or more parties, the inner parties may not move to the median voter position because they fear losing votes to more 'extreme' rival parties. For instance, a conservative party may not moderate its policies to appeal to the median voter if they fear that a rival right-wing party would then find space to secure some of their more right-wing voters' support. Usually there are more than two political parties because there is more than one dimension to political conflict. For example, a green party may form based on the environmental dimension, or a separatist party based on an ethnic dimension. Extreme parties can flourish in such cases, though much will depend on the particular configuration of parties and issues. There may still be incentives for parties seeking power to move to the centre ground – especially in countries with proportional representation systems, where governments require coalitions of more than one party to have a majority of votes in the legislature (we will discuss coalitions later in this chapter).

4 The simple exposition of the median voter results assumes that all citizens vote, which is unrealistic (except in countries like Australia and Belgium where voting is compulsory). People may instead abstain if there is no party close to their own position. If parties converge then eventually it will not matter who wins the election, so there is no point in voting – unless the relative effectiveness of the parties in actually achieving the positions favoured by the median voter is an issue. This argument may help explain the decline in voter turnout in many liberal democracies as ideological differences between parties narrow (discussed below). But any decline in turnout spread evenly across the spectrum will not stop parties converging on the median voter.

5 If many voters cluster at the extremes of the spectrum, then parties that move to the median position may well lose votes to more extreme parties. Thus parties will get locked into extreme positions. This kind of situation long characterized Northern Ireland, where parties that moderated their stance on the Protestant (Unionist) to Catholic (Republican) dimension often lost votes to parties that maintained more extreme positions on both sides.

Different voting systems

There are many different systems for organizing the election of representatives (for surveys see Grofman and Lijphart 1986; Dunleavy and Margetts 1995). There are three main categories in use: plurality rule;

proportional representation (which has a number of sub-categories); and preferential voting.

Plurality Rule voting is used in the United Kingdom, United States, Canada, Jamaica and India, but hardly anywhere else – for good reasons that will shortly become apparent. It is the easiest system to explain: the country is divided into constituencies with roughly equal numbers of voters, and whichever candidate gets the largest number of votes in a constituency is declared the winner. This system is often called 'first past the post' – but a key defect of the system is that there is no fixed winning post. In the United Kingdom it is not uncommon for members of parliament to be elected with as little as 26 per cent support in multi-party races with four or more parties. The legislature is composed of the winners from each constituency.

Plurality rule can also be used to elect a single office holder, such as the president of a country, governor of a state or mayor of a city. For the United States presidency, the mechanism is complicated by the presence of the electoral college, whereby the candidate getting the most votes in a state gets all the electoral college votes from that state (except for Maine and Nebraska, where there are provisions for splitting electoral college votes).

According to a famous 'law' named after Maurice Duverger (1955), plurality rule should produce a two party system, mainly because life is very difficult for third, fourth, or smaller parties. Voters whose first choice is a small third party are faced with the choice of wasting their vote on their real preference, or casting a vote more likely to make a difference in the contest between the two leading parties in their constituency. Riker (1982b) believes that Duverger's law is the closest thing political science has to a true scientific law. Riker was actually wrong even in 1982 – he admitted to anomalies such as India, where plurality rule produced a system with one dominant party (Congress) and several smaller parties. Today, the only plurality rule systems that have just two significant parties are the United States and a few small Caribbean islands. The United Kingdom is often misrepresented as a two-party system but has in fact looked this way for only short periods in the twentieth century. Today it has a strong national third party (the Liberal Democrats) and strong nationalist parties in Wales and Scotland. Duverger's law has been falsified – mainly because third parties with regional concentrations of votes can find it quite easy to get members elected to parliament.

With three or more parties, plurality rule often gives a party a comfortable majority of the seats in parliament while winning far less than 50 per cent of the citizens' votes. In the 2005 UK election Labour won 356 of 646 seats while winning only 35.2 per cent of the votes. Labour only had to obtain more votes than anyone else in enough constituencies to win the election. Across the UK as a whole, 65 per cent of voters chose other parties – yet Labour formed the government by itself. In societies with a shorter history of political stability than the United Kingdom this might well be a recipe for disaster, as representatives of that 65 per cent might call into question the legitimacy of the government. Defenders of plurality rule argue that it is conducive to stability because it disadvantages extremist third or fourth parties. Yet the opposite may in fact be true: only super-stable societies can tolerate the perverse counter-majoritarian results that plurality rule can generate.

Preferential majority voting also uses single member constituencies. However, instead of casting a vote for just one candidate, the voter can rank all the candidates. The candidate receiving the smallest number of first preferences is then eliminated, and his or her votes reallocated to the other candidates on the basis of the second preference listed on the ballots. In the Australian system the process is repeated until one candidate gets more than 50 per cent of the votes and is declared elected. This means that a first preference cast for a minor party with no chance of winning is not wasted. The preferential system can be effective in producing a two-party system, as in Australia. However, minor parties can still exercise influence while winning no seats. They do this by making deals with the major parties for the allocation of their preferences. In Australia, for example, the large Labour Party has often made an agreement with the small Green Party, which has never won a seat at a general election for the House of Representatives (it has won seats in the Senate, elected by proportional representation). The Labour Party agrees to adopt some Green policy positions. In return, the Green Party advises its voters to place Labour number 2 in their preference listing.

In many presidential systems preferential voting is achieved by a runoff election. This is actually a crude form of preferential voting. In France and Brazil, if no candidate receives over 50 per cent of the votes in the first round of voting, a second election is held between the top two candidates from the first round. Each supporter of the eliminated candidates then gets a chance to re-allocate his or her vote to one of these two candidates. The system used for electing London's mayor uses an instant runoff that avoids the need for voters to go to the polls twice. Voters mark their top two preferences, and if no candidate wins 50 per cent plus one vote on first preferences, all but the top two candidates are eliminated. Second preferences from these voters are added to the piles for the candidate still in the race. Whichever of these two candidates now attracts most first and second preferences then wins.

There are many varieties of *proportional representation*, which we will not explain in all their intricacies. Their common goal is to ensure that parties receive representation in parliament roughly in proportion to the number of votes they receive. So if a party receives (say) 35 per cent of the votes it ought to receive around 35 per cent of the seats in the legislature. The purest form of proportional representation is the national list system, used for example in Israel and the Netherlands. Each citizen can vote for one party list, and that party receives a number of seats in parliament directly proportional to the number of citizens who vote for it. In the Israeli case, this means that parties can get a representative into the Knesset with only around 2 per cent of the national vote.

Other mixed proportional representation systems (used in Germany, Scotland, New Zealand, and Wales) combine the election of half or more legislators in local constituencies with regional lists that ensure total votes and total seats match fairly accurately for each party. Germany also has a rule whereby a party must win 5 per cent of the votes nationally or some constituency seats to get any seats in the Bundestag (the rule was designed to prevent the resurgence of neo-Nazi and communist parties). In Japan a non-proportional mixed system is used, meaning the final number of seats is not proportional to number of votes. This system has helped keep the Liberal Democratic Party in power for decades.

Which kind of electoral system is best? In the 1950s and 1960s Anglo-American authors contrasted the simplicity and stability associated with plurality rule on the one hand with the fairness and enhanced legitimacy and inclusiveness of governments elected by proportional representation on the other. But proportional representation systems have over the past half century shown substantial propensity for stability, so the argument is now tipped in the direction of proportional representation. Moreover, the median voter analysis also points in the direction of proportional representation – because a government in a PR system must have majority support, and that majority will have to include the median voter. And as we have seen, there is a welfare-maximizing argument to be made in favour of pleasing the median voter (Colomer 2001). In contrast, governments supported by only a minority of voters need not include the median voter. Such governments are a normal feature in the UK. Even in the USA, if presidential elections feature a significant third party, the median voter will not necessarily be on the winning side. In 2000, the median voter was a supporter of Al Gore, not George W. Bush, because there was a concentration of votes for Ralph Nader, to the left of Gore on a left-right dimension. Yet Bush won the election. (This example is complicated by the fact that Gore actually won more votes than Bush, but the working of the electoral college and a controversial decision by the

Supreme Court awarded the election to Bush. The point is that even if Bush had won slightly more votes than Gore, the median voter would still have been a Gore supporter.)

Looking at trends in the electoral systems used in countries of at least 1 million people (i.e. excluding micro-states), research by Josep Colomer reported in Figure 7.5 shows clearly that plurality rule and other 'majoritarian' systems like preferential voting have not increased over time. By contrast, liberal democratic countries with PR systems have trebled in numbers since 1985, and mixed systems have also grown. In that time no new democracy has adopted plurality rule or even preferential majority voting, and several countries have switched away from using plurality rule.

Figure 7.5   *The numbers of liberal democracies using plurality rule/majority systems versus proportional representation to elect their legislatures*

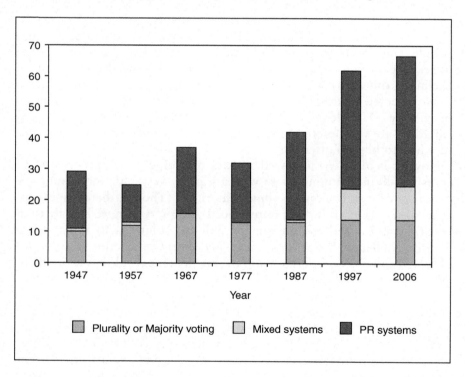

Note: The count of liberal democracies here excludes micro-states, those with fewer than 1 million citizens

Source: Colomer 2008: Appendix

Declining turnout

Turnout levels in formal elections have been falling substantially in many liberal democracies. In Switzerland, with its frequent elections and referenda, turnout in general elections has fallen from around two thirds of votes in the 1960s to only a third in the 1990s. Turnout in US presidential elections fell from around two thirds to only just over a half of eligible voters from the late 1950s to the 1980s, since stabilizing at this level. Japan and South Korea have also shown similar signs of falling voting levels since the 1990s. For a long time European states (mostly with proportional representation systems) had higher levels of voting and although their turnout levels ebbed and flowed it was difficult to spot a long-term trend. However, in most of these countries a downward movement can now be detected, with sharp falls in the UK in the 1990s, from over 75 per cent to 60 per cent.

For pessimists this trend signals increasing alienation from political life (see for example Chen 1992), with potentially negative consequences for political stability and the democratic credentials of states. However, it may also indicate a shift in the sorts of political action that people consider appropriate and likely to be effective. So while voting, political party membership and trade union membership may all be declining, other forms of activism may take their place. Membership of cause-oriented interests groups and informal sorts of activism may be on the rise. O'Toole *et al.* (2003) argue that young people in the United Kingdom are very interested in politics – but often believe *electoral* politics has nothing to offer.

Now, it is already the case that rates of voting participation tend to be especially low among those who are poor, very old, very young, or members of disadvantaged ethnic minorities. (Though there are exceptions to this rule. In India, poorer social groups vote more heavily than wealthier ones, perhaps hoping for political solutions to some severe social problems.) What this means is that the election results we observe can be very different from the results that would occur if all eligible citizens voted. For example, if the categories of people for whom non-voting is highest are those most likely to vote for left-wing candidates and parties (a plausible assumption in some countries, especially the United States), then their abstention advantages right-wing candidates. The Republican Party in the United States is quite aware of this, which is why it pushes measures to further suppress voter turnout. For example, in Florida in 2000, those with a criminal record (no matter how distant in their pasts) were not allowed to vote (and confusion over names meant that many with the same name as a convicted felon were also disenfranchised). Given that the proportion of African-

Americans with a criminal record is much higher than that of most other ethnic groups, and African-Americans vote heavily for Democrats, this measure advantaged Republican candidates – and indeed was decisive in allowing the installation of George W. Bush as President. Other measures to suppress turnout in the United States include requiring several specified forms of identification in order for an individual to register to vote – a requirement that poor and marginalized people find hardest to achieve.

Alternative representations of public opinion

The basic democratic justification of elections is that they are a way to ensure government responsiveness to the preferences of citizens – which in the aggregate we can describe as public opinion. But there are many different ways in which public opinion can be registered and transmitted to government. These may be attractive because there is a substantial informational deficit in election results. Voters do not get to express their opinion on issues, all they can do is cast a single vote – a very simple response to a very complex bundle of issues and attributes of parties and candidates. It is hard to infer from voting totals alone what they mean in issue terms. Other methods for ascertaining public opinion, some of which we have discussed already, include the following:

- *The activities of interest groups.* Pluralist theorists see groups as representing the preferences of their members, so the sum of group activity can constitute public opinion.
- *Opinion surveys.* If interest groups represent preferences weighted by the intensity with which they are held, opinion surveys represent the unweighted distribution of opinions. The problem is that they may often represent no opinions at all – that is, many people have no opinion on an issue until they are asked by a survey interviewer, but rather than say 'don't know' they may give a response determined by the way a question is worded. For example, a question worded 'do you favour free speech for all groups, irrespective of their beliefs?' will typically yield a much higher positive response than 'do you favour free speech for Islamic radicals?'. Bartels (2003) interprets the pervasiveness of such 'framing effects' in determining survey responses as a deficiency in the capacity of ordinary people to operate in a democracy. The obvious alternative explanation is that survey questions are a deficient means of ascertaining public opinion.

- *Focus groups*. Focus groups are a marketing tool. A group of consumers is convened to discuss proposals for products. Groups of citizens can be convened to 'market test' policies as well, giving insight into how ideas are connected and how opinion might change in response to changing policy positions.
- *Referenda*. A referendum gives a chance for citizens to vote directly on single policy measures. Decision-making referenda are used extensively in Switzerland and some American states. In California and Oregon, for example, majorities of voters have enacted property tax cuts that the politicians elected by those same voters were unwilling to adopt.
- *Deliberative innovations*. Recent decades have seen a wide variety of innovations in many countries that involve convening groups of deliberating citizens to make policy recommendations. The representation of public opinion that emerges is then informed and reflective – in contrast to the snapshot of responses in opinion surveys. We will discuss these innovations in Chapter 9.

All of these measures of public opinion are capable of giving different results.

The changing role of political parties

Political parties structure and simplify election campaigns, providing alternative packages of issues and leaders to voters. Elections are possible without parties, as for example in Papua New Guinea. The consequence is that elections in each constituency turn on who can best bring material rewards to the locally dominant ethnic group – of which Papua New Guinea has hundreds. Trying to form a government by gathering the support of a majority of such representatives is a real challenge; governments do not form on the basis of national issues, and so find it difficult to adopt any coherent national policies. Saudi Arabia held its first ever local elections in 2005, but parties remained illegal. Turnout was low, and the dozens of candidates were indistinguishable, except by their own tribes and families.

If convergence on the median voter of the sort we described earlier occurs, parties will end up providing few issue choices to voters. But this kind of convergence will only take place if parties are controlled by a coordinated leadership group interested in winning above all else. In practice, parties are not always like this. Some leaders may prefer ideological purity to winning an election, if they have to choose. Parties with democratic internal arrangements may also choose leaders and candidates who appeal to the median party activist – but not to the median voter in the electorate at large, likely to be more moderate than the average party member.

These considerations are important because political parties in some liberal democracies have adopted more internally democratic practices in the last 30 years. In Britain the Conservative and Labour party leaders were once elected only by the members of parliament (MPs) belonging to each party. And in the Conservative case, until the 1960s if the party needed a new leader to be prime minister because the party was governing, the new leader would 'emerge' from the machinations of party elites, rather than be elected by Conservative MPs. In the Labour Party, the platform constructed at the annual party conference was dominated by the 'bloc votes' cast by union leaders for hundreds of thousands of union members who were nominally affiliated to the party. The Conservative Party now elects its leader by a ballot of all party members. And the Labour Party uses a complex 'electoral college' in which one third of the votes come from individual party members, one third from affiliated union votes and one third from Labour MPs.

Party organizations in the United States have always been complex and fragmented. Once local and regional party bosses played prominent roles in selecting candidates for Congress and the Presidency. The national nominating convention for Presidential and Vice-Presidential candidates therefore featured complex jockeying, strategizing, and bargaining among local and regional party leaders, and the result could not be predicted in advance. All that has changed with the spread of primary elections, through which ordinary voters can register as a party supporter and cast a vote among alternative candidates for the party's nominations for both state and federal offices. In some states, 'open primaries' mean that to vote in a Republican primary one does not even need to be a registered Republican – and the same for the Democratic primary. Most states now hold primary elections (though some rely on caucuses of party members that are also hard for party leaders to control). For presidential elections, this means that the party's nominee is usually known before the party convention, which becomes simply a celebration of the nomination and a chance to put the candidate in the public eye.

On the face of it these kinds of changes in the selection of candidates and leaders are positive from a democratic point of view because they create open competition in which ordinary party members or registered voters can have a decisive voice. However, there is a downside. In the United States, the sums of money required to mount successful Presidential campaigns are vast and Congressional campaigns are also very costly – thus increasing the power of special interests with money at their disposal. Internal party processes for choosing candidates are almost the same as the general election process itself, and equally susceptible to being dominated by the media. Thus media corporations' and media professionals' influence has expanded. Media coverage, media 'spin' and media concerns (how leaders look on television), public opinion polls, focus groups and political marketing now dominate internal party processes.

The other major trend when it comes to parties in liberal democracies is a decline in supporters and members. Opinion surveys reveal the number of voters who identify strongly with a particular party has in most established liberal democracies been falling over time. In the early twentieth century leaders depended on their party organizations to recruit huge number of voters as members, supporters and election workers. Parties were 'mass' organizations. In Britain the Conservatives had more than 4 million members in the 1930s and the Labour party claimed 1.5 million individual and 5 million trade union affiliated members. Today these parties are hesitant about publicizing their true membership levels – the claimed figures are around 300,000 for the Conservatives and 200,000 for Labour, with around 70,000 for the third party, the Liberal Democrats. In the US both the Democratic and Republican parties once deployed huge numbers of election workers to knock on doors and hold large public meetings. These labour-intensive practices declined – until revived somewhat by Barack Obama's Presidential campaign in 2008.

The increasing importance of television in election campaigns from the 1950s onwards was the key factor here. The most important resource for party leaders became money from a few big donors (normally wealthy individuals and corporations, though unions remain important in some countries) rather than numbers of activists. This development concentrated power in the hands of party leaders, offsetting their loss of control resulting from any growth in internal party democracy. Leaders could surround themselves with an entourage of aides, speech-writers, 'spin doctors' and public relations experts, pollsters and fund-raisers. At the turn of the twentieth century, these dark arts were mastered by the US Republican Party (especially by Karl Rove, who orchestrated the two campaigns securing the George W. Bush presidency) and the British Labour Party as it won three consecutive elections under Tony Blair. In the United States, presidential candidates in particular developed their own personal organizational structure, consigning the formal party organization to handle only mundane bureaucratic tasks. Similar developments could be found in the party systems of Europe.

These developments have often been accompanied by scandals connected with the finance of politics and parties, with wealthy donors expecting tangible private benefits from government in return for their contributions. In the United Kingdom these concerned the awarding of peerages and knighthoods to large donors. In Italy the Christian Democratic Party that had dominated every post-war government for 40 years collapsed in the 1990s amid corruption scandals. Corruption is by definition the use of public office for illegitimate private gain. The response to these sorts of problems has led to the replacement of private funding of parties by state funding in some European countries. This development has problems of its own, for then parties come to look like arms of the state, rather than vehicles for the influence of civil society upon the state. They may seem to collaborate with each other in rigging the funding system, leading some political scientists to characterize them as 'cartel parties'. Especially in proportional representation systems, where coalitions of parties may stay in government for long periods whatever election results occur, state funding of parties may undermine any remaining sense that parties are organizations independent of the state.

Today, then, the landscape of electoral politics in liberal democracies is complex. Public opinion, conceptually central to democracy, can be quite elusive in practice. We turn now to the equally complex politics involving the interaction of elected representatives in legislatures.

Government and Policy Making: Legislative Politics

Votes cast in elections do of course determine office holders, be they legislators in an assembly or chief executives (such as presidents, governors, or mayors). But office holders have considerable discretion on what they do next.

The role of legislatures

Most liberal democracies are parliamentary systems, where the majority of representatives in an elected legislature chooses an executive to govern and to propose laws. If a government loses the confidence of a majority in the legislature then it must resign in favour of a different executive or call a general election to elect a new legislature. In the majority of the world's liberal democracies that use some form of proportional representation, coalition governments will normally need to be constructed through negotiations between different parties in the legislature (see below on coalitions). In Scandinavian countries and occasionally elsewhere, a minority government may be formed from parties with less than 50 per cent of the seats, though obviously it will need some acquiescence from other parties.

Legislatures vary in the degree to which they have autonomous influence on policy making. In corporatist systems policy was traditionally made through agreement between executive officials, business, and labour union federations, with parliament usually acting as a rubber stamp (see Chapter 6). In the United Kingdom, on some accounts the 'Mother of Parliaments', parliament has generally had little influence on budgets, and little (though occasionally important) impact on legislation and policy. The lower chamber, the House of Commons, is elected and has generally been dominated by around three parties, one of which usually has enough seats to form a government on its own. Party discipline over MPs in Britain is strong. The party cohesion score (which measures how often legislators of the same party vote together) is 97 per cent. The UK's upper chamber, the House of Lords, was disabled from influencing policy for the whole twentieth century because it was made up of a bizarre mix of unelected figures. Some were 'peers' by virtue of their aristocratic ancestry (and were only finally removed from the Lords in 1999), others were appointed for life to the Lords by one of the major party leaders. The Lords still lacks any democratic legitimacy (in 2009), and plays little role in policy making.

In presidential systems such as France, Mexico, Brazil, Russia and the United States, citizens directly choose who is to head the executive branch and form the government, and so the legislature cannot easily remove the president (except through a painful process of impeachment for wrong doing). However, the legislature can refuse to pass legislation proposed by the president, and may be able to amend budgets at will. Paradoxically, the country with one of the strongest presidential systems, the United States, is also the liberal democracy with the strongest legislature. The level of Congressional scrutiny of government operations is much greater than parliamentary scrutiny in most other liberal democracies. Party cohesion scores in Congress are low, with party members voting the same way only 65 per cent of the time.

Legislatures can debate bills (proposed laws) in the chamber as a whole, though normally bills are sent to specialist committees (on health, welfare policy, defence, environment and so forth) composed of a small number of legislators for closer scrutiny. Majority rule normally prevails, in that to be passed a bill needs 50 per cent of votes cast plus one. Occasionally there may be higher vote requirements. For example, in the US Senate, to achieve closure of a debate (and hence to stop opponents of a measure 'filibustering' a bill by talking until all the time allotted has been exhausted) a 60 per cent majority is needed. In many countries changes to the constitution require a two thirds majority (and often also ratification by states in a federal system, or by a majority of voters in a referendum).

Problems of majority rule

Majority rule seems commonsensical and it is often regarded as a cornerstone of democracy. But majority rule has been problematized by theoretical work on social choice. William Riker (1982a) argued that there is an extensive scope for manipulation of legislative voting by clever politicians. The reason is that most issues can in theory feature cycles between three or more options; and if no cycle exists, it is quite easy to craft an option to make sure that one does. A cycle is by definition when a majority can be found to support option A over option B, B over C, and C over A. For example, consider a vote on a war (say, Iraq) in which the legislature is divided into three roughly equal factions, facing three options. The options are the status quo (S), cessation of the war (C) or escalation (E). A 'dove' faction's ordering is C>S>E; an 'all or nothing' faction's ordering is E>C>S; a 'moderate' faction's ordering is S>E>C (where '>' means 'preferred to'). If a vote is taken of C versus S, then C wins two to one. If the vote is E versus C then E wins two to one. But if a vote is taken on S versus E then S wins two to one. So by majority rule, S beats E, E beats C, and C beats S. What, then, is the majority view? There is none; the outcome will depend entirely on the order in which the votes are cast. Procedures are open to manipulation by politicians who will craft options to try to make cycles happen, and then manipulate the order in which votes are taken.

This kind of analysis has received enormous attention from political scientists, despite the fact that in the entire political history of real-world liberal democracies it is almost impossible to find a single example of a cycle (Mackie 2004). Somehow, real-world legislatures find ways to overcome the theoretical problems caused by cycles. This can be a matter of the simple fact that legislators deliberate as well as vote (Dryzek and List 2003), or that legislatures create structural rules that limit opportunities to introduce new options (Shepsle 1979).

If anything, the problem with real-world legislatures is the opposite of that identified by social choice theory: they are too stable and predictable in making laws and budgets. In coalition governments, the largest party in the governing coalition plays the key role in deciding the legislature's agenda. In the United Kingdom, a government with a majority in the House of Commons can ensure that virtually every vote goes its way. In the United States Congress, policy stability is secured by powerful Congressional committees that draft laws (authorizing committees) and set budgets (appropriations committees). These committees are often dominated by legislators with constituency interests in the committee's subject, so that the Agriculture Committee consists mainly of legislators from farm states, the Energy and Natural Resources Committee is dominated by oil-producing states, and so on.

Market liberals are horrified by this sort of dominance by special interests (see Chapter 5). More optimistic pluralists see committees as capable of generating good information for Congress as a whole. If those pluralists are right then committees that simply protected vested interests would find their proposals overturned on the floor of Congress, where the median legislator will determine outcomes just as the median voter does in citizens' elections.

Coalitions

In proportional representation (PR) systems it is quite unusual for one party to win a majority of the vote outright. One exception is South Africa, where the African National Congress (ANC), which led the struggle against the previous apartheid regime, won the country's first three elections featuring universal adult franchise from 1996 to 2003 with almost two-thirds of the total votes. The ANC is also successful in inducing representatives from other parties to join it after they have been elected. But the more usual case in PR countries is that no single party has a majority of seats in the legislature, meaning that two or more parties must negotiate a coalition to form a majority. According to Riker (1962) the logical outcome is a 'minimum winning coalition', on the grounds that the spoils of office can then be shared among as few legislators as feasible. But this is not generally what we observe in practice, because coalitions also need to feature ideological proximity between their component parties. For example, it is rarely the case that parties of the left and right form a minimum winning coalition that excludes parties of the centre. If there is just one dimension along which parties are aligned (such as left to right), then the governing coalition will normally include the party containing the 'median legislator'. Coalition governments also tend to be supported by quite large majorities. Another less common outcome is that a majority coalition does not form, but that instead the largest single party forms a government even though it has only minority support. This sort of government is possible only in consensual democracies such as those in Scandinavia – facilitated by the fact that most important policy decisions are not made in parliament, but in corporatist bargaining between major social interests.

If parties in the legislature are divided on two or more dimensions – for instance, on left/right or class lines but also on ethnic lines – then matters are more complicated, but convergence around the median legislator can still operate. To illustrate, Figure 7.6 shows a highly simplified legislature with only seven members, L1 to L7. The black outline shows the 'Pareto set', the area bounded by the legislators' preference points moving into this space from outside will improve the welfare of all legislators at the same time. On the horizontal left-right dimension L4 is the median legislator, but on the vertical brown-green dimension (assuming environmental issues are important), L4 is not the median representative, but occupies a strong 'brown' position favouring industrial development. On the brown–green dimension L2 is the median legislator. This legislature ought to find a majority coalition that agrees on policy positions on the two dimensions located somewhere within the shaded area, known as the 'heart'. If we look closely at the figure, we see that any policy position within the core has majority support over any position outside it. (The heart is defined by looking at all the possible majority groups of 4 out of the 7 members here, always assuming that these winning coalitions would be composed of legislators relatively close to each other.)

What this analysis suggests is that in proportional representation systems with more than one issue dimension on which parties form (the normal case), there is a tendency toward moderation. As we will see in the next chapter, this leads many observers to advocate proportional representation for societies deeply divided on ethnic or racial lines. The situation is very different in countries using the plurality rule system. For instance, in the UK from 1979 to 2005 seven successive govern-

Figure 7.6   *The majority 'heart' and the 'Pareto set' in a simple legislature (with seven members, L1 to L7)*

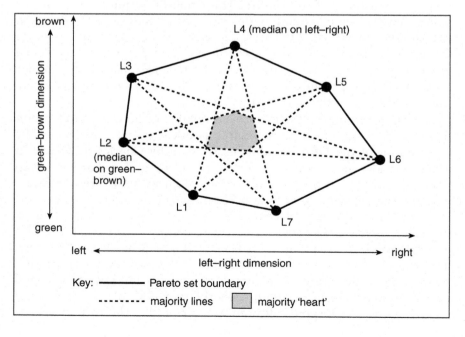

ments (headed by Margaret Thatcher, John Major and Tony Blair) were formed by one party with a comfortable majority of seats in the House of Commons, even though that party only received between 35 per cent and 42 per cent per cent of the citizens' vote. As Margaret Thatcher showed in pursuing a market liberal agenda, such governments can act like 'elective dictatorships' adopting extreme positions rejected by the majority of voters. Thatcher herself took pride in her 'conviction politics' that never sought accommodation with her opponents, be they inside her own party or in other parties.

Divided government

At first sight presidential systems may seem very different from coalition governments, because a single-office holder controls the executive. But in most such systems (like France and Korea) the president only controls a small range of issues directly, and still needs government ministers to have majority support in the legislature. Even in the USA, where the separation of powers between the executive and legislature is more complete, the president still needs to actively work with Congress to try and get his or her favoured legislation enacted and to produce budget outcomes in line with executive plans. And in all presidential systems 'divided government' situations can arise where one party wins the presidency, while another party (or coalition of parties) wins the majority of seats in the legislature. This situation is quite normal in the United States, where in addition different parties may have majorities in the House and Senate. However, the weakness of party discipline in Congress means that divided government does not necessarily make much difference beyond all the checks and balances that already induce moderation (except when it comes to foreign and defence policy, where the presidency operates with hardly any checks).

Divided government has also proved capable of inducing moderation in the historically much more volatile political system of France. The constitution of the Fifth Republic established by Charles de Gaulle in 1958 provides for a directly-elected president and a parliament to which the prime minister and his or her cabinet are also responsible – with no clear division of powers between president and prime minister. In 1981 French voters elected a left-winger François Mitterand as President and in 1986 chose a right-wing majority for parliament, creating a period of 'cohabitation' between left and right for the first time. This experience was then repeated in the 1990s the other way around, with a right-wing president (Chirac) and a left-wing government and parliamentary majority. In both cases the two sides managed to negotiate a division of responsibility quite successfully. The case of France suggests that divided government can act as a force for moderation and stability. French government was not paralyzed, and major new laws could still be passed – they just had to be negotiated between the two sides.

Consensual and majoritarian democracies

Democracy is sometimes equated with majority rule, such that the main legitimating principle of a decision is that it is supported by a majority of the voters, or a majority of their representatives. There are, indeed, some democratic systems and institutions that proceed along ruthlessly majoritarian lines – notably the 'Westminster systems' modelled on the United Kingdom. Paradoxically, however, we have seen that a system like the Westminster one that uses plurality rule voting to elect a legislature, whose largest party then authorizes an executive to govern without any significant checks and balances, ultimately features government by a minority, not a majority. For the majority party in the UK parliament has for over 30 years received no more than 42 per cent of the popular vote.

Even setting aside this paradox, democracy as majority rule can conceivably mean that the majority gets everything it wants, while the minority gets nothing. In deeply divided societies this is a recipe for separatism and violence. But in all societies, allowing minorities to receive nothing from government can look very unattractive from a democratic point of view. Thus most states feature consensual aspects that soften majoritarianism by trying to include all sides in key decisions. Lijphart (1984) suggests that all liberal democratic states can be arrayed on a continuum from majoritarian to consensual. The most consensual states would feature expansive corporatism (see Chapter 6) that tries to organize all social interests into government (not just the traditional corporatist trio of executive branch officials, business and labour); proportional representation; and a tradition of coalition government that includes more parties than necessary for a minimum winning coalition. The latter reaches an extreme in the idea of 'grand coalition' in which virtually all parties join in the governing coalition. Grand coalitions have been a long-lived feature of some societies trying to overcome deep divisions in their past (for example, Austria following World War II). It is used on a more temporary basis when two large parties of the left and right decide it would be preferable to govern with each, rather than with a more 'extreme' possible partner on their own side of the divide (as in Germany following the 2005 election). Consensual government (but without grand coalition) reaches a peak in the Scandinavian countries. It should be noted that consensual political cultures are not always accompanied by consensual government. For example, the Confucian countries of East Asia prize consensus culturally – but their political institutions and practices are often majoritarian and adversarial (the Taiwanese parliament is renowned for its fist-fights).

Agendas and Political Change

Electoral system reform

Electoral and legislative politics feature many proposals for institutional reform. The many varieties of voting systems all have their advocates. Some of these advocates have trouble convincing anyone beyond the academic world. For example, 'approval voting' is a favourite of a number of political scientists (Brams and Fishburn 1983), but it has never been adopted in the real world. (In approval voting, voters in single-member constituencies can vote multiple times for all the candidates of whom they approve, and the candidate with the highest number of voters wins. Thus candidates would be elected who secure broad approval, as opposed to sectional appeal.) We saw in Chapter 5 that some market liberals believe a unanimity requirement in voting (in the legislature) is more economically efficient than majority rule.

Often political parties will advocate voting systems that are in their own interest. It is no surprise that smaller parties in first-past-the post systems want to move in the direction of proportional representation. In the United Kingdom, the Liberal Democrats protest that even when they earn more than 25 per cent of the votes, they receive less than 10 per cent of the seats in parliament. It is equally unsurprising that parties who benefit from the established system block any such reforms. The only chance for the Liberal Democrats to enact electoral reform would be to catch the attention of a party that has a majority in parliament but believes it will lose it at the next election. To date this has not happened, perhaps because of the capacity of doomed politicians to overestimate their own chances of success.

Yet electoral system reform can sometimes happen. In 1993 New Zealand dumped the plurality rule system it had inherited from the United Kingdom in favour of a German-style proportional representation system with half the members elected in single-member constituencies, the other half allocated to ensure proportionality from party lists of candidates. This was largely a matter of citizen disgust with the two major parties (Labour and National) that had both implemented a strong version of market liberalism when in office – despite having promised no such thing at the previous election. New Zealand's move to proportional representation produced an increase in the number of significant parties in parliament, and the need for coalition as opposed to single-party government. The possibility of moving from plurality rule to PR has also been pursued seriously in the Canadian provinces of British Columbia and Ontario, both of which set up a 'citizen's assembly' of around 80 ordinary people selected at random from their citizenry, and charged them with recommending a system. The British Columbia Citizen's Assembly in 2004 recommended a German-style proportional representation system – which was endorsed by 57 per cent of the voters in a subsequent referendum. Unfortunately there was a 60 per cent requirement for adoption of the new system (an almost impossible hurdle for any constitutional measure to pass in a referendum). In Ontario a proposed new system was rejected by a majority of voters in a referendum.

It is also possible for systems already using PR to wish to curb its tendency to produce large numbers of parties. In 2006 the Netherlands government set up a citizen's assembly (on the British Columbia model) to consider changing the country's scrupulous form of list PR. In Italy in 1993 the electoral system was discredited, along with the corrupt Christian Democratic Party and its allies that had dominated Italian politics for four decades. In a referendum Italian voters chose to reduce the proportional representation elements of a mixed voting system, though 25 per cent of representatives continued to be elected by proportional representation. Though the number of parties in Italy remained stubbornly large, they did coalesce more into blocs of the right and left to contest subsequent elections.

Italy also illustrates the fact that sometimes electoral reforms can have the opposite result from that intended. Prior to the 2006 general election, the conservative Prime Minister Berlusconi introduced three changes. The first reverted to a complicated proportional representation system, but gave the winning coalition in the lower house a number of bonus seats so that it would not have to worry about any knife-edge majority. The second allowed Italians living abroad to vote for several special seats in the senate. The third was a specific provision designed to hurt coalitions specified in advance of the election that included very small parties – such as the coalition of his opponents. Much to his surprise Berlusconi's coalition of conservative, regional, and fascist parties lost the election in the lower house by a knife-edge, so his opponents received the bonus seats, and overseas Italians gave a majority of their senate seats to his opponents. Two years later the system worked as Berlusconi intended, returning him to power with an artificially boosted majority.

Increasing turnout

Other reform proposals are targeted at remedying the problem of declining voter turnout; though privately some parties may actually welcome falling turnout because they believe it will advantage them. The most obvious remedy is to make voting compulsory, as in Australia in Belgium, though this seems not to be on the agenda of most liberal democracies. Occasionally in Australia the conservative side of politics suggests abolishing compulsory voting – because it believes it would benefit. In countries where citizens have to make an effort to register in order to vote, such as the United States, there are various proposals to make it easier – such as 'motor voter', where citizens can register to vote at the same time that they renew their driving license. But as we have seen, there are also measures implemented in some states designed to suppress turnout and so benefit Republican candidates. For their part Republicans charge groups such as ACORN (Association of Community Organizations for Reform Now) that try to register poor and disadvantaged voters with 'voter fraud' – a charge made by the Palin-McCain ticket in the 2008 presidential race. Civic education for both school-age children and adults is also sometimes suggested as a cure for declining public interest in politics (though there is little evidence for this effect). In the United Kingdom, postal voting has been made easier and there have been experiments with Internet voting, though identification can be problematic.

In Caplan's (2007) market literal judgment, given the irrationality of most voters then declining turnout is a solution, not a problem. He frankly believes that voting should only be for the economically literate. And if most people cannot be educated in the right economics, the franchise should be restricted to those who do understand basic economic principles.

Controlling the impact of money

A final set of proposals has to do with curbing the influence of money in electoral and legislative politics. In the United States, where elections are more expensive affairs than anywhere else, campaign finance reform is a perennial topic, often involving caps on individual contributions to candidates. Such caps are easily circumvented by 'political action committees' that raise money and then distribute it to a variety of candidates. In addition, there is no limit on the amount of money an individual may spend on their own campaign – and very rich candidates take advantage of this. Elsewhere, there are worries about the influence of media monopolies on electoral outcomes. In a memoir of life in 10 Downing Street, Price (2006) recalls that any significant policy proposal from the Prime Minister had to meet with the approval of three other people: the Deputy Party Leader John Prescott, the Chancellor of the Exchequer (Treasurer) Gordon Brown, and Rupert Murdoch – a media baron who was not a British citizen and lived in the United States. Media influence on politics reached a peak in Italy in the early 2000s, when Prime Minister Silvio Berlusconi owned all three commercial television networks, tried to control the state-run television network (with dire consequences for journalists who opposed him), and owned several newspapers and magazines. This monopoly did not how-ever prevent his coalition narrowly losing the 2006 election, though it did return to power in 2008. Quite how the power of media barons might be curbed is a tricky question, especially given that most politi-cians fear confronting the power of the media. There may already be laws restricting monopolies – for example, prohibiting one company from owning both television stations and newspapers. Australia has such laws, but with time corporations have managed to dilute and cir-cumvent them.

Conclusion

For pluralists in particular the amount of energy devoted to election campaigns and legislative politics suggests that they do matter when it comes to steering the course society takes – even though elite theorists and Marxists might dismiss them as not really affecting the distribution of power. Electoral systems and legislatures are complex institutions that come in many varieties. We have briefly examined some proposals for reform that would involve taking the basic structure of elections and legislatures as given. But there are movements for democratic renewal in liberal democracies that go beyond voting as the central democratic act, which we survey in Chapter 9. But first, we need to examine another highly problematic aspect of contemporary states: the degree to which their existence and operation is bound up with poten-tially explosive questions of national, ethnic and cultural identity.

Chapter 8

Identity Politics

The classic theories covered in earlier chapters (pluralism, elitism, Marxism, and markat-liberalism) all miss what is arguably the most important fact about the modern state: that it is above all a *nation* state. Nationalists believe that each state (or at least their own state) should match a nation defined by history, community, language or ethnicity. In earlier eras some empires (such as the Habsburgs and Ottomans) could accommodate large numbers of different ethnicities. But modern state-building elites have often tried to homogenize identities within the territory they control or claim. Yet such homogenization has often been challenged by alternative or minority religions, language groups, ethnicities and cultures. Claims to nationhood associated with a state can be contested, sometimes bitterly. 'At present the fate of ethnic and national groups around the world is in the hands of xenophobic nationalists, religious extremists and military dictators. If liberalism is to have chance of taking hold in these countries, it must explicitly address the needs and aspirations of national minorities' (Kymlicka 1995: 195).

The four classic theories have little or nothing to say about this contestation, or how and why states come to organize the affairs of a particular, territorially-defined body of people in the first place. In Chapter 1 we mentioned a 'bottom up' perspective on state formation that sees in the emergence of states a search for a better fit between national, cultural, religious or linguistic categories and the boundaries of the state. These categories constitute identities that can be mobilized in support of any particular state's reach over a territory and its people. So to understand the formation, persistence and disintegration of states, we need to examine the politics of identity. As we will see, national identities themselves can also be mobilized from the top down, rather than just emerging out of societies, as a 'bottom up' description might always seem to imply.

The identity politics of the state emphasizes the role of national identities, which people often feel so passionate about that they are willing to both kill and die for them. Nations rarely coincide neatly with the boundaries of states, so we will also explore the particular problems of multi-national states. Of course national identities are not the only kind of politically-relevant identities – these can also involve religion, region, ethnicity, gender, voluntary subculture (of the sort that young people like to invent), age, sexuality and even social class. Today's states have to cope with a range of competing and sometimes conflicting identity claims. Yet few states have collapsed over identity, conflicts around gender or age, but many over nationalality, language and religion. We postpone our discussion of how relatively well-behaved identity groups are processed politically by contemporary liberal democratic states until Chapter 13, in the context of post-modern interpretations. Here we confine our discussion to those potentially explosive identities that either demand a state for themselves, or refuse to recognize the identity that goes with an established state. Identity politics of this sort can be far more divisive than the politics of social class, income distribution, and interest group competition, sometimes with catastrophic results.

Origins and Core Assumptions

Violent identity politics dates back to ancient times, notably in the struggles by the Jewish people to maintain their state against neighbouring empires. In the first century BCE, the Roman Republic's Italian allies fought a war against the metropolis in which their main demand was to be granted Roman citizenship, instead of the *socii* status to which they were confined. (Some material benefits went with access to Roman citizenship, so it was not just a war of identity.) Religious identity politics too pre-dates the modern state by several hundred years. For example the Muslim conquests under Mohammed and his successors that created a loose empire from Arabia to Spain. Subsequent Christian crusades then tried to push Islam back. The modern states system is often dated to the Treaty of Westphalia in 1648, which was designed to put an end to chronic wars of religion between Catholics and Protestants in central Europe. The Treaty endorsed the principle (first enunciated in the earlier 1555 Treaty of Augsburg) that the ruler could set the religion of the state – but it also specified that states should retain their religion as it existed in 1624. The presumption was still that each state should have one religion and possess sovereign authority that could be used as a protection against other states – especially states with a different religion.

Since 1648 identity claims for possession of a particular state have generally been pushed harder by political leaders and activists than by scholars (though scholars can often be found supporting different sides in identity conflicts). The Groups advancing particular national identities in politics are likely to see them as somehow basic and given; in the case of ethnic and national identities, as ancient and recurring (Smith, 1971; see O'Leary, 2001a). Scholars observing identity politics are much more likely to emphasize the socially constructed and changeable character of identities. There are exceptions though. Samuel Huntington's (1996) famous 'clash of civilizations' thesis takes civilizational identities as ancient and given, with no opportunity for negotiating identities. Robert Kaplan's (1993) book on the Balkans is credited with persuading President Bill Clinton to decide against United States intervention in the wars of a disintegrating Yugoslavia. It speaks (dubiously) of 'ancient hatreds' that underlie and explain contemporary conflicts (see Kaufman 2001 for a critique). But however identities are formed, and whether or not they are taken as fixed, any particular identity almost always finds both definition and validation in its rejection of some other identity. Christians reject other religions and atheism; fundamentalists reject sinful lifestyles; environmentalists reject conspicuous consumption; radical Islamists reject the West, nationalists reject cosmopolitanism; secessionists reject the national identity of the state they are trying to leave; and so forth.

Challenges to other theories of the state

The identity politics of the state does not involve a coherent theory of how the state works. However, the basic assumptions of identity politics do challenge some of the assumptions of the classical theories of the state discussed in Chapters 2 to 5, This critique goes beyond the inability of those theories to explain how states get defined, which we noted at the outset of this chapter. An identity refers to who a person is, rather than what he or she wants. Identities cannot therefore be reduced to interests; they are more basic and deeply held, less easily subject to compromise than are interests. In classical pluralist theory up to the mid twentieth century United States, interests were seen as mostly negotiable. Economic interests can always be met partially by material rewards; and it is quite easy for those with competing material interests to reach bargained solutions. But identity politics frequently have more of an all-or-nothing character. Either the state is a Christian state, or it is not. Either a particular nation has a state of its own, or it does not. This recognition does not mean that identity politics is intractable, just that it presents some especially difficult challenges.

Pluralists originally believed that modernization would inexorably blur identity conflicts, amalgamate ethnicities through migration, see religious conflicts displaced by secularism, and create more open-minded outlooks as a result of trade, travel and experience of other cultures. Contemporary pluralists try to rectify these over-optimistic views with a more sophisticated analysis of the origins and interactions of identities. Pluralists have also now developed strategies for permanently managing identity conflicts within constitutional politics, explored later in this chapter.

Identity politics also challenges Marxism and market liberalism. Marxists see social class defined by economic system as the basic driver of politics, and identity conflicts as a hangover from pre-modern times, or a cover for more basic class conflicts. But identities relating to nation, ethnic group and language cannot be reduced to social class. More problematic still for Marxists is the fact that people generally feel these identities more intensely and hold on to them much more tenaciously than they do to their class identification. In the Soviet Union, Lenin and his successors did grasp the extraordinary salience of nationalism, however, promising self-determination for nations in autonomous republics and other special districts (Walker 1984; Nimni, 1993). But these concessions meant little in light of the complete power of a unified Communist Party. Only in 1991, with the collapse of the Soviet Union, did these republics suddenly become (or in some cases reemerge as) nation states.

Market liberals for their part see politics only in terms of individuals pursuing their material self-interest. Identity politics simply does not register in the economistic world of the market liberal. Consistent market liberals should say that in a market economy individuals would outgrow the identities that seem to cause so much trouble, and get on with the serious business of pursuing material success (Breton *et al.*, 1995). But few if any market liberals have taken on identity politics in these terms. Albert Hirschman (1977) points out that political arguments for capitalism once emphasized the fact that a commercial society would replace the destructive pursuit of glory by aristocrats in feudal society with the more civilized and more easily managed pursuit of material interest. But while these arguments flourished several hundred years ago in Europe, they are rarely heard today.

Elite theorists have nothing good to say about identity politics. Inasmuch as they do approach these sorts of issues, they are likely to see identity in very instrumental terms: as something that can be manipulated to elite advantage. For example, elites interested in securing their power against potentially troublesome social movements or working class parties might well seek to cultivate a popular national identity that would help marginalize troublemakers as unpatriotic. This was how the Fascists in Italy and Nazis in Germany successfully crushed communist and social-democratic parties and unions in the 1920s and 1930s. More generally, elite theorists see state elite sponsorship of rituals, ceremonies, flags and mythical histories as a cinical way to mobilize the masses in opposition to out-groups.

Culture and identity

Identity politics is often discussed in terms of culture, but identity does not in fact reduce to culture (Moore 1999). In Northern Ireland, there are virtually no cultural differences between the two communities of a deeply divided society (McGarry and O'Leary, 1995). Protestants and Catholics look alike, wear the same sorts of clothes, speak English in the same accents, patronize the same kinds of shops, have equally conservative social attitudes, are equally ambivalent about the role of violence in politics, drink similar sorts of beer and whisky, eat equally bad food, and often have trouble telling which side a person is from when meeting them for the first time. But the identity difference here is massive. In the former Yugoslavia, there were hardly any cultural differences across Serbs, Croats, and a very secular Bosnian Muslim community – but huge differences in national identity opened in the 1990s amid murderous civil war. Identities are in fact a product of the discourses in which individuals move, not culture. These discourses can be manipulated by political leaders seeking to establish and expand their own power base – sometimes, by extreme ethnic nationalists or religious fundamentalists, with murderous consequences. But as we will see later, a more benign engagement across the discourses that construct identities is also conceivable.

Society and Politics

In our discussions of the relationship between society and politics in previous chapters, the emphasis was generally on how social forces come to be influential in politics. In identity politics, the emphasis is different, for identities that pervade society are often the product of politics – especially when it comes to identities that either lay claim to or dispute the legitimacy of a state.

A popular tradition in political philosophy, associated especially with Thomas Hobbes and John Locke, justifies the state as being formed in a 'social contract' by the members of society, to guarantee their security, liberty and prosperity. While the idea of a hypothetical social contract is a useful philosophical device, the real story is often precisely the opposite: societies are formed by states. That is, the state is historically prior to the national identity that normally accompanies the state.

This kind of claim will dismay nationalists who believe their own nation, be it German, Indian, Serbian, Welsh, Basque or French, has a primordial existence that justifies a state to accompany it. In fact, nations are often what Benedict Anderson (1983) calls 'imagined communities'. They are not genuine communities, which require direct and many-faceted relationships among people, though once constituted, the nation itself may have all the attributes of feeling 'real' to those who are part of it. An individual in a large nation will have no interaction at all with the vast majority of other members of the nation. Nevertheless, individuals imagine themselves members of a national community. Yet it is often very hard work for state-building elites to convince people that they are members of a nation. Some of Anderson's own work examines Indonesia, which began as a series of very disparate societies that just happened to be colonized by the Dutch, who as a matter of colonial convenience centralized their administration. Upon the Dutch departure, political elites had to convince the members of these disparate societies that they were in fact Indonesians – no easy task, and one that remains incomplete, as separatist movements in Aceh, West Papua, and elsewhere attest. Similarly, state-building elites in Turkey once insisted that no Kurds lived in the East of the country – rather, they were 'Mountain Turks'.

If we look at the history of European states, we see that the German nation was a long time in its production, eventually secured in the nineteenth century by Prussian elites. In the 1930s the Nazis managed to convince most Austrians (including the Austrian government) that they, too, were Germans and deserved to be part of the German *Reich*. We see similar stories of state building elites trying long and hard to establish national identities against persistent regional opposition in France, Italy, and the United Kingdom. While we have no opinion survey data from the late eighteenth century, it is probable that during the American revolution, many if not most residents of the former colonies considered themselves British, and so needed convincing that there was an American nation, and that they were part of it. In all these cases and many others, national historians cannot be trusted to tell the full story, because they will emphasize the unity and not the fractiousness and conflict that accompany nation building by states. They are also likely to tell the story in reverse, seeing state building as an accomplishment of the nation.

States homogenizing societies

It is normal for state-building elites to be confronted with populations in territories they claim who are not all convinced that they belong to the nation being constructed. Sometimes the result is very bad news for those remaining unconvinced. Rae (2002) recounts the history of what she calls 'pathological homogenization' by state-building elites. Her first case is fifteenth century Spain, where the new Spanish state sought to consolidate a Christian Spanish identity. Moors (Muslims) and Jews had three options: death; conversion to Christianity; or exile. At the end of the seventeenth century, Louis XIV believed that Huguenots (Protestants) were an affront to the singular French identity needed to accompany a modern state, and so the Huguenots were forced to convert to Catholicism or leave the country (Marx, 2003). In 1915, the Armenian genocide was organized by elites keen to establish a Turkish state (Akçam, 2006). And in the 1990s as Yugoslavia fell apart, state-builders showed once again the connection between constructing national identity and genocide. Consider in this light Hobbes's argument in *Leviathan* that the state should exist to prevent misery and death in a 'war of each against all'. The reality of the creation of the state is often the opposite, as the new state itself brings misery or death to those who do not share its prescribed national identity.

The modern notion of sovereignty established by the Treaty of Westphalia in 1648 provided a degree of license for states to act in this homogenizing fashion toward their subject populations. Designed to halt the wars of religion between Catholics and various protestant sects that had torn central Europe apart, the Treaty meant that those with a religion different to that of the state could not expect any support or protection from outside the state. The Westphalian sovereignty norm of non-interference in the internal affairs of a state remains strong today; though the norm has never been absolute (see Reus-Smit 1999 for a history of the sovereignty concept). Today, sovereignty can be conditional on a state not engaging in genocide against some of its own people – as attested by the 1999 NATO bombing campaign against Serbia over actions against ethnic Albanians in the then Serbian territory of Kosovo. But other clear cases of genocide (like Rwanda 1995) sparked so many interventions.

Now, some states have been quite successful in homogenizing their populations around a single national identity. So Spain eliminated its Moors and Jews, France its Huguenots and Nazi Germany its Jews. Poland and what is now the Czech Republic removed all their Germans after World War II. However, many states remain multi-national. So the United Kingdom includes Scottish, Welsh, Ulster Protestant and Irish Republican identities – as well as the majority English who tend to see little difference between Englishness and Britishness. Spain has substantial Catalan, Galician and Basque minorities. Canada has a large French-speaking Quebecois minority. Russia contains a host of non-Russian communities, especially along its southern edges. Some states have deep internal divisions between ethnic or religious groups. Historically, such deep division characterized Belgium, the Netherlands and Austria. Contemporary examples of deeply divided societies include Northern Ireland, Sri Lanka, parts of India, Fiji, many African countries, Lebanon and Georgia. Such societies are prone to civil war.

Large-scale migration has in many countries produced substantial immigrant populations not assimilated into the state's national identity (for example, in the United Kingdom, Netherlands, Denmark and

France), with no melting pot along nineteenth century United States lines. Thus there are very few states in today's world which can take the identity of their own population as given and unproblematic (McGarry *et al.*, 2008). Identity politics are now a major challenge in many states, including liberal democratic states. How, then, do states respond?

Government and Policy Making

If there is a dominant identity that key policy makers believe should accompany the state, and that government can try to manage, then it is citizenship (the problematic case where no such dominant identity exists is considered shortly). Citizenship is by definition the set of rights, privileges and obligations that accompany full membership of a political entity such as a state.

Managing citizenship

At the formal level, most governments decide who is and is not, can be and cannot be a citizen. In many states those born on the national territory automatically become citizens; but that is not true when states also apply an ethnicity test for citizenship. Such states may also enable those with no family connections to the territory but the requisite ethnicity to become citizens – examples would include Germany and Israel. Many states have provisions for immigrants to become citizens, though often tests will be applied relating (for example) to language, educational qualifications, social values, skills and family connections.

Governments also manage the content of citizenship, in many different ways. For example they may require the teaching of national history in schools; organize commemorations of key events in that history; construct and manage national cultural institutions such as museums and memorials; and generally propagate the symbols accompanying nationhood. State-owned television and radio networks may reinforce the national view (as may privately owned media). Such efforts may succeed – or they may fail. They are especially likely to be problematic when one or more substantial sections of the population have good reasons not to accept the general prescription for citizenship propagated by the government.

If conflicting identities exist, and their physical elimination is impossible, governments are faced with a range of possible strategies. At one extreme would be assimilation: the idea that minorities are to be integrated into the national culture. This is most straightforward when the minorities in question are immigrants who cannot appeal to an alternative identity that is deeply rooted on the state's territory. Assimilation can be promoted by policies that require all state education and all state business to be conducted in the national language; the physical dispersal of newly arrived immigrants, to prevent their clustering in particular neighbourhoods; and the absence of any categories in government policies sensitive to minority demands (concerning, for example, religious observances). At the other extreme would be separation. South Africa's apartheid regime tried this for several decades but eventually could not sustain white minority domination of a majority black population. More consensual forms of separation are conceivable, and we will discuss these when we turn to deeply divided societies. But in today's liberal democracies, the alternative to assimilation is generally defined as multiculturalism rather than separation.

Multiculturalism means that immigrant minorities in particular are expected and encouraged to retain aspects of the culture of their place of origin. Those aspects might be religious, linguistic, dietary and social. Government might encourage the formation of ethnic associations, subsidize teaching in the minority's language, translate government documents, provide interpreters where needed, and legally recognize differences in practices relating to (say) marriage and child-rearing. Conflicts concerning for example religious buildings and the overt display of religious symbols may then need to be managed.

Multicultural policies will not help much when it comes to societies deeply divided on the basis of religion, ethnicity or race. The hallmark of a divided society is that one identity finds its validation in complete rejection of the identity of the other side. Historically, when identities could not coexist, the solution has often been the formation of separate states (Pakistan and India, Ireland and the United Kingdom, Serbia and Croatia, etc). The process of separation can be very violent, and often substantial minorities are left on the 'wrong' side of the new border. Thus even after separation, deep divisions may remain. And if there is substantial geographical mixing of populations, separation may not be feasible. So how can divided societies manage their conflicts – short of one group using the state to dominate other groups? There are three main categories of solution currently available: consociational; electoral system engineering; and communicative.

The consociational model for divided societies

Consociational democracy was first identified by Arend Lijphart (1968) in an analysis of how political stability had been achieved in the once deeply divided society of the Netherlands. Since then, Lijphart (1977) and others have claimed that the model applies to many other societies – and it is often advanced as a solution for the ills confronting divided societies. Given that its democratic qualities can be questioned, we prefer to call it the consociational model rather than 'democracy'. The model may be defined in terms of 'grand coalition, segmental autonomy, proportionality, and minority veto' (Lijphart, 2000: 228). The idea is that the leaders of all the segments in the society reach an agreement among themselves to govern the state in consultation with one another. Below the elite level, 'segmental autonomy' means that each group will ideally have its own schools, universities, places of worship (if relevant), businesses, labour unions, sports teams and social organizations. Conflicts are chiefly managed at the elite level, and relationships across block lines lower down are minimized so as to avoid the possibility of conflict. The government may be comprised of a coalition of all the major parties, themselves organized on a segmental basis. Proportional representation is normally used as the voting system to ensure that the various blocks get represented in parliament in proportion to their numbers in the population. State offices, public employment, and government expenditures are allocated proportionately between the various blocks.

In the Netherlands, the blocks in question were Catholic, Protestant and secular. In Switzerland, they have been defined on the basis of language: German, French and Italian (though Switzerland differs from the Netherlands because geographical separation of the three language groups means that autonomous cantons can be defined). Language is also the basis in Belgium, divided between Flemings and French-speaking Walloons. The Good Friday agreement of 1998 was an attempt to reach a consociational settlement in Northern Ireland between Republicans (Catholics) and Unionists (Protestants). The power-sharing arrangement began to work almost a decade later, with the largest Protestant party receiving the first minister's position, the largest Catholic party the equally powerful second minister's slot (O'Leary, 2006). The consociational model has been applied in a less pure form outside these small west European settings. In Lebanon before 1975 an elaborate arrangement allocated political offices between Maronite Christian, Shi'ite, Sunni and Druze communities (this collapsed in civil war, but elements of it have since been revived). Lijphart claims that there were elements of consociationalism in South Africa's transition from apartheid in 1994–96 (though most have since been lost, given the dominance of the African National Congress in electoral politics), and that even India has had its consociational aspects (Lijphart, 1996). He asserts that the consociational model is 'the only workable type of democracy in deeply divided societies' (Lijphart, 1994: 222).

If consociationalism were indeed the 'only workable type of democracy' for divided societies seeking to escape violence and the threat of civil war, then there would be little point in dwelling on its defects. But if it is not in fact the only way, then it is worth pointing to its shortcomings. The first is its democratic deficit: block leaders can often govern in partnership with one another irrespective of the rise and fall of votes. This deficiency can be ameliorated to the extent there is more than one political party per block. So for example in Northern Ireland, Republicans have the choice of voting for the radical Sinn Fein or the moderate Social Democratic Labour Party. A second democratic shortcoming is that most key political decisions are taken in secret, for fear of inflaming inter-group passions, so that public debate may be suppressed, even in the legislature. A further deficiency is that in specifying particular identities at the constitutional level, consociationalism solidifies identities and the divisions between them. At worst it may actually reinforce the kind of identity conflicts it is designed to solve (Reynolds 2000: 169–70). Identity conflicts are the product of a particular kind of social learning (Kaufman 2001) and so ought in principle to be capable of amelioration through a different sort of social learning (Valadez 2001: 36–8) – but critics ask if consociationalism precludes the latter. Parties that are block-specific are promised a particular share of political offices, and so are advantaged in comparison to parties that are not sectarian and block-specific. In the case of Northern Ireland, this works against parties such as the Greens and Alliance that try to transcend the sectarian divide (Taylor 2006). An additional problem follows: given that the system is set up by block leaders to their own advantage, these leaders can be reluctant to dismantle the system when it is no longer needed as a result of declining inter-group hostilities (though this did eventually happen in the Netherlands). If block leaders are inflexible then consociationalism can descend into civil war, as happened to Lebanon in the 1970s, when its system could not adjust to the changing demographic realities of increasing Shi'ite population and the growing importance of Palestinian refugees. (Of course, Israeli an Syrian interventions from outside also created crises from outside).

Electoral system engineering

In Chapter 7 we looked at the political consequences of different sorts of voting systems. Consociationalists advocate proportional representation because it helps achieve the proportionality in political offices and the spoils of government required for an inter-block settlement. Another school of thought argues for the virtues of a system of preferential voting of the sort we also discussed in Chapter 7, especially when it comes to divided societies (Horowitz 1985; Reilly 2001).

Reilly (2001) argues that preferential voting motivates 'centripetal' electoral politics. Parties will still be based in society's blocks. However, rational candidates seeking to win elections ought to cultivate the second and third preferences of voters from the other side.

They can do this by adopting relatively moderate stances on inter-block issues, which should give them an advantage over more extreme politicians on their own side of the divide. In Papua New Guinea, upon independence, the country applied the preferential system of its former colonial master, Australia. Unfortunately in 1975 Papua New Guinea changed to plurality rule on the grounds of simplicity – with dire consequences for the intensity of inter-group conflict. The case of PNG is actually of questionable generalizability because it has so many politically-relevant ethnic groups – hundreds rather than the more normal case for divided societies of two, three or four. But the theoretical argument is that though preferential voting systems will normally produce a government of parties that do not represent all ethnic groups, yet those within that government will advance electoral platforms and so adopt public policies that are relatively moderate on inter-block issues.

However, if we look at the actual application of preferential voting to divided societies, matters are not so clear. Northern Ireland used the single transferable vote (STV) in multi-member constituencies in elections in 1973 and 1982 that did not succeed in advancing the fortunes of politicians appealing across the lines. This system was adopted again in 1998, when it seemed to work better – according to Reilly (2001: 136–7) because 'a core group of moderates emerges from both sides of the communal divide'. But then why did these moderates exist in 1998, but not earlier? Clearly factors other than the voting system must be called on to explain this change. Also the years following 1998 saw renewed polarization in Northern Ireland politics, with more strongly factional parties on both sides (Sinn Fein and the Democratic Unionist Party) advancing at the expense of the more moderate parties. Obviously the electoral system alone is not sufficient to induce moderation.

If we look at other ethnically divided societies where preferential voting has been tried the results are not always encouraging. Fiji in 1997 adopted the 'alternative vote' (AV) system; preferential voting in single-member constituencies. According to Horowitz, (1991: 189) this is better than STV because candidates cannot win with the support only of an extreme minority. The engineers of this system expected moderate ethnic Fijian parties to prosper in elections. But some technical details of the AV system unexpectedly proved to advantage ethnic Indian parties, which could then dominate the government (Frankel and Grossman, 2006). This was unacceptable to many ethnic Fijians, and the result was that a group of them carried out a coup in 2000. In light of the Fiji case (and a similar story with a slightly different system in Sri Lanka) Reilly remains optimistic, but concedes that the electoral system engineering has to be done exactly right to achieve the desired moderating effects. The problem is that the high-tension circumstances of deep inter-block conflict are hardly conducive to cool analytical thinking and precision policy implementation. Extremists on all sides (who are aware of a system being designed to frustrate their political ambitions) should do all they can to sabotage any such electoral reforms.

A communicative approach to deep division

Consociationalists admire states that may tend to suppress dialogue across difference; electoral engineers deal in the formal properties of voting systems, but otherwise ignore the content of political communication. A very different approach would seek to tame visceral identity clashes through the promotion of communication across block boundaries. Such communication can take a number of different forms. The first is labelled 'agonism', associated with Chantal Mouffe's (1999, 2000) proposals for divided societies. Essentially Mouffe seeks passionate exchange in which antagonism becomes agonism, enemies become respected adversaries and violence gives way to critical engagement. Individuals come to accept the legitimacy of the identity of different others as a result of a conversion experience (1999: 755). What this means is that one's own identity has to be flexible to the extent it no longer requires validation through suppression of the identity of the different other. Quite how all this could work in practice is left murky. What remains is a hope for engagement across difference that is energized and passionate, yet civil. Quite what a state would look like that embodied such principles is murkier still.

A more deliberative approach seeks communication across difference that is less passionate. It is more concerned with the practical questions of how to live together than with the validation of the identity of different others. Its starting point would be the observation noted earlier, that identities are the product of discourses, not culture. And what can be constructed in discourses can also be modified in engagement across different discourses (Dryzek 2005a). Deliberation is a particular kind of communication that involves recognizing the reasons advanced by those with whom one disagrees, even though one does not share them (see also Chapter 9 below). While argument is important, deliberation can also involve telling of personal stories, communicating personal experiences, and using rhetoric that appeals to emotions rather than reason. The aim is not consensus, but rather working agreements about how to resolve practical problems. Deliberation has to involve substantial social learning about the perspectives of those on different sides (Kanra 2005).

There are three sorts of location in which deliberation across difference might be sought: the formal institutions of the state (such as legislatures), designed forums that bring together participants from different sides (who can be ordinary people as well as political leaders), and the informal flow of communication in the broad public sphere, which may involve the media, political activism and even everyday conversation. For two reasons the public sphere might be emphasized rather than the institutions of the state. The first is that in the politics of the state, it is very difficult to avoid the sovereignty question; and in the world of modern states (ever since the Treaty of Westphalia in 1648), sovereignty has an all-or-nothing character (Dryzek 2005a). This explains, for example, why dialogue between political leaders from different sides of the sectarian/national divide in Northern Ireland often so unproductive: they could get beyond the sovereignty question in order to engage in joint problem solving. Only when representatives are put into an institutional context where sovereignty is not at issue, such as District Policing Partnerships, is productive dialogue possible. These partnerships address policing issues, traditionally among the most explosive in Northern Ireland. While not perfect, the partnerships do much better in deliberative terms than parliamentary politics. In a very different but still very divided context, Forester (1999) reports the case of a dialogue between fundamentalist Christians and gay activists in Colorado concerning HIV/AIDS policy. Even as each side continued to deny the validity of the identity of the other, they did manage to agree on some practical measures that could be taken on this policy issue. Progress was possible so long as both sides avoided the big question of how the issue was framed: as a moral issue by the Christians; as a public health issue by the gays.

To have any hope of moderating division in divided societies, deliberation must occur in the public sphere involving people from different sides – and this might be very different from consociationalism's 'segmental autonomy'. Examples might include mixed-race discussion groups in South Africa. In Turkey, activists from secular and Islamist blocks have been able to find some points of agreement when called upon to resolve particular problems, such as headscarves in universities (Kanra 2005). Such dialogue is not futile. As Benhabib (2002) stresses, cultures or identity groups are not monoliths. Internally they can be home to many voices, and this very polyvocality provides a point of entry for outsiders to participate in deliberation about issues that concern both the category of people in question and others in society.

The three approaches to moderating conflicts of identity in deeply divided societies – consociational, electoral systems engineering, and communicative or deliberative – are only mutually exclusive if one adopts a strong consociational programme with segmental autonomy at its core. One could imagine a power-sharing state coexisting with a deliberative public sphere encouraging engagement across the different sides, along with an electoral system that used preferential voting. O'Flynn (2006) shows how consociational systems might be made more deliberative, though he is more concerned with deliberation associated with the institutions of the state than in the broad public sphere.

Consociation and deliberation can also be applied to the international politics of identity. Huntington's (1996) solution to the clash of civilizations is to identify an elite leadership for each civilization. Ideally this leadership would come from the 'core state' of each civilization – the United States for the West, India for Hindu, possibly South Africa for African, Russia for Orthodox, China for Sinic and so forth. Institutions would then be designed for conflict management – in particular, something like the United Nations Security Council with one representative per civilization. Though Huntington does not cite the consociational literature, this solution resembles a consociational elite pact at a global level that suppresses interchange across civilizations at the non-elite level, a kind of segmental autonomy. (A particular challenge arises in the case of Islam, which has no core state.) A more deliberative (but critics say also overly optimistic) approach to international identity conflicts would look at the possibilities for the engagement of discourses across difference (Dryzek 2006). This would involve trying to build more deliberative practices into international politics at all levels, engaging non-governmental organizations, political activists, and the media as well as politicians and officials of intergovernmental organizations. Transnational civil society would be emphasized, not just negotiations between the leaders of states.

Agendas and Political Change

There are many conflicting agendas in the context of identity politics, aadditions to three (consociational, voting system design and communicative) reviewed so far. Two additional agendas point in somewhat different directions. The first encompasses those who seek to promote particular identities, especially three types of nationalists; ethnic; cultural; and liberal. The second agenda seeks ways to recognize conflicting identities, especially through granting rights to minority groups.

Nationalism

We noted earlier that the history of many states is characterized by the often coercive efforts of state-builders to craft an identity – usually national, though sometimes religious – to accompany their political project. While such efforts lie deep in the past of some established liberal democracies, to the point the nation is taken for granted, in other states they are a recent memory or in some cases still in progress. With separatist movements inspired by *ethnic nationalism* the process has to begin again. There are long-lived but as yet unsuccessful separatist movements (in the sense that they have yet to gain a state of their own, despite some political autonomy) in Quebec in Canada, the Basque country in Spain, Scotland and Wales in the United Kingdom. All seek to solidify identities separate from those of the state they are trying to break away from. In three out of these four cases the struggle is peaceful, but in the Basque country it has been accompanied by violence – targeting both the Spanish state and moderate Basques who sought some accommodation with it. The first task of separatists is to convince their target population that they do have an identity and a history different from that of the dominant identity and history of the state they share with others. One possible strategy is to provoke an oppressive state backlash that will gain sympathy for their cause.

Cultural nationalism is a bit different from ethnic nationalism because it does not restrict full membership of the nation to those with the right ancestry. Thus it can be inclusive of a variety of ethnic groups – provided they subscribe to the national culture. Assimilationist policies of the sort we discussed earlier in this chapter can be deployed by cultural nationalists. Cultural nationalism has long characterized France. Because the ideals of the French republic are also seen officially as universal ideals, there should be few barriers to anyone (from anywhere in the world) subscribing to them. But this universalism has a distinctively French cultural tinge – especially when it comes to the primacy of French language and the secular, unitary and republican character of the state.

Cultural nationalism is also very important in the United States, (like France), the USA also considers its own political ideals to be universal ones. US cultural nationalism received powerful expression in Samuel Huntington's (2004) book *Who Are We?* which portrays an historically protestant and liberal individualist culture being undermined by large-scale legal and illegal immigration from Mexico and elsewhere in Latin America. Huntington does not fear the catholic religion of these immigrants so much as the collectivist political traditions, weak commitments to individual liberty, and Spanish language they bring. His policy agenda could involve assimilation, or restrictions on immigration, or probably a mixture of both. The singing of national anthems at sports events, the construction of monuments, holidays to commemorate key events in the nation's history, patriotic ceremonies involving royals or presidents, can also play a part in solidifying cultural nationalism.

In established liberal democracies, cultural nationalism has often been a staple of conservative politics. If conservatives can convince middle and lower income people of their allegiance first and foremost to the culture of the nation, that ought to reduce the appeal of alternative identifications – such as social class, which might lead people to support social democratic parties seeking income redistribution. Conservative parties are correspondingly often hostile to multiculturalism. When it comes to education policy, they are likely to favour a curriculum that teaches a positive view of the nation's history and accomplishments, picking out its great leaders and individual geniuses rather than its slave owners, war criminals and madmen. In Australia, around 2000, conservative Prime Minister John Howard decried the 'black armband' view that he believed characterizes the overwhelmingly leftist academic historians of Australia. The discipline of Australian history has been engaged in 'history wars' (Macintyre and Clark 2004) as the left establishment has been challenged by conservative historians financed by private think-tanks, who particularly downplay the mistreatment of Aborigines by European settlers. However, it is also possible for those on the left of the political spectrum to try and claim the nation for themselves, and to associate it with possibilities for more progressive policies. The leftist author George Orwell was also a British cultural nationalist, contemplating socialist revolution even as he celebrated Englishness in his 1941 essay on *The Lion and the Unicorn* (Orwell 1990). More recently the radical British folk singer Billy Bragg (2006) has styled himself *The Progressive Patriot*.

Despite some contemporary associations with cultural conservativism, separatism, and ethnic assertiveness, nationalism also has strong historical connection with liberalism and democracy. In the days when empires covered much of Europe, nationalists, liberals and democrats could make common cause against both the despotism of empires and their overseas colonies and more local despotisms. Writing in the eighteenth century, Jean-Jacques Rousseau in *The Government of Poland* saw nationalism as a way for a beleaguered society such as Poland to secure the individual freedoms of its people. The Italian *Risorgiomento* (1848–1860) was both liberal and nationalist, as were the other attempted revolutions that swept France, what is now Germany, and the Austro-Hungarian Empire in 1848.

Liberal nationalism perhaps peaked in 1918 with the enunciation of the principle of self-determination for European societies by US President Woodrow Wilson. Some of the multi-ethnic states created at this time had troubled histories, and much later Yugoslavia disintegrated violently into its component parts; Czechoslovakia split more peacefully. Outside Europe liberal nationalism inspired independence movements in the 1930s and 1940s. Liberal, multi-ethnic and secular politics survived in India to shape its liberal democracy after independence in 1948. But in Pakistan, Africa and elsewhere, state independence saw liberal nationalism quickly extinguished by rival doctrines and dictatorships. Liberal nationalists played major roles in the collapse of the Soviet rule in eastern Europe in 1989.

Today, liberal nationalists can be found arguing that membership of a nation is instrumental to the individual wellbeing prized by liberalism. Kymlicka (1995) believes that only the nation provides the range of worthwhile choices that together comprise a culture – though he is especially attuned to the rights of minority nations and cultures within states, as we will see shortly. Miller (1995) claims that instruments of justice such as the welfare state require the support of a nation, because only a nation can yield the sort of social solidarity that social justice in practice requires. But beyond defending an emphasis on justice within the nation-state against cosmopolitans, who believe obligations should extend across boundaries to encompass all humankind, the prescriptions associated with such an approach are not substantial.

Group rights

There may be times when a state cannot achieve the kind of unified identity that ethnic, cultural and liberal nationalists in their very different ways all seek. Such an impasse is especially likely in developed liberal democratic states that abide by international norms forbidding repression, expulsion, genocide and forced conversion. Consociational power sharing, electoral system design and deliberation across difference (discussed earlier) may all play their parts managing the identity claims of such states' national minorities. But they do not address the question of recognizing minorities head-on.

A direct approach to this question would involve granting rights to particular minorities. The idea of group rights has been advocated for just about every oppressed category of people – based on gender, race, sexual orientation, disability, age, social class, and so forth (Young 1990). But the most compelling case for such rights applies to national minorities who do not accept the dominant national identity accompanying the state. The most well-studied case is that of Canada, in some ways an exemplary liberal democracy. Canada is home to Quebecois who reject Anglophone domination of the Canadian state, indigenous peoples who lay claim to territory and protection of a way of life, and legions of political philosophers who study these questions. So it is no surprise that much of the best work in this area has been done by Canadians (for example, Kymlicka 1995).

In the liberal tradition, rights are properly held only by individuals – to protect them against the state and against each other and to enable individual flourishing. The idea of group rights is that individuals can have different rights depending on which group they belong to. For example, an indigenous person may have rights to hunting and fishing, to collective sorts or property, and to ceremonial uses of land that are denied to non-indigenous people. Francophones in Quebec may have a right to impose their language on non-native speakers of French who live in the province, for example, in education and peoples' dealings with government. Liberal advocates of such measures rest their case upon the idea that a flourishing of the national group in question is instrumental to the wellbeing, self-respect, and autonomy of the individuals who belong to it. Thus liberals such as Kymlicka (1995) prefer to speak of 'group-differentiated rights' rather than group rights per se; the right is held by individuals, rather than by the group collectively.

Group rights are controversial. Orthodox liberals see in group rights the betrayal of the liberal ideal in which all individuals are treated equally. As we will see in Chapter 10, some feminists worry that practices oppressing women may be shielded by rights granted to cultural minorities. Conservatives and communitarians, discussed in Chapter 12, believe that group rights fracture the national community that should be associated with the state.

Conclusion

The politics of identity is almost by definition plural, in the sense of involving multiple identities. This is true even at the extreme when genocidal state-building elites are trying to construct a single national identity – this identity itself only makes sense in terms of rejection and repression of some other identity. So for radical Serb ethnic nationalists, the Croatian, Bosnian, Albanian and Yugoslav identities all had to be rejected for people who were to become part of the Serbian state. The rhetorical stakes were high. As Serb leader Slobodan Milosevic (later indicted for war crimes) put it: 'The loss of national identity is the greatest defeat a nation can know'.

Pluralism as a theory of the state can accommodate a politics of identity – but to do so it has to move beyond both its mid twentieth century focus on the material interests of groups, and the neo-pluralist emphasis on the power of corporations. In particular, the relationships between those holding different identities have to receive much more attention – especially when particular identities seem to require validation in the suppression of alternative identities. We have argued that identity conflict can be managed in a top down fashion only by violent means. Once the state could try to purge particular identities, but that is no longer possible in most liberal democracies. In a democratic era, identity conflicts really ought to be capable of being approached in a democratic fashion, although the challenge of how to do so is a major one that has not yet found a universally applicable or compelling solution. Consociational, electoral system, agonistic and deliberative approaches all offer some insights, but a widely applicable set of effective solutions has yet to be found.

Part III

Critiques of the State

In recent decades theories of the state have been expanded and enriched by several significant and thorough critiques, which expose some blind spots of both classical theories and the more recent pluralist developments covered in Part I. In Part III we take a close look at the content of these critiques, and the political changes they prescribe. The first takes seriously the democratic deficiencies of existing liberal democratic states. In Chapter 9 we look at democratic remedies, including proposals for basic income and stakeholder grants that would more effectively equalize opportunities in society, create more participatory democracy, and a republican invigoration of civic life. We pay special attention to deliberative democracy, which is both a normative political theory about how authentic politics should work, and a reform movement for the introduction of better and more inclusive communication in political life.

Chapter 10 turns to the feminist critique of the state, which liberals, pluralists, and others long failed to notice was dominated by male practices and male interests. Feminist critiques now come in many varieties, some of which can be linked to established theories (such as liberalism and Marxism), while others distance themselves from all previous theories of the state. Feminists have also generated plenty of ideas about how to rectifygender inequalities. Just as feminists point out that established theories failed to notice male domination, so environmentalists argue that these same theories failed to notice that human political and economic systems are embedded in larger ecological systems. Chapter 11 examines the ecological failings of contemporary states, and of all previous theories of the state. Environmentalism too comes in more or less radical varieties, with more or less radical political agendas.

Chapter 12 explores a very different kind of critique, a conservative stance that sees participatory democracy, feminism and environmentalism, (as well as market liberalism and identity politics run wild), as just further contributing to the woes of contemporary states and societies. This conservative reaction against progressive politics seeks instead a restoration of virtues grounded in harmonious communities and social morality. There is also a very different kind of neo-conservative approach to the state. It throws the caution of traditional conservatism to the wind, and wants to re-make the world in a hurry to re-establish traditional moral values and commitments to the collective good of society. Neo-conservatism flourished as an orientation in US foreign policy in the George W. Bush presidency, but at home it also sought to reverse a perceived moral decay of American society.

Chapter 9

Democratic Critique and Renewal

In 1989 Francis Fukuyama famously proclaimed 'the end of history', by which he meant the exhaustion of any serious global rival to liberal democracy plus capitalism as a political model (see also Fukuyama 1992). Though allowing variations on the liberal democratic model (encompassing, for example, Scandinavian social democracy), in Fukuyama's account the days of struggling for any qualitatively better form of democracy were over. Political scientists who studied the transition of post-communist societies and other countries escaping authoritarianism almost all treated democratization in terms of the spread of a standard liberal democratic model – free and fair elections plus a basic set of rights guaranteed in a constitution – to ever more parts of the world. After 2001, the USA under President George W. Bush enthusiastically took up democratization as a global project, again defining democracy in terms consistent with Fukuyama and the democratization scholars. In all of these endeavours, there was no sense that democracy itself might need deepening – not least in the homes of liberal democracy in the West. In this chapter we sketch the degree to which liberal democracies themselves may in fact fail to live up to democratic ideals – and what might be done about it.

The Democratic Deficit in Liberal Democracies

Yet all is not necessarily well with contemporary liberal democracies. The term 'democratic deficit' is often associated with the European Union, whose institutions initially grew up without many of the democratic trappings of its component states. Yet many states, in the European Union and beyond, may suffer democratic deficits of their own. In previous chapters we surveyed a number of democratic flaws that can be present to a greater or lesser degree in some or all liberal democratic states. All of them obstruct the effective realization of popular control in politics and public policy. These flaws include:

- Citizens who have little interest in or knowledge of political affairs.

- Domination of policy making by an elite, behind a democratic façade.
- Ideologies that pervade society, but serve some dominant interests.
- The privileged position of business in seemingly pluralist policy making.
- Policy making that has to please financial and capital markets, not the voters.
- Private interests that exploit the state for their own material gain, at public expense.
- Self-interested legislators pushing irresponsible spending proposals that will benefit their constituencies and financial backers.
- Bureaucracies that maximize their own budgets or pursue their own priorities, rather than serve the public interest.
- Arbitrariness and instability in aggregating the preferences of voters and legislators.
- Limited channels for social movements and organized interests to exercise influence on government.
- Lack of accountability in low-visibility networked governance, where it is not clear where power lies.
- Political parties that offer no real choice to voters.
- Electoral systems that can produce perverse results, such as governments supported by a minority of voters.
- Expensive election campaigns dominated by the need to raise money from wealthy interests.
- Declining turnout in elections.
- Falling memberships in political parties.
- Electoral politics that centre around spin, manipulation and negative advertising.
- The resolution of contested elections by legal manoeuvring rather than the will of the people.
- Repression of minorities on the part of state-building elites.
- The existence of alienated minorities with weak attachments to the state.
- Incivility verging on violence if the politics of identity goes bad.
- The attenuation of democratic rights in the name of 'security' – exacerbated by the 'war on terror' proclaimed in the United States and elsewhere.

These flaws are highlighted by different theories of the state, so it is highly unlikely that any particular commentator would think all of them important. One response to them might be to lower our expectations of democracy: to retreat to a minimalist model where at least there is some chance of particularly bad governments sometimes being thrown out by voters – but nothing more (see Przeworski 1999). However, it is possible to respond more positively. When we discussed these problems individually in previous chapters we also canvassed numerous solutions to them. In this chapter we take a somewhat different approach. Rather than address each flaw in isolation, we treat them as symptoms of some more general democratic malaise. Likewise, the remedies we address here have an across-the-board intent of democratic renewal. In the 1927 words of the American philosopher John Dewey, they contend that 'the cure for the ailments of democracy is more democracy'.

'More democracy' here refers in particular to the *authenticity* of democracy: the degree to which popular control is substantive rather than symbolic, engaged by critical, reflective, and competent citizens. This notion begs the question of where exactly such citizens might be found – and why they do not assert themselves spontaneously in the existing institutions of the state.

Civic education

Discovering where active citizens might be found starts from recognition that citizens are not like mushrooms; they do not just spontaneously appear from the ground, without cultivation. Citizens are the products of the societies in which they live (for immigrants, the story is more complicated). Most states have an education system designed to produce people with particular sorts of knowledge and capabilities. If the citizens of liberal democracies often seem uninterested, uninformed and apathetic, then perhaps that reflects in part a deficiency of education. A remedy might then be found in better education. As Barber (1992: 15) puts it, 'there is only one route to democracy: education'. Education for political participation is normally styled civic education, and there is a long tradition of advocacy on its behalf. Indeed, this has often been seen as one of the key tasks of political science (Leonard 1995).

Civic education of a fairly conventional sort involves the schooling of individuals in the fundamentals of the political system in which they live. Civics in US high schools is like this. Students learn all about federalism, the branches of government, the Bill of Rights, how laws are made and so forth. The problem with this sort of civic education is that it does nothing to enhance the critical capacities and political competencies of those at the receiving end (though Brody 2001 demonstrates a weak but statistically significant impact of participation in a civic education programme upon tolerance in US high school students). Typically the curriculum will contain a large measure of celebration of the institutions and the state being studied. At worst, such education – especially when combined with national history – can be put in the service of ethnic nationalism.

An alternative approach to civic education would focus more on developing the critical competencies of students. So Amy Gutmann (1999) advocates democratic education to produce qualities of openness to different ideas, awareness of diversity of opinion and identity, respect for those with different values and beliefs, enthusiasm for debate about ethical issues, along with more traditional historical knowledge. Benjamin Barber (1992) recommends an additional emphasis on community service for students: not as a matter of charity, but rather as a way of cementing a commitment to the common life of the republic. Unfortunately these sorts of civic education are quite rare. For good reason: why would those in positions of political authority promote a curriculum that would enable citizens to be more critical and challenging toward those in authority?

Basic income and stakeholder grants

The idea that the best way to reinvigorate democracy is through civic education is a very American one, and it is no coincidence that the best writings on democratic education are mostly American. A more European approach to raising the capacities of ordinary individuals to participate in politics would focus instead on their material endowments. In many ways the welfare state has been an instrument of economic and so political equality, though often it has been hedged with stigma attached to particular sorts of welfare, turning its recipients into supplicants rather than confident citizens. Welfare states vary in the degree to which they do this (Esping-Anderson 1990). The more generous universalistic welfare states of Scandinavia in particular have allocated benefits to all as a matter of right rather than need, and so avoid this problem. The most ambitious universalistic proposal, yet to be adopted anywhere, is for a basic income that every citizen would receive with no strings attached (van Parijs 1995). Basic income would be financed out of general taxation and administered by government. Every citizen would receive the same amount. It could be set at a level sufficient to provide the basics of a decent life – or indeed at some lower or higher level, though it is hard to see why it should be set at a level lower than that necessary for subsistence needs. Proponents of basic income argue that in van Parijs's (1995) terms it would help secure 'real freedom for all' by releasing everyone from worry about how to meet basic material needs. Because it is a matter of right for everyone, it would remove many of the paternalistic aspects of the welfare state by freeing recipients from the discretionary power of government bureaucrats. Critics would argue that a paternalistic element remains because individuals could still come to depend on a monthly allowance from government (Cunliffe and Erreygers 2003: 108). Opponents also argue that basic income is a largely inefficient means of taking money away from people and then giving it back to them; that it would enable many people to live a life of leisure without working or contributing to society.

As an alternative to a continuous stream of basic income, Ackerman and Alstott (1999) propose a scheme of stakeholder grants. They suggest that at the age of 21, every citizen with a high school diploma be given a large financial 'stake' by government – for the United Sates in 1999, they suggested $80,000 (paid for initially from a 2 per cent wealth tax). This would be paid in four annual instalments of $20,000. The individual can then do with this money what they please: invest it, use it to pay for education, buy a house, start a business or even squander it. The only proviso is that they have to pay it back to government when they die (with interest). The idea is that the money provides financial independence and security for young adults, and so promotes equality of opportunity. The scheme ought to encourage individual responsibility and independence, for individuals have to live with the consequences of any decision about what they do with their stake. Stakeholder grants may be more attuned to American ideas about individual responsibility and investment, though their unconditional nature would still raise strong objections from those who see it as potentially a subsidy to the workshy, and a handout of something for nothing. Basic income and stakeholder grants alike are seen by their proponents as instruments of social justice, but also as ways of inculcating a sense of confident citizenship by removing financial insecurity and promoting social belonging. Given that neither has been implemented anywhere, there is little evidence on such matters.

Civic education, basic income and stakeholder grants are all targeted at improving the endowments and capacities of the individual citizens who are the building blocks of a democracy. An alternative set of approaches to democratic renewal to which we now turn, emphasizes instead the political circumstances of citizen interaction.

Participatory Democracy and Civic Republicanism

There is a long tradition in political theory critical of the limited character of electoral democracy, viewing real democracy in terms of more direct participation by individuals in decisions that affect their own lives. As Jean-Jacques Rousseau put it in 1762 in his *Social Contract*: 'The people of England thinks itself free, but it is grossly mistaken; it is free only during the election of members of parliament'. Participatory democrats want people to be truly free much more of the time, through active involvement in public affairs. The participatory ideal actually goes back to ancient Greece. It was advocated by the foremost statesman of Athens, Pericles, who argued in his Funeral Oration for the War Dead of Athens: 'Here each individual is interested not only in his own affairs, but in the affairs of the state as well . . . We do not say that a man who takes no interest in politics is a man who minds his own business, we say he has no business here at all.'

Real-world participatory democracies have been historically rare. Workers' cooperatives have sometimes tried to manage economic enterprises on participatory lines, a development sometimes called 'economic democracy' (Dahl 1985). The largest such cooperative is at Mondragon in the Basque region of Spain, which employs around 20,000 workers in a variety of enterprises. Worker self-management was also widespread and official government policy in Yugoslavia until the country fell apart in ethnic warfare in the 1990s. Examples have also been found in the United States, where (for example) tree planters in the Pacific Northwest have organized as workers' cooperatives (Mackie 1994).

Workplace democracy can be justified in at least two ways. The first is that the workplace is itself a kind of political system, and that if democracy is desirable generally, then it should prevail in the workplace too (Dahl 1985). The second is that individuals who participate in decision-making in the workplace will gain confidence in their capacities which will make them better citizens of the larger political system, better able to understand public affairs and participate in public policy making processes (Pateman 1970). In this light, workplace democratization is a step on the road to the participatory democratization of the state. Evidence on this claim is scarce.

One of the more ambitious programmes for participatory democratization of the political system as a whole is advanced by Benjamin Barber (1984). He combines a scathing attack on the inadequacy of existing liberal democracy with a detailed programme for 'strong democracy'. Barber's programme involves, among other things, neighbourhood assemblies, universal access to communications technology, citizen-controlled criminal justice (which might easily be linked to later proposals for 'restorative justice'), referendums on a national scale, representation by lot at the local level (as in ancient Athens, where officeholders are selected at random), universal military service (with a civil option), volunteer community service programmes, workplace democracy and a transformed architecture for constructing physical public spaces where people might more effectively assemble and communicate. Together, these reforms would direct the attention of individuals toward their membership of the community and their tasks as citizens. One way of interpreting this programme is that it is the opposite of market liberalism, which stresses the individual, private self-interested motivation, and the joining of individuals in market transactions. The growing importance of market liberalism since the 1980s (discussed in Chapter 4) have therefore been very bad news indeed for the feasibility of the strong democracy programme.

One specific innovation that has received a great deal of attention since 2000 is participatory budgeting, which began in Brazil in the 1980s. It is most famously practiced in the city of Porto Alegre (Baiocchi 2001) and has since been copied in other countries. The process starts with a number of regional assemblies that anyone can attend. Participants in the regional assemblies elect representatives to regional budget forums, who in turn elect members of municipal budget councils. Participation rates by citizens in the initial regional assemblies approach 10 per cent. Such exercises seem much more feasible at the local level that at the larger state level.

Porto Alegre notwithstanding, enthusiasm for participatory democracy probably peaked in the 1960s and 1970s, when it was part of the programme of a 'new left' seeking an alternative to a socialism that had become associated with centralized economic planning and control by bureaucrats. Many of the cooperatives and social movement groups that organized themselves on a participatory, non-hierarchical basis proved very hard to sustain in the face of the sheer demands they imposed upon participants' time and generosity of spirit. The fate of such experiments was often to disintegrate, or to adopt more conventional, hierarchical management styles. Thus it would be easy to dismiss participatory democracy as passé – if it proves so hard to sustain even in small workplaces or groups of like-minded political activists on this basis, what hope is there for the participatory democratization of larger, diverse and complex societies? One answer may be that there is no need to democratize all political processes all of the time, just some of them some of the time.

In recent years the enthusiasm that once went into advocacy of participatory democracy has been channelled into two enterprises that share similar commitments to civic renewal in politics, but are a bit more guarded on how much participation is actually required of the ordinary citizen. These two alternatives are, respectively, civic republicanism and deliberative democracy.

Republicanism is actually older than democracy, dating back to ancient Athens and especially Rome. (It should not be confused with the US Republican party, which does not pursue republican ideals that have much to do with an active role for the citizenry). Republicanism can be defined in terms of mixed government (with checks and balances across different parts of government), the rule of law, and above all public-spirited citizenship. 'Republicans will attempt to design political constitutions that promote discussion and debate among the citizenry; they will be hostile to systems that promote lawmaking as deals or bargains among self-interested private groups' (Sunstein 1988: 1549). In the last 2,500 years republicanism has come in a number of varieties, some of which involve taming rather than promoting citizen involvement in politics – for example, the political theory of James Madison, as embodied in the constitution of the United States. Here we focus on the wave that began in the 1950s with the work of Hannah Arendt (1958). For contemporary civic republicans such as Sunstein (1988), Sandel (1996) and Dagger (1997), the hallmark of politics ought to be a commitment to the common good that is the essence of civic virtue, rather than partial interest, still less material self-interest. Thus civic republicans are hostile to any kind of pluralism based on material interest – and indeed, highly suspicious of pluralism in general, on the grounds that it obstructs community solidarity and the pursuit of common, civic ends. Individuals ought to subordinate their particular interests to a general good that is manifested in the institutions of the republic – not in any ethnic nationalism. Of course citizens can disagree about the content of the general good, so there is plenty of opportunity for vigorous political debate. Arendt's conception of republicanism was particularly heroic: she believed that only in such civic politics could human life find its true meaning.

But what exactly does civic republicanism offer when it comes to reform of the state, as opposed to exhortation on behalf of a certain kind of political action and behaviour? We might start by looking for positive historical examples. Beyond looking back to ancient Athens and the Roman Republic, Arendt believes that in the modern world, authentic republican politics can only be found in the spontaneous emergence of citizens' councils in revolutionary circumstances. Examples would include the Paris Commune of 1871, the Russian revolution of 1917 (before it was taken over by Lenin and the Bolsheviks), the Spanish Civil War of the 1930s, Hungary's rebellion against the Soviet Union in 1956 and the somewhat similar 'Prague spring' of 1967. The revolutions of 1989 in east central Europe could be applauded by civic republicans. In Czechoslovakia in particular, the main revolutionary body was the 'Civic Forum', and the revolutionary-turned-President Vaclav Havel espoused a politics of the common good against sectional interests – associated with a 'politics of truth' as opposed to interest. But as with previous civic republican moments, this kind of heroic politics did not last long before giving way to a more routine politics of sectional interests.

Beyond such fleeting moments, what do civic republicans have to offer consolidated liberal democratic states – other than criticism? In large part it is a matter of established institutions adopting different principles to guide their actions, as opposed to any drastic institutional overhaul. For example, Braithwaite and Pettit (1990) outline a republican approach to criminal justice that avoids retribution, does not discriminate in favour of wealthy white-collar criminals and against the poor and disadvantaged, and generally contributes to a more politically equal republican society. Sunstein (1988) endorses campaign finance reform in order to curb some gross inequalities of financial influence in politics. Civic republicans are also likely to favour the more activist civic education we discussed earlier, and strengthened public deliberation. Yet as a reform programme, civic republicanism has so far offered much less than its deliberative democracy cousin, to which we now turn.

Deliberative Democracy

Deliberation is a particular kind of communicative process in which individuals reflect upon their own views in the light of what others have to say, ideally in context free from coercion, manipulation and deception. Highlighting deliberation means that 'Talk-centric democratic theory replaces voting-centric democratic theory' (Chambers 2003: 308) – though voting is not ruled out.

Origins and core assumptions

Democratic theory took a deliberative turn around 1990, and works on deliberative democracy have mushroomed since then. However, the basic idea is as old as democracy itself: it is that central to democracy should be a particular kind of communication, involving the giving of good reasons and reflection upon the points advanced by others. The *polis* of Ancient Athens involved not just voting, but also vigorous political debate. And the Athenian ideal of citizenship involved engaging in argument about the common good. Two hundred years ago the conservative philosopher Edmund Burke put deliberation (interpreted as mature and calm reflection) at the heart of politics. In the nineteenth century, liberals such as John Stuart Mill highlighted the importance of extensive and informed public debate, although Mill himself also worried about it getting out of hand. In the early twentieth century, the leading American philosopher John Dewey saw democracy in terms of a community of problem-solving inquirers communicating with each other. (For a history of deliberative democracy, see the introduction of Bohman and Rehg 1997). But only very recently did the term deliberative democracy come to be used (first by Bessette 1980). The success of the deliberative turn was confirmed in the 1990s when the leading continental European philosopher (Habermas 1996) and the most important Anglo-American political philosopher (Rawls 1997: 771–2) both described themselves as deliberative democrats. Deliberative democracy could, then, draw on post-Marxist critical theory (via Habermas), liberalism (via Mill and Rawls) and even (via Burke) conservatism. Deliberative democracy is not just political theory: it has inspired a wide range of reforms in liberal democracies in recent years. A key testing ground might even prove to be China, where some claim it is being embraced by some in the Chinese Communist Party hierarchy as an alternative to standard western electoral conceptions of democracy. Citizen deliberation is increasingly found in local-level innovations in Chinese practice, though the core of the national state is not touched (Leib and He 2006).

Deliberative democracy is grounded in an assumption about individuals that stresses their capacity to reflect upon their own preferences, values and judgments in light of their participation in political dialogue with other individuals. This conception of individual action is completely different to that deployed by market liberals (see Chapter 5), who treat individual preferences as fixed and given, and see action solely in terms of individuals' pursuit of pre-given preferences. Deliberative action is also different from the kind of motivation assumed by mid twentieth century US pluralists, for whom interests were defined by groups that emerged from society, and once fixed by that process were then expressed in politics – not changed by politics. However, more flexible kinds of pluralism ought to be able accommodate deliberation about the content of interests. Elite theorists would see deliberative democracy as a sideshow, on the grounds that members of a ruling elite are perfectly aware of their own interests and how to go about achieving them, with no need to reflect upon them. Those who are not members of the elite would only be fooling themselves if they thought that their reflective preferences mattered much. Marxists would scorn deliberative democracy because they see interests defined by class positions, and a clash of interests between different social classes that cannot be reconciled in debate. Deliberative democracy does, then, challenge the sorts of individual motivation assumed by all the classical theories of the state.

Aside from its assumptions about individuals, deliberative democracy must also assume that public policy decisions can be affected by the outcome of deliberation. In some theories of the state talk is cheap and ultimately of little consequence. Of course public policy is talked about in the media and debated in the legislature and elsewhere – but mid twentieth century US pluralists, elite theorists, Marxists and market liberals alike believe that it is ultimately the pre-determined content of interests and the relative power of those who hold them that determine policy content. Now, for policy decisions to be affected by deliberation does not mean that deliberation must always be decisive in determining policy. But it must have some influence – otherwise deliberators themselves might begin to wonder about the point of all their communication and reflection. Quite where that influence comes from and how it takes effect in policy is a matter of disagreement among deliberative democrats, as we will see in the next two sections.

Society and politics

In a deliberative democracy, state and society ought to be connected by means that are themselves deliberative. In a deliberative democracy legitimacy depends on the right, opportunity, and capacity of those subject to a collective decision to participate in consequential deliberation about the content of the decision in question (Cohen 1989: 22; Benhabib 1996: 68). 'As political decisions are characteristically imposed on *all*, it seems reasonable to seek, as an essential condition for legitimacy, the deliberation of *all* or more precisely, the right of all to participate in deliberation' (Manin 1987: 352). Citizens need to be able to participate in deliberation about a decision, rather than simply vote upon it. Claims on behalf of particular policy options must be made in terms that, on reflection, the affected individuals can, accept (Gutmann and Thompson 1996).

Applied to contemporary large and complex societies, the theory of deliberative democracy immediately runs into a problem of scale. Face-to-face deliberation is easy to organize in small groups, of up to around 20 people. But what if millions of people have an interest in an issue? That is not easy. 'Deliberation is not an activity for the demos . . . 100 million of them, or even 1 million or 100,000, cannot plausibly 'reason together' (Walzer 1999: 68). However, there are a number of possible solutions to this problem of scale (Dryzek 2001).

The first obvious solution is to restrict the number of deliberators – perhaps to elected representatives. This would suit deliberative democrats who emphasize deliberation within the legislature (for example Bessette 1994). In his 1774 *Speech to the Electors of Bristol*, the conservative thinker and politician Edmund Burke described Parliament as a 'deliberative assembly of one nation, with one interest, that of the whole'. For Burke, legislators were to deliberate on behalf of their constituents, whose voice was not to be heard: 'Your representative owes you, not his industry alone, but his judgment; and he betrays, instead of serving you, if he sacrifices it to your opinion'. The prominent contemporary political philosopher Robert Goodin (2003) echoes Burke's conservatism in stressing 'deliberation within' – that is, deliberation as a matter of personal reflection in which a political leader thinks seriously about the interests of citizens and others, but does not seek to engage them in actual dialogue.

The problem with relying on elected representatives to deliver on the legitimacy claims of deliberative democracy is that election campaigns themselves are often not very deliberative. They feature image-making, deception, the making of empty promises that cannot possibly be kept, distortion of the record and positions of the other side, the scapegoating of unpopular minorities and character assassination. In the United States, the media campaign is dominated by negative advertising directed at the alleged personal failings of the other side's candidate. One solution would be to make campaigns more deliberative. Gastil (2000) suggests holding deliberative events in conjunction with campaigns; but this begs the question of how such events can make themselves felt against the weight of non-deliberative communication.

Elections are not the only way to identify deliberating representatives. Goodin's 'deliberation within' suggests that deliberation be conducted by the people best able to internalize the outlooks of the public. If we define the most important such outlook as the interests of the public as a whole, then experts in 'public reason' may be the best deliberators. This explains the enthusiasm of Rawls (1993: 231) for the US Supreme Court. The trouble with the Supreme Court is that it may be a deliberative institution, but it is not a democratic one. Moreover, the justices *only* 'deliberate within' – they do not converse with each other about their decisions.

A more democratic non-electoral way to identify deliberating representatives is to follow the ancient Athenian model and select them by lot – just as juries are selected for court cases. Many such designs are available, and we will discuss them later. The people so selected can be representative of the population in a statistical sense. But they are not representatives in the normal political sense, because they lack any accountability to a broader public outside the deliberative forum (Parkinson 2006).

Another solution to the problem of scale is to think of democratic legitimacy in terms of the resonance of collective decisions, with public opinion revealed in the engagement of discourses in the public sphere

(Dryzek 2001). This approach would fit with the emphasis placed by some deliberative democrats on broader debates involving social movements, the media, political activists, interest organizations, even conversations in cafes and pubs (Dryzek 2000; Benhabib 1996). Of course not all this communication is deliberative, and some might be very heavily manipulated by sensationalists, propagandists, public relations specialists and spin doctors. A discourse is a shared language-based form that enables understanding of the world, embodying assumptions, judgments, contentions, dispositions and capabilities. Those who subscribe to a particular discourse can then recognize and process sensory inputs into coherent stories or accounts, shared in intersubjectively meaningful fashion. Examples of discourses would include sustainable development in environmental policy, a restorative justice approach to criminal justice, or human rights in international politics. Market liberalism (discussed in Chapter 4) is a discourse that contains a theory of the state.

Rather than focus upon the electoral connection between the state and the public sphere, a number of other mechanisms for transmission of public opinion to government can be addressed. These involve communication rather than the counting of heads in elections. They might include government's fear of political instability, leading to policy that addresses the concerns raised by disadvantaged groups in society. (Piven and Cloward 1971 explain the rise of the welfare state in these terms at least in the United States). Social movement leaders can use rhetoric designed to move electoral majorities and their representatives. Consider, for example, the powerful rhetoric employed by Dr. Martin Luther King Jr. in the 1950s and 1960s, when African Americans were excluded from participating in electoral politics, especially in the southern states of the US. King appealed to the emotional attachment of white Americans to the Declaration of Independence and the Constitution, asking for them to be taken literally, as well as to Christian tradition. The engagement of discourses in the public sphere may also produce a cultural change that eventually pervades politics – many of the successes of environmentalism and feminism since 1970 can be explained in these terms. And occasionally the power of arguments made in the public sphere can be taken up by the state. 'Discursive legitimacy' is then secured when a public policy is consistent with the constellation of discourses found in the public sphere, but only to the extent this constellation is itself under the reflective control of competent actors (Dryzek 2001). The latter condition means attending to the conditions of communication in the public sphere, and the degree to which they are free from domination, propaganda, deception, manipulation, legal restraints on freedom of speech and association, and so forth. Public opinion can then be thought of as the outcome of the engagement of discourses as transmitted to the state. The scale problem is solved because the number of deliberating citizens is indeterminate. It could be very large – as when a social movement captures the public attention (environmentalism did this around 1970, and again around 1990 in many countries). More typically it will be quite small. But unlike the other approaches to the scale problem, no exclusions are required.

Government and policy making

Some deliberative theorists have been silent on the institutional specifics of a deliberative democracy, focusing on the activity of deliberation itself rather than where exactly it might be located. But institutional design matters a lot for deliberation, and the content of deliberation is likely to be very different in different institutional locations – and in settings outside formal institutions, such as the informal public sphere. Habermas (1996) outlines a 'two track' account of deliberative democracy that involves both the generation of public opinion in the informal public sphere and debate in the legislature.

It should be stressed that deliberative democracy is mainly a normative theory, capable of providing prescriptions and evaluations of existing practices. It has no stand-alone explanatory theory of how the state works and how policy gets made, though it can be deployed in connection with many such theories. For example, if we adopt a pluralist account of the centrality of organized interests in policy making, we could try to reform the avenues in which their influence is felt to make them more deliberative. This could be done by restricting backdoor access to legislators, penalizing material inducements offered by groups to legislators, and specifying that all interest groups active in lobbying make their cases in public hearings, where they can be challenged by one another and by sceptical legislators. A more heavy-handed approach might involve government intervention in associational life to subsidize the organization and argumentative ability of groups representing the underprivileged – a proposal we discussed in Chapter 6.

Let us now look at the various institutions where deliberation can be sought. Following Edmond Burke, the most obvious place to look for deliberation in the institutions of the state would be in the *legislature* (Bessette 1994; Uhr 1998). Legislatures after all are debating chambers. Yet members of disciplined parties there must vote the party line, even if they are persuaded that it is wrong. Other things being equal, we might expect legislatures where party discipline is weak (such as the US Congress) to have greater deliberative capacity than legislators where party discipline is strong. But even when votes are a foregone conclusion before debate starts – which will be the case when a government controls a parliamentary majority in a system with disciplined parties – debate still occurs. Arguments on behalf of the legislation must be advanced, and no government likes to provide the opposition with ammunition. There is a big difference between an elected government ruling by decree, and one presenting its policies for parliamentary debate – even when it knows in advance the outcome of the vote following debate.

The way the legislature is structured can make a difference to the quality of debate. A deliberative advantage of the upper house in bicameral legislatures is that it can be a 'house of review' not necessarily dominated by the discipline of the parties forming a governing majority and its opposition in the lower house. Members may therefore be comparatively free to craft their own arguments from a more detached standpoint. Of course partisan bile is not ruled out either, and upper house members may come from the self-same parties represented in the lower house. Where the upper house shares legislative responsibility, as in the US and Australia, it is less of a house of review and so likely to be no more deliberative than the lower house, for better or for worse.

Much of the work in legislatures is actually done in committees that prepare legislation before it is presented on the floor of the legislature as a whole. Because committees have comparatively low visibility there may be less incentive for legislators speaking there to try to score partisan points. One particular kind of committee that exists in many bicameral legislatures is the one designed to reconcile differences in the language of legislation as passed in the upper and lower houses: in the US Congress, this is called a Conference Committee. This kind of committee may be among the most promising locations for constructive deliberation because there is a clear practical task at hand not defined in terms of opposing parties or coalitions, but simply different versions of proposals. For this reason, such committees are emphasized by Steiner *et al.* (2004) in their comparative empirical studies of the deliberative quality of legislative debates: they deploy a 'discourse quality index' based on a coding of every intervention in a debate.

In Chapter 7 we saw that parliamentary democracies can be arrayed on a continuum from majoritarian to consensual. Legislatures in consensual democracies are normally multi-party because they are elected by proportional representation. They may be more effectively deliberative since the fight between government and opposition does not dominate all parliamentary debate. On the other hand, debate may be so moderate and technical that it induces little reflection on the part of those participating or listening. Steiner *et al.* (2004) find that the former effect dominates, and that legislatures in consensual democracies are generally more deliberative than their more majoritarian counterparts.

In corporatist systems, discussed in Chapter 5, legislatures are less central and so their deliberative capacities are less crucial. Equally important is the degree of deliberativeness in the *corporatist institutions* that integrate executive officials, business and labour federations – and sometimes other groups. These institutions often operate in greater secrecy than does parliament. Secrecy is not necessarily a bad thing, because participants can explore positions without always worrying about the members of their federation or group looking over their shoulders, or the glare of media publicity (Chambers 2004). Yet any deliberative qualities they do possess are attenuated by any lack of democratic representativeness of the non-governmental officials present.

Courts too can be sites of deliberation, especially constitutional courts. We saw earlier that Rawls treats Supreme Court judges as experts in public reason – that is, reasoning about what is in the true interest of society as a whole. Given that public reason is the main deliberative virtue, there is then little need to worry that members of courts are appointed, not elected; and are at least in principle unresponsive to the weight of public opinion. Other deliberate democrats would on these grounds dismiss the deliberative democratic credentials of courts.

Designed forums are a means of securing the direct deliberative participation of non governmental actors; they are sometimes termed 'discursive designs' (Dryzek 1990) or 'deliberative designs' (Hendriks 2002). These can be of two types, partisan and non-partisan (Hendriks *et al.* 2007). Partisan forums bring together stakeholders who take opposing points of view on an issue – for example, environmentalists and developers on a city planning dispute, or gay activists and fundamentalist Christians on HIV-AIDS policy. Such exercises go by different names: mediation; consensus-building; stakeholder dialogues; principled negotiation; alternative dispute resolution. The idea is to bring the different sides together under the auspices of a mediator or facilitator, and get them to reason through their differences. The mediator will normally enforce some rules of discourse, ruling out personal attacks, deception, withholding of information, shouting down and so forth. The record of such processes in producing agreement across hostile parties is impressive (Susskind 1999).

In contrast, non-partisan forums involve lay citizens recruited at random from a larger population. They are brought into an information-rich setting and given access to advocates for different sides and expert witnesses. In most cases the citizens then deliberate among themselves on the issue and produce a set of recommendations for public policy. The number of citizen-deliberators ranges from 15 to several hundred – when large numbers are involved, they have to be split into several deliberating sub-groups. Examples include consensus conferences (invented by the Danish Board of Technology), citizen's juries (invented in the United States, used most widely in Britain), deliberative polls (invented by Fishkin 1991) which conclude with a questionnaire rather than a citizens' report, planning cells (invented in Germany), and citizens' assemblies (invented in British Columbia in Canada, where one was used to recommend a new voting system for the province). (See Goodin and Dryzek 2006 for both a catalogue and examples of their impact on public debates.) The issue deliberated most frequently by lay citizen forums to date has been that of genetically modified foods; normally lay citizens come up with recommendations more sensitive to the risks of the technology than the positions taken by governments. Lay citizens turn out to make exceptionally good deliberators in such forums, because they are not encumbered by any prior partisanship on the issue, and so approach it with an open mind amenable to being persuaded.

Governance networks of the sort introduced in Chapter 6 are also a potential site for deliberation. Such networks are informal and communicative, featuring mixes of conflict and cooperation among the actors involved. They are rarely designed with deliberation in mind (unlike the forums we have just discussed). However, it is possible to apply deliberative standards to the evaluation of particular networks (though to the best of our knowledge nobody has yet done that). This is an important task if (a) networks are becoming increasingly important in producing collective outcomes in today's world; (b) all forms of authority in today's world must be democratic to be legitimate; and (c) the dominant model of democratic legitimacy is deliberative.

Agendas and political change

Our discussion of institutions and policy making suggests there are many locations where deliberation can be sought: in election campaigns; in legislatures; in corporatist bodies; in courts; in designed forums; in policy networks. We should add mechanisms for public consultation (such as public hearings on administrative or legislative proposals), public inquiries, and (bearing in mind our previous discussion under 'state and society') the broader public sphere – which itself need not be confined. What this might seem to suggest is that the deliberative democracy agenda involves a commitment to political reform that involves more authentic deliberation wherever politics is found. There is a set of deliberative virtues that could be promoted universally across all political locations. For Gutmann and Thompson (1996) the key virtue is 'reciprocity', which means making arguments in terms that others can accept. This rules out, for example, arguments based on religion in a multi-faith society. So when it comes to a contentious issue like abortion, arguments that it is contrary to God's plan cannot be made. Those motivated by such religious concerns will have a find another different way to couch their arguments – for example, in terms of the intrinsic value of respect for life.

Mansbridge (1999) speaks of the 'deliberative system' that links the many locations of politics, from ordinary conversations among citizens to the legislature. She treats authentic deliberation in multiple locations as mutually reinforcing, but that may not in fact be the case. For example, very inclusive state institutions may promote deliberation within the state – but at the same time impoverish the public sphere. An actively inclusive state (such as Norway) organizes a wide range of political concerns into governmental institutions, and funds organizations to express particular points of view (see Chapter 6). The result is that there is little autonomous social movement activism of the sort seen in other countries – and so critical debate in the public sphere is impoverished (Dryzek *et al.* 2003). To take another case, environmental mediation in the United States involves recruiting environmental representations into face-to-face deliberations with their opponents, such as polluters or developers. Critics suggest that in entering such forums environmental leaders are co-opted and in danger of losing touch with their grass roots, becoming too accommodating and again losing their capacity to participate in critical debate in the broader public sphere (e.g. Amy 1987). Thus in promoting deliberation in a particular institution, we need to be mindful of the possibility of negative as well as positive effects elsewhere in the deliberative system.

In efforts to promote more authentic political deliberation, there turns out to be no one-size-fits-all recipe as to what sort of practices and designs are best. The lessons of practice may be tough ones, for particular designs are often deployed and take effect in ways that their advocates would see as far from ideal. For example deliberative citizen's panel are sometimes used by clever government officials to produce a different picture of public opinion that can be used to sideline troublesome advocacy groups (Parkinson 2006). Deliberative democratization should therefore itself be a deliberative and participatory process, and any proposals require reflective validation by a broader public.

Conclusion

We have surveyed a number of proposals for democratic renewal in established liberal democracies, some of which seek better citizens, some better institutions and some both. Making such proposals at the level of political theory is relatively easy, actually putting them into practice is much harder. But many innovations are being tried, and there is much that democratic innovators can learn from this productive mix of theory and practice.

Chapter 10

Feminist Theory of the State

Politics has generally been dominated by men, practiced according to patterns of male behaviour, and structured by male interests. For all their differences, pluralism, elite theory, Marxism and market liberalism had little or nothing to say about the gendered nature of politics, and how it affects the way that the state works. Feminists argue that as a result they all missed one of the key foundational facts of politics, in the liberal democratic state no less than elsewhere. The feminist theory of the state involves explication and criticism of male domination, together with prescriptions about how it might be remedied. Beyond this common core, feminism is a diverse body of thought whose adherents differ on some matters of theory and practice. It is also an evolving social movement as well as an academic outlook. Some feminists have sought to link their ideas to liberalism, pluralism, elite theory (at least in its later form involving critique of elite dominance) and Marxism. Feminist links to market liberalism are harder to discern. Other more radical feminists keep their distance from all of these classic positions in the theory of the state, treating the state as bound up with patriarchy, hierarchical rule by men, in its very essence.

Whether or not feminism actually has a theory of the state of its own is a different question. Catharine MacKinnon (1989: 249) believed that 'a feminist theory of the state has barely been imagined; systematically, it has never been tried'. Radical feminists, including MacKinnon, would reject all the theories of the state we have surveyed so far. Some would turn their backs on the irredeemable patriarchal state in the name of women organizing and living in separate spheres of society – though advocates of this position ought to have a theory of the state to justify their rejection of it. An explanatory theory of the state can in fact be found in feminism, which links the state as it has evolved so far to patriarchy, and it is this we emphasize here.

Origins and Core Assumptions

Since the rise of organized agriculture, most human societies have been dominated by men. Some feminists (for example, Starhawk 1987) look back to pagan times when goddesses were honoured and the sexes were more equal (though occupying different places in a division of labour). but such history is contentious, not least among feminists themselves. Since the time of ancient kingdoms and empires organized governments have generally been run by men, and this is no less true of states in the modern era. Though female monarchs such as Elizabeth I of England or Catherine the Great of Russia might occasionally come to power, their sex made little or no difference to the way they had to work, and the male-dominated governmental apparatus they had to work with. The affairs of state were a public realm for men only, while women were confined to the private realm of the household.

Within the household women were subservient to husband or father. Women had fewer rights than men. Married women were treated as the property of their husbands, single women as subordinate to their fathers. Early modern male proto-democratic thinkers saw no need to change this presumption. For example, writing in the eighteenth century, the radical republican Jean-Jacques Rousseau, argued that women should be excluded from politics. He also proposed different education systems for boys and girls, with girls to be trained for keeping house and entertaining, rather than for any intellectual pursuits. Such states of affairs were long accepted and unchallenged by women as well as men. Women might have occasionally crafted separate social realms where male domination was held at bay, but they never challenged male-oriented political power – and perhaps never conceptualized the possibility of such challenge.

The publication in England of Mary Wollstonecraft's *A Vindication of the Rights of Women* in 1792 indicated that matters were beginning to change. Wollstonecraft made an essentially liberal argument for the equality of men and women: 'I do not wish women to have power over men; but over themselves.' Yet male liberal thinkers continued to resist. In the early nineteenth century James Mill could still argue that women needed no rights to representation of their own, because their interests could be taken care of in electoral politics by the votes of their husbands or fathers.

In nineteenth century Britain sons at least were free to speak against fathers, and John Stuart Mill did so in 1869 in his *The Subjection of Women*, like Wollstonecraft's earlier book an essentially liberal argument for the equality of the sexes before the law and the state. In socialist thinking during the nineteenth century, Karl Marx himself said little about women. However, in his 1884 book *The Origins of the Family, Private Property, and the State*, his co-author Friedrich Engels argued that gender inequality in families and households was used by the ruling class to help bind working class men to the capitalist social order. Men who were subservient in the factories where they worked could none the less exercise power within their households. Thus were the seeds of Marxist feminism sown, a strand which re-appeared toward the end of the twentieth century (Hartsock 1985). In the early twentieth century socialist and communist political thought stressed the equality of men and women, especially in terms of access to paid work and labour rights. Later, socialists would often stress rights to contraception and abortion (though sometimes more guardedly in Catholic countries).

'First wave': The suffrage movement and beyond

As an organized social movement feminism really only took off in the late nineteenth century in Europe, Australasia and North America, though women had long been active in political campaigns, especially for the abolition of slavery. The women's suffrage movement campaigned for votes for women on the same terms as for men, and organized women in ways that transcended party lines and social class divisions, involving large demonstrations and occasional civil disobedience. This movement was unsurprisingly concentrated in the few liberal democracies existing at the time. Women gained the vote in New Zealand in 1893, Australia in 1902, Finland, Norway, Denmark and Iceland between 1906 and 1915, and Canada, the United States, Germany, Austria, the Netherlands, Sweden, Czechoslovakia, and Ireland during 1918 to 1922. The UK enacted voting rights for women aged over 28 in 1918, but only in 1928 reduced the eligible age to 21, as for men.

The suffragettes also called for equal civil rights for women, equalization of property rights and legal standing, and the removal of restrictions on educational opportunities for women, especially in universities. They also argued that women should be able to enter the professions and have careers in their own right. The emergence of a substantial number of women in the arts and literature aided their case. The mobilization of women into factories in many of the participating countries in World War I strengthened the credibility of women's rights in the workplace. However, after the end of the war women were generally moved back out of workplaces, in order to provide jobs for men at a time of growing unemployment. Opportunities in universities and the professions remained highly restricted.

While the suffrage movement is today remembered as the most important aspect of 'first wave' feminism, the related temperance movement actually mobilized more women, and found it easier to secure political influence. In the United States and Australia, the suffrage movement was often involved with evangelical Christians seeking more responsible and less sinful male behaviour, through restrictions on drunkenness, prostitution and gambling. The Women's Christian Temperance Union linked men's heavy drinking to the abuse of women and children, and so campaigned for restrictions on alcohol or outright prohibition. In 1920 the United States adopted a constitutional amendment forbidding the sale of alcohol. With the manifest failure of Prohibition to end alcohol consumption and the strong impetus it gave to organized crime, which took over alcohol supply, the temperance movement subsequently went into decline in the United States and elsewhere. However, a lasting feminist legacy of the temperance movement is the idea that that what goes on inside the household is not just a private matter, but also a matter for public regulation.

With the success of demands for suffrage, the impetus of the women's movement faltered in the 1920s and 1930s. Women became enmeshed in conventional left-right political conflicts. Communist parties pronounced their commitment to equality of the sexes, and the Soviet Union claimed to advance gender equality in the workplace, for a time attracting some radical feminists. Campaigns for welfare state benefits favourable to women, such as family allowances for children and equal old age pensions, pulled many west European feminists into a social democratic orbit. However, feminist campaigning did continue in efforts to disseminate knowledge of birth control among low income women, which ran up against opposition from churches, conservative politicians and the media. Feminists also campaigned to liberalize divorce laws and to protect women and children within households from being physically abused by their husbands and fathers.

World War II again radically changed the terms on which women participated in the workforce and military. In 1945 women achieved the vote in another wave of countries (except a few odd cases, such as Switzerland where the need to win a referendum to change the constitution meant that men there could carry on denying women the vote until 1973). The wartime and post-war expansion of the welfare state materially helped women, with better pensions, benefits for families and expanded education and health care services. The welfare state also provided many job opportunities for women, in both caring occupations and the bureaucracies that organized them. The war was followed by a 20 year pause in large-scale feminist organizing, before the next 'second' wave of feminism began in earnest in the late 1960s, in a way that made some pluralists uncomfortable.

Second and third waves

The new left radicalism of the 1960s in many liberal democracies was at first mostly devoid of feminism, but that glaring absence soon led to a feminist response that became a major contribution to the social movements that developed in the 1960s and 1970s. Second wave feminism stressed not just formal equality between the sexes, but also that women should have parity in careers, life chances, pay and political representation. Mothers should not have to sacrifice their careers to bring up children, nor should women have to give up work to care for sick or elderly parents. Housework and parenting should be shared equally. Women should no longer be judged by their appearance nor treated as sexual objects, in pornography or elsewhere. Laws against rape and sexual assault and harassment should be strengthened and enforced. One controversial slogan from the second wave is that 'the personal is political'. 'The millennial feminist has to be aware that oppression exerts itself in and through her most intimate relationships, beginning with the most intimate, her relationship with her body' (Greer 1999: 330).

Policy changes in response to this agenda included legislation for equal pay and career opportunity, subsidized or government-provided childcare, reforms in family law, and more equal pension rights. Rights to contraception and abortion have generally been secured, though requiring constant defence against conservative reactions in the United States. Sexism in the media and public discourse has been ameliorated but not eliminated. Controversy continues over the enforcement of laws against rape and sexual assault. But almost everywhere political representatives are still mostly male. Substantial pay gaps between men and women with the same qualifications remain. Culturally, sexist attitudes in the media have made something of a comeback. Above all, the reforms that improved the lot of women in developed liberal democracies have not spread to the rest of the world, and in many societies women remain subject to extreme forms of oppression.

Contemporary feminists see gender as still a dominant fact of contemporary societies. A distinction can be drawn between biological sex differences, which are incontestable, and socially constructed gender differences, which are highly contestable. Gender roles and expectations are embodied in laws, customs, traditions and social conventions. Generally these gender differences have constructed women as inferior to men, confined to subordinate roles in society and excluded from full participation in politics. One such gendered role assigns the primary responsibility for child-rearing to women, meaning that women who have children are disadvantaged in the competition for positions of power and influence in politics, business and elsewhere. The lower social status ascribed to women and their work can mean too that many jobs carried out mainly by women (nursing, cleaning, primary school teaching, etc.) are assigned low status and low pay. By contrast, high status positions often come with masculinist conventions attached to them – to be 'one of the boys' in drinking together, making jokes, behaving aggressively, competing for status points and so forth.

A parallel can be made with Marxism as discussed in Chapter 4. Just as Marxists stress class divisions, feminists stress gender divisions. But while Marxists believe that class divisions can eventually be overturned in revolutionary action, feminists are both cautious and divided on this point. Moreover, some feminists are wary of the idea that 'women qua women constitute a giant "sisterhood" waiting to be mobilized' (Zerilli 2006: 112), on the grounds that differently-situated women have different experiences and interests, tied to variations in race, religion, age, social class, sexuality and the kind of society in which they live. This multiplicity of interests may help explain why the political exclusion of women was so total for so long.

Difference or equality?

One very basic point of disagreement among feminists concerns whether one believes men and women are basically different, or basically the same; and if they are different, whether the difference is socially or biologically constructed. Some feminists associate a different paradigm of personhood with women, one that is nurturing and caring, rooted in the capacity to bear and raise children (Gilligan 1982). This model of the individual is contrasted with a masculine self that is striving, competitive and potentially violent. Immediately we can see why such feminists would want to reject market liberal theory discussed in Chapter 4, on the grounds that the latter is based on a masculinist model of man. If this alternative model of a nurturing and caring individual is accepted, the next question that arises is whether or not men can learn to share in this kind of behaviour, or whether they cannot change. If they are irredeemable, then the political consequences would point in the direction of a radical separatism of men and women – though such a conclusion is reached by a relatively small number of feminists, including some lesbian feminists (for example, Daly 1993). If men are redeemable, and masculinist models of behaviour are social rather than biological constructions, then the agenda can become one of changing society (including the state) to bring out this better side. Citizenship could become feminized (Ruddick 1980). But for Camille Paglia (1994: 15), 'I have intensely disliked the tendency of many feminists to want men to be remade in a kind of shy, sensitive form, to become, in essence, new kinds of women, contemporary eunuchs which is less inconvenient for women.'

Arguments about an essentially different male and female nature make some feminists very nervous. Liberal feminists who have been fighting long and hard for equality and the political irrelevance of gender differences can see in such arguments a mirror image of the arguments long used by men to keep women in subordinate positions, on the grounds that the sexes are indeed essentially different. A common position in contemporary 'third wave' feminist politics denies 'a pre-given feminine subject (rooted in the experience of being a woman)' (Zerilli 2006: 112). Recognizing a plurality of subject positions suggests that feminism needs to adopt some kind of pluralism – but not a pluralism of competing material interests to be reconciled in conventional state politics, still less a pluralism in which 'women' are treated as one interest group among others. Rather, a feminist pluralism is one where identities somehow need to be negotiated within the politics of the women's movement itself. Here there are affinities with the plural politics of identity introduced in Chapter 8, as well as the post-modern politics we will discuss in Chapter 13.

Society and Politics

While some feminist theory strongly suggests that men and women ought to be different in how they approach politics, conventional survey measures of voting and other kinds of political behaviour suggest the differences are slender. Feminist scholars sometimes reply that opinion surveys are masculinist instruments (Oakley 1972).

For the first four or five decades after getting the vote, in most established liberal democracies women tended to support conservative parties more than men did. Part of the explanation may have been that women live longer than men, and that older people are generally more conservative. Eventually this difference disappeared. Inglehart and Norris (2003) found that in most established democracies, women now more left-leaning than were men. But in most countries the differences are slight. In the United Kingdom, Campbell (2006: 132) concludes that, 'Gender has a subtle and pervasive influence upon attitudes and behaviour'. Younger women are more pro-Labour and older women more pro-Conservative, but gender effects are filtered through many other aspects of social locations. Women tend to prioritize public services and construe politics in terms of its implications for a web of relationships with close family and friends, while men assign more weight to the economy and see politics in more individualistic and strategic terms.

For radical feminists, state and society are linked mainly by the notion of patriarchy. Patriarchy literally means rule by a male head of family and has long been used in religious affairs (note the Patriarchs of

Greek and Russian Orthodox Christian Churches). Patriarchy for feminists now means not just male domination, but a hierarchy organized on masculine lines with particular kinds of men (richer, socially well-connected or older) at the top (Millett 1970). This is how society's institutions are mostly organized – be they families, corporations, churches, or non-governmental bureaucracies. And in a patriarchal society, this is how states are organized too. Calling a state liberal or democratic makes little difference; no less than overtly authoritarian regimes, liberal democracies too are generally patriarchies. They are organized by men, contain large hierarchical bureaucracies, and rarely recognize the distinct and different interests of women. In this light, states are not the creation of patriarchal societies, or vice versa. Rather, the patriarchal aspects of state and society help constitute and reinforce each other. Because this pattern is deeply rooted in many institutions, it cannot be changed by single pieces of legislation, but rather must be contested in multiple settings.

Feminists highlight another crucial aspect of state-society relations: the public-private split that has helped define the 'liberal' aspect of liberal democracies. According to this split, there is a private realm of life, including the family and the household, where the state has no business. Feminists point out that the household and family can be sites of power, oppression and violence – as well as patriarchy. So many matters traditionally classified by liberals as 'private' ought also to be of public concern, and the private-public split does not hold up.

The sexual contract

One way of conceptualizing feminism's challenge to the public-private split here is through reference to Carole Pateman's (1988) notion of a 'sexual contract' that underpins the justification of the liberal state. That state was famously justified in terms of a hypothetical 'social contract' by the liberal philosopher John Locke, in his 1689 *Two Treatises of Government*. In this social contract, individuals forego some of the liberties they have in a hypothetical 'state of nature' in exchange for the security, property rights, civil liberties and predictable social environment that the state provides for them (see Figure 10.1). The contracting individuals take on the obligations of citizenship, to obey the law, pay taxes and (for example) meet any requirements of military service.

Locke's account is superficially gender-neutral. But as Pateman points out, Locke's theory actually requires an additional and separate sexual contract, in which women and children are seen as having contracted with their husbands or fathers for protection and care in return for their being governed by a man (see Figure 10.2). The man then deals

Figure 10.1   *How Locke portrayed the social contract*

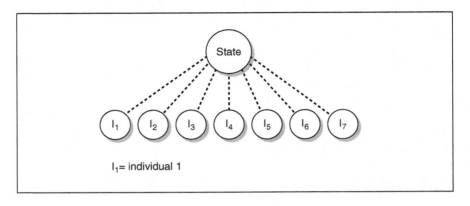

Figure 10.2   *How Pateman argues that Locke's social contract in fact relies on a sexual contract*

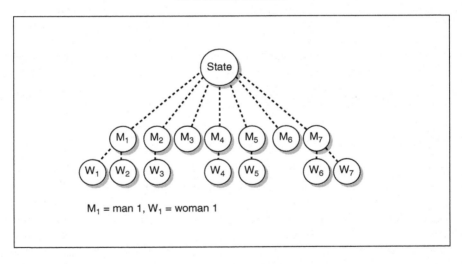

with the state on behalf of women and children, as well as himself. Because this sexual contract is between men and women in the private sphere, Locke's attempt to put all individuals on an equal footing in relation to the state collapses. Under liberal assumptions about the public-private split, the state cannot intervene to regulate the relations between men and women within the household. The state cannot guarantee equal rights to women and children, because in Locke's eyes that would be a tyrannical violation of the core liberal principle of a limited state, which respects the rights of the males who have consented to the state in their hypothetical social contract. Thus, the liberal social contract that seemingly guarantees human rights for all actually guarantees rights only for men. And protection of the rights of those men means they are free to engage in tyrannical behaviour within the household, which the state is powerless to prevent. Locke's liberal social contract allows oppression not in a way that is merely incidental or not covered by his theory, but in a way that is actually required by his theory. So Pateman could conclude that the social 'contract is the specifically modern vehicle for creating and maintaining relationships of domination and oppression' (interview in *Cosmopolis*, 2007).

Organizing women

This deficiency of the liberal state has adverse consequences for women. It can be remedied in part through the political organization of women. Such mobilization may involve constituting conventional interest groups to push for public policies that are in women's interests – such as the National Organization for Women (NOW) in the United States, founded in 1966, and today with half a million members. Feminism is also a social movement that can adopt a more radical critique of the state. Some feminists turn their back on the state in favour of women's self-organization, where individual women can find their voice in cooperatives, self-help ventures, and social organizations (Young 2000: 155). Rejecting conventional interest group action does not have to mean passivity and lack of effect. Arguably the biggest impact of the past several decades of feminism is cultural: in changing the ways many people, men and women alike, conceptualize gender roles in the household, the economy, social life and politics (Tesh 1993). This cultural change can also come to pervade the understandings of politicians and government bureaucrats, and so affect the content of public policy.

In Europe, the social democratic and labour movement connections since the 1980s have become progressively more important. Unions have helped secure equal pay, better pensions and maternity provisions. Social democratic and green parties have fielded increasing numbers of female candidates. An advocacy coalition for women's rights has been effectively constituted in many liberal democracies.

Feminist mobilization must sometimes be defensive, however. This is especially true in the United States, where Christian conservatives have repeatedly tried to restrict abortion rights and access to contraception (promoting abstinence instead). Globally, the Catholic Church makes similar efforts.

The Feminist Critique of Government and Policy Making

Traditionally the public realm was dominated by men, and as we have seen, even votes for women were a long time coming in all liberal democracies. The achievement of universal adult suffrage has not meant equal female representation in politics. however, Feminists believe a necessary (but not a sufficient) condition for more effective promotion of women's interests is parity in the numbers of women and men in positions of power. No woman has yet been elected President or Vice-President of the United States (Geraldine Ferraro in 1984 and Sarah Palin in 2008 were unsuccessful Vice-Presidential candidates for major parties). There has been only one female Prime Minister of the United Kingdom – Margaret Thatcher (1979–1990). Her successor had only two women in his cabinet, though subsequent Labour governments in the UK had much better female representation.

Nor has the picture been much better in legislatures; in 1992 there were only two female US Senators. Until 1997 female representation in the UK's House of Commons was only around 10–15 per cent, but then it jumped to 30 per cent. The situation is worst in countries like the USA and UK with single member constituencies and plurality rule. In proportional representation systems women do better because parties are under pressure to show that their slate of candidates treats women equally.

However, the trend in most liberal democracies is for a gradual increase in the proportion of female representatives. In some cases, such as Scandinavian social democrat parties, party policy has been to specify a proportion of women candidates for winnable seats in legislative elections. Not coincidentally, the proportion of women in parliament reaches a high point in the Nordic countries; for example, in 2005 45.3 per cent of the members of the Swedish parliament were women. In list system proportional representation (see Chapter 6) it is possible to 'zip' lists of candidates with alternating men and women. Politics could also be made more welcoming to women by conducting business in family-friendly fashion – and not, say, running legislative sittings into the evening. Some feminists argue that there is a 'tipping point' in terms of percentage of female parliamentarians that should actually make a clear difference to how parliament operates (Lovenduski and Norris 2003), somewhere between 20 per cent and 40 per cent.

When it comes to the public service, the term 'femocrats' was coined in Australia to describe female bureaucrats in charge of social service delivery agencies (Sawer 1990) – which are also largely staffed by women at lower levels. Especially service delivery agencies, government is often more hospitable to the employment of women than are large corporations in the private sector.

Even when women have succeeded in achieving high-ranking positions in government, the price of success has often been the need to adopt competitive and adversarial, male-oriented norms of behaviour, requiring an element of bullying when dealing with opponents inside and outside one's own party. This is especially true in democracies that are 'majoritarian' rather than 'consensual' (see Chapter 7 for this distinction), because members of other parties have to be treated unremittingly as adversaries. Margaret Thatcher exemplified these sorts of behavioural characteristics, though in her case it was probably not much of an effort to adopt them. The male members of her cabinet lived in constant fear of her.

Beyond these behavioural adaptations, a wider *'fraternalism'* can mean that men in positions of authority tend to recruit personnel in their own image, valuing 'male' qualities. Fraternalism is bound up with *androcentrism*, the belief that male norms are actually the universal norms by which everything is to be judged. This may mean the prioritization of technology, logic and instrumental rationality over intuitions, emotion, empathy and more 'feminine' sorts of knowledge. Androcentrism applies in the definition of the business of the state to the degree it is thought to involve war, policing and growth of the market economy, rather than changes in childcare duties in the household or the availability of contraception and basic health care. Worst of all from a feminist point of view is *misogyny*, the hatred of women. While overt misogyny is increasingly rare in liberal democratic politics, it still exists in liberal democratic societies – manifested in male violence against women, especially within households. The misogynistic practices of some men have the effect of intimidating all women in a society – for example, when it comes to fear of venturing into parts of cities after dark or without a male companion.

Patriarchy in political institutions and policies

Institutions can be male-ordered in their structure as well as their composition and the behavioural norms they feature. Patriarchy is a form of hierarchy (arguably *the* basis of hierarchy) in which strong leadership is expected at the top, and subordinate behaviour is expected at lower levels, though ambitious subordinates are supposed to try to impress those at the top. Most contemporary states still depend largely on bureaucratic forms of organization (networked governance of the sort described in Chapter 5 notwithstanding). Bureaucracy is criticized by many theorists of the state, from market liberals (see Chapter 5) to pluralists. There is a feminist critique of bureaucracy (Ferguson 1984) that stresses bureaucracy's objectification of individuals both within and outside the agency and its suppression of caring relationships. On this critique, bureaucracy embodies control, dominance, subordination and dehumanization.

Sceptics might point to the fact that bureaucracies in practice do not work as the rigid organizational chart would suggest: that it is informal interaction that actually enables them to function, despite the organization chart. Moreover, it is not clear to what extent such a critique ought to be pursued when it comes to social service bureaucracies, now delivering services to women and often largely staffed by women. It is still less clear what the feminist attitude to networked governance should be. Networks often work in a more decentralized and informal way than bureaucracies; but they are not necessarily any more women-friendly. It is possible to identify particular policy networks largely made up of women. Boles (1994) identifies feminist policy networks operating on issues of sexual assault, domestic violence and child care. These networks are composed of feminist interest organizations, elected officials, public servants, and women's service organizations. But what if anything feminists should think about the basic idea of networked governance is not at all obvious.

The social policies of governments can sometimes reinforce particular sets of assumptions about households and the different roles of men and women. For example, in Australia, a pioneering egalitarian approach to income distribution adopted by government in the 1900s set minimum wage rates (Castles 1985). For men, the rate set was sufficient to support a family; for women, sufficient to support one person. Thus even this seemingly progressive legislation reinforced gender inequality in income, and ruled out the possibility of households being supported by a woman's income.

Welfare state arrangements designed on a household rather than individual basis can be discriminatory in their effects. For example, many welfare state programmes adopted in the 1940s and 1950s assumed a male wage earner living with a woman who has no income or works part-time. The male would pay income taxes and health insurance and in return receive coverage for himself and his dependents. Women would generally have few personal entitlements of their own. If the family splits up, the woman may be left caring for children, but have no access to employment insurance or health benefits in her own right. Women in this situation would often have to fall back on less generous and more heavily stigmatized forms of welfare, thus implicitly categorizing women without a male partner as of lesser social status, as objects of poor relief rather than citizens with rightful claims on social insurance. Such women would suffer further as they aged, lacking old age pension entitlements because they had not participated in paid employment long enough to accumulate a worthwhile pension in their own right. Feminists argue that these sorts of policies were not acci-dental. Instead they constituted a whole coherent complex that extended across government to work systematically in favour of men (MacKinnon 1989)

With time, women's political activism did change such policies in many cases. The most far-reaching reforms have been achieved in the Nordic social democracies, Norway, Sweden and Finland (Hernes 1987). These states are 'actively inclusive' in their orientation to social movements (see Chapter 6) – especially in relation to the women's movement. Their relatively generous welfare states had little problem in re-organizing monetary contributions and entitlements in a way that did not discriminate against women. The solution was bureaucratic and administrative, and like all social movements incorporated into Nordic states the price paid was in terms of the critical edge of the movement, renouncing any possibility of a more radical transformation of society along feminist lines.

While a feminist critique of the state is well-developed, it should be noted that there is also a male-centred critique which sees the state as having moved too far in a women-centred direction. This critique is especially evident when it comes to family law and custody disputes, when fathers complain about the complicity of the courts and govern-ment more generally in denying them access to their own children. The presupposition is that the children will live with their mother, while fathers will be required to make financial contributions. The British group Fathers 4 Justice has been especially vocal on such issues.

Agendas and Political Change

Since the first wave of feminism began well over a century ago, one con-sistent theme has been the effective representation of women in politics. As Mary Wollstonecraft put it a century earlier: 'Women ought to have representatives, instead of being arbitrarily governed without any direct share allowed them in government'. At first equal representation just meant votes for women citizens. However, once achieved, votes for women did not lead to greater numbers of women in elected offices and other positions of power. We have seen that even in Nordic countries women still occupy less than half of the seats in parliament, and the per-centages are generally much lower elsewhere. Anne Phillips (1991) pro-poses quotas of women in political parties to secure women a certain proportion of legislative seats. Phillips (1995) speaks of a 'politics of presence': it is not enough that women's interests be represented. Rather, women themselves actually need to be there in legislatures to represent their own interests and provide their own perspectives on policy issues. More radically, Iris Young (1989, 1990) proposes that women's representatives, like those of all oppressed groups in society, should be guaranteed an additional veto power over all policies affecting them.

From equal rights to cultural change

The liberal feminist agenda, especially that of the 'second wave' that began in the 1960s, emphasizes equal rights for women in all areas of life. Equal rights apply to employment, citizenship and social benefits. In employment, this agenda demands that women should be paid the same as men for the same sort of work, have the same kinds of opportunities to enter different sorts of occupations, and be protected against discrimination and harassment of all kinds in the workplace.

However, ending discrimination on the basis of gender may not end women's disadvantage. For example, women are more likely than men to interrupt careers to bear and raise children. This can be a matter of choice rather than necessity, but government can try to compensate for the disadvantage so caused, for example, by legislating parental leave and promoting schemes for women's return to the workplace. Second wave feminists also advocated access to contraception and family planning, and an end to the exploitation of women's bodies by the media and advertisers. More radical feminists such as Pateman (1988) point out that equal rights are not enough to counter the sorts of inequalities and oppressions often found within households. As Rowbotham (1986: 86) argues, 'democratic control has to be extended to the circumstances of everyday life'. Okin (1989) believes that this politicization of the household requires a state that is very interventionist in what had traditionally for liberals constituted the private sphere immune from government interference. Second wave feminists sought a more equal division of labour in the household, and tried to change assumptions that it was women who would take on the entire burden of housework, caring for children or looking after aged parents.

In its drive for political equality, liberal feminism may leave the masculinist style of politics untouched. This is not enough for some feminists, who want 'to release from the realm of taboo, for incorporation into political discourse, a host of experiences and referents related to intimate personal connection' (Mansbridge 1993: 368–9). Such referents would include care and empathy as political principles, as opposed to competitive striving and the maximization of power and interest in relation to others. The target of women's activism is not just the state and public policy, but also cultural assumptions about the relative roles in life of men and women.

A prescriptive state?

Some feminists believe that a moralistic and prescriptive state can change culture and patterns of behaviour in the required direction. Certainly a century ago the women's temperance movement thought that prohibitions on alcohol, gambling and prostitution could change men for the better. More recently, feminists such as Catharine MacKinnon (1989) have simultaneously criticized the recalcitrant patriarchy of the liberal democratic state while seeking a moralistic and prescriptive state that would enforce feminist norms. Such a state would crack down on pornography, strip clubs, prostitution, and all forms of the exploitation of women in advertising and the media, as well as effectively enforcing laws against rape, sexual assault, sexual harassment and violence against women.

Thus a prescriptive state would reach deep into what for liberals was traditionally a private sphere off-limits to governmental intervention, and, it would override free speech for the sake of women's interests. Thus idea begs the question of whether there are any limits to the reach of the state. If we ally the extensive and prescriptive state with a feminist 'maternalist' ethic of care, then the political model starts to look like benevolent despotism (Dietz 1985)

If the state is deemed truly recalcitrant and hopelessly patriarchal, the option that remains is to organize feminist politics apart from the state. At an extreme, this leads to separatism – perhaps facilitated by advances in genetic technology that reduce the male involvement in reproduction. More frequently, separatism takes the form of women-only subcultures, cooperatives and networks.

Feminism and multiculturalism

Feminists may condemn liberal democratic states and societies for their patriarchal deficiencies, but they recognize that matters can be far worse for women in other cultures: 'In its demand for equality for women, feminism sets itself in opposition to virtually every culture on earth' (Pollitt 1999: 7). Forced marriages, 'honour' killings, punishment for being the victim (as opposed to the perpetrator) of rape or sexual assault, female infanticide, selective abortion in favour of male children and female genital mutilation are just some of the things that women have to suffer. When members of such cultures move to liberal democratic societies they sometimes bring these oppressive practices with them and demand government recognition of these practices. Government policies of multiculturalism may mean there is an effort to accommodate minority cultures and their oppressive practices. Okin (1999) asks 'Is multiculturalism bad for women?', and concludes that it most certainly is. Okin's feminism is universalistic: she believes that the pursuit of equality for women is much more important than respect for cultural difference (see also Nussbaum 1999). Thus while feminists may in principle value pluralism, it only goes so far, and does not mean accepting the legitimacy of cultural practices that oppress women.

Conclusion

There are, then, several dimensions to the feminist critique of state institutions and policy making. (See Dietz 2003 on the sheer variety of contemporary feminist points of view.) The critique is profound: 'Feminism provides democracy with its most important challenge and most comprehensive critique' (Pateman 1989: 210). Can we envisage feminist concerns moving beyond critique and becoming attached to the core business of the state? Certainly the more radical feminist critiques often seem to treat the liberal democratic state as irredeemably masculinist. But there have been times when feminist concerns could find support in the state's core. We saw in Chapter 1 that one core priority of the liberal democratic state is necessarily the economic one of providing the conditions for markets and so economic growth to flourish. If we look back to the first wave of feminism of a century or more ago, we find that the association of women with temperance was instrumental in producing disciplined and responsible men who would be steered away from the vices of alcohol, gambling and prostitution. As Max Weber famously pointed out in *The Protestant Ethic and the Spirit of Capitalism*, it is such responsible individuals striving to better themselves and their families who are especially functional when it comes to building a capitalist economy. Thus could feminist concerns be joined to the core economic priority of the state.

In the 1970s and 1980s, liberal feminist demands for equality in the workplace and provision of childcare also led to a greater and more flexible workforce for capitalist economic production. In this light, the patriarchical family actually resembles a lingering feudal remnant that obstructs the free use of labour in the market economy (Fraad *et al.* 1994). So again, feminist concerns might be joined to the state's economic priority.

Feminism today is a diverse movement, with liberal, radical, moderate, and lesbian separatist wings; and with theorists extending into Marxism and post-modernism. Its present and likely future involve action within the conventional institutions of government and interest group politics; plus radical action that occasionally challenges government; and continued development of separate spheres of political life at some distance from the state.

Chapter 11

Environmental Theory of the State

States are some of the main institutions that affect society's interactions with the ecosystems that sustain human and non-human life on this planet. And just as the political economy can generate crises that re-shape the state in powerful ways, so can the political ecology. From the ecological point of view, the degree to which humanity will flourish or diminish depends crucially on political responses to these crises, prominent among which is climate change. Political responses here are not confined to the policy actions of states, and as we will see many environmentalists have developed a critique of the state which stresses the need for political action above the level of the state in global action, below the level of the state in local activism, and across states in transnational coordination. 'The possible political arrangements in a sustainable society seem to range all the way from radical decentralisation to a world government' Dobson (1995). But for better or for worse, the state is going to play a central part in any re-shaping of the political ecology (Eckersley 2004).

Origins and Core Assumptions

Nonhuman nature has of course existed for much longer than humanity itself, and humanity would not exist without it. Yet the idea that there is such a thing as 'the environment' is actually of very recent origin. Prior to the late 1960s, the environment was simply not conceptualized as a political issue. Particular public policy initiatives relating to pollution control and the protection of natural areas pre-dated this transformation, often by several decades. Beginning in the late eighteenth century, the Romantic Movement across Europe celebrated nature and wildness in literature, music and art in contrast to industrialization and urbanization, and eventually this put nature protection on the political agenda. In the United States in the late nineteenth and early twentieth century, John Muir, founder of the Sierra Club, celebrated the natural areas of the American West and sought their protection. At the same time the 'Conservation Movement' flourished, associated with the US Forest Service's Chief Forester, Gifford Pinchot.

This movement sought conservation of natural resources such as timber and rangeland for the sake of future human use, but it lacked the deep respect for nature that Muir promoted (Taylor 1992). Muir was 'eco-centric' (human-focused), Pinchot 'anthropocentric'. In many liberal democracies, urban and regional planning along with anti-pollution laws was introduced in the 1950s.

For a long time there was no sense of interconnection across all these sorts of concerns, still less that there could be such a thing as an environmental crisis or indeed environmentalism. Around 1970 many threads came together in a new vocabulary and environmental politics began in earnest. The radical and ecocentric wing of environmentalism could sometimes identify a common cause with the new left social movements that began in the 1960s and 1970s. By contrast moderate and anthropocentric environmentalism was more easily assimilated into conventional pluralist politics.

The most important assumption of contemporary environmental theory is that there is indeed such a thing as the environment that constrains human activity. Given that the major theoretical accounts of the liberal democratic state predate 1970, none of them copes adequately with the environmental issue – treating environmental policy as an ordinary area of governmental activity is not adequate. Effectively, this means that all these perspectives, be they pluralist, elitist, Marxist, or market liberal, effectively treat the Earth on which we live as an unlimited source of wealth that can be used and abused at will, bouncing back after all but the most reckless forms of exploitation. Taking the environment seriously means scrapping these industrialist presumptions and instead treating human society, economy and politics as subsystems of global and regional ecosystems which are crucial for the wellbeing of these human systems. As Lewis Mumford (1964: 393) put it, 'all thinking worthy of the name must now be ecological'.

Given that the environmental theory of the state so far consists mainly of critique, most of its key assumptions pertain to the vantage point from which critique is constructed, rather than to the basic building blocks of the state itself. The critique is actually not especially concerned with how the state got to be the way it is and why it does the things it does – except insofar as such explanations help diagnose the inadequacies of the state as it confronts ecological issues. In this light, it is probably enough to say simply that the modern state in all its variations is a product of an industrialist era in which economic growth and technological change were unquestioned goods. That state must now be re-thought as we enter an ecological era. To Beck (1992), this passage is from semi-modernity to (potentially more rational) modernity proper. In modernity proper, there are no traditions – including the traditions of economic growth and technological progress – that are off-limits to rational scrutiny and collective control.

The arrival of environmental policy

Before the environment was recognized, there could be no environmental theory of the state. In the 1970s, two very different environmental accounts of the state developed. The first followed closely on the heels of actual policy developments. Governments responded to heightened and intense public concern with environmental issues by setting up agencies to regulate pollution, passing pollution control legislation to be implemented by these agencies, establishing or strengthening professional resource management bureaucracies, and making both public and private development proposals subject to the new device of environmental impact assessment. The United States was the pioneer in all these respects, with an outpouring of federal legislation including the National Environmental Policy Act of 1970 (which instituted impact assessment and an advisory Council on Environmental Quality), the Clean Air Act of 1970, the Water Pollution Control Act of 1972, the Environmental Pesticides Control Act of 1972, the Coastal Zone Management Act and a Marine Protection, Research, and Sanctuaries Act in 1972, and the Endangered Species Act in 1973. The federal Environmental Protection Agency was founded in 1970, soon followed by state-level counterparts. However substantial, these innovations involved using established tools of government. In that sense, an environmental account of the state pointed mainly to the deployment of governmental powers in new areas. In the United States, environmental policy soon came to feature a greater capacity for legal challenge to government decisions (by polluters and developers as well as environmentalists); the assertion of congressional micro-management of the federal EPA to prevent its capture by special interests (Ackerman and Hassler 1981); and greater opportunities for public comment on and input into policy making than was traditional in other policy areas. But these were marginal changes in the structure and operation of government. Moreover, these particular features generally did not appear when similar environmental policy initiatives were pursued in other developed societies – though we will see that the tendency of environmental issues to democratize the liberal state is actually quite pervasive.

Limits and survival

A very different kind of environmental theory of the state was developed in the 1970s by analysts who believed that ecological crisis demanded immediate and drastic measures to forestall catastrophe. Such warnings were backed by the deployment of global models that predicted catastrophe as exponential growth in human populations and economic activity eventually encountered limits directly imposed by the finite nature of the earth. In the language of ecology, overshoot and collapse in human population would result once global 'carrying capacity' was exceeded (Catton 1980). Most famous among these analyses were the computer models whose predictions were summarized in *The Limits to Growth* (Meadows *et al.* 1972), which soon sold four million copies worldwide.

The *Limits* report actually contained little in the way of political analysis, but the force of global limits could easily be linked to social scientific models of the state grounded in microeconomics. For market-oriented economists, the classical justification of the state in the first place is in terms of the need to correct for 'externalities' and provide 'public goods'. To these could be added the model of the 'tragedy of the commons' made famous by the biologist Garrett Hardin (1968), but actually a staple of natural resource economics long before that. All three concepts (externalities, public goods, and common pool resources) point to the degree to which rationally egoistic human behaviour, which should produce such beneficial results through the operation of Adam Smith's 'invisible hand', could in some cases produce collectively bad results. And in each case, the bad result in question found perfect illustration in the environmental area. The classic example of an externality is pollution, which unintentionally harms third parties as a result of a market transaction that leads to a good being produced. The classic example of a public good is environmental quality, which is in everyone's interest, but hard to get market actors to provide, because there is no profit to be made in producing it. And the tragedy of the commons applies most easily to 'commons' resources such as the atmosphere, watersheds, publicly shared space, and the oceans, to which individuals and firms have unrestricted access. Given that each actor reaps the entire benefit of his or her exploitation of the commons, but shares the costs of his or her action in degrading the resource with all other users, rational actors will continually increase their exploitation of the resource – until the resource is destroyed. And that is why in Hardin's (1968: 1244) words: 'Freedom in the commons brings ruin to all.' A good example of the tragedy in operation is ocean fisheries, many of which have been destroyed by over-fishing. The global atmosphere is the most problematic commons resource, because the damage of each polluter's contribution to greenhouse gas build-up is shared by everyone in the world.

In all three of these models the state is recognized as the collective authority that can step in to ensure that externalities are internalized, as in anti-pollution legislation, which forces polluters to recognize the harm caused by pollution, and either cut back or pay for it. Similarly, government action can ensure that public goods are provided, and the commons protected. Now, if environmental problems are not very severe, all this can be done by ordinary policy making in the liberal democratic state – exactly the policy response that began in the United States in 1970, and was soon followed elsewhere. But if overshoot and collapse are looming, this incremental and limited response may not be enough to prevent catastrophe.

In particular, polyarchy with multiple veto players may mean that self-interested actors try to ensure that others pay the costs of environmental protection, while continuing themselves to pollute and to exploit the commons. If all rational actors have the same incentive, the tragedy of the commons is simply replicated within the state, as special interests seek access to resources such as forests and rangelands without responsibility to care for them. Such considerations led some theorists ineluctably toward authoritarian prescription. In the words of Garrett Hardin, 'mutual coercion, mutually agreed upon' was the only solution. Robert Heilbroner (1974) foresaw a grim future that could be navigated only by authoritarian government combining 'religious orientation with a military discipline' to stop people abusing the commons.

Such eco-authoritarian thinking could not stop at the level of the nation state, for many of the most severe ecological problems arise at international and especially global levels. Thus the prescription had to involve authoritarian international bodies too. If the existing international system makes this unlikely, then the solution for countries that saw the light was to cut themselves off from the rest of the world, to act as lifeboats whose occupants should ignore those drowning in a sea of ecological misery Hardin (1977) saw the Third World as consigned to such misery.

Beyond limits: Markets, community, sustainable development

Both eco-authoritarianism and the limits perspective that helps to underwrite it eventually ran into hard times. The challenge they posed to existing states (embedded in a political economy that made economic growth the first policy priority) proved just too radical. Their social scientific theory also was attacked from two directions. Market economists argued that the price system is perfectly capable of inducing corrections for resource scarcity. As resources become scarce their price goes up, so there is money to be made in developing substitutes or ways of using existing resources more efficiently (for an extreme statement, very influential in the USA under the Reagan administration in the 1980s, see Julian Simon 1981). Falling commodity prices in the 1980s and 1990s lent support to this kind of thinking. However, after 2000, aspects of the limits perspective began to seem more plausible as the price of oil and other natural resources increased, and the prospect of passing the peak in world oil production loomed.

The second direction of criticism accepted the existence of limits but criticized the associated politics. Analysts of commons resources pointed out that in many cases, the users of commons resources themselves are capable of developing cooperative arrangements for managing the resource that do not require any governmental intervention at all, still less an authoritarian state (Ostrom 1990). This kind of analysis resonated with a strand in green political thinking that dates back to the very beginning of the environmental era and believes in cooperative, 'small is beautiful' human social arrangements (Schumacher 1973), perhaps even eco-anarchism (Bookchin 1982). These arrangements enable human communities to live in a harmonious, low-stress relationship with the natural world in a way that the very large-scale social structures of industrial society do not.

Though the existence of global ecological limits has never been refuted, they received progressively less prominence as environmental discourse in both theory and practice emphasized the idea of sustainable development. The key marker here is the Brundtland Commission report to the United Nations, *Our Common Future*, published in 1987. It argued (or, rather, assumed) that economic growth and environmental conservation did not have to conflict – that economic development could be made environmentally sustainable, and could achieve social justice both within and across generations for good measure. As Brundtland (1987: 8) put it: 'Humanity has the ability to make development sustainable – to ensure that it meets the needs of the present without compromising the ability of future generations to meet their own needs'.

A complementary discourse of ecological modernization began moving environmental policy in several North European countries at around the same time (notably Scandinavia, Netherlands and Germany) (Weale 1992). According to ecological modernization, 'pollution prevention pays' in economic terms because pollution indicates inefficient use of materials. Moreover, a clean and pleasant environment means happy, healthy and productive workers. And there is money to be made in pollution control technology. This shift to ecological modernization and sustainability had no impact in the United States, which remained stuck in a conflict between defenders and critics of the regulatory system established in the 1970s (Andrews 1997). Sustainable development and ecological modernization can underwrite a moderate environmentalism in association with the state – though both can also be bent in more radical directions.

While the idea of global ecological limits was at its most influential in the 1970s, its softening in the subsequent era of sustainability and ecological modernization did not quite mean that these limits were no longer recognized as real and important. For if sustainable development is to mean anything more than 'business as usual' in pursuit of economic growth, there has to be some recognition that human economic activity is environmentally constrained. Where sustainable development differs from the older discourse of limits and survival is in its assumption that it is possible for collective political action to redesign economic development so that it respects ecological limits. Economic growth could go on, but it has to be the right kind of growth. Thus the idea that there are some ecological limits is a basic assumption that ought to be shared by environmentalists in all their variety, from the most moderate, business-friendly advocate of sustainable development to the most radical green eco-anarchist. The idea of ecological limits became especially plausible with the increasing prominence of the climate change issue on political agendas worldwide after 2000. The capacity of the atmosphere to absorb greenhouse gases without potentially catastrophic climate change is one inescapable ecological limit on human economic activity.

Human nature

Though having a lot to say about the character of non-human nature, environmental theory of the state is quite varied when it comes to assumptions about human nature. Environmentalism as a movement is home to all kinds of wishful thinking about how humans could behave in a more environmentally sound fashion. This might come about by adopting a particular kind of environmental ethic; or a more empathetic eco-feminist sensibility (Diamond and Orenstein 1990); or a deep ecological identification with nature as a larger 'Self' (Devall and Sessions 1985); or a more modest, indeed conservative, approach to human needs (Schumacher 1973; Ophuls 1977); or a more cooperative attitude in human community. When it comes to humans as they currently are, analyses of public goods, externalities, and the tragedy of the commons can assume a homo economicus model of rational egoism. But many environmental analyses are actually quite agnostic on the essence of human nature, treating it (like Marxists) as having a history rather than an essence, and thus the product of particular social circumstances.

Arguably, a true homo ecologicus would be able to reflect upon these circumstances and their ecological consequences. In this sense, a commitment to full individual autonomy becomes part of the foundation for an ecological political economy, more secure than either a homo economicus echo of the industrial era or wishful thinking about how human sensibilities could be more benign toward nature.

Society, Politics and Ecosystem

Given that environmental theory lacks a distinctive explanation of how public policy gets made in the liberal democratic state, it also takes an eclectic approach to how social forces can and do influence the structure and operation of the state. But as environmentalism, in all its varieties, rejects of the unqualified industrialism of an earlier era, then it ought to recognize the pervasive influence of industrialism upon the state. Until environmental critique appeared around 1970, that influence was barely recognized; it was so pervasive that it infused even seemingly radical critiques of capitalism, such as Marxism. Though a commitment to economic growth now needs defending, and the content of scientific and technological change is increasingly questioned rather than simply accepted, many industrialist ideas have proved to die hard, and their influence is still overwhelming. It is still widely accepted that the first task of government is economic management, and that the key indicator of success or failure is the level of economic growth.

Of course, there is plenty of variation in the rhetoric that accompanies such commitments. In the United States, the presidential administrations of Ronald Reagan and later George W. Bush were quite unapologetic and forthright in putting economic growth above environmental concern – for example, injustifying why the United States was no longer interested in participating in global efforts to tackle the climate change issue in 2001–2002. Elsewhere, government officials may have accepted the validity of environmental concerns, but they still put economic growth first. The problem here is one of time scale. If a state fails to secure economic growth, it is punished quickly and publicly by global financial markets, the decisions of corporate investors, and voters at the next election. If public policy contributes to causing ecological disaster, the negative effects are likely to be diffused across national boundaries, felt in the long term, and are difficult to pin on particular policy decisions. The global political economy possesses powerful economic police officers (the World Trade Organization, the World Bank, the International Monetary Fund and financial and capital markets) ready to pounce on any state that departs from the liberal capitalist, growth-oriented orthodoxy. International environmental police officers are very weak in comparison. There is no World Environment Organization. All we have is a set of treaties whose enforcement depends solely on the continued active consent of the governments that have signed them, and networks of non-governmental organizations exerting moral pressure on governments and corporations.

Environment and economy reconciled?

How might ecological interests and values compete more equally with economic interests and values in their struggle to influence the state? One answer is that the struggle can be dissolved (or at least re-framed) by making environmental values compatible with economic ones. This rhetorical achievement was enabled by the rise of sustainable development discourse in the 1980s, and given precision by the idea of ecological modernization that took hold in several north European governments around the same time. In Norway, for example, this meant that environmental groups could have representatives on the committees that are the real driving force of public policy in that country. Though differing in details, increased access and influence for environmentalists also occurred in other Nordic countries too, Germany and the Netherlands, and was reflected in environmental policy performance. Summary measures relying mostly on pollution levels and emissions control, (occasionally measuring also the stress imposed on ecosystems) put these countries at the top of international league tables. For example, the environmental sustainability index computed for the World Economic Forum in 2002 rated Finland, Norway and Sweden as the top three performers (see http://www.ciesin.org/indicators/ESI/rank.html). The United States, once a pioneer in the 1970s, lagged far behind at number 45 out of the 142 countries surveyed, as environmentalists and their opponents continued their decades-old confrontation in Congress, state houses, executive agencies, the courts and elsewhere.

So is the key to effective environmentalist influence and (ultimately) the development of a green state to adopt sustainable development and ecological modernization principles? For several reasons such adoption may not be enough. Only moderate environmental concerns can readily be incorporated into the state through such means. Moderation here means steps reconciled to the basic structure of the liberal capitalist political economy – and the priority it gives to economic growth. Writing in the ecological modernization idiom (though they do not use the term), what Hawken *et al.* (1999) call 'natural capitalism' is really only a more efficient form of capitalism, using fewer resources to yield greater social welfare. Green visions of a more thoroughly transformed political economy living in harmony with nonhuman nature would have to be shelved. Why should this matter? Aside from the intrinsic congeniality of the radical green vision, there remains the thorny question of the ultimate existence of ecological limits. Ecological modernization simply neglects global limits in order to focus on practical policy questions in the short term within tight geographical boundaries – extending at most to the whole of the European Union, certainly not beyond. Improved efficiency in fuel and materials use may delay any encounter with global limits, but not indefinitely. Sustainable development may be conscious of the need for the world to change the composition of economic growth in a more environmentally friendly direction – but in practice limits are simply forgotten in policy deliberations. With time, the centre of gravity of sustainable development has become ever more business friendly and mindful of the priority of economic growth, until the 'sustainable' aspect of sustainable development becomes forgotten. This slippage was pronounced at the 2002 World Summit on Sustainable Development in Johannesburg, where business partnerships with governments and NGOs were highlighted (Wapner 2003).

Environmental legitimation crisis and the limits of moderation

Such criticisms notwithstanding, if sustainability and ecological modernization are the only games in town when it comes to effective environmental influence on public policy, should not environmentalists simply buy into them? Yet environmentalists, especially green radicals, are reluctant to make any complete commitment here. To see why moderation does not always pay most, let us return to what happened in the United States at the beginning of the modern environmental era. The puzzle here is why Richard Nixon, a conservative president with no environmental sympathies, should have presided over the world's first great expansion of environmental legislation and institution building. The answer is that, to borrow some post-Marxist language (see Chapter 4), this was his administration's response to a legitimation crisis that beset the United States in the late 1960s.

This crisis was not occasioned by environmentalism, which in itself did not have the capacity to destabilize the political economy. However, the movement against the Vietnam War coalesced with the more radical aspects of the new left, women's liberation, black power and environmentalism to constitute a 'counterculture' that was widely perceived as a threat to political stability (see, for example, Crozier *et al.* 1975). The Nixon administration sought to remove the least radical of these movements, environmentalism, from the grasp of the counter-culture by enacting a series of policy measures. This strategy was successful in that it immediately converted environmentalism into a well-behaved set of interest groups. But it also produced real payoffs in policy content. No other developed liberal democracy had the same kind of legitimation crisis as the United States in that era, so none matched the power of its environmental policy implementation. As the legitimation crisis waned in the 1970s, so did US environmental policy.

This fate notwithstanding, the moral of this American story is that one means for environmentalism to influence public policy in a profound fashion is by taking advantage of opportunities that legitimation crisis provides; and at least in the first instance, this dynamic may be advanced by radicalism, not moderation. Is there anything in environmental affairs in the early twenty first century that constitutes such a crisis? The best candidate here may be found in risks involuntarily experienced by the public. Such risks might relate to nuclear technology, food safety, toxic pollution, genetically modified organisms and other biotechnologies. It is not so much that the risks are of greater magnitude today than in previous eras; more that public reaction to them is different. Every new risk-related scandal increases public scepticism, be it asbestos in schools, mad cow disease/BSE in the UK, or toxic wastes buried under housing developments in the United States.

Though he does not use the language of legitimation crises, Ulrich Beck (1992) argues that our 'risk society' brings severe crises of confidence in the authority of scientists, technologists and the governments and corporations that employ them. Risk society is peopled by critically aware citizens who no longer accept the inevitability and desirability of economic growth and technological change. Rather, they call the content of social and economic development into question. Beck believes that new forms of democratic 'subpolitics' might result, that in turn presage a 'reflexive modernity' in which fundamental questions about the political economy require rational justification and public scrutiny. While his analysis here is short on specifics, and involves selective exaggeration of a few trends, the general point is important that risk issues can threaten the legitimacy of the state and the political economy in which it is embedded. And such crises constitute opportunities for enhanced environmentalist access to the state, and so may expand the range of values that can influence public policy. Moreover, 'subpolitics' can involve the direct engagement of environmental groups and other activists with corporations in political efforts that can produce quasi-governmental outcomes without reference to the state – as, for example, when a group organizes a boycott of a company until it changes its ways, and then certifies the improved behaviour.

The capacity of risk issues to cause legitimation crisis is enhanced to the degree there is a radical social movement ready to pick up on them. This combination of highly salient risks and a radical social movement operating in a public sphere has characterized Germany since the 1970s. The heyday of broad-based radical social movements was perhaps in the 1970s and 1980s, but the anti-nuclear movement could still mobilize large numbers to protest against shipments of nuclear materials in 2001. Germany is where Beck's risk society scenario appears to make most sense. Subpolitics there features interactions involving radical and moderate movement representatives, ecological research institutes, and corporations. Germany's combination of moderate environmentalism pursuing ecological modernization at the heart of government and radical social movements highlighting risk issues and critique of the political economy is a fertile one. This is not to say that Germany has achieved anything like a comprehensive ecological transformation of the state, still less a reflexive modernity; but it has the potential to move further in this direction than just about any other country (Dryzek *et al.* 2003). And part of the reason for this is the continued presence and still stronger memory of a radical social movement.

Organizing environmental lobbies

The environmentalist or green movement has a proliferation of different forms of organization, ranging from small-scale, local groups lobbying over specific pollution, conservation, species-protection or sustainability issues through to national-level coalitions mounting major protests against nuclear power, airports or losses of green spaces and wilderness. Established national groups such as the National Wildlife Federation in the United States and National Trust in the United Kingdom have millions of members, dwarfing the membership of political parties. More radical groups still have hundreds of thousands of members (Carter 2001: 132–3). Groups such as Friends of the Earth, Greenpeace and the World Wide Fund for Nature organize internationally and take on international issues such as whaling.

The methods used by green groups also range widely. At one end of the spectrum, direct action involves (for example) harassment of Japanese whaling ships, occupying sites threatened by development, or tree sitting in the path of logging of old-growth forests. At the other end of the spectrum, moderate green groups maintain think tanks, links with environmental scientists and technologists, and connections to mainstream party politicians. At the international level, green non-governmental organizations are welcomed in a consultative role with organizations such as the World Bank.

In organizing members, green groups share the problems of any 'endogenous' group that appeals to a diffuse set of potential members, united only in their concern for an issue – as shown in Figure 11.1. Unlike a trade union, for instance, whose potential members may be conveniently grouped by employers into large factories or workplaces, there are no particular locations in society where green activists or members are concentrated for easy recruitment. And people who care about the environment at present may simply change their mind next month, transferring their attention to other issues or reverting to a focus on their own private concerns. Recruiting from everywhere in society is exactly what is so hard to do. Free-riders who benefit from the efforts of environmental groups are likewise hard to identify, let along bring into line. Unsurprisingly many environmental groups have quite high levels of 'churn' in their membership, losing up to a quarter of members each year and having to recruit new ones.

Environmentalists also have to contend with the 'issue attention cycle' in public opinion that Anthony Downs (1972) identified. This starts with 'alarmed discovery' over a new environmental problem. Under pressure from voters, governments make some policy response to improve matters. Subsequently policy discussions become more technical and public interest wanes. The issue does not disappear, but it becomes routinized. Hirschman (1982) detected long (10 to 15 year) cycles in developed liberal democracies, with attention oscillating between public action spheres (such as environmentalism) and private materialism.

Figure 11.1   *The problem of organizing 'endogenous' groups*

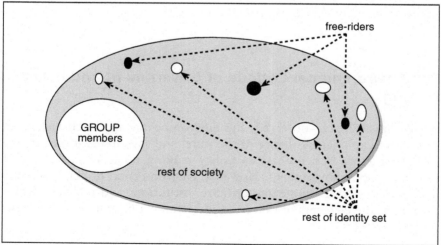

Since the 1970s green parties with environmental commitments at their core have challenged more established parties. Under plurality rule elections (see Chapter 7), citizens who cast their vote for small green parties do so in the knowledge that their chosen candidate cannot win. Green parties exist in the Anglo-American plurality rule countries, but they have a mountain to climb in terms of securing political representation. The more established parties may however try to make green appeals – during 2006 to 2008 the British Conservative Party deployed the slogan 'Go green, vote blue'.

Green parties do better where proportional representation (PR) is used (see Chapter 7). Greens have been elected to the Australian Senate (which uses a PR system) and to UK seats in the European Parliament and London Assembly in the UK (also using PR voting). Greens flourished in New Zealand once its electoral system changed from plurality rule to proportional representation, and joined a governing coalition led by the Labour Party. In the coordinated market economies with PR systems of mainland Europe green parties have been much more successful in establishing themselves as significant political forces, because vote shares of 5–10 per cent can translate into seats in the national legislature. The German Greens formed a national governing coalition with the Social Democrats that lasted from 1998 to 2005, having earlier joined coalitions at city and state level. The Greens were the minor partners, but they supplied Germany's foreign minister, Joschka Fischer. After 2005 the Greens still had 51 seats in the German Bundestag. Green parties have experienced divisive internal debates about the degree to which they should participate in conventional legislative politics or form coalitions with other parties, but in Germany and elsewhere these debates were eventually resolved in the conventional direction.

The Environmental Critique of Government and Policy Making

As we have already observed, the environmental approach lacks any distinctive explanatory theory of the state, and this observation extends to the structure and process of policy making no less than to social influences upon government. However, environmental principles can be deployed to both evaluate and criticize institutions and policies. Before turning to the elements of this critique, we take a brief look at the comparative evaluation issue.

The comparative environmental capacity of states

The best systematic comparative evaluation of the ability of different sorts of states to cope with environmental problems has been carried out by Martin Jänicke, Helmut Weidner, and their associates (1997). For them, a state possesses environmental capacity to the degree that it can effectively deploy social learning about ecological problems. Such a state ought to have well-developed and well-funded institutions that can generate and use knowledge, and the ability to ensure policy implementation. There should be integration across actors and policy areas, culminating in integrated environmental planning across the whole of government. All this requires a flourishing scientific and engineering establishment, environmentalist organizations working with the state (rather than against it), as well as an acceptance of environmental values that range across all administrative agencies, not just those with an environmental mission. Ideally such agencies should operate in a framework provided by a constitutional recognition of environmental rights, and formalized understandings – such as the precautionary principle, which specifies that scientific uncertainty is not an excuse for inaction on an environmental risk. Capacity does then depend on a consensual approach to policy making, underpinned by a shared commitment to environmental values within government and beyond. It is no coincidence that Jänicke himself was one of those who first identified and named ecological modernization in the early 1980s. Ecological modernization denies the necessity of conflict between economic and environmental values – and so between industry and environmentalists, or between the economic and environmental agencies of government.

In these terms, environmental capacity is clearly highest in north European countries that have pursued ecological modernization. As a corollary, the more adversarial approach characterizing environmental policy in the Anglo-American countries (and especially the United States) is clearly problematic. The Anglo-American countries are further downgraded by their reluctance to embrace the precautionary principle. The traditional approach to science in the United States and particularly the United Kingdom is that sound science is needed before action can be taken, meaning that scientific uncertainty about (say) global warming or acid rain is routinely used by politicians as an excuse for policy inaction. A defender of the Anglo-American countries might argue that the capacity building model discriminates against them from the outset. But the obvious reply is that comparative national performance indicators of the sort discussed in the previous section corroborate the capacity building story, as do comparative case studies of the sort compiled by Jänicke and Weidner (1997).

The capacity building analysis demonstrates that some kinds of public institutional arrangements do better than others when it comes to environmental affairs. But this does not mean that the performance of even the best states is necessarily good enough. To see why not, we turn now to the more thorough environmental critique of the modern state, beginning with its territorial boundaries and the kind of sovereignty that accompanies them.

The critique of boundaries and sovereignty

From an ecological point of view, state boundaries are arbitrary, the legacy of historical accident, and they do not correspond to ecosystem boundaries. For example, a watershed such as that of the Rhine or Danube encompasses parts of many countries. Even if policies make some environmental sense within one country, they may make no sense in terms of the basin as a whole. For example, upstream countries can solve their own toxic waste problems by dumping wastes in the river as it leaves their border. A country such as the United Kingdom can rely on prevailing westerly winds to take care of some of its air pollution problems – at the expense of Scandinavians who live downwind.

The ecological problem posed by the sovereign state is most acute at the global level, where many of the more severe and intractable ecological problems reside, especially those relating to climate change. Recent decades have seen some successes in terms of agreement among sovereign states producing global environmental accords. The most notable was the 1987 Montreal Protocol for the Protection of the Ozone Layer, banning chlorofluorocarbon chemicals that depleted stratospheric ozone. However, such agreements have to be essentially self-enforcing, there being few sanctions that sovereign states are prepared to accept in the environmental area. This is especially problematic when it comes to climate change, where the economic stakes are orders of magnitude greater than on the ozone issue, because most national economies depend so heavily on fossil fuels, whose use would have to be curtailed.

In 1997 many countries signed the Kyoto Protocol, which committed developed countries to a target of a 5.2 per cent reduction on 1990 levels of greenhouse gas emissions, to be achieved by 2010. But in 2001 the United States, by far the biggest emitter of greenhouse gases, withdrew, citing the priority of its economic interests. The George W. Bush administration was influenced by powerful oil and coal interests that denied the reality of climate change. Even the countries that remained nominally committed to the Kyoto principles showed few signs of moving toward, let alone meeting, the 2010 targets. And any efforts the European Union and Japan made to cut their emissions were more than offset by rapid economic growth based on fossil fuels in China, India, and other developing economies not subject to Kyoto restrictions.

Within sovereign states, sub-national boundaries often cut across ecosystems and similar kinds of problems arise, for example, as different US states in the arid Colorado River Basin fight over allocation of limited water flows. One solution in such cases is to place policy making authority at a higher level. But then in large countries that can often mean empowering a central government agency that has no local sensibilities, and which applies principles and regulations in a way that is insensitive to local ecological variations and incapable of making use of local knowledge. However, effectively co-ordinated efforts may sometimes work at the level of large regional blocs – as in the EU's success in managing down the risks posed by Soviet-designed nuclear power plants across central and eastern Europe. The EU found it harder to create a working European market in permits for carbon dioxide emissions. Effective action along such lines at the global level would be harder still.

The state's rationality in question

The modern state is also vulnerable to ecological critique about the degree to which it embodies a particular analytic view of rationality that dominates the modern world. Max Weber argued a century ago that the best way to approach complex problems is to divide them into simpler sub-problems, devise solutions to the sub-problems, then piece together these solutions into a grand solution. Indeed, this is what the word 'analysis' means. To Weber, this kind of analytical principle was the basis on which rational bureaucracies are organized, producing the familiar hierarchy and pyramid-shaped organization chart. Bureaucracy is rational because it can produce coordinated solutions to problems that would overwhelm the cognitive capacities of any individual or small group. Most large organizations, including those in the modern state, continue to follow this logic, at least when it comes to setting up their basic structure. This approach to solving complex problems has also been advocated by Herbert Simon (1981), who spoke of 'problem decomposition' as a basic strategy for confronting complexity.

The problem is that the very complexity which is the justification for problem decomposition and Weberian bureaucratic organization can overwhelm the analytical approach to task organization. Complexity exists to the extent of the number and variety of elements and interactions in the environment of a decision system. Environmental problems often feature great complexity, because they arise at the intersection of complex human systems and complex ecosystems. What happens under extreme complexity is that bureaucratic coordination fails. Solutions arrived at, in the various locations into which the overall problem has been decomposed, fail to add up to a coherent whole. Indeed, particular sub-units may be working at cross-purposes, as when an air pollution authority mandates a technology that removes suspended particulates by 'washing' emissions, which creates a water pollution problem. Or tall smokestacks might reduce pollution locally while creating it at long distance. Or mandating solar energy may lead to severe pollution in the production of photovoltaic cells. Or insisting on geologically secure repositories for radioactive wastes may mean that they pile up (and disperse) at their points of generation, because no secure geological site can be found. The net result is not convergence on a better situation, but endless displacement across the boundaries of the sets and sub-sets into which the original complex problem has been disaggregated (Dryzek 1987).

Now, the Weberian model of state organization is arguably being undermined from several directions. The decentralized problem-solving associated with networked governance (discussed in Chapter 6) can be coordinated with some environmental institutional agendas, of which more later. But other developments actually reinforce the Weberian approach, even as they are justified in opposition to it. The market liberal version of public choice theory, especially influential in the Anglo-American countries, in practice involves an enhanced role for the apex of the governmental hierarchy, now charged with overseeing contracts and competition in service delivery according to tight design specifications (see Chapter 5). So the Weberian model is still with us. Most environmental agencies still operate under a series of single-medium statutes. For example, the United States EPA has to implement the Clean Water Act, Clean Air Act, Resource Conservation and Recovery Act and other pieces of legislation – none of which takes any of the others into account. Yet as Barry Commoner (1972) put it long ago, the first law of ecology is that 'everything is connected to everything else'.

The environmental critique of the liberal democratic state is deepened by pointing to the kind of interests it is incapable of representing – however responsive it may be to ordinary voters. Environmental problems often have long term aspects. So decisions made today concerning what to do with long-lived nuclear wastes, or whether or not to control greenhouse gas emissions, or how much to exploit fossil fuel resources, will have consequences that are felt in the decades or centuries to come. The problem is that future generations cannot vote.

Neither can non-human entities. Yet one of the key aspects of ecological crisis is human destruction of the non-human world. Biodiversity is lost, habitats are destroyed and species become extinct. Nature has no direct voice in policy making – only advocates who try to speak on its behalf, but who are usually listened to only when they speak in terms of (enlightened) human interests. So for example rainforest is more likely to be protected if it can be shown to sustain eco-tourism, provide genetic resources for pharmaceutical companies, act as a buffer against local climatic fluctuations, or protect watersheds. Its intrinsic value or simple right to exist is rarely enough.

These aspects of the critique of the state – relating to its territorial definition, its inability to deal with transnational and global issues, its priorities, its underlying analytic theory of knowledge, and its inability to represent future generations and non-human nature – have inspired a multi-faceted agenda for transformation of the state, to which we now turn.

Agendas and Political Change

Environmentalism comes in many varieties, and so its agenda is not easily mapped onto conventional left-right classifications. The original slogan of the German Green Party, *Die Grünen*, was 'Neither left nor right, but in front.' Like most other green parties, *Die Grünen* themselves were actually more left-libertarian than anything else. But liberal, Marxist, conservative and even fascist environmentalisms are also possible. Ophuls (1977) took the epigram for his pioneering book on environmental political theory from the founder of conservatism, Edmund Burke: 'Men of intemperate minds cannot be free'. Conservatism involves an organic view of society that can be connected to ecological views about the organic character of ecosystems. And its fundamental impetus, to conserve what is best and not meddle with it recklessly, can be applied to complex ecosystems just as easily as to complex social systems (Scruton 2006). A romanticized view of Aryan nature once found a corner in the Nazi party (which of course cared nothing for other peoples' nature). Recent attempts to reinvigorate Marxism have emphasized ecological causes of crisis in the capitalist political economy (see, notably, the journal *Capitalism, Nature, Socialism*, founded by leading eco-Marxist James O'Connor). Of course, eco-Marxists must distance themselves from the very poor environmental record of past Marxists states.

The best environmental record can be found in liberal open societies, though critics would say this has often been as a result of their ability to export their destruction, for example, by getting their goods produced in highly-polluting factories in poorer countries. Liberal environmentalists take a more positive view (Wissenburg 1998). 'Free market environmentalists' (Anderson and Leal 2001) believe the solution to the tragedy of the commons that underlies many ecological problems is to divide the commons up and establish private property rights to all component pieces of the environment – not just land, oceans, and forests, but to air, flowing water and migratory species. Owners of those rights will then have every incentive to protect the resource in question and find its best (most profitable) use. Eco-anarchists such as Bookchin (1982) see the root of environmental evil in the rise of hierarchy that enables human domination of nature as well as other humans; so they recommend the abolition of all hierarchies – including that of the state over society. Eco-feminists believe that the particular hierarchy of patriarchy is to blame.

In short, just about every conventional political ideology can be linked to environmentalism. In this light, it remains paradoxical how hard it has been to get contemporary states to take environmental crisis seriously. Rather than canvass ideologies any further, we will focus now on agendas for the structural transformation of the state and its relation to society that respond directly to the environmental critique of the state as set out above. This means looking beyond mere advocacy of better environmental policy – and beyond the viewpoint that environmental policy can be pursued straightforwardly in existing states, provided only that enough political force is mobilized (for example, Goodin 1992).

The centralizing agenda and its problems

The seeming refusal of the liberal democratic state to change its system of priorities in response to ecological crisis might be countered by the centralized imposition of ecological priorities. Such a course was advocated most famously in the 1970s by authors such as Garrett Hardin (1977), Robert Heilbroner (1974) and William Ophuls (1977). Centralization would also overcome the problem of territorial fragmentation that runs across ecosystem boundaries. Indeed, this logic would point ineluctably to the development of a global super-state to deal adequately with global problems. This kind of eco-authoritarianism is easily extended beyond coercive solutions to the tragedy of the commons; it could also curb the consumer appetites that are one driving force of exponential growth in the stress imposed on resources and ecosystems. So for Ophuls (1977: 163): 'The steady-state society will not only be more authoritarian and less democratic than the industrial societies of today ... but it will in all likelihood be much more oligarchic as well, with only those possessing the ecological and other competencies necessary to make prudent decisions allowed full participation in the political process.'

Eco-authoritarianism mostly failed to outlast the 1970s; its association with a grim discourse of limits and survival was just too great a challenge to the primacy of economic growth in the dominant liberal capitalist order. It is also a direct challenge to fundamental precepts of liberal democracy, and so is hard to sustain in a liberal democratic era. But it is also suspect from the point of view of environmentalism itself. For the only administrative technology currently available to organize a strong and highly centralized state is a Weberian one, involving problem disaggregation and task allocation within a pyramid-shaped bureaucratic structure. Yet just such an analytic approach to problem-solving is one of the main targets of the ecological critique of the modern state, notes in the previous section.

A look at real-world evidence can also shed light on the issues here. While there are plenty of examples of bureaucratic-authoritarian regimes in human history, there is no example of an authoritarian regime effectively pursuing ecological values. It might be argued that none has ever had the commitment and motivation; none has ever been controlled by, in Ophuls's (1977: 163) words, the right kind of 'ecological mandarins'. But how exactly might such mandarins come to power? How is their permanent and unwavering commitment to ecological values to be ensured? What is to stop such rulers pursuing their own interests instead?

Ecological democracy and networks

What the history of the past four decades does reveal is that the environmental policy area has been at the forefront of the further democratization of the liberal democratic state, and in particular its administrative agencies (Paehlke 1988). Key innovations were all pioneered in the environmental area such as, public comment on proposed legislation, right-to-know laws, citizens' juries and other devices such as consensus conferences that involve deliberation by a group of randomly selected citizens, mediation of policy disputes, regulatory negotiation, public inquiries and policy impact assessment with guaranteed public input, and policy dialogues of various kinds. Thus the 'greening' of the administrative state in this era has also meant its democratization.

From the viewpoint of many environmental agendas this democratization is mere incremental tinkering, yet it is perhaps indicative of the possibilities for more extensive political-ecological reform. In the 1990s, the environmental theory of the state turned decisively in a democratic direction (Mathews 1996; Lafferty and Meadowcroft 1996;

Minteer and Taylor 2002). The exact kind of democracy that is required remained a matter of dispute, with boundaries set by existing liberal democracy on one side and radical, participatory, discursive democracy on the other. The case for the latter can begin with the complexity problem that ultimately overwhelms the capacities of Weberian bureaucracy and conventional liberal democratic problem-solving (which is equally compartmentalized, if not quite so rigid as bureaucracy). The idea here is that the interactions across the sets and subsets into which complex problems are divided can be matched by more effective decentralized dialogue between individuals concerned with these various sets and subsets. This dialogue would involve not just public officials concerned with the issue in question, but citizens who are closer to the problem.

Such closeness might involve being a victim of toxic pollution, a member of an indigenous community with accumulated traditional knowledge of an ecosystem, a wilderness advocate concerned with the ethical as well as scientific aspects of nature protection, an engineer, or a citizen who has surveyed their own neighbourhood to get stories of environmental illnesses. This decentralized approach to problem-solving meshes quite easily with ideas about networked governance. But networks can also involve social movement activism, as exemplified by the environmental justice movement in the United States (Schlosberg 1999). The latter explicitly rejects the more traditional kind of centralized environmental interest group, adopting instead a 'bottom up' kind of organization with no central coordination, let alone executive leadership. Beginning in the 1980s, and based on a series of local actions, the environmental justice movement raised concerns about the inequitable distribution of toxic risks across lines of race and social class, proving remarkably successful in bring new issues to the agenda, and eventually achieving (some) public policy response.

Effective problem-solving in such decentralized networks will prosper to the extent of competent and authentic participation and communication encompassing a variety of perspectives – and this is its discursive democratic aspect. This aspect can be realized in institutionalized deliberative forums – discursive designs (see Chapter 8). Such designs might involve parties to a dispute, sitting down together in order to reason through their differences and try to arrive at a solution to which all sides can assent. For example, this is the basic idea of environmental mediation, though many other kinds of dialogue follow this core model. Normally a neutral mediator or facilitator oversees the process. Environmental mediation has been widely used in the United States, mostly in site-specific disputes concerning the construction of a dam or shopping mall or over local air pollution control. Such processes can be discursive but not necessarily very democratic, because only representatives of the main stakeholders take part – and in the case of environmentalists they may be self-appointed. Such processes may still fall short of the kind of discursive ideals that appear in environmental democratic theory because some participants (for example, polluters or developers) are at the table only because of their environmental misbehaviour, and their underlying concern to turn a profit, rather than to contribute to ecological wellbeing. The dangers of becoming co-opted by their opponents are pervasive, because in the very act of sitting down with a developer or polluter on equal terms, an environmental or community group is accepting the presumption that their interest is legitimate, and have the moral equivalence of environmental protection and private profit (Amy 1987).

These sorts of hazards perhaps explain the more recent interest in deliberative processes that select lay participants from the larger population (usually at random), of the sort discussed in Chapter 8. Such processes have been applied to issues such as the release of genetically modified organisms into the environment, container deposit legislation, river basin management and wetland protection.

Democracy and the green public sphere

However far they fall short of discursive democratic ideals, these sorts of processes do indicate a democratic opening of the state – especially its administrative aspect. But any limits to authentic deliberation caused by close attachment to the state and its priorities, not to mention the possibility of co-optation, mean that environmental democrats are often interested too in other locations. Deliberation can be located not just in or close to the institutions of government, but also in the public sphere constituted by environmental and community activists and others at a distance from the state (see Chapter 8). In environmental affairs no less than elsewhere, the public sphere can be considered as a repository of authentic democratic communication, a source of critique of public policy. Indeed, this is where environmentalism began – as a social movement, initially confronted with a state that was fairly recalcitrant (except, for reasons we have already discussed, in the United States). Torgerson (1999) endorses the kind of 'carnival' aspect often found in the green public sphere, involving not just deliberation over serious matters, but also protests and performances. Examples of the latter would be members of Earth First! sitting in treetops in old growth forests threatened with logging, or many Greenpeace actions (such as installing solar panels on the roof of the Australian prime minister's house in protest against his government's stand on energy policy). Such activity may be welcomed by mainstream groups. As Duncan McLaren of

Friends of the Earth UK put it: 'From my perspective there is a great synergy with what the Direct Action people do – them being in the trees and us being in the Treasury' (quoted in Dryzek *et al.* 2003: 156).

There remains the question of how all this activity in the public sphere may then come to influence collective outcomes such as public policies. But such connections can be made, if not always obviously and directly. Part of it is simply changing the terms of discourse in society, which then comes to pervade the understandings of policy makers. Indeed, this may be the single most important achievement of four decades of environmentalism; there is now a language for discussing pollution, risk, wilderness, indeed the environment itself, that simply was unavailable before. One other trend pioneered in the environmental area is societal governance that does not involve government – except perhaps to confirm practices already in operation. For example, the transnational regulation of forest products guarantees, that wood products come from sustainable forestry rather than the destruction of virgin rainforest. It is carried out mostly by a network of non-governmental activists who certify products that companies can then sell with a seal of approval (often in the form of a sticker) to reassure consumers (Meidinger 2003).

This kind of societal self-regulation is consistent with a far more radical strand in green thinking about the state that dates back to the beginning of the modern environmental era (Goldsmith *et al.* 1972). Impressed by the degree to which small-scale human communities once appeared to live in greater harmony with the natural world than their successors, this approach seeks a radical decentralization of human affairs, to be organized on a cooperative, communal basis, downplaying the role of both markets and hierarchies. The state is seen only as part of the problem, thoroughly enmeshed with the large technostructures of the industrial political economy. The most radical strand here is eco-anarchistic (Bookchin 1982).

A practical approach to reorganization consistent with this radical communitarianism is bioregionalism (McGinnis 1998). Bioregionalism begins with the critique of the ecologically arbitrary fixing of political boundaries (discussed above). Bioregionalists propose redefining the boundaries of the state and other political units to reflect ecosystem boundaries. For example, instead of Oregon, Washington, northern California, and British Columbia dividing up the west coast of North America, we would have Cascadia, defined by the temperate coniferous forests that are its basic natural ecosystem west of the crest of the Cascade mountain range. Other parts of these states and province would fall into different bioregions. Of course, such re-drawing of boundaries is not enough to ensure better environmental outcomes without a change in outlook on the part of political leadership. And this is why biorgeionalism also stresses changed public consciousness, to emphasize awareness of one's bioregion, rather than one's culture or nation.

Tentative forms of bioregional organization already exist, mainly in the form of river basin authorities such as the Murray-Darling Basin Commission in Australia. Similarly the Northwest Power Planning Council oversees the Columbia River basin in the Northwest United States, a basin that cuts across the forests of Cascadia and mid-continent deserts. Here the Council has attempted to pursue ecosystem management for the whole basin, complete with inputs from discursive designs that enable citizens and users of basin resources to have their say (Lee 1993). However, this kind of management eventually foundered in the face of more powerful and still competing jurisdictions with different interests – the different upstream and downstream states in which the basin is located, the federal government and its agencies, and interest groups based outside the basin pursuing their interests within it. The trigger for the end of ecosystem management in the Columbia basin was actually a lawsuit filed by a national environmental group seeking better protection for salmon under the terms of the federal Endangered Species Act.

Conclusion

Eco-authoritarianism, eco-anarchism, green democracy, and bioregionalism all challenge quite directly some of the fundamental organizing principles of the contemporary liberal democratic state, and the political economy in which it is located. Beginning in the 1980s, a more reformist structural agenda has sought accommodation with the state rather than confrontation. Eckersley (2004) points to the inescapability of the state as a site for environmental action – indeed, the site that provides the preconditions for activism at all other levels, such as in civil society, and which acts as the main bulwark against the market imperatives pushed by and in the global liberal capitalist order. After endorsing the capacity-building approach, Eckersley sketches what a green state might look like. Such a state would operate with a constitution that embodies information rights about hazards, rights to litigation for third parties as well as those directly affected by a risk, 'temporary citizenship' rights for those affected by transboundary effects, the precautionary principle, the polluter pays principle, and recognition of the rights of nature itself. Eckersley's green state would also be cosmopolitan, a good international citizen on environmental affairs.

Whether or not one endorses Eckersley's specifics, sustainable development and ecological modernization have major implications for the environmental theory of the state, because they dissolve the conflict between environment and economy that had generally kept environmental concerns away from the core economic business of the state and public policy. As we have already seen, in countries where these ideas have been taken seriously, environmentalists came to be accepted as major players in cooperative policy making operations. Whether this is adequate from the point of view of the environmental agenda is another question entirely. While a country like Norway leads the world in environmental quality indicators, and has pioneered initiatives such as green taxes, it may have reached the limit. Norwegian environmental groups help make and implement policy – indeed, most groups are so thoroughly integrated into the state that they often behave like parts of it. What is lost is the radical critique that provides the main impetus for environmental reform to begin with. This is retained in Germany, where a state mostly committed to ecological modernization (whether or not the Green Party forms part of the government) still confronts a degree of radicalism in the public sphere, and so retains greater dynamism in environmental politics (Dryzek *et al.* 2003).

These developments notwithstanding, substantial scepticism remains among political ecologists concerning the ability of the contemporary state – whether it is it styled an administrative state, a liberal democratic state, or a capitalist state – to confront environmental crisis in sustained and effective fashion, especially the aspects of that crisis that transcend the boundaries of developed Western democracies. The climate change issue in particular puts the limitations of these states in stark perspective. Many governments have recognized the severity of the issue, but despite their signing up to international agreements and committing to cutbacks in emissions levels, targets are not met and emissions continue to increase. Thus to environmentalists, the contemporary liberal democratic state still looks like an ecological failure, and the first task of the environmental theory of the state is still critique.

Chapter 12

The Conservative Reaction

Conservatives are those who adopt a moralistic approach to politics that is often combined with strong appreciation of the role a particular society's traditions play in assuring social cohesion and political stability. Contemporary right-wing political parties (such as the British Conservative Party and US Republican Party) often feature an uncomfortable mix of true conservatives and market liberals (described in Chapter 5). Market liberals are not true conservatives because they care nothing for communities, public morality and traditions, only for individuals and markets. Some true conservatives want to turn the clock back to a world where social order was firmly established and everyone knew their place in it. Other conservatives accept that the world changes and that there is a need to adjust, slowly and carefully. More recently a third offshoot of conservatism has convulsed the United States and, through US foreign policy, the world. This 'neo-conservatism' is highly moralistic and opposed to the civic decay of contemporary societies, but unlike more established conservatism it happily embraces radical policies to achieve its goals.

Origins and Assumptions

Conservatism was founded by the British political philosopher and politician Edmund Burke, who in 1790 published his most famous work, *Reflections on the Revolution in France*. In that book Burke warned that any proposals for the wholesale reform of society, such as those enacted by the liberal revolutionaries in France, would lead inevitably to misery and death. The reason is that society is like a complex organism that cannot be understood by any single theory, let alone redesigned in its entirety. Even well-meaning radicals will find that their reforms have unexpected and unwanted consequences. The temptation is then for these radical reformers to resort to coercion to make the world fit in with their schemes. Or, as Burke puts it: 'In the groves of their academy, at the end of every vista, you see nothing but the gallows.' This process was exemplified in France, where the guillotine rather than the gallows was employed. Burke believed that political reform was necessary in response to a changing world, but that such reform should proceed slowly and carefully: 'Approach to the faults of the state as to the wounds of a father: with pious awe and trembling solicitude.' This attitude to reform was adopted by the British Conservative party – which helps to explain its extraordinary political success over the subsequent 200 years, as it managed to cope with the gradual extension of the franchise to all adult citizens, and attract substantial support even from relatively poor voters, thus securing its position as the 'natural party of government'. Continental European conservatives throughout the nineteenth and early twentieth century tended to be much more reactionary, defending the privileged classes against democracy, and the landed aristocracy against the rise of first capitalism and later socialism. As a result they were much less successful than the British Conservatives in attaining and keeping control of government, and often found themselves opposed by revolutionary movements.

Of course, the nineteenth and twentieth centuries did witness major social, economic and political changes to which conservatives everywhere had to adjust. These changes included the rise and expansion of capitalism, the growth of electoral democracy and the development of welfare states. Governments became large and interventionist in their dealings with society. So conservatives could often find themselves defending institutions and practices whose origins they might once have opposed. Most fundamentally, they eventually accepted the basic contours of the liberal democratic state, and the range of individual rights that accompany it. Many conservatives came to accept the welfare state – and even played key roles in the expansion of social welfare programmes. However, eventually there arose a conservative reaction against the alleged excesses of an individualistic, rights-based society and political system on the one hand, and against an excessively active and expensive state on the other. It is upon this reaction that we focus in this chapter.

British Prime Minister Margaret Thatcher once claimed famously that 'There is no such thing as society', by which she meant that all that mattered were the rights, interests and wellbeing of individuals. Despite being leader of the Conservative Party, Thatcher was a market-oriented neo-liberal (see Chapter 5), not a true conservative of any sort. True conservatives believe there *is* such a thing as society, created over the generations by the contributions of many individuals to particular social traditions and political practices. Unlike market liberals, who believe that people are basically the same everywhere (i.e. rational and egoistic), conservatives believe that individuals are the product of their own particular society. Conservatives recognize the webs of social obligation that bind people together: shared culture, shared religion, shared festivals, shared language, shared prejudices, shared outlooks and shared sports teams. The specific content of these binding factors will vary in different societies, and so will the moral commitments they generate.

Society and Politics

The stress on society as existing prior to the individual is stated in its strongest form by *communitarians*. Communitarian political philosophers (for example, Sandel 1982) begin with a critique of all liberal political philosophies based on the rights and obligations of abstract individuals. Communitarians do not deny the importance of rights, but believe that individuals are created by the web of social relationships into which they are born and develop. Individuals thus have strong obligations to their community. Society is composed of families, churches, voluntary associations and neighbourhoods – not isolated individuals. Communitarianism is a political movement as well as a philosophy. In the United States, communitarians have claimed Presidents Bill Clinton and George W. Bush among their number. Communitarian William Galston was Clinton's domestic policy advisor, and communitarian Amitai Etzioni consulted with Bush. Communitarians protest that they offer a 'third social philosophy' that 'leapfrogs the old debate between left-wing and right-wing thinking' (Etzioni 1996: 7), but the continuity from classical conservatism as articulated initially by Edmund Burke is obvious.

This emphasis on obligations to community above individual rights is also shared by Confucian political ethics influential in east Asian societies (Bell and Hahm 2003). The communitarianism of East Asia has been most strongly advocated against Western individualism by former Singapore Prime Minister Lee Kuan Yew (Bell 2006: 265), who believed that governments in Asian societies should keep tight control over a unified society. 'Asians have little doubt that a society with communitarian values where the interests of society take precedence over that of the individual suits them better than the individualism of America' (Lee Kuan Yew, quoted in *International Herald Tribune*, 1991) .

Western thinkers including John Stuart Mill and Max Weber had long supposed that this sort of importance placed on family and community above the individual would preclude effective capitalist development in east Asia, because it would rule out the individualistic striving and competition necessary to make capitalism work. Recent decades have of course shown this supposition to be wrong, as capitalism in east Asia has boomed. And if the thesis is wrong in east Asia, it might also be wrong when applied to other parts of the world where the bonds of community enmesh individuals tightly.

In the strong sense emphasized by conservatives, community is only ethically defensible to the degree that there is a consensus on social values; otherwise communal obligations can only be secured by repressing dissidents. Thus an underlying social consensus is a key conservative assumption, though the content of this consensus can vary from society to society. Edmund Burke spoke of the 'wise prejudices' formed by social traditions that define each society and constitute the shared understandings that enable it to function and flourish in its own unique way.

The density of the social ties that connect individuals to their society has in recent years been described under the heading of *social capital* (Putnam 2000). Societies can have different amounts of social capital. A society heavy in social capital will have high levels of membership in social organizations, be they sports clubs, choral societies, churches, youth groups, trade unions, service organizations, consumer cooperatives, professional associations or social clubs. It is these organizations that link the individual to the larger society, and help teach individuals the virtues of trust and social cooperation. Social capital is also built through associating and networking in informal ways: by talking with others in a café or bar, by inviting friends to dinner, even interacting with one's family. Social capital is both reflected and reinforced in high levels of volunteering and giving to charity.

The contention of social capitalists is that individuals who learn the virtues of sociability and community will have a generalized trust in other members of their community, and so be better citizens. They will make society as a whole more productive, prosperous, educated, peaceful, harmonious and free from crime. The originators of this thesis, Robert Putnam and colleagues (1994), believe that the reason Northern Italy is a better society than southern Italy is because the former has a great deal of social capital, the latter hardly any. This difference can be traced back over several hundred years, and so is grounded in the very different histories of the two parts of Italy. The quantity of social capital can rise and fall with time, however. So Putnam (2000) charts and laments the decline of social capital in the United States since the 1950s. As he puts it, Americans may be still be bowling, but they are 'bowling alone' rather than in clubs. Membership of associations, volunteering, charitable giving as a proportion of income, even simple sociability and spending time with friends have been falling steadily. And even when individuals do belong to associations, they are often mere 'checkbook' members, giving money but none of their personal time – so political associations have 'astroturf' instead of 'grass roots'. They have no local chapters where individuals might meet and construct shared actions, only national offices that fund a professional staff.

Partly Putnam's story is one of generational change, as the civic-minded and public-spirited generation that grew up amid the hardships of depression and war was succeeded by more self-centred, individualistic generations. In this light, social capitalist analysts sought and thought they detected a civic upturn in the United States in the wake of the terrorist attacks of 9/11, though the effect did not seem as profound as that of the Great Depression and World War II. However, Putnam's US story is also one of negative social trends that affect everyone. One of the main culprits is the way that television isolates people from their society, exacerbated more recently by the Internet and other forms of electronic entertainment. Putnam disparages the idea that new sorts of community can be found on the Internet. Similarly, Sunstein (2007) argues that the Internet induces people to congregate in like-minded sectarian enclaves that reinforce prejudices, but never expose anyone to others who do not share their point of view. For Sunstein, there are no multi-faceted communities on the Internet.

Also important to Putnam in explaining the decline of social capital is the increasing employment of women outside the home, undermining family life and the traditional leading role that women play in community-building. Suburban sprawl contributes to the isolation of individuals from each other, because there is no need for them to interact with neighbours with whom they share nothing except residential location. This kind of analysis drives home the communitarian and conservative antipathy to the rampant individualism of contemporary Western societies.

Finding yet another nail for the coffin of American social capital, Putnam (2007) discovers in a wide-ranging study of neighbourhoods in the United States that the more ethnically diverse a neighbourhood, the lower its levels of trust (even trust in members of one's own ethnic group), and hence civic commitment and the engagement of individuals with others. Diversity leads people to become like turtles, withdrawing into their individual shells. Putnam himself is uncomfortable with this finding, and hopes that in the long run these negative effects of diversity can be overcome.

The notions of community, consensus and social capital that are the building blocks of conservatism have substantial implications for the structure and operation of the state. Essentially, a flourishing state requires a flourishing community with plenty of social capital. Individuals schooled in trust and cooperation will bring these virtues to politics, be it as voters, public servants, or politicians. Voters should seek what is in their community's interests rather than their own narrow material self-interest. Ordinary people in general should be willing to make personal sacrifices for the common good (especially in wartime). Public servants should serve the public – and not seek mainly to advance their own careers, or line their own pockets. Politicians should govern in ways that seek and obtain the broad support of the public, and not engage in needless partisan conflict with one another. Everyone should know their place in the social and political order, and not seek to disrupt this order for the sake of their personal advantage, or the wellbeing of their social class, occupational category, religion or ethnic group.

In this conservative light, the key social influences on public policy come not from competing interest groups, or the material self-interest of voters, or the demands of the economic system, or the sectional interest of the ruling class. Instead, they come from the traditions and social values into which members of the society are socialized. So citizens of France should accept and value the ideals of republican social solidarity enforced by a centralized state that are the legacy of the French Revolution, Napoleon, and Charles de Gaulle. Britons, in contrast, ought to accept monarchy and the associated hierarchy based on birth. Ideally, these traditions and values would be virtuous – though conservatives recognize that real-world societies and states may fall far short of the ideal, especially if they are under the influence of nefarious disruptive doctrines such as pluralism, Marxism, market liberalism or feminism.

The Conservative Critique of Government and Policy Making

Conservatives are not committed to any particular explanatory theory of the state, and they have no general explanation of how public policy gets made that would apply to even a single state. For conservatives, the world is too complex to yield to any such general theory. Yet in keeping with our stress on treating conservatism as a reaction against the excesses of contemporary liberal democracies, we should highlight the important tendencies in contemporary states that conservatives identify and criticize. Conservatives believe that the state should respond to and reinforce common community interests, but there are many aspects of contemporary states that undermine the proper conduct of government in the community's interest. This list of evils includes the following.

The liberal democratic state can accommodate groups pursuing many different purposes, but common purposes that unite rather than divide society are harder to generate. A commitment to freedom might seem to be one such purpose, but all too often freedom itself is interpreted in terms of a set of rights that individuals have against the state, and against each other. Thus if all freedom means is 'rights talk' (Glendon 1991), conservatives believe it will lead to further division and individual isolation in society. Matters are exacerbated to the extent that the first task of the state is seen in terms of promoting economic growth and so better satisfying the material needs of its population. For any loyalty to particular governments or the state as a whole is then going to be simply a matter of material calculation – voters will only be pleased when their income is increasing. This ever-changing calculation is a very weak basis for individuals' commitments to society and politics, compared to the much stronger loyalties that a common culture and way of life ought to generate.

The liberal state's neutrality across competing doctrines is often manifested in the idea of *secularism*: that the state should embody no religion as its own. While the remnants of a state religion cling to some states (such as the Church of England), in general liberal states seek to distance themselves from any particular religion. To many conservatives, this distancing compounds the lack of common purpose and morality that would bind a people together, and to its state. For many modern conservative thinkers, the content of the religion in question is much less important than the simple fact of its existence, such that it is fine for different states to be guided by different religions. However, for more committed religious conservatives, especially fundamentalist ones, the content of the religion and the moral guidance it supplies to the state are crucial. In the United States, conservative Christian fundamentalists seek to impose a radical religious agenda on government, one that would forbid (among other things) abortion, human biotechnology, any recognition of the rights of gays and lesbians, sex education in public schools, and the teaching of biological evolution unless it is on equal terms with 'intelligent design'. To date, Islamic fundamentalists in countries such as Saudi Arabia and Iran have been far more successful than US Christian fundamentalists in imposing their religious beliefs upon their state.

While the existence of *rights* as such does not necessarily dismay conservatives, the universalistic and overarching way in which rights are sometimes specified certainly does. If rights are universal, that means they are politically and legally more important than the particular traditions of societies valued by conservatives. East Asian conservatives in particular are very critical of universal human rights, treating them as essentially Western constructs that can only destabilize Asian societies. For political rights to free expression and association provide the space for political dissidents to oppose government and so disrupt the harmony of the social and political order. Conservatism in this context can help justify authoritarianism.

Conservatives fear the consequences of a *proliferation of interest groups*, especially if those groups are making financial demands on government, or threaten to block government action in areas of concern to them. Crozier *et al.* (1975) raise the spectre of liberal democracies becoming 'ungovernable' as a result of this proliferation – though their criticism was directed mostly at social movements and lobby groups representing the poor and previously marginalized. They argued that the extension of political power to ever-increasing numbers of groups will lead to chaos in policy making, and if all the demands were met, bankruptcy for the state.

Multiculturalism means that government recognizes the validity and political standing of a variety of cultures, notably those of immigrants, national minorities and indigenous peoples. Cultural minorities may therefore be granted government support for education in their particular language or religion, government recognition of their customs, traditions and legal codes, and representation in government bodies. In such policies Conservatives see a further dilution of the common culture and identity that binds individuals to their society and its state. Conservative opposition to multiculturalism is often accompanied by worries about immigration, if the immigrant minority in question is culturally different from the majority. For example, Samuel Huntington (2004) asks *Who Are We?* in relation to the United States. Huntington believes that the United States is an essentially liberal democratic protestant country and state, whose character is being undermined not just by multiculturalism, but also by large scale legal and illegal immigration, especially from Mexico and elsewhere in Latin America. This kind of analysis does not necessarily mean hostility to immigration – but it does require that immigrants assimilate to the political culture of their new society, rather than demanding public recognition of and retaining primary loyalty to their culture of origin.

Conservative worries about the negative effects of cultural diversity are reinforced by Putnam's findings we noted earlier about the negative effects of ethnic diversity in a neighbourhood on social capital. Putnam (2007) believes that in the long run these effects can be overcome, but only to the degree that diverse groups are assimilated into a common framework of life. Multicultural policies that perpetuate the separateness of ethnic groups only delay that assimilation.

Historically, conservatives played a part in the creation and expansion of *welfare state* programmes. The first social insurance programmes were pioneered by the authoritarian conservative government of Otto von Bismarck in late nineteenth century Germany as a way of drawing working class support away from the Social Democratic Party. But many contemporary conservatives believe that too extensive and too generous a welfare state means that responsibilities now fall upon the state which once fell upon individuals, communities and families. In particular, the old and the sick are seen as the responsibility of government, rather than their families. Advocates of 'Asian values' note the degree to which care of the elderly is important within Asian families, while it seems to have been taken over by government in the West. And a generous welfare state means that individuals are allowed to be irresponsible when it comes to decisions affecting their own lives, because if things go wrong government can always step in to help. This critique of excessive welfare state dependency is one point of commonality between conservatives and market liberals (see Chapter 5).

To conservatives, *feminism* has contributed substantially to the individualization of society and loss of community and common purpose. Putnam (2000) points out that if women work in paid employment outside the home, they have less time to participate in voluntary associations that are key to a society's social capital. Feminism further disrupts the social order by pushing for a more extensive welfare state, by criticizing the gender-biased nature of many social traditions, and affirming the universal rights of women in all political contexts. At its most destructive, feminism is seen as joining multiculturalism in pushing for special treatment in public policy to advance the employment opportunities, social standing, and political representation of women and ethnic minorities alike, thus further dividing the political community.

In Chapter 5 we saw that in many countries since the 1980s market liberals have had some success in re-making the state in the image of the *market*, through devices such as privatization, contracting out of government services, internal markets, compulsory competitive tendering for service provision contracts and across the board budget cuts. Though much of this programme has been carried out by governments claiming to be conservative, true conservatives worry that this programme not only contributes to the decay of common purpose in society – because it converts citizens into consumers or customers of the state – but also corrodes the state from within. It does so by destroying any notion of public service on the part of government officials, who are treated as self-interested rational egoists unworthy of any trust. If they are treated like this, they may come to behave more like this. Political morality and common purpose are again the casualty in conservative eyes.

The communitarian basis of the conservative reaction against the excesses of contemporary liberal democracies is quite easily attached to the 'imagined community' of the nation-state. It is much less easily attached to governing structures above the level of the state, and the idea of a 'global community' is weak or non-existent in conservative eyes. So conservatives generally oppose *international government* above the level of the state. They are hostile to the United Nations, to the World Trade Organization and to the European Union. For these international governmental organizations are seen as making policies that are based on abstract trans-national values, such as economic theories of the benefits of free trade, or universal human rights. These policies then override the traditions and values of national communities. For example, it is hard for a state to subsidize its farmers so as to produce traditional products in an attractive countryside – for that will be interpreted by the World Trade Organization as a subsidy for unfair competition in international agricultural markets. In the United Kingdom, 'Euro scepticism' defines a large, nationalistic section of the Conservative Party, who see British national traditions, policies and practices being overruled and broken up by a European bureaucracy.

We turn now to what conservatives think might be done to counter all these negative trends associated with liberal democratic states.

Agendas and Political Change

Conservatives traditionally believed in defending the status quo, and reforming it only gradually to cope with new problems and changing circumstances. But the cumulation of the negative developments outlined in the previous section means that conservatives have had to develop a more active political programme. Communitarians in particular have articulated a comprehensive set of proposals. The communitarian political agenda involves re-establishing the claims of the concrete community as a whole above the abstract human rights of individuals. Communitarians see virtuous and socially committed citizens subscribing to an ethics of personal responsibility and social obligation as the bedrock of a good society. And so much of what they propose in the way of institutions and policies consists of social engineering to promote virtue and morality. The US-based Communitarian Network has developed a detailed 'Responsive Communitarian Platform' (online at www.gwu.edu/~platformtext.html). Values education is crucial, not just through formal schooling, but also through religious and community organizations. For example teenagers should be schooled in responsible sexual behaviour. Public policies should strengthen two-parent families and support the role played by extended families. Private interests such as corporations, unions and lobby groups should be made more responsive to public interests, rather than simply their own self-interest. The role of private finance in politics (especially in campaign finance) should be curbed, for therein lies a corruption of politics in support of narrow sectional interests and material self-interest. Earlier we noted conservative suspicion of an excess of democracy, but according to the Responsive Communitarian Platform 'communitarians favor strong democracy . . . more representative, more participatory, and more responsive to all members of the community'. Such a democracy is not a problem for communitarians if it is composed of virtuous, public-spirited, community-minded citizens.

While communitarians seek a balance between individual rights and social responsibilities, they believe that in many liberal democracies the balance has swung too far in favour of rights. Communitarians want to curb individual rights run wild – extending even to the right to own guns in the United States, which for other kinds of conservatives is sacred. Conservatives in general are uneasy with the degree to which institutions such as the United States Supreme Court make individual human rights the bedrock of decisions. Traditional conservatives would be happy with the idea of judicial review of legislation because it imposes a check on the excesses of democratic majorities, but they believe that the terms of that review should take into account community interests, not just individual rights.

In the wake of the terrorist attacks of 9/11, communitarians were generally supportive of restrictions on individual liberties for the sake of collective security. Members of the US-based Communitarian Network debated online the issue of whether it was acceptable to torture terrorist suspects if the information elicited could forestall future attacks.

Communitarians should be suspicious of political systems structured in adversarial fashion, because adversarial politics guarantees that sectional interests get heard (for example, a right-wing party dominated by large corporations, and a left-wing party dominated by labour unions), rather than the voice of the community as a whole. In terms of the categories we surveyed in Chapter 7, communitarians should advocate consensual rather than adversarial parliamentary systems.

The communitarian stress on *consensual government* acting in the interests of the community as a whole appears very strongly in east Asian political thinking and practice. The implication can be authoritarian, if opposition to the governing consensus is interpreted as unwarranted disruption of the prevailing political order. While some east Asian Confucian societies do indeed feature adversarial politics (for example, South Korea and Taiwan), others allow little if anything in the way of organized political opposition or criticism of the government (China and Singapore). Japan has institutionalized a system whereby one ruling party essentially monopolizes political power – though managing to do so in conjunction with free elections that the Liberal Democratic Party always wins. The legitimacy of the state in such systems turns on its efficacy in meeting the needs of the people as a whole – so even authoritarianism is tempered by a degree of solicitude for what is in the interests of the people, rather than their rulers (Ng-Quinn 2006).

Promoting morality and building social capital

The contemporary conservative reaction against the excesses of liberalism seeks a state that would do a better job in inculcating morality in its citizens. There are historical examples, and some contemporary examples, of states that have tried to do this very directly. Lindblom (1977: 276–90) speaks of 'preceptoral' systems such as Mao's China that devote substantial energy to inculcating in their people the kinds of values that the regime considers desirable, though the threat of coercion for those who do not comply is mostly not far away. (Obviously conservatives would not approve of the particular kinds of radical leftist values associated with Mao). Christian theocracies were once highly preceptoral, and contemporary Islamic theocracies in Saudi Arabia and Iran police morals very carefully – with drastic penalties for those who do not conform.

Contemporary liberal democracies find such moral instruction from above much harder, precisely because of their more pluralistic character. Thus policies to induce more moral sentiments and behaviour must be more indirect. In the United States, this has led to specific policy measures such as 'welfare to work' or 'workfare', under which the right to welfare payments for the poor comes with an obligation to work most of your life and to seek work actively when unemployed. The idea is to reduce individual dependency on bureaucratic decision, and to create more responsible members of society. US conservatives have long criticized welfare policies that encourage the growth of single-parent families by eliminating the need for a male breadwinner (Murray 1984). On this analysis, one major consequence is a high rate of violent crime among young African-American males, who have grown up without any role model of a responsible male. When it comes to crime, the policy of 'zero tolerance' for minor infractions that began in New York City under Mayor Rudy Giuliani has been widely adopted. Here the idea is to show that any degree of criminal or anti-social behaviour is intolerable. Moralizing conservatives can also join forces with some feminists in passing laws to restrict pornography and prostitution – though of course the conservatives' broader agenda is anti-feminist. The administration of George W. Bush advanced 'faith-based initiatives' – the delivery of publicly-funded social services by religious organizations, which would dole out moral instruction along with material benefits to the poor.

Moralistic social engineering may increase virtuous citizen behaviour, but what can be done about declining social capital? Critics of Putnam *et al.*'s (1994) analysis of Italy suggest (tongue in cheek) that it is important for a society to get itself a good history – one in which there are plenty of legacies of social commitment and consequently civic virtue to build upon. Putnam (2000) himself issues a clarion call for civic renewal in the United States. However, it is often hard to see how exactly this can be translated into public policy content, still less public policy that could counteract the powerful social trends (television, the Internet, suburban sprawl and women's employment outside the home) responsible in Putnam's eyes for declining social capital. Moreover, individuals often join associations not because they want to be more civic, but because the association has some more instrumental purpose for them (be it in terms of social standing, developing useful business contacts, protecting against employment insecurity, or advancing a public policy they favour). The contribution to social capital is often a by-product of this instrumental action. So if individuals do not believe that associating with others will serve any personal interest, they are unlikely to do it. Yet perhaps governments could adopt a more interventionist policy in civil society to help create the 'right kind of associations' (Walzer 1994); ones that integrate communities rather than pull them apart, that create what Putnam (2000) calls 'bridging' as opposed to 'bonding' social capital. Government should then subsidize neighbourhood watch groups and community associations – but not the Ku Klux Klan or other sectarian groups.

We should also note a religious conservative agenda reacting against the secular nature of the state – though not all conservatives are religious, and communitarianism as a political philosophy does not have to involve religion. The joining of religion with conservative politics is mostly confined to the United States, where it animates opposition to homosexuality, abortion and the teaching of evolutionary biology. Though the United States is constitutionally secular and liberal, as Morone (2003) reminds us, it is also a 'hellfire nation'; subject throughout its history to moral panics and religious crusades against sinful minorities.

Beyond such prescriptions for the re-moralization of society and the rebuilding of community and social capital, conservative approaches to political change since Edmund Burke have generally emphasized limited and piecemeal reform, curing particular problems rather than trying to re-shape society. We turn now to a doctrine that is nominally conservative but adopts a very different and much more radical approach to political change.

Neo-conservatism

We treat the agenda of neo-conservatism separately in this chapter because although 'conservative' is part of its name, it categorically rejects some of the key tenets of the conservative reaction rooted in community, consensus and scepticism discussed so far. As Paul Weyrich, first President of the Heritage Foundation and later Chairman of the Free Congress Foundation, put it in 1984: 'We are different from previous generations of conservatives. We are no longer working to preserve the status quo. We are radicals, working to overturn the power structure of the country'. Neo-conservatism radicalizes some core conservative beliefs, but rejects the traditional conservative emphasis on piecemeal reform attuned to the complexity and organic unity of societies. Moreover, it embraces with enthusiasm some aspects of liberalism and democracy with which other conservatives have traditionally been uncomfortable. And it discards the communitarian emphasis on the particularity of cultural traditions in favour of a moral universalism believed to be right for the whole world. This doctrine came to prominence in 2003 with the US-led invasion of Iraq, justified in part on the grounds that it would bring democracy to the Middle East. But the roots of neo-conservatism can in fact be found in a diagnosis of some of the ills of US society and its domestic politics.

Neo-conservative ideals

Neo-conservatism begins with a standard conservative critique of the loss of common moral purpose in the modern world (see for example Kristol 1983). Some of its prominent exponents learned this lesson first from the political philosopher Leo Strauss, who inspired a generation of talented students at the University of Chicago from the 1940s to the 1960s with tales of the timeless wisdom of great political thinkers. Rather than advocating a communitarian agenda or return on the part of all societies to their own particular traditions, neo-conservatives selectively embrace modern liberalism and democracy (Williams 2005: 311–21). They reject liberalism's stress on individual self-interest and a pluralism of social interests, and also the idea that democracy is just a way of aggregating material interests. Instead, they seek to recover the more heroic side of liberalism. Here they can point to Adam Smith's account of morality developed in the eighteenth century. Smith is celebrated by market liberals as the father of the free market, but he also thought that a successful commercial society required widespread moral sentiments, a commitment to community values and concern with the wellbeing of others that provides essential social glue (Williams 2005: 315–16). But neo-conservatives go further than Smith in arguing that such commitments to the community can only be inspired to the degree that there is a common national project – something worth fighting and sacrificing for.

There is a clear echo here of a tradition of republicanism extending back to ancient Rome, where a republican citizenry is a body of confident equals, armed and ready to take on the world, secure in the knowledge of its superior political system, and contemptuous of other political models. The American national project is seen as being established over 200 years, as one of bringing liberty and democracy to the world. So neo-conservatives are American nationalists – but they believe that American values are also universal values, right for everyone, and that it is always in the US national interest to extend these values to the rest of the world. Correspondingly, it is wrong to tolerate those who hold anti-liberal and anti-democratic values, be it at home or abroad. The end of the Cold War in the 1980s can be interpreted as a triumph of this idealism, as Soviet communism eventually crumbled in the face of an unwavering commitment to liberal and democratic principles, latterly lead by the Reagan Administration. Neo-conservatives have nothing but scorn for international institutions such as the United Nations and European Union, which they believe equivocate in the face of evil and compromise with authoritarian regimes (Frum and Perle 2003). They also despise their adversaries in the foreign policy establishment in the United States, which in the past had sought authoritarian allies in the Cold War. Some of these alliances eventually came back to bite the United States – most notoriously in the form of Osama bin Laden and Islamic radicalism emanating from Saudi Arabia and those armed by he USA to fight the Soviet invasion of Afghanistan.

After the Cold War, more of the world came to be governed by liberal democratic regimes – though there were still large parts of the world living under repressive states. But neo-conservatives found it hard to mobilize Americans to any new national project in the absence of any clear adversary. They argued that the USA should use its military power to re-make the world, especially in the 2000 manifesto *Rebuilding America's Defenses* published by their Project for the New

American Century think tank. But they gained little support outside a small circle of intellectuals. All this changed after 9/11 in 2001, an opportunity immediately seized by neo-conservatives with access to and influence upon the Presidency of George W. Bush. International terrorism backed by Islamic extremism became the new enemy. Yet neo-conservatives were interested in confronting and changing states rather than terrorist networks, and so orchestrated the invasion of Iraq in 2003. Iraq may have been a slightly odd choice, given that it was a secular regime with no ties to Islamic terrorism. But Iraq was initially a relatively easy sell to the American people, given its alleged possession of weapons of mass destruction that could be deployed to threaten the US, the clearly dictatorial character of Saddam Hussein's regime and the recent history of the 1991 Gulf War when a US-led coalition defeated Iraq's invasion of Kuwait. The neo-conservatives were not actually interested in any of these things. Rather, they wanted to show that a US-friendly liberal democracy could be built in an Arab society, and so begin the transformation of the Middle East as a whole into a region of democracy, capitalism, and political stability.

The conservative critique of neo-conservatism

The neo-conservative contention was that removing Iraq's dictatorship would lead almost immediately to the flourishing of Iraqi democracy. In retrospective the contention was clearly wrong, but more to the point it was completely inconsistent with just about the entire body of conservative thinking of the previous two centuries. This is why a number of prominent US conservatives could be found opposing the invasion of Iraq. To bring democracy to Iraq required the possibility of social engineering on a massive scale – the denial of which pretty much defined traditional conservatism. Alternatively, neo-conservatives would have to assume that democracy is the natural condition of all societies, to which they will happily and easily turn as soon as dictatorship can be removed, as the onetime neo-conservative Francis Fukuyama eventually admitted (Fukuyama 2006). The second of these contentions is just as problematic as the first, given that most human societies and states throughout history have not been democracies, making it hard to maintain that democracy is in some sense natural. This would be an especially odd assumption for traditional conservatives, given the differences across national traditions that such conservatives always stress.

   Such differences writ large are at the heart of Samuel Huntington's (1996) 'clash of civilizations' thesis, through the lens of which the conflict between radical Islam and the West could also be interpreted. Huntington was a conservative – but not a neo-conservative. He believed the world is increasingly divided into a number of civilizational blocks, each with its own political traditions. Liberal democracy and human rights help define Western civilization. But they are not universal ideals, they are not at home in other civilizations, not in Islam, the Eastern Orthodox Christian World, or Japanese, Chinese, African, and Hindu civilizations. Huntington argued that the West in particular should not intervene in internal conflicts in other civilizations, still less try to remodel their societies along Western lines (1996: 316). Such meddling could only ever have the consequence of exacerbating inter-civilizational conflict (and, in one of his scenarios, instigate world war). Thus Huntington's particular brand of conservatism ought to rule out adventures such as the invasion of Iraq.

Communitarians too ought to oppose neo-conservative adventurism. Against both Huntington and the neo-conservatives, the leading communitarian Amitai Etzioni (2006) argues that the real split in the world is not between liberal democracies and dictatorships (as neo-conservatives believe) or civilizations (as Huntington believes), but rather between moderates and radicals within 'civilizational' blocks. Moderates believe in persuasion, while radicals (be they neo-conservatives or radical Islamists) believe in coercion and violence. Etzioni's approach to international relations would involve uniting moderates to underwrite international agreements – and that includes illiberal but moderate governments that do not believe in human rights or democracy.

On the face of it, the insurgency, terror and civil war in Iraq after 2003 constitute a clear falsification of neo-conservative doctrine. By 2006 the neo-conservative hope for an American citizenry united in virtuous promotion of democratic ideals in international struggle was over, as US public opinion turned firmly against American involvement in Iraq. Moreover, public opinion and elite opinion almost everywhere in the world turned against the United States, rather than joining the administration of George W. Bush in its crusade. Some neo-conservatives, notably Fukuyama (2006), essentially recanted in the face of this reality. Others, such as Richard Perle (in a 2006 interview in *Vanity Fair* magazine) argued that there was nothing wrong with the doctrine – only the incompetent way it had been implemented in Iraq (see also Muravchik 2006). But the latter escape is again inconsistent with core conservative principles, because true conservatives always stress that the lessons of experience are a much better guide to action than the conjectures of a theory, however elegant and appealing the theory might seem on paper.

Conclusion

The spectacular rise and equally spectacular fall of US neo-conservatism in the early to mid 2000s should not obscure the enduring force of the conservative reaction against the character of the contemporary liberal democratic state. But with neo-conservative policy prescriptions refuted by the test of experience, conservatives find fewer levers for policy and institutional change to fall back upon. Thus conservatism's theory of the state comes to resemble environmentalism and feminism (which it otherwise generally reviles) in at least one important way: the critique is powerful, but the agenda for feasible change is weak.

Conservativism has traditionally been most comfortable when defending a generally satisfactory status quo against proposals for radical change, and this is how it prospered for two centuries (most successfully in the United Kingdom). But when conservatives find the status quo has itself become unsatisfactory, they become less confident and more divided about what to do. Conservatives at the turn of the twenty first century saw a political status quo in liberal democracies riddled with the decline of community and social capital, the rise of secularism, universal human rights run wild, pluralism, multiculturalism, an over-extended welfare state, feminism, the marketization of the state and the growth of international government overriding national traditions. Lamenting and criticizing these trends is relatively straightforward, and conservatives have been eloquent in their critique. Developing a practical programme to role back these trends is much harder.

Part IV

Beyond the State

The very idea that the state is the focal point of contemporary politics has seen profound challenge from two directions. The first is from post-modernism, which we address in Chapter 13. Post-modernists seek to undermine any 'grand narratives' about the state of the sort that all the classical theories offer – as indeed do feminist, environmentalist and conservative critiques of the state. In place of grand narratives, we get particular discourses that can construct politics in a variety of ways, and which are manifested in many places within and across societies. We focus most on post-structural accounts that see contemporary liberal democratic societies in terms of a pervasive 'governmentality' that constructs individuals in particular kinds of ways, as well-disciplined subjects of the liberal order, whose capacity to make autonomous choices is an illusion. Post-modernists have plenty of ideas about how a pluralistic politics of discourses and identities might be constituted in response to these problems, though some of them are not very optimistic about the prospects for its achievement in practice.

Globalization entails the increasing importance of cross-national flows of money, goods, people and ideas that increasingly elude the control of the state. Thus globalization may mean that the real political action is no longer to be found at the level of states, which are forced to behave in particular ways by global economic processes in particular. One response is that global political institutions should be strengthened to match global economic forces. Another is to re-assert the capacity of the state to choose whether to implement or resist the forces of globalization. We explore all these issues and their consequences for established theories of the state in Chapter 14.

Chapter 13

Post-modernism

Somewhat like the conservatives, post-modernists point to the unique features of particular cultures, and criticize universal practices and principles that ride roughshod over differences. However, unlike conservatives, post-modernists see little or no value in any traditions that characterize the community as a whole, still less any national community, still less any national community to which a state is attached. Post-modernists see their own task mainly in terms of disrupting established understandings of this sort, rather than reinforcing such understandings after the conservative fashion. But this disruption is generally not in the name of universal principles that attract liberals, deliberative democratic reformers, Marxists, greens and feminists (though some creative thinkers try to stretch post-modernism in the direction of all five of these schools of thought). What this disruption is in the name of is not always clear. Different thinkers have supplied different answers, but disruption for its own sake is one possible answer.

In this chapter we include the school of post-structuralism, associated especially with the French philosopher Michel Foucault and his followers, under the post-modern heading. While practitioners of these two schools of though might stress the fine differences between them, from the outside their similarities are much more striking. Both are essentially sceptical points of view, casting doubt on ideas of progress in human affairs, and committed to destabilizing any alleged rationality in modern government and the state. Post-structuralism actually supplies post-modernism with an explanatory theory of the state of the sort conspicuously absent in feminist, green and conservative critiques of the liberal democratic state (discussed in earlier chapters). This explanatory theory is organized around the key concept of 'governmentality'. However, building any kind of positive programme for political change and reform of the modern state to accompany this explanatory theory proves very difficult, as we shall see.

Origins and Core Assumptions

The roots of post-modernism as social theory can be traced to nineteenth century reactions against the Enlightenment and modern notions that saw society as properly organized on the basis of reason – for example, the German philosopher Nietzsche. However, as an academic school of thought, post-modernism flourished only in the last quarter of the twentieth century in a variety of social science and humanities disciplines, though its stronghold was in studies of language, literature and culture. Because post-modernism emphasized its scepticism toward all grand systems of thought, its adherents disdained any comprehensive doctrinal statements. Indeed, post-modernism was defined by Jean-François Lyotard (1984) in terms of its 'incredulity toward meta-narratives'. What this meant in practice was a celebration of variety in social practices and ways of looking at and acting within the world. Correspondingly, history was stripped of any meaning and direction. This attitude immediately puts post-modernism at odds with Marxism, which of course highlights a meta-narrative, in its depiction of an historical trajectory that produces capitalist society and then its downfall at the hands of the working class. Marxists and other socialists have often reacted angrily against post-modernism, which they see as a betrayal of the progressive legacy of the left. But post-modernists can be equally hostile to liberal ideas of progress that stress ever-expanding human rights, constitutional government, personal security and economic prosperity. As a result, they believe that liberal democratic states should not be celebrated, but rather criticized for their repressive tendencies.

The fact that there are exceptions to this generalization concerning post-modernism's anti-liberalism shows how hard it is to pin down this approach. For example, the US philosopher Richard Rorty (1983) describes himself as a 'postmodern bourgeois liberal', favouring US-style liberal democracy on the grounds that compared to other political systems, it allows a variety of understandings of the world to flourish. Here Rorty links post-modernism to pluralism; and the kind of critical pluralism we touched on in Chapters 8 and 9 shows that this kind of rapprochement does make some sense.

Post-modernism is not just an approach to social theory and literary criticism. It is also supposed to capture something about the contemporary era. If modernity is defined in terms of the rational justification of social and political arrangements, the universal applicability of reason in human affairs, constitutional government, a familiar set of individual rights, individualistic action, progress, and an economy based on science and technology, then post-modernism sees its task as the de-stabilization of this ensemble. Post-modernism seeks to relativize this state of affairs; to show that it is just one way of being in the world, not necessarily better than other kinds of social arrangements. For post-modernists there are multiple ways of both living in and interpreting the world. In practice, post-modernists often privilege the perspective of those who are oppressed by dominant systems, be they indigenous peoples, gays and lesbians, racial and ethnic minorities, the disabled – but rarely a subordinate social class whose perspective was key for Marxists (see Chapter 4). This inattention to the working class further antagonizes Marxists.

Post-structuralism

Post-structuralism is a 'post' school of thought that resembles post-modernism in its sceptical evaluation of the blessings of modernity. Their theoretical devotees are likely to highlight the differences between these two schools of thought, but to outsiders their commonalities are more readily apparent. Post-structuralism is associated with Michel Foucault, a philosopher who first came to prominence with his histories or 'genealogies' of madness, medicine and sexuality – but not initially of politics or the state. Foucault was mainly concerned with uncovering the social construction of taken-for-granted ideas about disease, mental illness, sexuality and so forth. With the benefit of several centuries' hindsight, old classifications of diseases and mental conditions and their treatments, can look quite bizarre. But Foucault sees the same arbitrary and repressive forces still at work in defining what constitutes received wisdom and common sense in today's world. History to Foucault is mostly a parade of repressive understandings (discourses). Certainly progress of the sort to which most liberal democrats and Marxists are committed is ruled out. What looks like progress is in reality just a narrative of the past designed to serve some powerful interest in the present; to show that today's dominant order is rational.

Eventually Foucault himself turned his attention to politics and the state, which he interpreted in light of a concept he called 'governmentality'. We will attend to the details of this concept shortly. For the moment it is sufficient to note the continuity between Foucauldian analyses of madness, illness, sexuality – and politics. In each case, the dominant reality is one of widely-shared oppressive understandings that it is the task of genealogical analysis to uncover and destabilize.

Post-modernists share the conservative and Marxist scorn for the liberal idea that free and rational individuals are the building blocks for society and politics. Instead, individuals are very much the creation of social forces. For post-structuralists, the social world is always constituted by discourses. A discourse is defined not just in terms of an arena of talk, but rather in terms of a set of taken for granted presuppositions. Those presuppositions condition the way individuals talk, think and act. There is no rationality that can assess critically the content of a particular discourse from the outside, because rationality itself is constituted within discourses. As Foucault (1972: 216) put it, 'Nothing has any meaning outside of discourse.' Post-structuralists speak of power-knowledge formations. The knowledge generated therein always serves some particular interest. For example, a discourse that defines radical political behaviour as deviant and psychologically abnormal serves the political status quo. In fact this is how domestic radicalism was defined in US politics and political science at the height of the Cold War (see, for example, Almond 1954).

Discourses operate so as to organize attention in a particular direction, and so away from other directions. For example, when it comes to environmental affairs, a discourse about responsible environmental behaviour is pervasive in contemporary Western societies. This involves recycling, minimizing waste generation, installing insulation in houses, using public transport where possible, conserving fuel and water, contributing to wilderness preservation lobby groups and so forth. To the post-structural sceptic, this kind of discourse is itself a form of discipline, an 'environmentality' (Luke 1997) that deflects attention away from the structural causes of environmental decay that are intrinsic to the capitalist political economy. So what looks like benign and rational individual and community responses to environmental crisis in fact is a form of social control.

Now, discourses do not have to be repressive – but the kind of history recounted by Michel Foucault and those following in his tradition almost inevitably treats discourses in these terms. The ensemble of discourses characterizing a particular historical era is referred to as the *episteme*. So for example the modern era that began in Europe in the seventeenth century features particular views of science, technology, means-ends rationality, secularism, individual morality, human rights and economic competition that to liberals look progressive – and with the ensuing centuries becomes improved, though still not perfect. But liberals are looking at this episteme from the inside, so it is no surprise that they favour it. To post-structuralists, this modernity simply disciplines subjects in new ways. Individual rights and responsibilities mean mainly that the individual internalizes his or her own repression by taking on a particular kind of moral responsibility that serves the dominant order. The modern episteme marginalizes all kinds of alternative modes of behaviour, by categorizing them as clinically or psychologically abnormal. These might include alternative approaches to sexuality, the pursuit of pleasure, and rebellion against school, work, or political authority.

For the most part individuals are treated by post-structuralists as being in the grip of discourses so powerful that they are not even aware of the existence of the discourses in question, which are accepted as the natural way of the world. There is a parallel here with Marxist notions of false consciousness instilled in the working class (or other subordinate classes) by the bourgeoisie (or other dominant classes) (see Chapter 4). The difference is that for Marxists, it is possible for members of the working class to see through this false consciousness and come to an awareness of their true class position. For post-structuralists, there is no true awareness – just other discourses that might sometimes be available, but probably will not be. While resistance to dominant discourses is conceivable (see below), it is a much harder matter than Marxist resistance to false consciousness, because dominant discourses are ingrained so deeply into the psyche of society and its members. Even those who think themselves radicals may in fact adopt most aspects of the dominant discourse. For instance, in a post-modern light, Marxists share with liberals strong commitments to industrialism, economic growth, scientific rationality and secularism – all of which are central to the oppressive character of modernity.

Post-modernists generally accept this sort of depiction of the constraining character of modernity. But they may see modernity itself as being on the way out, or at least having its universalist pretensions laid bare, such that post-modernity also describes an emerging historical era, not just a school of thought. Post-modernists stress the plurality of ways of experiencing, assessing and acting in the world. So when studying literature, there is no one right way to read and assess a text; everything depends on the viewpoint of the observer. When it comes to science, holistic therapies can be granted equal standing to modern reductionist science. When it comes to politics, what may look like freedom or neutral institutions to liberals can look like oppression to sexual minorities, radical feminists and indigenous peoples. Post-modernists generally celebrate marginal understandings as alternatives to the (old) status quo of modernity. The notion of deconstruction began in studies of literature as a way of revealing the implicit political commitments in texts such as novels or poems. But politics too can be deconstructed. For example, parliamentary customs might be shown to privilege the speaking style of old, upper-class males. When deployed by corporate leaders, the discourse of sustainable development in environmental affairs might be shown to equate 'sustainable' with continued, and 'development' with growth – and so to be ultimately empty of real environmental content (Torgerson 1995).

Society and Politics

The most comprehensive analysis of politics and society in a post-struc-
turalist idiom comes in Michel Foucault's (1982, 1991) notion of *governmentality*. This concept has major implications for the relationship
of the state to society, but not in any conventional way, for it dissolves
the state and society into each other. The term 'governmentality' combines government, rationality and mentality. Government in this light is
what Foucault termed 'the conduct of conduct', where the second 'conduct' is individual behaviour. And that process is everywhere: it is not
something the state does to society, but rather a process that pervades
society, including the bits of society that used to be called the state.
Governmentality proceeds in realms that we can recognize as political
(party competition, voting and elections, debates over the content of
public policy). But it is equally present in realms of life not normally
classified as political, such as religion, individual health, morality, medicine and psychology. Economics contributes through the ethos of self-
discipline, hard work, self-improvement, assiduousness and punctuality
instilled by the experience of markets. The 'conduct of conduct' does
not require the exercise or threat of force. Instead, individuals and
groups monitor and regulate their own behaviour. Paradoxically, then,
the discipline imposed by governmentality actually requires the appearance and feeling of freedom (Brown 2006, 73). Laws promulgated by
government may exist, but more important are all the invisible micro-
processes that keep individuals in line.

In this idiom, power is pervasive and insidious. Power is not something exercised by actor A over actor B to make B conform with A's
wishes. Instead, power is diffused in all the understandings that shape
peoples' lives. This diffusion of power is not however democratic, for
typically it takes a disciplinary and repressive form. Some interests will
be served, and others denied. In particular, those who might disrupt the
established political and economic order are made to feel deviant and
irrational. So those who benefit in material terms from the established
order also benefit from this diffuse power; but they do not actually
have to do anything to keep on benefiting.

In this light, the state still exists, but the state, and so the theory of
the state, is 'de-centred' (Brown 2006: 72). No longer is the state *the*
locus of political power. Instead, the state too is enmeshed in wider
processes of governmentality. Foucault criticized the alleged continuing
obsession of political theory with the construction and limitation of
sovereign political economy. He recommended that political theory
should 'cut the head off the king' and cease this obsession. Instead, the
emphasis should be on the 'microphysics of power' – all those practices

through which power is constructed and maintained. These practices might include the collection of statistics to monitor the wellbeing of populations in the aggregate, schooling, the categories through which populations are classified for purposes of social policy, processes that turn individuals into consumers, socialization mechanisms that condition how people come to feel about their bodies and their identities. Dean and Hindess (1998) catalogue a variety of such practices in Australian government, involving (for example) welfare policy that tries to make its recipients more like market actors, education that creates corporate toadies and consumers rather than citizens, and policies toward indigenous peoples that try to make them more like settlers.

There would seem to be no limit to what can be studied under the governmentality heading. The relevant practices are multiple and complex. The institutions of the state have no unique role in all of this, and certainly the separate institutions of the state do not rule over society. There are things that parts of the state can do – for example, in determining how population statistics should be collected. But the same functions can be carried out by non-governmental actors – for example, a professional society of statisticians, or individual academics or journalists. The formal powers of government combine with all kinds of informal processes to constitute the governance of society (Rose 1999). The relevant processes can be highly elusive and unbounded. But some practitioners of the governmentality approach have made connections with the idea of governance networks that were discussed in Chapter 6. So Sørensen and Torfing (2007) suggest that one way of interpreting networked governance is as a development in governmentality, whereby the network is used as a site for inducing behavioural conformity, and reducing the need for the overt exercise of more conventional forms of power by government. Networks, like governmentality, mix private and public actors, and feature dispersed and often elusive responsibility for the production of collective outcomes.

The end of progress?

Is the kind of governance identified by the governmentality school a good or bad way to organize society? This question is hard to answer, because in the modern world there may not in fact be any alternative to dominant sorts of governance. One might then take a step back to ask, is this world in which governmentality is pervasive getting better or getting worse? This is not a question that post-structuralists, or post-modernists more generally, themselves are especially interested in asking, given their hostility to grand narratives and their associated wide-ranging scepticism. Evaluations of progress or regression could in this light only be made internally, within particular discourses, so there is no sense in asking the question in the abstract. If we pose the question within the liberal democratic tradition, according to liberal democratic standards, the answer might be that things are getting better, that progress is being made. Look, for example, at the ever-increasing proportion of the world's population that lives under constitutional, democratic regimes. On the other hand, even if we stay firmly within the liberal democratic idiom, we can see signs of regression. Some of the excesses perpetrated by the United States in its reaction to terrorism after 2001 fall into this category. In holding 'enemy combatants' indefinitely in Guantanamo Bay, the US violated liberal precepts by putting detainees beyond the reach of the Geneva Convention regulating the treatment of prisoners of war, beyond any protection under international law, and unable to seek redress through US domestic law. In arranging the 'rendition' of terrorist suspects to countries where they could be tortured, basic liberal notions of human rights were cast aside.

Here, many post-modernists would express little surprise at such backsliding, on the grounds that liberalism has always had a dark side that it shows toward those not considered modern or rational enough to enter the liberal order. Remember that in the nineteenth century, the celebrated liberal John Stuart Mill said in his book *On Liberty* that 'despotism is a legitimate mode of government in dealing with barbarians, provided the end be their improvement'. Hindess (2001) points out that liberal states have always repressed not just those in their colonial populations, but also their indigenous peoples, urban poor, criminal underclass, and new immigrants, among others. Thus the relative freedom of being subject to governmentality applies only to those not in these severely repressed categories. Liberal states have to decide who is governed in a relatively benign fashion through 'the conduct of conduct', and who requires treatment through overt authoritarian repression.

Government and Policy Making

Post-modernists generally downplay the importance of the detailed formal structure of the institutions of government. However, institutions can still be treated and analyzed in terms of the shared understandings of people that they reflect. These understandings may be unstable over time. For example, the institution of 'sovereignty' is often treated in mainstream political and even academic discourse as somehow sacrosanct and unchanging, meaning that a state has the authority to do what it likes within its own borders. But as Reus-Smit (1999) shows, the content and meaning of sovereignty have changed over time – and have never been absolute. Keene (2002) points out that sovereignty in this sense has only ever applied to Western states, and states that abide by Western norms. The rest of the world has been treated in colonial terms, with no sovereign rights of the sort enjoyed by Western states. More recently, sovereignty for many states has become contingent on abiding by norms defined in the West (as Iraq found out in 2003). Institutions like sovereignty are social construc-tions. The particular social construction that is the sovereign state may actually be on its way out, according to post-structuralists of the gov-ernmentality school. For the institutions of the state increasingly blend and dissolve into the myriad micro-practices of governance. The sover-eign state is diffused into power networks that do not stop at national boundaries.

Institutions may be further destabilized when confronted with changing conditions surrounding joint problems. Hajer (2003: 177) suggests that contemporary processes of 'globalisation on the one hand and individualisation on the other', multi-level governance (where formal power is distributed and shared across levels of government, from the local to the international), complexity, novelty in the char-acter of policy problems, new sites and forms of political action and undermining of expert authority often lead to an 'institutional void'. That is, when a problem arises on the political agenda, it may be unclear where (if anywhere) responsibility for its resolution can be located, and the character of the polity itself must be negotiated along with the nature of the problem and possibilities for collective action. Hajer gives examples ranging from the trans-national negotiation of intellectual property rights to planning issues in the Netherlands, where actors such as social movements take on quasi-governmental roles, and architects find themselves organizing public participation and indeed representing the public.

Frames and discourses

When it comes to determining the content of public policy, the key influence for post-modernists is likely to be the way that an issue gets framed, not formal institutional structure, and not any calculation on the part of policy makers or policy analysts. A frame is the scheme through which a problem or set of problems gets constructed, inter-preted and so solved. A frame embodies judgments, values, and action repertoires (Schön and Rein 1994). For example, in criminal justice policy, one frame would stress that crime is a matter of rational calcu-lation on the part of potential criminals. What this means is that as the probability of being caught and the severity of expected punishment increase, the relative attractiveness of the criminal act should fall. Any problem solution then lies in effective law enforcement and severe punishment. A second frame would instead stress the sources of anti-social behaviour in the deprived upbringing of criminals, in which case the solution lies in social policies to address these conditions. Such policies might involve the redistribution of wealth, alleviation of poverty and provision of schooling. A third frame would stress the psychopathology of criminal behaviour, locating the source of problems in individual minds, not in social conditions. The key then becomes to treat offenders with rehabilitation or therapy or, if that does not work, simply lock them away so that they can do no further damage. A fourth frame stresses the roots of the problem in the criminal's inability to understand the consequences of crime for his or her victims, which stems in turn from the criminal's isolation from the community. Under the heading of 'restorative justice', this fourth school believes 'reintegrative shaming' (Braithwaite 1989) is better than simple punishment. That is, the criminal enters a process in which the victim of the crime explains how it has damaged his or her life, while (ideally) friends, family, and community members who know the perpetrator participate in a process that both shames the criminal act but seeks to reintegrate the offender into a community. Each of these frames has its own rationality that begins with interpretation of the problem and ends in the selection of a solution. The frames themselves are tied up with larger ideologies and perspectives. For example a frame stressing rational calculation on the part of the criminal is consistent with rational choice theory and market liberalism discussed in Chapter 5.

The language of 'discourses' as well as 'frames' is also very popular in the public policy literature. So for example Hajer (1995) explains the differences between Dutch and British environmental policy in terms of the different discourses that dominate in each country. In Britain, policy making is dominated by a discourse that emphasizes scientific certainty as a precondition to action, and sees environmental and economic values pulling in opposite directions. In the Netherlands, a discourse of ecological modernization embodying a precautionary principle is more important, such that economic and environmental values are seen as complementary rather than competing, and action against pollutants should not await conclusive proof of their harm.

The precise definition of 'discourse' differs across individual authors, but most would agree that a discourse can be thought of in terms of shared concepts, categories and ideas that yield a way of comprehending situations. A discourse will therefore contain and be defined by particular judgments, assumptions, capabilities, dispositions and intentions. The individuals subject to a particular discourse will weave the fragments of information they receive into 'storylines' that are meaningful to others who share the discourse in question. In this light, there are numerous discourses present in the world of public policy. In environmental policy, they would include sustainable development, an older discourse of ecological limits and survival, and green radicalism (see Chapter 11). In economic policy, market liberalism is a powerful and pervasive discourse, especially in international economic affairs (see Chapter 5). Discourses can also be organized around religious or ethnic identity – for example, Islamic and Christian fundamentalism, or ethnic nationalism of the sort that in an extreme form caused war in the former Yugoslavia in the 1990s. Discourses establish what kinds of knowledge can be accepted as legitimate, define common sense, identify who can take action, differentiate these agents from those who can only be at the receiving end of actions, and point to the ways that different actors can be related – for example, through hierarchy, or competition, or cooperation (Milliken 1999).

Actions as well as words matter in discourses (and words can be kinds of actions), and actions are given meaning by the words that accompany them. Particular actions can involve accepting or challenging a discourse. Routine actions reinforce discourses; so driving carefully in Canada and flamboyantly in Italy in both cases reinforces a locally dominant discourse.

Our earlier discussion of governmentality showed how discourses are tied up with power; followers of Foucault refer to 'power-knowledge formations'. Particular discourses serve some interests and marginalize others. So for example a discourse of criminal justice that emphasizes rational action (see above) advantages economists, judges and law enforcement agencies. One stressing criminal psychopathology advantages therapists, and so forth. So for better or for worse, discourses help coordinate the activities of large numbers of people, who never need meet or communicate directly, do not belong to the same formal organization, may be citizens of different states and live in quite different societies. Consider, for example, the role of market liberal discourse in coordinating international financial affairs involving individuals in far-flung corners of the world.

A reasonably conventional way of viewing the roles of frames and discourses in public policy would allow that they offer a range of responses to a problem or set of problems. But this would be to miss the role of frames and discourses in *defining* problems. Moreover, frames and discourses can be produced and reproduced by the content of policy itself. So the logic of public policy making is reversed from its conventional, problem solving sequence. Public policies do not respond to problems: they create problems. Schram (1993) illustrates this post-modern sequence in a discussion of social policy in the United States. A framing of the 'feminization of poverty' was at the time popular in social policy circles: the notion that poverty in the United States was increasingly a matter of households headed by a single female. What Schram demonstrates is that this is not actually a new phenomenon, and that the absolute number of such households in poverty has changed little with time. What has changed are classifications of poverty and the decline in poverty rates for other sorts of households. So the 'feminization of poverty' is not symptomatic of a disintegrating social fabric of the sort some conservative social analysts suggested. Government policies directed at poverty-stricken, single female-headed households take on punitive form, 'stigmatizing and denigrating mother-only families for being the cause of their own problems' (Schram 1993: 257), thus making it less likely that such families can actually escape poverty. In this light, the 'feminization of poverty' frame suits a conservative political agenda for family structure – but does nothing to alleviate the poverty of women and children in single female-headed households, and in fact makes their material situation worse.

Reframing and discursive contests

'Frames', 'perspectives', 'paradigms', 'discourses', and 'ideologies' are concepts that now pervade attempts to explain the content of public policy. One does not have to be a post-modernist to find these useful. Some post-modernists take the concepts and run with them to an extreme, stressing the exclusiveness and incommensurability across different frames, so that no adjudication across frames is possible. Thus hard-line post-structuralists tell historical stories (genealogies) of discourses in ways that emphasize the hegemonic power and remorseless evolution of dominant discourses. However, it is possible to depart from this hard line to treat frames or discourses as multiple and competing. The explanation of public policy then lies mostly in the results of this kind of discursive contest. For example the story of environmental policy can be told in terms of the relative weight on governments assign to discourses of limits and survival, pragmatic problem-solving, sustainable development and green radicalism (see Chapter 11).

It is possible for the relative weight of discourses to change over time, and for reframing to occur. Sometimes the process can be quite sudden. For example, Litfin (1994) explains the history of the issue of ozone layer protection in international affairs, particularly the adoption of the 1987 Montreal Protocol for the Protection of the Ozone Layer, in terms of a sudden shift to a 'precautionary' discourse on the part of negotiators representing the United States, the European Union and other countries. The key impetus was the rhetorical force of the idea of an 'ozone hole' over Antarctica – a way of redescribing abnormal seasonal fluctuations in ozone concentrations in the stratosphere of the southern hemisphere. Other observers tell a story where rational argument based on scientific knowledge played a bigger role than rhetoric in this re-framing of the issue.

This ozone case is one where a single discourse eventually proved decisive. But ongoing contestation across different frames and discourses is also possible. Consider for example the four frames for criminal justice policy introduced earlier. They have mostly been contested for several decades (although with re-integrative shaming a relatively late entrant), suggesting that it is hard to find decisive evidence or rhetoric that would lead partisans of any frame to question their faith. Each frame is also quite capable of recruiting new adherents as old adherents die off.

In light of the determination of policy by the balance of competing frames or discourses, the key capacity in government is the ability to define situations in particular ways, so that a particular frame or discourse dominates (Hajer and Laws 2006: 252). This capacity may be centralized, and certainly political leaders often devote huge efforts to the framing task. For example, in the wake of the 2001 attacks on the World Trade Center, President George W. Bush and his administration framed responses in terms of a global 'War on Terror'. This did not have to be the response: the attacks could have been treated as isolated criminal acts, rather than cause for wholesale panic and mobilization. Together, the US and its adversaries (such as Osama bin Laden in al-Qaeda) managed to construct a frame of Manichean global struggle between good and evil (though each saw evil in the other). This frame suited *both* sides. The resulting Bush–bin Laden discourse coalition then came to dominate international security affairs in the ensuing years.

Agendas and Political Change

Post-modernism is sometimes equated with an unrelenting scepticism toward political arrangements of all sorts, delighting in exposing the repressive side of everything. In the light of the ubiquitous nature of repressive discourses, the only defensible response is to *Resist!* with a capital R and an exclamation mark. This is how Michel Foucault often conceived of politics: resistance should be local in response to particular oppressions. But resistance could never add up to any grand positive project of the sort to which Marxists among others are committed.

For all that could be constructed would be another repressive discourse. Resistance should be enjoyed for the release it provides, but not because it would then lead to anything better. However, some post-modernists have tried to explore more positive agendas, and it is these authors we focus on in this section.

The cultural left and identity politics

In Chapter 8 we explored the rise of identity politics in contemporary states. Post-modernists have devoted substantial attention to the ways in which particular identities are constructed as the social norm, and other identities correspondingly stigmatized as deviant. So in Western liberal democratic states the norm has often been white, male, middle class, heterosexual, secular, with a particular kind of two-parent family structure – or at least it was. Post-modernists side with the repressed, marginalized, and colonized – member of minority ethnic groups, women, gays and lesbians, minority religions, and so forth. They can support not just *Resistance!* on behalf of such groups – but also attempts to promote their standing through public policy. Such policies might involve recognizing gay marriage, reforming textbooks to validate the place of downtrodden minorities in history, more equitable welfare delivery that does not stigmatize single mothers, multicultur-alism, and educational reform to stress society's diversity. Such policies are the programme of a 'cultural left' that has largely given up on both Marxist revolution and socialist material redistribution. (Indeed, white working class males can easily find themselves counted among the oppressors by the cultural left.) The new push is felt not just in an agenda for the state, but also within institutions such as universities. A wave of what opponents styled 'political correctness' peaked in US universities in the 1990s. This was an extreme example, where all kinds of oppressions surfaced and were reflected in all areas of university life, from the regulation of social relationships to curriculum reform. (The very label 'political correctness' suggests that post-modern scepticism could then be turned on these sorts of developments, which in the end helped constitute a new kind of oppressive discourse.)

Laclau and Mouffe (1985) construct a radical political programme that tries to combine a Marxist emphasis on liberation with a post-modern recognition of the variety of oppressive discourses. They argue that in the contemporary world, the grand unifying logic of Marxism (reducing everything to the economic mode of production) no longer holds. Instead, contemporary states and other political units can piece together different sorts of political, economic and social structures. So an economy might be planned, mixed or ruthlessly competitive; a state might feature power sharing or adversarial politics. Many economic, political, and social practices will occur in the vicinity of the state. 'Hegemony' is what they call an attempt to impose meaning on any such situation. This hegemony may be oppressive – as in the traditional Marxist sense of a system of ideas that systematically favours the ruling class developed by the Italian theorist Gramsci in the 1920s. But hegemony of this sort can also be recognized and contested by radical oppositions to prevailing oppressive practices. Laclan and Mouffe felt that a radical and plural politics can be built from the bottom up. The variety of oppressions is matched by variety of responses; but progressive groups ought to be able to negotiate joint and mutually beneficial actions. In doing so they might also create collective meanings to counter dominant hegemony. The political struggle is not unified under the social class banner as it is for Marxists, but always remains decentralized and in a state of ferment, as new oppressions are discovered, old ones redefined, and new possibilities for linking different movements combined. In a way this analysis simply describes the practice of the array of new social movements (feminism, radical environmentalism, peace movements, etc.) that flourished in the 1970s and 1980s, together with a hope that such movements might together amount to something more than the sum of their parts. It also describes a democratic communicative practice of grassroots politics. Generally that politics will be oppositional; it will exert pressure on government to produce particular policies, but it is difficult to see how it could ever enter the conventional institutions of government, or reform them in any systematic way.

From culture wars to agonistic democracy

The struggle of differently situated social groups to recognize one another provides grist for post-modern theories of agonistic democracy (Connolly 1991; Honig 1993; Mouffe 2000). Agonism starts with the potentially problematic nature of conflict across groups. To Connolly (1991) the basic problem is one of assertions of identity and denial of the identity of others being a matter of often deadly earnest, featuring both dogmatism and resentment. So even in liberal democracies, the United States in particular, such interplay can take the form of 'culture wars'. On one side can be found multiculturalists and those seeking validation of the political claims of gays, lesbians, ethnic minorities, Native Americans, women and the non-human environment. On the other side are cultural conservatives, among whose number can be found large numbers of fundamentalist Christians. For these Christians, many contemporary identity claims are anathema, in the case of gays and lesbians tantamount to seeking government endorsement of sin, and they simply unacceptable in a Christian society where the traditional nuclear family should be privileged. The conflicting agendas arise on issues such as affirmative action, anti-discrimination legislation, family law, marriage or the recognition of civil unions for same-sex couples, pornography (where feminists and fundamentalist Christians can actually be found on the same side, though for very different reasons), HIV-AIDS policy, sex education in schools, curriculum issues in public universities, and rules for the distribution of taxation and public expenditures (for example, when it comes to single-parent families). On each issue there are particular cases to be argued concerning the advantages and disadvantages of different policy options. Always in the background is how the policy in question affects the standing of different identity groups in society – and so the character of American society as a whole. Different sides will also try to invoke particular sorts of identity issues in order to disadvantage other sides. For example, cultural conservatives know that same-sex marriage is opposed by majorities of voters in almost all states. Thus it is to conservative advantage if this issue is highlighted around election time. This explains referendum measures and motions brought to legislatures in support of a constitutional ban on same-sex marriage.

For agonistic democrats, the solution to these sorts of problems is a vibrant but respectful engagement across different groups. To Mouffe (2000), the antagonism of enemies needs to be changed into the agonism of adversaries; indeed this conversion should be at the heart of what we mean by democracy. As a postmodernist, Connolly wishes that individuals and groups could recognize the fluidity and contingency of identities, treating them as something to explore rather than assert dogmatically. Ideally, individuals involved in this engagement should be open to conversion in their attitude toward others. This does not mean they have to accept or agree with the identity of the others, which can still be contested. Quite what this means in practice is somewhat murky. It is not clear where the requisite passionate yet respectful attitude toward others can originate, in particular when some of the groups involved (such as fundamentalist religions) repress their own members and do not readily let go of dogma (Kapoor 2002: 472–3). If interchange between opposing groups can be engineered at all – a big 'if' – it might just as easily reinforce conflicting identities as transform them.

So Agonism does have an other-worldly feel about it. Agonist theorists can point to some examples of real-world practices that exemplify their proposals for critical interchange. For example, Schlosberg (1999) shows how very different ethnic groups managed to negotiate their differences and devise common actions in the US environmental justice movement. Hasidic Jews and African-Americans could for example carry out joint actions against proposals for a toxic waste incinerator close to their neighbourhoods. But contemporary liberal democratic societies are a long way from a more generalized agonism when identities clash. Connolly himself accepts that while there is a conceivable world in which agonism would flourish, it is very different from the kind of world that actually exists – especially in his own United States. From the point of view of theory of the state, agonism is also problematic because it describes only inter-relationships between different identity groups – but it is silent on what the state should do, or what should be done inside the state, when it comes to this engagement. As a theory of democracy agonism is incomplete because it says little about how collective decisions should be made.

Whither the democratic agenda?

At some level post-modernists and post-structuralists are almost all committed to democracy. But they are held back by their scepticism and suspicion of any sort of positive proposals – especially those that involve formal political institutions – for fear of becoming complicit in new sorts of oppression. It is possible to manage this tension – but the cost, as for agonists, may be in terms of relating their proposals to real world practices. Two other alternative paths are available.

The first would involve a more whole-hearted embrace of scepticism, and an associated abandonment of any positive political programme. This scepticism would extend to social movements trying to change the world for the better. So for example Luke (1997) sees in environmentalism only new forms of discipline. For Luke, environmentalists at best want to turn the world into a more pleasant playground for themselves at the expense of government (wilderness preservation advocates), at worse want to subject the world to hierarchical management by themselves, guided by an alleged science of ecology. Not surprisingly, environmental activists are appalled by this kind of analysis, which in their view comforts polluters and despoilers. Scepticism would also have to extend to democracy itself, and any particular proposals for democratic reform. So in a case study of democratization in Thailand, Connors (2003) sees only 'democrasubjection', the creation of new kinds of disciplined subjects who will fit into the sort of political economy required by capitalist development in compliant fashion. Hindess (2001) treats liberalism, and so presumably liberal democracy, as repressive in their essence – not just repressive in some of their historical applications.

The other direction would involve renunciation of scepticism and appreciation of the degree to which it is possible for individuals, groups and societies to reflect upon the discourses to which they are subject. Ulrich Beck (1992) treats what post-modernists call modernity as only semi-modernity. In the semi-modernity of industrial society, individuals are indeed often subject to the constraining force of dominant social traditions – such as one that sees economic growth allied to technological advance as necessarily progressive and good. Beck believes that in modernity proper, or what he calls 'reflexive modernity', it is possible to call traditions into question – and that is what we see happening in recent decades, especially when it comes to growing resistance to the unwanted risks imposed upon society by economy and technology. If we grant this capacity, then such critical questioning can be channelled into democratic reform that begins in civil society, but eventually challenges the state.

Engagement across discourses can also be linked to notions of deliberative or discursive democracy that we introduced in Chapter 9. Some versions of deliberative democracy stress the engagement of discourses in the public sphere, with the outcomes of that engagement being transmitted to the state by a variety of mechanisms, such as rhetoric and argument, fear of political instability by dominant state actors, cultural change, and the myriad activities of social movements. The problem here is that many post-modernists (such as Mouffe) believe that 'deliberation' is a repressive form of communication, one that disciplines participants to behave in civil fashion, to repress their passions, to conform to norms of liberal politics. In Chapter 9 we pointed out that deliberative politics does not have to be like this. It can be much more expansive in the kinds of communication it allows, and the sorts of subject positions that can be stated.

Conclusion

Post-modernism is capable of generating some unique and profound insights into the character of politics and the operation of the state. Post-structuralism in particular has developed a strikingly original analysis of the nature of power, which can be connected fruitfully to work on the way that governance networks can transform the state. Post-modernism is less compelling when it tries to suggest what should be done about the problematic states of affairs it has identified, beyond some limited state validation of the identities of oppressed groups. Many post-modernists endorse radical and plural agonistic democracy, but they are not always especially optimistic about the prospects for advancing such democracy.

Chapter 14

Globalization

Globalization is the process of integrating social, cultural, economic and possibly political systems into a single global system that extends across the boundaries of states. Interactions across the boundaries of states increase in frequency relative to interactions within states. So globalization is a process rather than an accomplishment. This recognition begs many questions: how far along this path are contemporary societies? Is there resistance to such integration, and if so are reverses possible? Have such reverses indeed already occurred, and if so when? Is convergence on a single global system now inevitable, or can it be resisted? Does globalization apply to some societies more than others? Will the state wither away in the face of globalization, or will the state retain important roles in globalizing and globalized systems? Clearly there are potentially major consequences for states – and also for the theory of the state. At one extreme, globalization threatens to render the national sovereign state obsolete, dissolving the state into global or transnational forms of power. As yet, this outcome remains remote. But globalization does not leave any state unscathed. In this chapter we look at its consequences for contemporary liberal democratic states, and how states might respond to these challenges.

Origins and Assumptions

At one level, globalization as a process is as old as human history. Ancient societies traded with each other, often across very long distances. Vast empires sought to integrate political systems. Trade between Europe and East Asia is over 2,000 years old, along the overland silk roads that linked China to Rome.

From the sixteenth century onward European powers sought profit and territory in distant parts of the world. Trade routes then extended from metropolitan centres in Europe to north, central and south America, Africa and south and east Asia; and large territories were incorporated into European empires. By the nineteenth century, the spread of capitalism meant a further scramble for sources of raw materials for production processes and for markets for finished goods. Thus globalization especially accelerated in the late nineteenth century. Indeed it is probable that the world just prior to World War I was just as globalized in economic terms as the world is today – perhaps more so (Hirst and Thompson 1996: 18–50). The economic difficulties of the interwar years then led to protectionism and economic nationalism, so economic globalization decelerated, at least temporarily.

The current era of accelerated globalization is sometimes traced to 1971 with the collapse of the Bretton Woods system of fixed exchange rates that operated since 1945 and had acted as something of a brake on international economic integration (Steger 2005: 29). Since the 1970s, economic globalization has been aggressively promoted by policy makers in the United States and elsewhere, especially by governments under the influence of market liberal ideology. Globalization in non-economic realms remains much more of a mixed bag.

There remains some dispute about how far globalization has proceeded. The school of thought sometimes labelled 'hyper-globalization' stresses the degree to which we already have a single global system in economics and finance, in which all players compete on equal terms. As Friedman (2005) puts it, 'The World is Flat', with no barriers. At the other extreme, sceptics point out that most of the world's population, especially in the Third World, is not well integrated into the global economic system. They engage in limited and partial interaction with the global system on unfair terms, and in many cases are not integrated at all. It is also a matter of some contention how novel globalization really is, especially if we think of it as a process, rather than as the outcome of that process. Hirst and Thompson (1996) claim that there is actually little new in the contemporary economy. Any increases in trade and capital mobility are largely within the already developed countries, leaving out most of the Third World. And even multi-national corporations are still largely tied to their country of origin.

Nevertheless, the consciousness of globalization exists today in a manner unprecedented in human history. So globalization is widely felt, regardless of the extent of its actuality – and this widespread feeling or discourse of globalization itself helps constitute globalization. Postmodernists would say that it is the discourse that makes the reality (see previous chapter), and in this post-modern era the discourse of globalization is very powerful. The number of books and articles with 'globalization' in the title has exploded since around 1990, and the term pervades discussions among politicians, journalists and corporate executives as they think about finance, economics and trade. (For a flavour of the literature, see Held and McGrew 2000.)

The limitations of classic theories of the state

The classic theories of the state, (whether pluralist, elitist, Marxist, or neo-liberal), see the primary forces that constitute the state and then determine its character and actions as originating within that particular state's society and territory. These theories allow that states may have to look outward in terms of foreign policy, security and trade, but these policy areas are mainly treated as just another set of outputs, determined by domestically-constituted forces. Pluralists recognize only domestic groups as influencing policy. For elite theorists, elites are almost always national elites for better or for worse. Marxists have long recognized the role of economic imperialism for almost a century (beginning with the work of Lenin). But imperialism as an influence on state action is a problem only for exploited countries and colonies – not for states in the prosperous core of liberal democracies. For market liberals, the key (negative) influences on policy are selfish groups constituted within a state's territory by its own people, keen to maximize rewards to themselves at the expense of the public interest. Market liberals recognize international markets, but only in terms of domestic markets writ large: to be valued for the competition, freedom, and prosperity they provide. At the end of this chapter we give a fuller account of how globalization is received within different theories of the state, but to do that we need to explore its implications for the state in many dimensions.

Globalization theory inverts thes relationship between domestic and international factors. For globalists (who we can define as those committed to a greater or less degree to the globalization thesis), the key influences on the state are now international in their origins, and consequently domestic forces are downplayed. What this means is that global systems are regarded as fundamental. These systems may be markets, or they may be networks, or they may involve communications (such as the Internet), or they may mix economic, cultural and political aspects. Many aspects of the global system can be measured and tracked over time: for example, levels of international trade, investment, financial flows and the movements of people across national boundaries. It is less easy to measure the relative significance of such flows compared to their non-international counterparts. Thus globalists insert assumptions about the relative importance of international flows, systems and networks compared to their domestic counterparts. The elusive character of global networks in particular means that they are hard to capture and measure, still less determine accurately their influence on states. Castells (1996) has highlighted the networked character of global economic and financial systems, and writers in this idiom can provide all sorts of illustrations of network linkages that span the globe. It is less easy for them to measure and demonstrate systematically how such financial and economic networks translate into policy networks that influence the actions of governments.

Social, political and cultural globalization

While economics and finance are central to globalization, the global system does not just involve the movement of goods, investment and finance. Globalization also involves information. The Internet has been a key driver making information from sources all over the world instantly available to anyone with access to a computer (unless they live under an authoritarian regime that seeks to censor Internet communications). Media such as television, newspapers and radio also have a global reach. In some cases this development is relatively recent (as with global television channels such as CNN, BBC World, and al-Jazeera), in other cases long-established (as with the World Service of BBC Radio). Cultural globalization also accompanies these developments, with English the lingua franca of global business and culture alike. Cultural globalization is heavily Americanized, in the form of Hollywood movies and television shows.

Globalization can also involve the movement of peoples. Again this is something that has happened throughout human history, and migration levels in the late nineteenth century were as high as today. Now, however, movement for business, pleasure or education is increasingly pervasive – though only for a globalized elite. Movement across national boundaries for the poor is still a much more hazardous matter, often involving the dangers of illegal migration. Diseases too can now have rapid global reach, as fears of a bird flu pandemic illustrate.

Globalization is also political in the sense of the development of global institutions. Such institutions have been around for a long time – the League of Nations was founded after World War I. The International Labour Organization, founded at the same time, is still operating. The end of World War II saw a burst of global institutionalization with the establishment of the United Nations, the International Monetary Fund, the World Bank and the General Agreement on Tariffs and Trade (GATT). Since then the number of international governmental organizations has mushroomed, though their formal power is often weak and contested. Political globalization is currently no match for economic globalization, and the only global governmental organizations with real teeth are the ones with an economic mandate. So the WTO can authorize sanctions against states violating principles of free trade, and both the IMF and World Bank can advance funding to states in financial need that follow their economic recipes, while withholding funds from states that refuse to abide by these recipes. These recipes have generally involved market liberal soltions, as described in Chapter 5.

Globalists assume that the net effect of all these forces is to undermine the sovereign character of the state. Increasingly, states are enmeshed in transnational forces that mean they no longer have complete and effective control of what goes on inside their own territories. Sometimes aspects of sovereignty are formally ceded to global or international bodies. So when a state joins the World Trade Organization, it relinquishes full control over its own economic policies, renouncing measures that would be defined by the WTO as protectionist. Member states of the European Union must now abide by regulations in single-market, transportation, pollution, work safety, food safety and a host of other areas, promulgated at the EU level. But the attenuation of sovereignty can be more insidious, as states find they must pay more attention to what global markets think of their actions, or find themselves subject to the influence of transnational governance networks (described in Chapter 6).

(International) Society and Politics

All states in today's world must respond to both internal and external social forces. This Janus-faced nature of the state has actually existed since the dawn of the modern era (Skocpol 1979), because one of the first tasks of every sovereign state is to survive in a potentially hostile world composed of other states. Globalization means that the security threat facing most states fully integrated into the global economy have diminished to the point where state survival is secure. States not in this core are not so lucky. They still face a situation more like the insecure 'state of nature' portrayed by Thomas Hobbes in the seventeenth century, where violent attack remains an ever-present possibility (Goldgeier and McFaul 1992). However, the gain in autonomy for the integrated states on the security dimension is counteracted by a loss of autonomy on the social and economic dimensions. Globalization means that transnational social forces are increasingly important in comparison to their nationally-generated counterparts.

We can see this transfer of influence operating in several arenas:

- *Multi-national corporations.* Many large corporations operate across national boundaries, marketing their products in multiple countries, and locating their manufacturing plants where labour is cheap, taxes are low and regulations weak. The annual sales figures of large corporations can be bigger than the gross national product of many countries. Globalization is epitomized by global brands such as Nike, Starbucks and McDonald's.

- *Global elites.* Classical elite theory (discussed in Chapter 3) traditionally assumed that elites were constituted within state territories. But globalization is accompanied by the emergence of a global elite, symbolized by the annual gathering of the World Economic Forum in Davos, Switzerland. This elite comprises the leaders of states, international organizations, multi-national corporations, large foundations and banks, with a sprinkling of academics and celebrities. Conspicuous charity, for example, operating through the Bill and Melinda Gates Foundation, or the 'Live 8' concerts against poverty in Africa in 2005, are part of this global elite culture. The elite may not operate in close unison in the way that classical elite theory requires. But within this global elite there is a degree of common understanding about the need to coordinate actions across national boundaries and international institutions. This elite is very closely connected to the networked world of international finance described by Castells (1996).
- *International non-governmental organizations.* International NGOs organize with the intention of pushing particular causes in many countries, and are specifically targetting international institutions. Examples include Amnesty International, active on human rights issues; Greenpeace, working on global environmental issues; the Red Cross, working on humanitarian aid; Oxfam, concerned with global food issues; and the World Business Council on Sustainable Development, which combines a political agenda with the financial interest of its member corporations. NGOs can influence states both directly and indirectly, and can also provide a conduit for 'boomerang' effects. So social movements struggling against their own governments in Third World societies can forge alliances with well-resourced NGOs from rich countries, who in turn lobby their own governments and relevant multi-national corporations to exert pressure on the Third World government in question. The Ogoni people in Nigeria have been particularly successful in forging alliances with international NGOs, which in turn have influenced the Shell oil corporation. The firm has both changed the way it operates in Ogoni territory and tried to induce the Nigerian government to be less repressive.
- *Social movements.* Social movements are the more radical counterparts of NGOs, though the two categories do shade into each other. Economic globalization has engendered its own kind of global opposition. This is sometimes referred to, mostly by its critics, as the 'anti-globalization movement'. However, members

of the movement would mostly say they are against only particular aspects of globalization – such as unfair terms of trade that disadvantage Third World producers; the imposition of genetically modified organisms on agriculture; the exodus of industry from developed countries to parts of the world where wages are lower; – or the sweatshops, and environmental degradation accompanying free trade. Since the 'Battle of Seattle' at the World Trade Organization meetings in 1999, gatherings of the WTO, WEF, G8, and other international economic institutions are routinely accompanied by street protests. But these protests are just one visible manifestation of the anti-globalization movement, which organizes internationally, making good use of the Internet. The movement has little in the way of formal organization, and so actually represents a wholly new kind of social movement, different again from the 'new social movements' (environmentalism, feminism, peace movement) that began in the 1970s. It is an aspect of what Falk (1999) refers to as 'globalization from below'.

Conspicuously missing from this list are political parties, which are nowhere organized across national boundaries. This is true even in relation to elections to the European parliament, which are contested only by national parties, and whose votes depend mostly on the dynamics of national politics, not European issues. This absence of international political parties symbolizes the decline of electoral politics in a globalizing world; perhaps democracy may have to be sought in locations other than elections. We return to democratic agendas associated with globalization at the end of this chapter.

The forces emanating from this list of transnational influences in the state do not necessarily pull in the same direction. In particular, social movements and international NGOs may pull in the opposite direction to multi-national corporations and global economic elites, the latter seeking the support of market forces. These cross-pressures could conceivably give the state some degree of autonomy in deciding which way (if any) to move. For instance, a government contemplating radical free trade reforms might reconsider given the likely negative reaction of social movements.

Government and Policy Making

Globalization implies a degree of institution building at transnational and global levels, with a corresponding shift in authority away from the state and into such institutions. However, this shift does not necessarily connote a loss in the *formal* authority of states. For the most part, formal international institutions are still the creation of the states that subscribe to them. And if they so choose states can withdraw from these institutional arrangements. Think, for example, of the US withdrawal from the Kyoto Protocol on climate change in 2001.

The most well-developed set of international institutions and organizations can be found in the European Union, and it is conceivable that the EU could one day evolve into a federal state itself. But currently the EU is not like that. Most of its key decisions are made by representatives of its component states, so it is still very much an inter-governmental body, without settled, state-like sovereignty of its own. For example, it lacks, political parties that campaign across national boundaries; the European Parliament is composed of elected representatives from national parties, only loosely grouped into EU-wide blocs. The EU can offer a united face to the world when it comes to economic and environmental policy – but not when it comes to security issues. Some deep divisions occur between governments that look to the US alliance (especially the UK), and those that seek a more independent European voice. Internally, regulation in areas of health, environment, transportation and safety are increasingly matters for determination by EU bureaucracies. And there is quite a degree of integration of economic policy, especially because of the single European market and since many members of the EU adopted the Euro as their common currency in 2002.

However, the EU does not pre-figure global institutional integration. Nothing else remotely like the EU currently exists anywhere else in the world. And it is quite conceivable that regional integration of the EU kind might actually impede global integration, if a 'Fortress Europe' were to raise economic and political barriers against the rest of the world.

Currently there are three global institutions with real teeth, all of them economic. Both the International Monetary Fund and World Bank can make assistance to countries in economic trouble, conditional on the recipient governments abiding by a particular set of policy prescriptions. This conditionality undermines both sovereignty and democratic control (Stiglitz 2006: 12). Since the beginning of the 1980s the dominant prescriptions have followed the 'Washington Consensus', so called because it was forged by three Washington-based institutions: the IMF; the World Bank; and the US Treasury Department. Until some soul-searching prompted by social movement protests in the early 2000s, the medicine always involved free trade, free access for foreign investors, restrictive monetary policy, de-regulation of the economy and privatization of government assets. Governments are not allowed to impose restrictions on flows of 'hot' money (Stiglitz 2006: 20–1). Effectively, this recipe is a radical form of market-oriented neo-liberalism as discussed in Chapter 5 – indeed of a radicalism that has never been tried in wealthy countries such as the United States.

The United States is never on the receiving end of IMF and World Bank decisions, but it has placed itself at the mercy of the World Trade Organization, and indeed the USA has complied with WTO rulings against its policies on numerous occasions. In economics, unlike issues relating to human rights, security and the environment, America does comply with the decisions of global institutions. And this illustrates the degree to which globalization is currently driven by economics. The WTO was set up in 1995 to oversee the liberalization of global trade, and obviously the US government believes that its benefits from free trade to itself outweigh the costs of compliance with the occasional anti-US ruling. Other developed countries have made the same calculation. The WTO operates according to an economic mandate, and must subordinate values pertaining to (for example) environmental protection or social justice when making its decisions. So if an importing country wants to ensure that the timber it brings in does not involve destruction of tropical rainforests, that is not admissible.

Automatic constraints on governments

More important than the decisions of formal international institutions in restricting the autonomy of states are the impersonal and automatic forces generated in the international economy. The more a state becomes integrated into the global economy, the more it has to worry about the reactions of international markets to its policies. And markets worry only about what is good for business, not for social justice, human rights or environmental protection. Friedman (1999) calls this a 'golden straitjacket', golden because this integration allegedly fosters the generation of wealth. For Friedman, nobody is policing the global system, which responds only to the movements of the 'electronic herd' of bankers, traders, analysts, financiers, and investors. If the herd does not like a country's policies, it will stampede away from the country, which will experience capital flight, attacks on its currency and disinvestment. This anticipated reaction is an intensification of the economic constraint that all states must operate under in the context of a market economy, be it national or global (see Chapter 1). Consistent with the herd metaphor, Giddens (2000) speaks of a 'runaway world' beyond the control of any powerful actor (or small set of actors) to manipulate. The speed with which this system can both grow and react is captured in the further metaphor of 'turbo-capitalism' (Luttwak 1998). In light of these forces: 'It has been said that arguing against globalization is like arguing against the law of gravity' (Annan 2006).

There is some dispute as to whether this system lacks any central steering (Steger 2005: 67–71). After all, the Washington Consensus did begin with the conscious adoption of a set of policy principles in three closely international ??? organizations. And the USA has linked the promotion of free markets to its international security agenda, for example in the *National Security Strategy of the United States of America, September 2002*. Its first sentence proclaims a 'single, sustainable model for national success: freedom, democracy, and free enterprise'. The US wants to re-shape the world to its liking in these terms. For example, since the invasion of Iraq in 2003, US policy toward the Middle East has sought the more effective integration of the region into global market capitalism, with Iraq originally intended to be at the forefront. Such efforts to plan globalization notwithstanding, once a transnational market system has been designed and the plan brought into being, the electronic herd can largely take over; and it can be hard to move once it does.

States integrated into the global economic system find themselves subject to a number of requirements that are not easily resisted. They include:

- Free trade: no tariffs on imports or subsidy of exports.
- Acceptance of investment from multi-national corporations.
- A variable exchange rate for the currency.
- Acceptance of international standards for financial systems.
- No restrictions on flows of money across borders.
- Tax rates no higher than internationally competitive levels.
- Provision of communications infrastructure.
- Ease of international travel.
- Higher education to conform to international norms of recognized qualifications.
- Restrictions on the capacity of trade unions to raise wage rates.
- Restrictions on the generosity of welfare state programmes.

The discourse of economic globalization

Those invoking the force of economic globalization often claim that there is no alternative to this kind of recipe (Hay 1998). 'No alternative' is an undemocratic claim, for its intent is to silence debate and the exploration of options. Clearly, when adopted by a particular society the measures just listed benefit some and hurt others. Those benefiting can then use the rhetoric of 'no alternative' to push for policies that are in their own material interests. Market liberalism is an ideology that is held by some political actors and contested by others; obviously it suits market liberals to suggest that there really is no alternative to their position. If a policy proves unpopular, a leader can always say 'globalization made me do it'.

In this light, economic globalization may take effect first and foremost because it is a discourse, a set of concepts, assumptions, ideas, dispositions, contentions and capabilities that is widely shared by key political actors (Hay and Rosamond 2002; Marsh and Smith 2004). Yet the fact that economic globalization is a discourse does not mean that it is any less real. Marsh *et al.* (2006: 187) are wrong to distinguish between 'discourse' and 'reality' in globalization, because reality can be constituted by discourses. Globalization discourse is not just invoked by policy makers to advance the cause of particular measures they favour. If that were the case, it could be unmasked and contested quite easily. The problem is that the discourse is also accepted by key decision makers dispersed throughout the global system, people whose confidence is necessary for a state's economy to be held in high esteem by Friedman's 'electronic herd'. Vulnerable governments fear the reactions of this herd, and so feel they must adopt policies to please it. For example, after the 1997 East Asian financial crisis the IMF offered financial aid to Indonesia, which came with the usual market liberal conditions attached. The government of Indonesia thought the IMF-prescribed policies were wrong, but accepted them for fear of the reaction of international markets if it did not (Dalrymple 1998). Market reaction in turn would be determined by the discourse of globalization that key market actors share.

But are all states this vulnerable? Globalization sceptics such as Hirst and Thompson (1996) believe they are not, so that the discourse of globalization can be resisted. Some developed countries have retained a generous welfare state, yet remained economically competitive in the globalizing era. Stiglitz (2006: xv) points to Sweden as an example. In fact Sweden in the 1990s had trouble maintaining its traditional social bargain, with large businesses withdrawing from centralized wage determination and seeking more competitive processes. Hall and Soskice (2001) argue that two national political-economic models can flourish in the context of economic globalization. The first is the liberal market economy beloved of economic globalists; the second is the cooperative market economy that is the legacy of corporatist states of the kind discussed in Chapter 6. Corporatism entails a response to external economic pressures that is coordinated across government, business and labour unions. For example, wage rates can be kept down as part of the corporatist bargain to keep industry competitive; labour receives in return guarantees of a social safety net and planning for low unemployment. Even a non-corporatist country like Australia managed to pursue a policy of economic liberalization in response to global pressures while moderating wage rates under a series of formal Accords between the Labour government and Australian Council of Trade Unions in the period 1983 to 1996 (Capling and Galligan 1992). From this viewpoint, it is possible for liberal democratic states with capitalist economic systems to continue to regulate business and control their own economies in much the same way as they always have. All that is stopping them is globalist ideology.

In late 2008, the looming insolvency of many banks and other major financial institutions in the United States and Europe was met by nation states taking some very assertive action, bringing major banks and financial institutions under much tighter governmental regulation and control, and in some cases taking over all or part of their operations. Far from simply adjusting to the global financial storm, governments in liberal democratic states sought to bring matters under their direct control, revealing the degree to which they might still seek to regulate globalized markets if they chose to do so.

Consequences for the distribution of power within states

Even if states lack the degree of autonomy that globalization sceptics (such as Hirst and Thompson) believe they still possess, economic globalization does not necessarily mean that the state becomes weaker in relation to its domestic society. The state may lack autonomy but still be strong. Applying the precepts of the globalization discourse may meet with strong domestic opposition, from labour unions, environmentalists, social justice activists, even business owners likely to be hurt by international competition. Thus the implementation of economic globalization policies may call for a strengthening of the state and a centralization of its powers, in order to squash this sort of domestic opposition. Implementing an economy that is 'free' in economic terms may require a very coercive state (Gamble 1994).

Globalization has consequences too for the distribution of power between different branches of government. Normally it is the executive branch of the national government that interacts with international political institutions. As these interactions become more important, the central government's hand is strengthened in relation to sub-national units (such as local governments, or states in federal systems). In Australia, for example, the federal government can use the fact of its having signed up to an international treaty to overrule contrary policies adopted by states, under the foreign affairs power in its constitution. This power was confirmed by the High Court in a case in 1983 where the government of Tasmania wanted to build a dam in a location that had previously been classified as a World Heritage area, under the World Heritage Convention that Australia had signed. The federal government successfully opposed the plan. Within national governments, it is only the executive branch that sends representatives to key international negotiations. Given that formal global institutionalization is much more advanced on questions of economics, trade, finance and investment, it is normally officials from the economics, trade, and finance ministries who represent national governments. So those ministries are advantaged relative to other departments covering (for example) social policy, environment culture. Thus economic globalization in particular can mean the centralization of state power in the executive branch, which from any normative pluralist point of view has negative consequences for democracy (see Chapters 2 and 6).

Agendas and Political Change

Several well-defined and often competing political agendas exist in the context of globalization. They range from an endorsement of the current trajectory of economic globalization, to nationalist protectionism, to concerns with global justice and democracy. The ideology that accompanies advocacy of economic globalization is globalism (Steger 2005), which has a clear normative agenda linked to market liberalism (set out in Chapter 5). However, this agenda does go beyond neo-liberalism in important ways. Globalization's central claim is that global economic integration is good for everyone, rich and poor alike. Evidence that globalization in recent decades has been accompanied by growing gaps in the wealth and income of rich and poor countries is dismissed as a transitional phenomenon, as is evidence of increasing inequality within rich countries. What is good for international business is seen by globalists as good for the world – not just in spreading prosperity, but also in spreading the political freedom and democracy that are the necessary accompaniments of economic freedom. There is a long (and contested) literature on the relationship between economic development and democracy; the consensus today seems to be that prosperity does not cause democracy, but it does act as a bulwark against a democratic regime reverting to authoritarianism (Przeworski *et al.* 2000). Thomas Friedman (1999: 187) claims that the 'electronic herd' in global economics and finance demands constitutional liberal democracy in states, because democracy provides a stable and predictable environment for business. However, multi-national corporations have been perfectly happy to operate in stable-looking authoritarian regimes, so Friedman's claim seems highly dubious.

As noted earlier, Friedman's 'electronic herd' metaphor suggests that economic globalization is remorseless and impersonal. But we also saw that aspects of globalization have been steered very consciously. That steering persists. One elite group is quite self-consciously the guardian of economic globalization: the World Economic Forum, meeting annually in Davos in Switzerland. The WEF brings together leading figures from international institutions, governments, corporations, finance and (economic) academia. The WEF has no formal role in governing the world, but is rather an informal site for discussing and potentially harmonizing globalizing agendas, and for bringing into being global policies even in the absence of global bodies that might implement them.

Globalization with a human face

The celebrities such as Bono who regularly show up at Davos and meetings of the G8 countries are not there to advocate turbo-capitalism or flat-earth economic liberalization. Nor are they anti-globalization. What they want to do is convince the movers and shakers of the economic world order to have a social conscience, to shift resources in the direction of their favoured projects. That project might involve debt relief for Third World countries, the alleviation of global poverty, targeting the myriad problems that beset Africa, action on global climate change or more effective international action against HIV/AIDS. Clearly there are those attending Davos meetings who control financial resources that could make a large contribution to any and all of these projects. The money may be in public or private hands. The funds available for private social projects may be huge. Biggest of all is the Bill and Melinda Gates Foundation, which devotes vast sums to health projects, especially in the Third World. However noble their ends, these kinds of private initiatives have no political accountability of the sort that governments and even inter-governmental institutions provide; they are an aspect of the privatization of government.

A more systematic agenda for globalization with a human face is presented by Joseph Stiglitz, former Chief Economist at the World Bank, turned critic of the Washington Consensus (see Stiglitz 2002: 200). He criticizes the way globalization has worked in practice, mainly on the grounds that the global trade regime currently favours the very rich at the expense of Third World countries, the poor in rich countries and especially the poor in Third World countries. Stiglitz points out that market liberal free trade recipes are urged upon poor countries, while rich countries still put tariffs upon goods from the Third World and subsidize their own farmers, with devastating consequences for Third

World agriculture. Stiglitz calls for globalization that is managed more effectively and more fairly. He recognizes that changes in the terms of trade will hurt unskilled workers in rich countries, whose jobs will be exported to poor countries. The solution lies in more interventionist governments in rich countries seeking to increase the skill level of their workforces, to construct a social welfare system for those thrown out of work, and to redistribute income through a progressive taxation system (Stiglitz 2006: 275).

Stiglitz also wants stronger and more democratic global government to regulate international capitalism. Currently international institutions are weak. He believes stronger global government can be financed by a reform to the global reserve system. Currently most poor countries put their reserves in US Treasury Bills, which are secure but yield low interest. A global reserve currency could yield higher interest, and at the same time be controlled by an international body and used to finance its own governmental activities. Stiglitz's global government would be more democratic than existing international economic institutions – but within tight limits. Mainly he wants to see greater weight for Third World votes in the International Monetary Fund (currently dominated by rich countries); the representation of all ministries and not just trade ministries when governments send delegations to key international nego-tiations; and the more effective representation of blocks of poorer coun-tries at such negotiations, which again have been dominated by rich countries (Stiglitz 2006: 281–2). So international democracy for Stiglitz is at one remove, attained only through the representation of more or less democratic states in international negotiations and institutions. As we will see shortly, others have greater or more creative hopes for transnational democracy that would transcend this limitation. For the moment it should be stressed that Stiglitz-style 'globalization with a human face' would actually involve strengthening the role of states in managing the consequences of globalization for their own societies, and in steering and regulating globalization itself. Stiglitz also advocates greater transparency, openness, accountability and law in international governance.

Reactions against globalization

The more radical protestors against economic globalization – credited by Stiglitz (2002) with putting a number of neglected issues on the global agenda – want to go much further than him in changing the tra-jectory of globalization. Quite where they want to go remains a matter of some contention. The protestors have raised a range of concerns relating to poor terms of trade for the Third World, income insecurity in developed countries, sweatshops and poor working conditions in Third World factories owned by global brands such as Nike, and the environmental degradation caused by global capitalism. These concerns do not constitute a harmonious whole, and some appear to point in opposing directions. For example, workers in rich countries may lose if a better trade deal is secured by producers in poor countries. But such differences have actually been grist to the mill for deliberations within an emerging global justice movement. Interchange across difference itself has helped constitute the essence of a democratic, discursive politics in a transnational public sphere (Dryzek 2006: 124–5). This public sphere confronts the established centres of power in the global system, be they the national governments of wealthy countries, multi-national corporations, or international organizations such as the IMF, WTO, G8, or WEF. The global justice movement is not necessarily protectionist. Moreover, its own way of organizing across national boundaries (making good use of the Internet) is itself an illustration of globalization, though political rather than economic. Falk (1999) refers to all this as 'globalization from below', a matter of grassroots social movement activism rather than economic integration.

While economic globalization is pushed by neo-liberal forces often most at home in right-wing political parties, there is also a segment of the right that wants to resist globalization and strengthen national control of the economy. In the United States, this movement is personified by the pundit and occasional presidential candidate Pat Buchanan (Steger 2005: 95–102): 'With the money we are pumping out for imports, foreigners are buying up America . . . to maintain and increase their share of the US market and to continue to suck production out of the United States' (Buchanan 2004: 204). Buchanan opposed free trade and wants increased tariffs on imports, as well as powerful restrictions on immigration, both legal and illegal. Internally, he favours a low-tax market economy. American workers would have their jobs, wages and security protected against foreign competition.

Hostility to globalization and international integration is also found in many far-right European political parties. Within the British Conservative party, a powerful 'Eurosceptic' faction opposes the European Union, defending the autonomy of British government against regulation from Brussels, and resisting economic integration (for example, by opposing Britain's adoption of the Euro currency). The British picture is complicated because some Eurosceptics are also market-oriented liberals who object mainly to the EU's intrusive governmental role. For most right-wing anti-globalization forces, the struggle is a matter of identity as well as economics. They champion national identity against the cosmopolitan forces that would undermine it, seeking in the end a re-assertion of the power and sovereignty of the nationstate.

Defenders of the autonomy of the nation state against economic globalization can also be found on the left, among those who see in the nation state the last, best hope for redistributive politics. In this viewpoint, neo-liberal globalization amounts to an attack on the welfare state that must be resisted (Gray 1998: 87–92).

Transnational democracy

The Stiglitz approach discussed earlier is very thin and conventional, interpreting democratic control as first and foremost a property of states, with transnational democracy possible only at one remove through a more egalitarian distribution of power across states in global negotiations. There are several more ambitious agendas for global democracy.

Cosmopolitan democracy is a model of the global political order and an agenda for political globalization that has been well developed by normative theorists (Held 1995; Archibugi *et al.* 1998), though it has yet to see much in the way of implementation. Cosmopolitan democrats seek first of all a much stronger set of global institutions (such as the United Nations) and regional institutions (such as the European Union). When it comes to the United Nations, the Security Council should be more effective and inclusive, and not dominated by the veto of a few great powers as at present. Ideally the General Assembly would be replaced by a global parliament. Global military authorities would be subordinate to this strengthened UN structure. There would be international referenda and courts with international jurisdiction. All these institutions would be cosmopolitan in the sense of being subordinated to a common, global legal framework, and directly accountable to the peoples of the world – not just to national governments, as at present. Held (2004) takes cosmopolitanism one step further in advocating a globally social-democratic economic policy, committed to intervention in markets so as to secure global social justice through income redistribution.

Cosmopolitan democracy is a long term project, and some aspects – for example, a global parliament – currently seem very distant aspirations. At present the only truly cosmopolitan global institution is the International Criminal Court, from which the United States has exempted itself, for fear that members of its military could be tried by this tribunal for war crimes. Cosmopolitanism has been severely damaged by US unilateralism more generally in the years after the 9/11 terrorist attacks. The administration of US President George W. Bush sought to subordinate international organizations such as the UN to

American desires, and if they did not comply, declared them irrelevant. The exception to this rule is the World Trade Organization; on economics and free trade the US does abide by WTO rulings, as noted earlier. US anti-cosmopolitanism dominates when it comes to security, terrorism, human rights and the environment, but not when it comes to economics. However, cosmopolitan democrats are reluctant to endorse the WTO (at least as it currently works) because it is so clearly undemocratic and not committed to global justice and equality of the kind that cosmopolitans favour.

States would still exist in a cosmopolitan democracy. However, they would be just one level of political authority among many – local, subnational, regional and global. A cosmopolitan system would not be federal, with lower levels being subordinate to higher levels. Rather, power would be dispersed across and shared between different levels, in 'a system of diverse and overlapping power centres shaped by democratic law' (Held 1995: 234). The primacy of this legal framework means that nothing like sovereignty as we currently know it would apply to the state. Indeed, the concept of sovereignty, and so the sovereign state, would fall into disuse. And the theory of the state would dissolve into the theory of multi-level government.

Transnational discursive democracy involves a more de-centred, bottom up approach to democratizing of the global system. The emphasis would be on transnational public spheres rather than the construction of formal international governing bodies. In Chapter 8 we characterized the public sphere in terms of an arena of political communication oriented to public affairs but not seeking a formal share in state authority, extending from the media to social movement activism. Public spheres have traditionally been defined in relation to particular states, but the concept can also be stretched to apply in transnational politics. Examples of international public spheres include those defined by concerns with global justice, opposing corporate globalization; with global environmental affairs; with the behaviour and misbehaviour of particular corporations, such as the oil industry; with international human rights; with very particular issues such as female genital mutilation; or with the onset of the invasion of Iraq in 2003. Public spheres can take more or less oppositional form in relation to dominant institutions – the global anti-war movement that flourished in 2003 would seem to be like this. However, this movement was met with sympathy by the governments of many states (for example, France and Germany).

Transnational discursive democracy sees international public spheres as potential sites of deliberation across national boundaries, providing arenas for the engagement of different discourses. Examples of discourses that might develop and contest each other in such settings would include sustainable development, currently the dominant global discourse on environmental affairs; market liberalism (as in Chapter 5); the international human rights discourse; counter-terror; and global justice. The engagement of different discourses can be more or less democratic, engaging a more or less broad variety of competent actors. It can also involve propagandists, deceivers, public relations experts and spin doctors. Particular discourses may be oppressive. So it is important to keep a critical eye on the conditions of communication in transnational public spheres. The legitimacy of decisions can then be assessed by seeing how far decisions resonate with the balance of discourses in the public sphere, and to what extent this balance is under the dispersed control of critical and competent political actors. This approach to democracy has real-world bite to the degree that transnational political affairs are ordered by discourses rather than by formal authority. The weakness of formal international institutions means that discourses such as sustainable development and neo-liberalism play a much larger part in ordering international affairs than they do in ordering politics within states. Democratization at the international level is only ever a matter of degree; there is no global equivalent to universal suffrage. The claim is only that discursive democratization can render collective decision making in the international system more democratic over time: not that any ideal model of democracy is being achieved or constructed.

Transnational discursive democracy has an advantage over cosmopolitan democracy because its institutional requirements are much less demanding. It can co-exist and feed into many sorts of formal institutions, which do not have to be organized at the international level. Among those institutions are states. So transnational discursive democracy could be strengthened in a world where states continue to be the dominant locus of formal or legal political authority.

Globalization's Consequences for Theories of the Democratic State

We are now in a position to summarize the implications of globalization for the theories of the state covered in previous chapters:

- *Pluralism in its classic form* looks limited, because as it is based on the assumption that group interests are constituted within a well-defined national political system.
- *Elite theory* can be reinforced to the extent that globalization is creating a new global elite. Again the national level of analysis needs re-

thinking, because the new global elite has little regard for national boundaries. However, national elites may use the discourse of globalization to consolidate their power, claiming that the demands of the global economy mean that (for example) the demands of non-elites for income redistribution cannot be met, for fear that redistribution will upset international investors and financiers.

- *Marxism* can draw comfort from the degree to which the dynamics of capitalist development now culminate in an integrated global system. All the crisis tendencies of capitalism can therefore be played out at the global level – but without any global state to manage these contradictions. For example, there are no mechanisms for creating systems of social welfare to prevent workers developing a revolutionary consciousness. Globalization also means that national states increasingly have to serve the interests of the global economic system, so they too are in no position to ameliorate the class struggle between workers and global business.

- *Market liberalism* should welcome the global expansion of markets. If globalization does force states to be more competitive by reducing levels of taxation and spending, then for market liberals this is a big step in the right direction – toward states that serve the market and are not held back by rent-seeking domestic interests (such as organized labour).

- *Contemporary pluralism* can be home to some very mixed reactions to globalization. For neo-pluralists, globalization simply reinforces the privileged position of business in polyarchies, because multinational corporations in particular become ever stronger in relation to any domestic political forces. Conversely, analysts of multi-level governance see globalization as potentially reinforcing pluralism, inasmuch as it adds new levels of power, and so more countervailing interests into the political system. Transnational social movements might further strengthen this pluralist mix. Theorists of networked governance who believe that the conventional state is increasingly 'hollow' see globalization as increasing the importance and power of transnational networks, further undermining the power of the sovereign state. Corporatists and defenders of 'cooperative market economies' argue in contrast that states acting together with nationally-organized business corporations can still weather the storm of globalization by creating cooperative political-economic structures to produce high-quality, internationally marketable goods while keeping social benefits for workers. In short, different aspects of globalization may both reinforce and undermine pluralism.

- *Electoral politics* is diminished in importance in a globalizing world, if power is increasingly transferred to international institutions that are not elected (such as the WTO or IMF). The global-ization of media may mean that people pay less attention to their own elections than to those in larger countries (such as the United States), whose results may actually have far more consequences for them than the elections in which they are allowed to vote.

- *Identity politics* may intensify in importance due to globalization. One reaction to the insecurities produced by globalization is a retreat to an extreme form of attachment to one's own traditions – and this may help explain the rise of religious fundamentalism in a globalizing world. The more interaction there is across the bound-aries of 'civilizations' as identified by Samuel Huntington, the more arenas there are in which the 'clash of civilizations' can be played out. Yet if globalization means more migration, then glob-alizing societies may also become more multi-cultural.
- *Democratic renewal* tries to meet the challenge of a globalizing world by seeking new forms of democracy for an international system that has historically resisted democratization. Examples include the cosmopolitan and transnational discursive democracies discussed in this chapter.
- *Feminism* shares aspects of the anti-globalization critique that we have discussed, for example, because women suffer from the decline of the welfare state or exploitation in sweatshops pro-ducing goods for multi-national corporations.
- *Environmentalism* too joins the anti-globalization critique, pointing to the environmental destructiveness of international cap-italism. But environmentalists can also support transnational social movements in an approach to political action that is itself globalized. And sometimes, transnational environmental action can influence the policies of states much more effectively than can green activism confined to the national level.
- *Conservatives* are uneasy with the many aspects of globalization that undermine the self-contained and distinctive character of national communities. Thus Conservative Party 'Eurosceptics' resist the power of the European Union in the UK; and in the United States, globalization and free trade are opposed by conserv-ative such as Pat Buchanan and his sympathizers. By contrast, US neo-conservatives see globalization as something that can and should be organized in the interests of the United States, by making sure that US-style liberal democracy plus capitalism is adopted everywhere.
- *Post-modernists* interpret the discourse of globalization as just another form of oppression, conditioning people to behave in par-ticular kinds of well-disciplined ways that serve the liberal capi-

talist system. Post-modern advocates of agonistic democracy see some possibilities for renewing democracy in anti-globalization movements, especially given the need for such movements to organize people internationally from very different social backgrounds, whose differences could be the basis for the development of agonistic respect.

Conclusion

Globalization has major consequences for the theory of the state. At one extreme, it could lead to a dissolution of the state (and so the theory of the state) into multi-level governance. That prospect still remains distant. In the meantime, globalizing forces often make themselves felt through the medium of the state. It is states that negotiate treaties, enforce the prescriptions of global institutions, apply the ideology and discourse of globalization, and (sometimes) resist globalizing pressures. At the time of writing we do not know how the story ends; we only know that the story is profound and important in its consequences for the state.

Chapter 15

Current and Future Debates about the State

Writing about debates in academia (and philosophy in particular), the sociologist Randall Collins famously formulated an 'intellectual Law of Small Numbers'. Its central proposition is that 'the number of active schools of thought which reproduce themselves for more than one or two generations in an argumentative community is of the order of three to six' (1998: 81). The lower limit must be two (because you cannot argue with yourself) and the number is almost invariably three in any reasonably creative period. The upper limit reflects recurring evidence that although intellectuals may spawn more positions in creative periods many will struggle to acquire adherents over the long term. When more than six positions exist some are reclassified as variants of bigger views and others 'are not propagated across subsequent generations'. Thus: 'Positions appear and disappear, grow stronger or weaker in adherents. The Law of Small Numbers holds sway amidst the flux' (Collins 1998: 81). These propositions seem relevant for the landscape we have described here.

Once upon a time there were just a few classic theories of the state — pluralism, elite theory, Marxism and market liberalism. In the late 1960s cracks in this configuration began to appear. In nearby sociological theory at the same time the numbers of positions suddenly increased from three key schools to six or more, many of them overlapping significantly with the positions covered here (Taylor 2001). Today the theory of the state seems more complex and we have now reviewed 10 positions, if we count neo-pluralism as different from its classical forebear, and nine if we do not. This number is larger than Collins suggests is sustainable over the longer term, reflecting the creativity of the last 40 years, especially in multiplying critiques of classical state theories. So can we expect the number of strands to slim down in future, and if so, at whose expense? We are as bad as most social scientists at predicting the future course of events, and the sheer variety of contemporary forces means that combinations of positions may emerge which have novel and unforeseeable consequences. But we can offer some thoughts about how matters currently stand.

The Fate of the Classical Theories

Of the four classic theories of the state, pluralism is probably in the best of health, though only at the cost of some substantial modifications to its basic tenets. As Chapter 6 showed, pluralism has moved away from complacent celebration of the openness of liberal democracies in general (and the United States in particular) towards accepting inputs from a much wider variety of actual and potential interest groups. Pluralism is now much more guarded about the equality of access and influence achieved in any real world polity, but remains adamant that a wide variety of inputs to policy making is desirable. Quite how that variety can and should be organized remains a matter of some dispute. Different answers are provided by liberal corporatists who want to organize varying numbers of 'social partner' groups into the policy process; analysts of advocacy coalitions who believe the effective number of groupings in debate will normally remain small but vary from issue to issue; and neo-pluralists most concerned to counter the privileged position of business corporations in policy making. Pluralism also takes on a somewhat different kind of life in the politics of identity, as different groups vie for recognition. Of course, some identity groups and (especially) their leaders still sometimes seek the eradication of other groups, rather than plural coexistence. This creates tough problems for all liberal views. Many liberals now seek to confront such intransigent identity groups robustly, even pre-emptively, at home and abroad. The 'soft power' version of pluralism developed in the European Union (and increasingly deployed to try to stabilize the EU's neighbours) may prove more lasting than the 'hard power' approach enabled by the United States' dominant military power and potentially 'imperial' status (discussed later).

Marxists and elite theorists are in much worse shape than pluralists. Marxism has still not recovered from the demise of the Soviet bloc, no matter how hard its dwindling number of serious contemporary proponents insist that their analysis of the character of the liberal capitalist state stands on its own merits, irrespective of the fate of authoritarian regimes that once termed themselves Marxist. The draining of influence away from Marxist economics and its labour theory of value, and the inability of class analysis to explain the character of many contemporary political mobilizations, has increasingly left Marxist theory as a political critique of the limits and defects of capitalism (see for example Hardt and Negri 2001). In this sense, empirical Marxist political analysis has increasingly converged with the elite theory critique, with little sign of the materialist and dialectical thinking that were previously the signatures of orthodox Marxist thought.

Post-1945 elite theory has never faced the kind of decisive moment that fascism posed for classical elite doctrines in the 1930s, or that Marxism had to grapple with after the collapse of communism in 1989. The world is undeniably still mainly run by elites. The idea that there is a single unified elite controlling each nation state has never been refuted, partly because elite theorists have never really stated their theory in an easily refuted way. And since there is always some form of ruling group or network in every society, the claim has a near-tautologous quality – as the leading modern elite theorist C. Wright Mills noted. In a 'celebrity' culture where political finance scandals recur apparently incessantly and where media corporations (and even parties in some countries) are still owned and run by tycoons, the political dominance of rich people has rarely been more widely perceived by Western public opinion. At one level contemporary neo-elite critiques have not lost their resonance or sales appeal, as in Naomi Klein's exposés of how corporations use branding power (Klein 2001); or how corporations and market liberal governments together exploit 'shocks' like national emergencies to push hard-line capitalist solutions (Klein 2008). But for whatever reason, elite theory has lost much of its intellectual appeal. Even radicals disenchanted with the status quo are now more attracted to feminist, environmental, radical pluralist and postmodern critiques of the state. If elite theory has new momentum, it is at the global level, where we may be witnessing the emergence of a global *uber*-elite composed of the heads of large corporations, financiers, and politicians riding the globalization wave.

Market liberals might claim that their analysis of the state remains compelling, and many of those who flocked to this theory in the 1980s remain in positions of academic and political power. But the market liberal ascendancy has peaked. In the United States, one of its bastions, the events of 11 September 2001 led Republican Party politicians and others on the political right to a renewed appreciation of the need for a strong state, for example, one that did not outsource airport security to private contractors. Worldwide, the rising prominence of the climate change issue has been accompanied by increasing recognition of the central role that governments (and inter-governmental arrangements) must play in counteracting irreversible adverse shifts in the condition of the human habitat. Left to themselves markets cannot tackle these problems, notwithstanding the possible use of market-type instruments such as carbon trading as part of the policy packages deployed.

Yet it is in the core area of market operations under 'light touch' regulation that the greatest difficulties have arisen for market liberals. During the Asian financial crisis of 1997 European and American market liberals looked on condescendingly as what they styled 'crony capitalism' pervasive in east Asia suffered a sudden and acute crisis of confidence. A diet of more market liberal deregulation was prescribed. Yet in late 2008 the USA and almost all European countries suffered their own cascade of crisis, as bad debts from the American housing market triggered a catastrophic slump in trust in the banking sector, where highly leveraged strategies had run wild under market liberal deregulation. These strategies featured financial derivatives and other complex instruments poorly understood by almost everyone involved in the markets for them – including government officials. The traumatic stabilization of the main crisis in October 2008, too late to avoid a significant worldwide recession, underpinned an essential truth. Behind every contemporary market economy stands a state. In the end it was only the state's tax-raising powers that protected banking systems across the United States and Europe from collapse. This highly inconvenient truth for market liberals is likely to sap simplistic 'Market good/ State bad' doctrines for many years ahead – at least until the lessons of the 2008 crisis are forgotten by new generations of exuberant market actors and their supporters in academia and government.

Another foundation of market liberalism was the seeming impossibility of the extent of central calculation needed to operate a planned economy effectively. But that cornerstone, once so solid, begins to look a bit shaky in light of the ever-growing computational capacities associated with effective use of information technology. In a matter of a few decades some of the most apparently utopian political musings of a cluster of IT visionaries almost unknown in the social sciences have been implemented in uncannily similar ways and on a global scale (Brate 2002). The political, economic and cultural implications of these epoch-making shifts in access to the world's information are still working out in real-time. But already there are claims that 'super-crunching' the vast piles of data now accumulating can decisively expand human cognitive limits (Ayres 2008)

To date it is mostly large corporations that have reorganized their affairs along these lines. For example, large retailers can now gather transactional information that tells them everything they need to know in precise detail about each of their customer groups, and how to ensure that shelves are re-stocked in optimal fashion to take advantage of customer behaviours. Most of this can be done automatically, with little need for managers to intervene, and it confers a degree of market power on the largest companies that smaller firms simply cannot begin to emulate. In the future there is every prospect that the same technologies could translate into radically improved performance within government, which is likely to become ever-more capital intensive and information-dependent. 'Digital-era governance' systems are increasingly run by global IT companies but on behalf of government bureaucracies, whose informational incompetency can no longer be taken as a given (Dunleavy *et al.* 2008). By contrast, exaggerated claims of a new age of 'e-democracy' or of radical changes in political mobilization on the Internet have yet to be borne out, with mostly smaller, incremental effects showing on the radar so far. Yet in the longer term the decreasing information costs of collective action may still have major implications.

However, the financial crash of 2008 may also hold a silver lining for followers of Friedrich Hayek in their protracted guerrilla war against the analytic over-confidence of mainstream economics. It will not prevent the resurgence of the 'commonsense regulation' demanded by President Obama in his 2008 election campaign, and with it a hugely increased economic role for western governments, at least for a time. But at least the crisis may renew a pervasive scepticism about whether financial and economic risks can ever be adequately modelled or controlled by any form of human agency. The complex structure of financial derivatives and elaborate models designed to parcel out and distribute risk failed to reduce (still less eliminate) the risks themselves. So the Hayekian scepticism about human knowledge (discussed in Chapter 5) may enjoy a resurgence within the diminishing ranks of market liberals themselves.

Persistent Critiques and New Agendas

Some of the more contemporary theories of the state, notably environmental, feminist, post-modern, and neo-conservative approaches, take the form of critique rather than offering comprehensive explanatory theories in their own right. Environmentalism and feminism expose some pervasive shortcomings of modern states, whether they are liberal democratic or authoritarian. The environmental critique is given added force by the increasing salience of climate change since the late 1990s, joining other problems involving pollution, the destruction of biodiversity, water and energy. The unfolding significance of these global issues should grow in coming decades, raising the prospect that environmentalism will absorb many globalization discussions. If so, the environmental theory of the state will become an increasingly coherent and influential pole of debate.

No such boost has been received or is likely to be received by feminism, which has therefore had to rely on the intrinsic power and plausibility of its analyses. The same might be said of post-modern analyses of the 'governmentality' that pervades liberal societies. For feminists and post-modernists, the critique may well persist, but many of their lessons have already been absorbed in advanced industrial countries. This is not in any way to downgrade the real impacts of feminism, especially when it comes to cultural change over recent decades. But it seems unlikely that the liberal democratic state will undergo further radical change as a result of the further development of these schools of thought.

We have seen that moralistic conservatism too is now largely a matter of critique, as conservatives lament rather than defend the liberal democratic status quo. When neo-conservatives in particular moved from critique to prescription and then a particular kind of implementation under the George W. Bush presidency, the results were disastrous, not just for Iraq, but also for the credibility of any international moral crusade originating in the United States. The powerful strands in American life that sustain evangelical religious conservatism continue to be influential. But it is hard to see where else neo-conservatism and religious fundamentalism can go.

Reform agendas associated with democratic renewal and globalization (beyond ecological issues) are perhaps in better shape, though generally pointing in different directions. Democratic renewal seeks more authentic democracy, in a variety of locations — including but not limited to the state. However, there are plenty of forces that want to roll back democracy, rather than deepen it. Some of these are associated with globalization, and especially a globalist discourse according to which all societies must follow the same economic priorities, irrespective of what their citizens may say they want. Globalization too engenders resistance, not least from those defending democracy in the state and civil society. Theorists have only just begun to seriously imagine how to globalize democracy to match the globalizing economy.

Liberal Democracy in Question

At the turn of the twenty first century liberal democracy's political and intellectual ascendancy seemed at last to be secure. Of course there remained plenty of authoritarian governments around the world, but they looked like remnants rather than any model for a world to come. Yet within a few years liberal democracy's prospects on the global stage no longer looked so rosy. The aftermath of the invasion of Iraq in 2003 discredited the muscular universalists who would seek to impose liberal democracy at the point of a gun. And even more peaceful 'soft power' proponents of liberal democracy suffered from the fallout of what had been done in the name of the political model they cherished. In the Middle East and beyond, non-democratic models of governance gained confidence and support precisely because they were not associated with the United States. In Asia rulers and publics alike drew their own conclusions about the 'realpolitik' that underlay protestations of western democracy's moral superiority.

Authoritarian alternatives to liberal democracy also prospered, with the continuing economic rise of China, which alone includes more than one in every five people in the world. In Russia, a resource-led boom resting on exports of oil and natural gas of vital significance for Europe accompanied the hollowing out of liberal democracy after 2000. Both these large states combined rapid economic growth with authoritarianism. Equally important was the influence that Russia and China have been able to exercise beyond their borders. Some of Russia's neighbours, once organized into the Soviet bloc, could be more comfortable with their democratic deficits of more or less severity as Russia slipped back into authoritarianism. And China provided a model for developing countries, especially in Africa, that had never been able to follow any western model of the political economy with much success. China could also afford to provide financial assistance to such countries, without the liberal democratic strings attached to aid offered by the International Monetary Fund and World Bank. Such conditions are often unpalatable to African governments not keen on transparency, the rule of law or reducing corruption.

The reinvigoration of economic growth in India, the world's largest if still flawed polyarchy, and the consolidation of democratic government across most of Latin America (albeit with low levels of public confidence), have posted some gains for liberal democracy. Some authors maintain an optimism that China itself will become more democratic in future, as its increasing economic clout requires openness in all branches of thought and social organization (Hutton 2006). China's 'socialist' character has been largely written off in the west as no more than a tattered ideological façade. But Lin (2006) points out that never in the history of the world have around 350 million people moved from poverty into basically adequate incomes in a few decades — an accomplishment that easily dwarfs that of nineteenth century industrialization in Europe. But any democracy that does develop in China may well be different from liberal democracy as it has developed in much of the rest of the world. In particular competitive elections may be a long time coming. And even could such elections come into being, the examples of Japan and Singapore show how one-party dominance can co-exist with elections in countries with strong Confucian traditions of hierarchy and consensus. Finally, the example of India shows that governing a single nation-state with over a billion citizens is no easy task, and that local authoritarianism can sometimes coexist with national democracy.

The Return of Empire?

In Chapter 1 we showed how the modern state had emerged as the dominant global political form, leaving behind tribal societies, communes, the complex webs of monarchy, feudal obligation, and theocracy that characterized medieval Europe and empires. After 1989 the collapse of the militarily-enforced Soviet bloc, and the subsequent disintegration of the USSR itself into its component republics, seemed to confirm that the age of empire was over. However, empire may be making a comeback (Lal, 2004). Some proponents of United States hegemony after 2001 were happy to see the world in terms of the expansion of American empire (for example, Ignatieff 2003). Such an empire would not come in the form of direct rule, but rather with nominally independent states being in practice subservient to the United States. Other empires of this sort might be centred on Russia, the European Union and China. Russia sees its former 'near abroad' as its own sphere of influence, and from 2000 on its re-found domestic stability and prosperity enabled it to intervene with more effect (though with some resistance) in these countries. Yet an invasion of Georgia in 2008 proved economically costly, as international investors took flight from a possible 'new Cold War'.

For many centuries before 1800 China, the 'middle kingdom' (or in other words 'centre of the earth' for Chinese rulers and intellectuals), exercised suzerainty over most of its east Asian neighbours. With the success of its authoritarian economic development and the rise of Chinese finance comes renewed Chinese political influence, though its near neighbours remain perhaps more resistant to this than are more distant states in sub-Saharan Africa. The extension of Chinese influence into Africa, and its limited influence so far closer to home, emphasizes the fact that any resurgence of empire is not the same as Samuel Huntington's alleged 'clash of civilizations', which would predict that any emerging empire would be confined within the boundaries of a particular civilization.

Finally the European Union is not exactly an empire, or even a federation. Nor does it have any one dominant country to serve as imperial headquarters. But the EU is still reasonably effectively run by shifting coalitions of its largest states (Germany, France, Britain and Italy) and the remaining middle-sized countries. Despite persistent internal criticisms and occasional public opinion backlashes against its operations, the EU also increasingly governs the affairs of its component states and speaks with one voice in international affairs. And the number of those states keeps expanding, as we write 27 countries, with more on the way. Moreover, the EU pursues a strong 'neighbourhood policy' toward the states in its own 'near abroad'. These states include all the countries bordering the Mediterranean, encompassing the Islamic countries of the north African littoral (whence acute migration issues emanate), and also the countries on its eastern and Balkan fringes. The EU offers its prospective 'partners' the lure of greater economic access to European markets if they will only bring their education systems, industrial production, trade systems, and systems of human and civil rights into greater accord with European standards. This is an attractive 'soft power' proposition that is widely taken up by its targets. The countries either within the EU itself or decisively within its 'neighbourhood' sphere of influence may soon number 50 or more.

New Kinds of Governance

Changes in the character and configuration of the international system have all kinds of consequences for states. The modern state's origins in seventeenth century Europe owed much to the recognized need to establish some kind of solution to violent conflicts between different religious sects. The subsequent development of states in Europe and beyond was conditioned by ever-present threats from other states, and the danger of war between states. But war between states is now extremely rare (though still common between factions within states). This is not just a matter of the 'democratic peace', under which liberal democracies (allegedly) do not go to war against one another. Outright wars between democracies and authoritarian states, and among authoritarian states, are now also rare, although aggressive border clashes continue to occur, as between Russia and Georgia in 2008 or between Israel and Lebanon in 2006. Perhaps the 2003 invasion of Iraq by the United States, the UK and a few supporters was one of the last gasps of full-scale inter-state warfare, demonstrating just how costly such war can prove even for the seeming 'winner'.

If inter-state war is no longer such a significant threat, then states have less need to organize themselves militarily or governmentally to protect against it. Thus there is one less obstacle to emerging forms of organization that transcend state boundaries. Such forms are best developed so far within the European Union, especially when it comes to formal government at a layer above the state. In the EU and perhaps elsewhere, governance networks can increasingly be effective across the boundaries of states. And within states, such networks can increasingly operate with some degree of independence from a national government that no longer has to claim sovereign authority with such exclusivity or urgency as in the recent past.

The global system also features ever-increasing economic transactions across state boundaries. Such economic trans-nationalization and globalization may be accompanied by parallel political changes. Impetus toward a genuinely global pattern of governance has already been observed, albeit with multiple, largely uncodified governance arrangements still operating in many diverse ways and in a range of transnational institutional forms. This change is furthered by the rise of global issues such as climate change. However, economic and even ecological globalization may not necessarily undermine the authority of the sovereign state. States may re-assert themselves as the managers of globalization, just as in the 1980s states that wished to implement market liberal principles had to centralize their domestic authority and coerce those internal social interests that were resistant to marketization. And in cooperative market economies, governments may join with national corporations to position themselves effectively in relation to global markets – in a way that maintains the state's coordinating role, in both managing the economy and providing social welfare. Yet still across such efforts there looms the shadow of climate change and ecological degradation, from which no country, however large or powerful, can stand aloof.

Conclusion

If we were to project present trends at the time of writing (2008), we might conclude that:

- (Variants of) pluralism will continue to be a central strand in thinking about the liberal democratic state, perhaps now more centred in European Union countries than in the USA.
- Elite theory and a de-economized Marxism will survive in an increasingly merged form as a powerful radical critique of the social and power inequalities of capitalist polyarchies.
- Environmental theory will grow in significance and may in time absorb many aspects of globalization theories.
- A re-merged market liberal and neo-conservative position, an integrated 'new right' akin to that of the 1980s, will survive the twin adverse shocks of the financial crash of 2007–08 (on the one hand) and the USA's imperial over-reach in Iraq and Afghanistan (on the other) to maintain an incessant critique of pluralism from the right, especially in the United States.

If Collins's limit of six or seven major theory slots holds good, then feminism, conservatism, postmodernism and (non-ecological) globalization theories must continue to scrap for the remaining one or two slots.

However, we are also aware of the frequency of unanticipated developments and sudden shocks that can alter quite fundamentally the relative standing of different theories of the state, and in some cases call forth new theories. Starting in the 1960s, such surprises include civil unrest followed by the rise of new social movements (including environmentalism and feminism) in the late 1960s, the collapse of the post-1945 international economic order in the early 1970s, energy shocks in the mid-1970s, the election of Prime Minister Thatcher in 1979 and President Reagan in 1980, the collapse of communism in 1989, the resurgence of ethnic nationalist politics of identity in the 1990s, the 9/11 terrorist attacks on the United States in 2001, the neo-conservative-orchestrated invasion of Iraq in 2003, and the global financial crisis of 2008. The sheer frequency of such developments and events should make us pause before making predictions of any sort about where the theory of the liberal democratic state might go next.

In the 1990s it was fashionable to speak in terms of a global triumph of liberal democracy that would see all states converging on a common pluralist model, which also featured competitive elections and a capitalist market system. No such conclusion seems so plausible any longer. In part this is because there are actually many different sorts of liberal democratic state, as we have seen: federal and unitary; majoritarian and consensual; corporatist and pluralist; exclusive and inclusive; minimalist and interventionist. All are the targets of critiques and reform movements, concerned not just with the content of public policies but with the basic structure of the polity and political economy. All have to respond to challenges presented by identity politics, environmental crises, and globalization — but they do so in different kinds of ways. Among liberal democracies, there are also big differences between states that aspire to empire (if no longer by that name), giant states that are already continental in scale (like India or the USA), states that lock themselves into supra-national unions (such as the European Union), states retaining substantial autonomy as stand-alone nation-states, and micro-states. Beyond liberal democracy may be found illiberal democracies (with competitive elections but little respect for human rights and no effective constitutional restraints on government), failed states, rogue states and authoritarian states in several forms. If the contemporary theory of the state looks to be complex and multi-faceted, that only reflects the complexity of the world it confronts.

Bibliography

[Numbers in square brackets, e.g. [211] show pages in the chapters above where the source is cited as relevant.]

Ackerman, Bruce and Anne Alstott. 1999. *The Stakeholder Society*. New Haven, CT: Yale University Press. [211]

Ackerman, Bruce A. and William T. Hassler. 1981. *Clean Coal, Dirty Air: or How the Clean Air Act became a Multibillion-Dollar Bail-Out for High-Sulfur Coal Producers and What Should Be Done About It*. New Haven, CT: Yale University Press. [245]

Akçam, Taner. 2006. *A Shameful Act: The Armenian Genoicde and the Question of Turkish Responsibility*. Translated by P. Bessemer. New York: Henry Holt.

Alford, John and Deidre O'Neill. 1999. *The Contract State: Public Management and the Kennett Government*. Geelong: Deakin University Press. [122]

Allison, Graham T. 1972. *Essence of Decision: Explaining the Cuban Missile Crisis*. Boston: Little, Brown. [49]

Almond, Gabriel. 1954. *The Appeals of Communism*. Princeton, NJ: Princeton University Press. [292]

Almond, Gabriel A. and Sidney Verba. 1963. *The Civic Culture*. Princeton, NJ: Princeton University Press. [45–6]

Amy, Douglas J. 1987. *The Politics of Environmental Mediation*. New York: Columbia University Press. [224, 265]

Anderson, Benedict. 1983. *Imagined Communities: Reflections on the Origin and Spread of Nationalism*. London: Verso. [188–9]

Anderson, Terry L. and Donald R. Leal. 2001. *Free Market Environmentalism*, rev. edition. New York: Palgrave. [121, 262]

Andrews, Richard N.L. 1997. United States. In Martin Jänicke and Helmut Weidner, eds, *National Environmental Policies: A Comparative Study of Capacity-Building*. Berlin: Springer, pp. 24–44. [249]

Annan, Kofi. 2006. *Opening Address to the 53rd Annual Department of Public Affairs/Non-Governmental Organizations Conference*. New York: United Nations. [315]

Archibugi, Daniele, David Held and Martin Köhler, eds. 1998. *Re-Imagining Political Community: Studies in Cosmopolitan Democracy*. Cambridge: Polity. [322]

Arendt, Hannah. 1951. *The Origins of Totalitarianism*. New York: Harvest Books, 1973 edition. [39]

Arendt, Hannah. 1958. *The Human Condition*. Chicago: University of Chicago Press. [214]

Arendt, Hannah. 1978. *The Life of the Mind, I: Thinking*. New York: Harcourt, Brace, Jovanovich. [39]

Arrow, Kenneth J. 1963. *Social Choice and Individual Values*, 2nd edition. New York: Wiley. [112]

Axelrod, Robert. 1984. *The Evolution of Cooperation*. New York: Basic Books. [17, 54]

Ayres, Ian. 2008. *Super Crunchers: How Thinking by Numbers is the New Way to be Smart*. London: Bantam. [332]

Bachrach, Peter and Morton A. Baratz. 1963. Decisions and Nondecisions: An Analytical Framework. *American Political Science Review*, 57: 632–42. [65]

Baiocchi, Gianpaolo. 2001. Participation, Activism and Politics: The Porto Alegre Experiment and Deliberative Democratic Theory. *Politics and Society*, 29: 43–72. [213]

Barber, Benjamin R. 1984. *Strong Democracy: Participatory Politics for a New Age*. Berkeley: University of California Press. [212–13]

Barber, Benjamin R. 1992. *An Aristocracy of Everyone: The Politics of Education and the Future of America*. New York: Oxford University Press. [209–10]

Bartels, Larry. 2003. Is 'Popular Rule' Possible? Polls, Political Psychology, and Democracy. *Brookings Review*, 21: 12–15. [169]

Bauer, Raymond A, Ithiel de Sola Pool and Lewis A. Dexter. 1963. *American Business and Public Policy*. Chicago: Aldine-Atherton, 1972 edition. [48]

Beck, Paul Allen. 1986. Choice, Context, and Consequence: Beaten and Unbeaten Paths Toward a Science of Electoral Behavior. In Herbert F. Weisberg, ed., *Political Science: The Science of Politics*. New York: Agathon, pp. 241–83. [156]

Beck, Ulrich. 1992. *Risk Society: Towards a New Modernity*. London: Sage. [244, 253–4, 306]

Bell, Daniel A. 2006. East Asia and the West: The Impact of Confucianism on Anglo-American Political Theory. In John S. Dryzek, Anne Phillips and Bonnie Honig, eds, *The Oxford Handbook of Political Theory*. Oxford: Oxford University Press, pp. 262–80. [271]

Bell, Daniel and Hahm Chaibong, eds. 2003. *Confucianism for the Modern World*. New York: Cambridge University Press. [271]

Benhabib, Seyla. 1996. Toward a Deliberative Model of Democratic Legitimacy. In Seyla Benhabib, ed., *Democracy and Difference: Contesting the Boundaries of the Political*, pp. 67–94. Princeton, NJ: Princeton University Press. [219]

Benhabib, Seyla. 2002. *The Claims of Culture: Equality and Diversity in the Global Era*. Princeton, NJ: Princeton University Press. [197]

Bentley, Arthur F. 1908. *The Process of Government*. Chicago: University of Chicago Press. [45]

Berelson, Bernard. 1952. Democratic Theory and Public Opinion. *Public Opinion Quarterly*, 16: 313–30. [43–4]

Berelson, Bernard R., Paul F. Lazarsfeld and William N. McPhee. 1954. *Voting*. Chicago: University of Chicago Press. [156]

Berlin, Isaiah. 2007. *Political Ideas in the Romantic Age: Their Rise and Influence on Modern Thought*. London: Pimlico. [40]

Bessette, Joseph M. 1980. Deliberative Democracy: The Majoritarian Principle in Republican Government. In Robert Goldwin and William Shambra eds, *How Democratic is the Constitution?*. Washington, DC: American Enterprise Institute, pp. 102–16. [216]

Bessette, Joseph M. 1994. *The Mild Voice of Reason: Deliberative Democracy and American National Government*. Chicago: University of Chicago Press. [217, 220]

Block, Fred. 1977. The Ruling Class Does Not Rule: Notes on the Marxist Theory of the State. *Socialist Revolution*, 33: 6–28. [95, 134]

Bohman, James and William Rehg. 1997. *Deliberative Democracy: Essays on Reason and Politics*. Cambridge, MA: MIT Press. [215–16]

Boles, Janet K. 1994. Local Feminist Policy Networks in the Contemporary American Interest Group System. *Policy Sciences*, 27: 161–78.   [238]

Bookchin, Murray. 1982. *The Ecology of Freedom: The Emergence and Dissolution of Hierarchy*. Palo Alto, CA: Cheshire.   [248, 262, 266]

Bragg, Billy. 2006. *The Progressive Patriot*. New York: Bantam.   [200]

Braithwaite, John. 1989. *Crime, Shame, and Reintegration*. Cambridge: Cambridge University Press.   [298]

Braithwaite, John and Peter Drahos. 2000. *Global Business Regulation*. Cambridge: Cambridge University Press.   [144–5]

Braithwaite, John and Phillip Pettit. 1990. *Not Just Deserts: A Republican Theory of Criminal Justice*. Oxford: Clarendon Press.   [215]

Brams, Steven J. and Peter C. Fishburn. 1983. *Approval Voting*. Cambridge, MA: Birkhauser.   [180]

Brate, Adam. 2002. *Technomanifestos: Visions from the Information Age Revolutionaries*. New York: Texere.   [332]

Braybrooke, David and Charles E. Lindblom. 1963. *A Strategy of Decision: Policy Evaluation as a Social Process*. New York: Free Press.   [51]

Brennan, Geoffrey and Loren Lomasky. 1993. *Democracy and Decision*. Cambridge: Cambridge University Press.   [113]

Breton, Albert, Jean-Luigi Galeotti, Pierre Salmon, and Ron Wintrobe, eds. 1995. *Nationalism and Rationality*. Cambridge: Cambridge University Press.   [187]

Brody, Richard A. 2001. Civic Education and Political Tolerance: The 'We the People' Curriculum. *The Good Society*, 10(1): 29–34.   [209]

Brown, Wendy. 2006. Power After Foucault. In John S. Dryzek, Bonnie Honig and Anne Phillips, eds, *The Oxford Handbook of Political Theory*. Oxford: Oxford University Press, pp. 65–84.   [294]

Brundtland Commission 1987. *Our Common Future*.   [248]

Buchanan, James M. 1991. Politics Without Romance: A Sketch of Positive Public Choice and its Normative Implications. In Alan Hamlin and Philip Pettit, eds, *Contemporary Political Theory*. New York: Macmillan, pp. 216–28.   [105]

Buchanan, James M. and Gordon Tullock. 1962. *The Calculus of Consent*. Ann Arbor: University of Michigan Press.   [111]

Buchanan, Patrick J. 2004. *Where the Right Went Wrong: How Neoconservatives Subverted the Reagan Revolution and Hijacked the Bush Presidency*. New York: St. Martin's.   [322]

Bull, Hedley. 1977. *The Anarchical Society: A Study of Order in World Politics*. London: Macmillan.   [17]

Burke, Edmund. 1790. *Reflections on the Revolution in France*. Stanford, CA: Stanford University Press, 2001   [269–70]

Burnham, James. 1941. *The Managerial Revolution*. Bloomington, IN: Indiana University Press.   [64]

Butler, David and Donald Stokes. 1971. *Political Change in Britain: Forces Shaping Electoral Choice*. Harmondsworth: Penguin.   [157]

Callinicos, Alex. 2006. *The Resources of Critique*. Cambridge: Cambridge University Press.   [90]

Campbell, Angus, Philip E. Converse, Warren E. Miller and Donald E. Stokes. 1960. *The American Voter*. New York: Wiley.   [157]

Campbell, Rosie. 2006. *Gender and the Vote in Britain*. Colchester: ECPR Press. [232]

Caplan, Bryan. 2007. *The Myth of the Rational Voter: Why Democracies Choose Bad Policies*. Princeto, NJ: Princeton University Press. [158, 182]

Capling, Ann and Brian Galligan. 1992. *Beyond the Protective State: The Political Economy of Australia's Manufacturing Industry*. Cambridge: Cambridge University Press. [317–18]

Carothers, Thomas. 2002. The End of the Transition Paradigm. *Journal of Democracy*, 13: 5–21. [25]

Carter, Neil. 2001. *The Politics of the Environment: Ideas, Activism, Policy*. Cambridge: Cambridge University Press. [254]

Castells, Manuel. 1996. *The Information Age, Volume I: The Rise of the Network Society*. Oxford: Basil Blackwell. [142, 309–10, 212]

Castles, Francis G. 1985. *The Working Class and Welfare*. Sydney: Allen & Unwin. [238]

Catlin, George E.G. 1927. *The Science and Method of Politics*. New York: Knopf. [44–5]

Catton, William R. 1980. *Overshoot: The Ecological Basis of Revolutionary Change*. Urbana, IL: University of Illinois Press. [246]

Chambers, Simone. 2003. Deliberative Democratic Theory. *Annual Review of Political Science*, 6: 307–26. [215]

Chambers, Simone. 2004. Behind Closed Doors: Publicity, Secrecy, and the Quality of Deliberation. *Journal of Political Philosophy*, 12: 389–410. [222]

Chen, Kevin. 1992. *Political Alienation and Voting Turnout in the United States 1960–1988*. San Francisco: Mellen Research University Press. [168]

Chong, Dennis. 1991. *Collective Action and the Civil Rights Movement*. Chicago: University of Chicago Press. [55]

Cohen, Jean. 1985. Strategy or Identity? New Theoretical Paradigms and Contemporary Social Movements. *Social Research*, 52: 633–716. [139]

Cohen, Joshua. 1989. Deliberation and Democratic Legitimacy. In Alan Hamlin and Philip Pettit, eds, *The Good Polity: Normative Analysis of the State*. Oxford: Basil Blackwell, pp. 17–34. [217]

Cohen, Joshua and Joel Rogers. 1992. Secondary Associations and Democratic Governance. *Politics and Society*, 20: 393–472. [152]

Collins, Randall. 1994. Why the Social Sciences Won't Become High-Consensus, Rapid-Discovery Science. *Sociological Forum*, 9(2): 155–77. [x]

Collins, Randall. 1998. *The Sociology of Philosophies: A Global Theory of Intellectual Change*. Cambridge, MA: Belknap. [329

Colomer, Josep M. 2001. *Political Institutions: Democracy and Social Choice*. Oxford: Oxford University Press. [166]

Colomer, Josep M. 2008. Electoral systems, Majority rule, Multiparty systems. *International Encyclopedia of the Social Sciences*. [167]

Commoner, Barry. 1972. *The Closing Circle*. New York: Bantam. [260]

Connolly, William E., ed. 1969. *The Bias of Pluralism*. New York: Atherton. [36]

Connolly, William E. 1991. *Identity/Difference: Democratic Negotiations of Political Paradox*. Ithaca, NY: Cornell University Press. [303–4]

Connors, Michael. 2003. *Democracy and National Identity in Thailand*. London: Routledge. [305]

Converse, Philip E. 1964. The Nature of Belief Systems in Mass Publics. In David E. Apter, ed., *Ideology and Discontent*. Glencoe: Free Press, pp. 206–61. [157]

Crozier, Michel, Samuel P. Huntington and Joji Watanuki. 1975. *The Crisis of Democracy: Report on the Governability of Democracies to the Trilateral Commission*. New York: New York University Press. [23, 252, 276]

Cunliffe, John and Guido Erreygers. 2003. 'Basic Income? Basic Capital!' Origins and Issues of a Debate. *Journal of Political Philosophy*, 11: 89–110. [211]

Dagger, Richard. 1997. *Civic Virtues: Rights, Citizenship, and Republican Liberalism*. New York: Oxford University Press. [214]

Dahl, Robert A. 1956. *A Preface to Democratic Theory*. Chicago: University of Chicago Press. [44, 46–7, 158]

Dahl, Robert A. 1961. *Who Governs? Democracy and Power in an American City*. New Haven, CT: Yale University Press. [46–8]

Dahl, Robert A. 1971. *Polyarchy*. New Haven, CT: Yale University Press. [132]

Dahl, Robert A. 1985. *A Preface to Economic Democracy*. Berkeley: University of California Press. [212]

Dahl, Robert A. 1989. *Democracy and its Critics*. New Haven, CT: Yale University Press. [21]

Dahl, Robert A. and Lindblom, Charles. 1953. *Politics, Economics and Welfare*. New York: Harper & Brothers. (Second edition, 1976.) [50–1]

Dalrymple, Rawdon. 1998. Indonesia and the IMF: The Evolving Consequences of a Reforming Mission. *Australian Journal of International Affairs*, 52: 233–9. [127, 317]

Daly, Mary. 1993. *Pure Lust: Elemental Feminist Philosophy*. San Francisco: Harper. [231]

De Tocqueville, Alexis. 1945. *Democracy in America: Volume I*. New York: Knopf. [36]

Dean, Mitchell and Barry Hindess, eds. 1998. *Governing Australia: Studies in Contemporary Rationalities of Government*. Cambridge: Cambridge University Press.

Devall, Bill and Sessions, George. 1985. *Deep Ecology: Living as if Nature Mattered*. Salt Lake City, UT: Peregrine Smith. [249, 295]

Dewey, John. 1917. The Principle of Nationality. In John Dewey, *The Middle Works*. Carbondale, IL: Southern Illinois University Press, vol. 10, pp. 285–91. [38]

Diamond, Irene and Gloria Feman Orenstein, eds. 1990. *Reweaving the World: The Emergence of Ecofeminism*. San Francisco: Sierra Club Books. [249]

Dietz, Mary G. 1985. Citizenship with a Feminist Face: The Problem with Maternal Thinking. *Political Theory*, 13: 19–35. [241]

Dietz, Mary G. 2003. Current Controversies in Feminist Theory. *Annual Review of Political Science*, 6: 399–431. [242]

Dobson, Andrew. 1995. *Green Political Thought*, 2nd edition. London: Routledge. [243]

Domhoff, G. William. 1978a. *The Powers That Be: Processes of Ruling Class Domination in America*. New York: Random House. [71, 74]

Domhoff, G. William. 1978b. *Who Really Rules? New Haven and Community Power Re-Examined*. New Brunswick, NJ: Transaction Books. [71]

Downs, Anthony. 1957. *An Economic Theory of Democracy*. New York: Harper and Row. [159–63]

Downs, Anthony. 1972. Up and Down with Ecology: The Issue-Attention Cycle. *The Public Interest*, 28: 38–50. [255]

Dryzek, John S. 1987. *Rational Ecology: Environment and Political Economy*. New York: Basil Blackwell. [259]

Dryzek, John S. 1990. *Discursive Democracy*. Cambridge: Cambridge University Press. [222]

Dryzek, John S. 2000. *Deliberative Democracy and Beyond: Liberals, Critics, Contestations*. Oxford: Oxford University Press. [218]

Dryzek, John S. 2001. Legitimacy and Economy in Deliberative Democracy. *Political Theory*, 29: 651-69. [217–9]

Dryzek, John S. 2005. Deliberative Democracy in Divided Societies: Alternatives to Agonism and Analgesia. *Political Theory*, 33: 218–42. [196–7]

Dryzek, John S. 2006. *Deliberative Global Politics: Discourse and Democracy in a Divided World*. Cambridge: Polity. [198, 322]

Dryzek, John S. and Robert E. Goodin. 1986. Risk-Sharing and Social Justice: The Motivational Foundations of the Post-War Welfare State. *British Journal of Political Science*, 16: 1–34. [103]

Dryzek, John S. and Christian List. 2003. Social Choice Theory and Deliberative Democracy: A Reconciliation. *British Journal of Political Science*, 33: 1–28. [175]

Dryzek, John S., David Downes, Christian Hunold, David Schlosberg with Hans-Kristian Hernes. 2003. *Green States and Social Movements: Environmentalism in the United States, United Kingdom, Germany, and Norway*. Oxford: Oxford University Press. [137, 139, 224, 254, 266, 267]

Dunleavy, Patrick. 1980. *Urban Political Analysis*. London: Macmillan. [49]

Dunleavy, Patrick. 1982. Part I: Perspectives on Urban Studies. In A. Blowers, C. Brooks, P. Dunleavy and L. McDowell (eds), *Urban Change and Conflict: An Inter-Disciplinary Reader*. London: Harper & Row, pp. 1–16. [40–1]

Dunleavy, Patrick. 1986. The Growth of Sectional Cleavages and Stabilization of State Expenditures. *Society and Space*, 4: 129–44. [90]

Dunleavy, Patrick. 1991. *Democracy, Bureaucracy and Public Choice: Economic Explanations in Political Science*. London: Pearson, direct edition 2001. [48, 133, 255]

Dunleavy, Patrick. 2003. *Authoring a PhD*. Basingstoke: Palgrave Macmillan. [x]

Dunleavy, Patrick and Helen Margetts. 1995. Understanding the Dynamics of Electoral Reform. *International Political Science Review*, 16: 9–29. [163–4]

Dunleavy, Patrick, Helen Margetts, Simon Bastow and Jane Tinkler. 2006. New Public Management is Dead: Long Live Digital Era Governance. *Journal of Public Administration Research and Theory* 16: 467–94. [322–3]

Dunleavy, Patrick, Helen Margetts, Simon Bastow and Jane Tinkler. 2008. *Digital-era Governance: IT Corporations, the State and e-Government*, revised edn. Oxford: Oxford University Press. [332–3]

Dunn, John. 2005. *Setting the People Free: The Story of Democracy*. London: Atlantic Books. [20]

Duverger, Maurice. 1955. *Political Parties*. London: Methuen. [27, 164]

Dye, Thomas R. and L. Harmon Ziegler. 1987. *The Irony of Democracy: An Uncommon Introduction to American Politics*, 7th edn. Monterey, CA: Brooks/Cole. [76, 157]

Easton, David. 1953. *The Political System: An Inquiry into the State of Political Science.* New York: Knopf.   [7, 77]

Easton, David. 1991. Interview. in Michael A. Baer, Malcolm E. Jewell, and Lee Sigelman, eds., *Political Science in America: Oral Histories of a Discipline.* Lexington: University Press of Kentucky. pp. 195–214   [7, 77]

Eckersley, Robyn. 2004. *The Green State: Rethinking Democracy and Sovereignty.* Cambridge, MA: MIT Press.   [243, 267–8]

Edelman, Murray. 1964.*The Symbolic Uses of Politics.* Urbana: University of Illinois Press.   [1]

Engels, Friedrich. 1884 *The Origins of the Family, Private Property and the State.* London: Lawrence & Wishart, 1972.   [227]

Esping-Andersen, Gosta. 1990. *The Three Worlds of Welfare Capitalism.* Cambridge: Polity Press.   [210]

Etzioni, Amitai. 1996. *The New Golden Rule: Community and Morality in a Democratic Society.* New York: Basic Books.   [271]

Etzioni, Amitai. 2006. The Global Importance of Illiberal Moderates. *Cambridge Review of International Affairs,* 19: 369–85.   [28]

Evans, Peter, Dietrich Rueschemeyer and Theda Skocpol, eds. 1985. *Bringing the State Back In.* Cambridge: Cambridge University Press.   [7]

Falk, Richard. 1999. *Predatory Globalization: A Critique.* Cambridge: Polity.   [313, 322]

Ferguson, Kathy. 1984. *The Feminist Case Against Bureaucracy.* Philadelphia: Temple University Press.   [237–8]

Finer, S.E. 1997. *The History of Government* (three volumes). Oxford: Oxford University Press.   [8]

Fiorina, Morris P. 1977. *Congress: Keystone of the Washington Establishment.* New Haven, CT: Yale University Press.   [115]

Fiorina, Morris P. 1981. *Retrospective Voting in American National Elections.* New Haven, CT: Yale University Press.   [158]

Fishkin, James. 1991. *Democracy and Deliberation.* New Haven, CT: Yale University Press.   [223]

Flathman, Richard. 2005. *Pluralism and Liberal Democracy.* Baltimore: Johns Hopkins University Press.   [39–40]

Follett, Mary Parker. 1918. *The New State: Group Organization and the Solution of Popular Government.* New York: Longmans, Green.   [43]

Forester, John. 1999. Dealing with Deep Value Differences. In Lawrence Susskind, ed., *The Consensus Building Handbook.* Thousand Oaks, CA: Sage, pp. 463–93.   [197]

Foucault, Michel. 1972. *The Archeology of Knowledge.* London: Tavistock.   [292]

Foucault, Michel. 1982. The Subject and Power. In Michel Foucault, *Beyond Structuralism and Hermeneutics.* Chicago: University of Chicago Press.   [294–5]

Foucault, Michel. 1991. Governmentality. In Gordon Burchell, Colin Gordon and Peter Miller, eds, *The Foucault Effect: Studies in Governmentality.* Chicago: University of Chicago Press.   [244–5]

Fraad, Harriett, Stephen Resnick and Richard Wolff. 1994. *Bringing It All Back Home: Class, Gender and Power in the Modern Household.* London: Pluto.   [242]

Fraenkel, Jon, and Bernard Grofman.2006. "Does the Alternative Vote Foster

Moderation in Ethnically Divided Societies? The Case of Fiji." *Comparative Political Studies* 39 (5):623–51. [195]

Frantzius, Ina von. 2004. World Summit on Sustainable Development Johannesburg 2002: A Critical Assessment of the Outcomes. *Environmental Politics*, 13: 467–73. [144]

Freeman, John R. 1989. *Democracy and Markets: The Politics of Mixed Economies.* Ithaca, NY: Cornell University Press. [138]

Freud, Sigmund. 1989 [1930]. *Civilization and its Discontents.* New York: W. W. Norton. [62]

Friedman, Milton and Rose Friedman. 1962. *Capitalism and Freedom.* Chicago: University of Chicago Press. [104]

Friedman, Milton and Rose Friedman. 1979. *Free to Choose.* New York: Harcourt, Brace, Jovanovich. [100, 108, 123–4]

Friedman, Milton and Rose Friedman. 1984. *Tyranny of the Status Quo.* New York: Harcourt, Brace, Jovanovich. [23–4, 119, 124]

Friedman, Thomas L. 1999. *The Lexus and the Olive Tree: Understanding Globalization.* New York: Farrar, Straus and Giroux. [315, 219]

Friedman, Thomas L. 2005. *The World is Flat: A Brief History of the Twenty-First Century.* New York: Farrar, Straus and Giroux. [308]

Frum, David and Richard Perle. 2003. *An End to Evil: How to Win the War on Terror.* New York: Random House. [283]

Frynas, J. George. 2003. Global Monitor: Royal Dutch/Shell. *New Political Economy*, 8: 275–85. [145]

Fukuyama, Francis. 1989. The End of History? *National Interest*, summer: 3–18. [81, 207, 284]

Fukuyama, Francis. 1992. *The End of History and the Last Man.* New York: Free Press. [207, 284]

Fukuyama, Francis. 2006. *America at the Crossroads.* New Haven, CT: Yale University Press. [284]

Gambetta, Diego. 1993. *The Sicilian Mafia.* Cambridge, MA: Harvard University Press. [6]

Gamble, Andrew. 1994. *The Free Economy and the Strong State: The Politics of Thatcherism,* 2nd edn. Basingstoke: Palgrave Macmillan. [318]

Gastil, John. 2000. *By Popular Demand: Revitalizing Representative Democracy through Deliberative Elections.* Berkeley: University of California Press. [218]

Giddens, Anthony. 2000. *Runaway World: How Globalization is Reshaping our Lives.* London: Routledge and Kegan Paul. [315]

Gilligan, Carol. 1982. *In a Different Voice: Psychological Theory and Women's Development.* Cambridge, MA: Harvard University Press. [231]

Glendon, Mary Ann. 1991. *Rights Talk: The Impoverishment of Political Discourse.* New York: Free Press. [275]

Goldgeier, James M. and Michael McFaul. 1992. A Tale of Two Worlds: Core and Periphery in the Post-Cold War Era. *International Organization*, 46: 467–91. [31]

Goldscheid, Rudolf. 1917. *Staatssocialzmus oder Staatskapitalismus.* Vienna. [5]

Goldsmith, Edward, Robert Allen, with Michael Allaby, John Davoll, and Sam Lawrence. 1972. *Blueprint for Survival.* Boston: Houghton Mifflin. [266]

Goodin, Robert E. 1992. *Green Political Theory.* Cambridge: Polity. [262]

Goodin, Robert E. 2003. *Reflective Democracy*. Oxford: Oxford University Press. [218]

Goodin, Robert E. and John S. Dryzek. 2006. Deliberative Impacts: The Macro-Political Uptake of Mini-Publics. *Politics and Society*, 34: 219–44.   [223]

Goodnow, Frank. 1904. The Work of the American Political Science Association. *Proceedings of the American Political Science Association*, 1: 1–17.   [42]

Grant, Wyn and Marsh, David. 1977. *The Confederation of British Industry*. London: Hodder & Stoughton.   [45]

Gray, John. 1998. *False Dawn: The Delusions of Global Capitalism*. London: Granta. [323]

Greer, Germaine. 1999. *The Whole Woman*. London: Doubleday.   [230]

Griffiths, Hugh. 2006. Introduction. In *Karl Marx: Selected Writings*. London: CRW. [99]

Grofman, Bernard. 1993. Lessons of Athenian Democracy. *PS: Political Science and Politics*, 26: 471–4.   [19]

Grofman, Bernard and Arend Lijphart, eds. 1986. *Electoral Laws and their Political Consequences*. New York: Agathon .   [163–4]

Gutmann, Amy. 1999. *Democratic Education*. Princeton: Princeton University Press. [224]

Habermas, Jürgen. 1976. *Legitimation Crisis*. London: Heinemann.   [97]

Habermas, Jürgen. 1996. *Between Facts and Norms: Contributions to a Discourse Theory of Law and Democracy*. Cambridge, MA: MIT Press.   [216, 220]

Hajer, Maarten. 1995. *The Politics of Environmental Discourse: Ecological Modernization and the Policy Process*. Oxford: Oxford University Press.   [298]

Hajer, Maarten. 2003. Policy Without Polity? Policy Analysis and the Institutional Void. *Policy Sciences*, 36: 175–95.   [297]

Hajer, Maarten and David Laws. 2006. Ordering Through Discourse. In Michael Moran, Martin Rein and Robert E. Goodin, eds, *The Oxford Handbook of Public Policy*. Oxford: Oxford University Press, pp. 251–68.   [301]

Hall, Peter A. and David Soskice, eds. 2001. *Varieties of Capitalism: The Institutional Foundations of Comparative Advantage*. Oxford: Oxford University Press.   [137–8, 317]

Hall, Rodney Bruce. 2003. The Discursive Demolition of the Asian Development Model. *International Studies Quarterly*, 47: 71–99.   [127]

Hanson, Russell. 1989. Democracy. In Terence Ball, James Farr and Russell Hanson, eds, *Political Innovation and Conceptual Change*. Cambridge: Cambridge University Press, pp. 68–89.   [21]

Hardin, Garrett. 1968. The Tragedy of the Commons. *Science*, 162: 1243–8.   [246]

Hardin, Garrett. 1977. Living on a Lifeboat. In Garrett Hardin and John Baden, eds, *Managing the Commons*. San Francisco: W. H. Freeman, pp. 261–79.   [247, 262]

Hardt, Michael and Antonio Negri. 2001. *Empire*. Cambridge, MA: Harvard University Press.   [330]

Hartsock, Nancy. 1985. *Money, Sex and Power*. Boston: Northeastern University Press. [228]

Hawken, Paul, Amory B. Lovins and L. Hunter Lovins. 1999. *Natural Capitalism: Creating the Next Industrial Revolution*. Boston: Little Brown.   [251–2]

Hay, Colin. 1998. Globalization, Welfare Retrenchment, and the Logic of No Alternative. *Journal of Social Policy*, 27: 525–32. [316]

Hay, Colin and Ben Rosamond. 2002. Globalisation, European Integration, and the Discursive Construction of Economic Imperatives. *Journal of European Public Policy*, 9: 147–67. [127, 317]

Hayek, Friedrich A. von. 1944. *The Road to Serfdom*. Chicago: University of Chicago Press. [103]

Hayek, Friedrich A. von. 1960. *The Constitution of Liberty*. Chicago: University of Chicago Press. [100]

Heilbroner, Robert. 1974. *An Inquiry into the Human Prospect*. New York: Norton. [247, 262]

Held, David. 1995. *Democracy and the Global Order: From the Nation State to Cosmopolitan Governance*. Cambridge: Polity. [322–3]

Held, David. 2004. *Global Covenant: The Social Democratic Alternative to the Washington Consensus*. Cambridge: Polity. [322]

Held, David and Anthony McGrew, eds. 2000. *The Global Transformations Reader*. Cambridge: Polity. [308]

Hendriks, Carolyn M. 2002. Institutions of Deliberative Democratic Processes and Interest Groups. *Australian Journal of Public Administration*, 61: 64–75. [222]

Hendriks, Carolyn M., John S. Dryzek and Christian Hunold. 2007. Turning up the Heat: Partisanship in Political Deliberation. *Political Studies*, 55(2): 362–83. [222]

Hernes, Helga M. 1987. *Welfare State and Woman Power: Essays in State Feminism*. Oxford: Oxford University Press. [239]

Higley, John. 1984. The Ruling Class Revisited. *Contemporary Sociology*, 13(2): 143–6 [65]

Hindess, Barry. 2001. The Liberal Government of Unfreedom. *Alternatives*, 26: 93–111. [296, 305]

Hirschman, Albert O. 1977. *The Passions and the Interests: Political Arguments for Capitalism Before its Triumph*. Princeton: Princeton University Press. [187]

Hirschman, Albert O. 1982. *Shifting Involvements: Private Interests and Public Action*. Princeton: Princeton University Press. [255]

Hirst, Paul. 1994. *Associative Democracy: New Forms of Economic and Social Governance*. Cambridge: Polity. [152]

Hirst, Paul and Grahame Thompson. 1996. *Globalization in Question: The International Economy and the Possibilities of Governance*. Cambridge: Polity. [308, 317]

Hix, Simon. 2008. Towards a Partisan Theory of EU Politics. *Journal of European Public Policy*, 15(8): 1254–65. [147]

Hobbes, Thomas. 1969 [1680]. *Behemoth, or the Long Parliament*. ed. Ferdinand Tonnies. New York: Barnes and Noble. [20]

Hobbes, Thomas. 1651. *Leviathan*. Harmondsworth: Penguin, 1968. [190]

Honig, Bonnie. 1993. *Political Theory and the Displacement of Politics*. Ithaca, NY: Cornell University Press. [303]

Hood, Christopher C. and Helen Z. Margetts. 2007. *The Tools of Government in a Digital Age*, 2nd edn. Basingstoke: Palgrave Macmillan. [3]

Hoover, Kenneth R. with James Mania and Kristen Parris. 1997. *The Power of Identity: Politics in a New Key*. Chatham, NJ: Chatham House.

Horowitz, Donald. 1985. *Ethnic Groups in Conflict*. Berkeley: University of California Press.   [**194–5**]

Horowitz, Donald. 1991. *A Democratic South Africa? Constitutional Engineering in a Divided Society*. Berkeley: University of California Press.   [**194–5**]

Hunter, Floyd. 1953. *Community Power Structure*. Chapel Hill, NC: University of North Carolina Press.   [**76**]

Huntington, Samuel P. 1996. *The Clash of Civilizations and the Remaking of World Order*. New York: Simon and Schuster.   [**284–5, 327**]

Huntington, Samuel P. 2004. *Who Are We? The Challenges to America's National Identity*. New York: Simon & Schuster.   [**199, 276**]

Hutton, Will. 2006. *The Writing on the Wall: China and the West in the 21st Century*. London: Abacus.   [**335**]

Ignatieff, Michael. 2003. *Empire Lite: Nation-Building in Bosnia, Kosovo, and Afghanistan*. New York: Vintage.   [**336**]

Inglehart, Ronald and Pippa Norris. 2003. *Rising Tide: Gender Inequality and Cultural Change Around the World*. Cambridge: Cambridge University Press.   [**232**]

Innes, Judith E. and David E. Booher. 2003. Collaborative Policymaking: Governance Through Dialogue. In Maarten A. Hajer and Hendrik Wagenaar, eds, *Deliberative Policy Analysis: Understanding Governance in the Network Society*, pp. 33–59. Cambridge: Cambridge University Press.   [**142**]

Jänicke, Martin. 1996. Democracy as a Condition for Environmental Policy Success: The Importance of Non-Institutional Factors. In William M. Lafferty and James Meadowcroft, eds, *Democracy and the Environment: Problems and Prospects*, pp. 71–85. Cheltenham: Edward Elgar.   [**145**]

Jänicke, Martin and Helmut Weidner, eds. 1997. *National Environmental Policies: A Comparative Study of Capacity Building*. Berlin: Springer.   [**257**]

Jessop, Bob. 1990. *State Theory: Putting Capitalist States in Their Place*. Cambridge: Polity Press.   [**98**]

Kanra, Bora. 2005. Democracy, Islam and Dialogue: The Case of Turkey. *Government and Opposition*, 40: 515–39.   [**196–7**]

Kaplan, Robert D. 1993. *Balkan Ghosts: A Journey Through History*. New York: Random House.   [**186**]

Kapoor, Ilan. 2002. Deliberative Democracy or Agonistic Pluralism? The Relevance of the Habermas-Mouffe Debate for Third World Politics. *Alternatives*, 27: 459–87   [**304**]

Katzenstin, Peter J. 1985. *Small States in World Markets*. Ithaca: Cornell University Press.   [**137**]

Kaufman, Stuart J. 2001. *Modern Hatreds: The Symbolic Politics of Ethnic War*. Ithaca: Cornell University Press.   [**194**]

Keene, Edward. 2002. *Beyond the Anarchical Society: Grotius, Colonialism and Order in World Politics*. Cambridge: Cambridge University Press.   [**297**]

Kennedy, Paul. 1989. *The Rise and Fall of the Great Powers: Economic Change and Military Conflict from 1500 to 2000*. London: Fontana.   [**10**]

Keynes, John Maynard. 1936. *The General Theory of Employment, Income and Money*.   [**102**]

Kinder, Donald R. and David O. Sears. 1983. Public Opinion and Political Action. In

Gardner Lindzey and Elliot Aronson, eds, *The Handbook of Social Psychology*, 3rd edn, vol. 2, pp. 659–741. New York: Random House. [157]

Klein, Naomi. 2001. *No Logo*. London: Flamingo. [331]

Klein, Naomi. 2008. *The Shock Doctrine: The Rise of Disaster Capitalism*. London: Penguin. [331]

Krasner, Stephen. 1978. *Defending the National Interest: Raw Materials Investments and US Foreign Policy*. Princeton: Princeton University Press. [73]

Kristol, Irving. 1983. *Reflections of a Neoconservative*. New York: Basic Books. [282]

Kymlicka, Will. 1995. *Multicultural Citizenship*. Oxford: Oxford University Press. [184, 201–2]

Laclau, Ernesto and Chantal Mouffe. 1985. *Hegemony and Socialist Strategy: Towards a Radical Democratic Politics*. London: Verso. [302–3]

Lafferty, William M. and James Meadowcroft, eds. 1996. *Democracy and the Environment: Problems and Prospects*. Cheltenham: Edward Elgar. [623–4]

Langenbacher, Eric. 2001. Disenchanted Liberals: Alexis De Tocqueville and Max Weber. *International Journal of Politics and Ethics*, 1: 27–45 [62]

Laski, Harold J. 1917. *Studies in the Problem of Sovereignty*. New Haven: Yale University Press. [43]

Lassman, Peter and Ronald Speirs. 1994. Introduction. In Peter Lassman and Ronald Speirs, eds, *Weber: Political Writings*. Cambridge: Cambridge University Press. pp. vii–xxv. [61]

Lasswell, Harold D. 1936. *Politics: Who Gets What, When, How*. New York: McGraw Hill. [64]

Lasswell, Harold D. 1941. The Garrison State. *American Journal of Sociology*, 46: 455–68. [73]

Laumann, Edward and David Knoke. 1987. *The Organizational State: Social Choice in National Policy Domains*. Madison, WI: University of Wisconsin Press. [50, 141]

Lee, Kai N. 1993. *Compass and Gyroscope: Integrating Science and Politics for the Environment*. Washington, DC: Island Press. [267]

Lehmbruch, Gerhard. 1984. Concertation and the Structure of Corporatist Networks. In John H. Goldthorpe, ed., *Order and Conflict in Contemporary Capitalism*, pp. 60–80. Oxford: Clarendon. [137]

Leib, Ethan J. and Baogang He, eds. 2006. *The Search for Deliberative Democracy in China*. New York: Palgrave Macmillan. [216]

Leonard, Stephen T. 1995. The Pedagogical Purposes of a Political Science. In James Farr, John S. Dryzek and Stephen T. Leonard, eds., *Political Science in History: Research Programs and Political Traditions*, pp. 66–98. Cambridge: Cambridge University Press. [6]

Levi, Margaret. 1988. *Of Rule and Revenue*. Berkeley: University of California Press. [29]

Levitsky, Steven and Lucan Way. 2002. The Rise of Competitive Authoritarianism. *Journal of Democracy*, 13: 51–65. [25]

Lezard, Nicholas. 2007. A Reluctant Controversialist. *Guardian*, 7 April. [39]

Lijphart, Arend. 1968. *The Politics of Accommodation: Pluralism and Democracy in the Netherlands*. Berkeley: University of California Press. [192]

Lijphart, Arend. 1977. *Democracy in Plural Societies: A Comparative Exploration*. New Haven, CT: Yale University Press. [192–3]

Lijphart, Arend. 1984. *Democracies: Patterns of Majoritarian and Consensus Government in Twenty-One Countries*. New Haven, CT: Yale University Press. [179]

Lijphart, Arend. 1994. Prospects for Power Sharing in the New South Africa. In Andrew Reynolds, ed., *Election '94 South Africa: An Analysis of the Results, Campaign and Future Prospects*. New York: St Martin's. [193]

Lijphart, Arend. 1996. "The Puzzle of Indian Democracy: A Consociational Interpretation." *American Political Science Review* 90 (2):258–68. [193]

Lijphart, Arend. 2000. Varieties of Nonmajoritarian Democracy. In Markus M. L. Crepaz, Thomas A. Koelbe, and David Wilsford, eds., *Democracy and Institutions: The Life Work of Arend Lijphart*. Ann Arbor: University of Michigan Press, pp. 225–46. [193]

Lin, Chun. 2006. *The Transformation of Chinese Socialism*. Durham, NC: Duke University Press. [99, 335]

Lindblom, Charles E. 1959. The Science of 'Muddling Through'. *Public Administration Review*, 19: 79–88. [50–1]

Lindblom, Charles E. 1977. *Politics and Markets: The World's Political-Economic Systems*. New York: Basic Books. [50–2]

Lindblom, Charles E. 1982. The Market as Prison. *Journal of Politics*, 44: 324–36. [132, 142, 280]

Lipset, Seymour Martin. 1960. *Political Man: The Social Bases of Politics*. Garden City, NY: Doubleday. [46]

Litfin, Karen T. 1994. *Ozone Discourses: Science and Politics in Global Environmental Cooperation*. New York: Columbia University Press. [300–1]

Locke, John. 1688–90. *Two Treatises of Government*. Cambridge: Cambridge University Press, 1988, ed. Peter Laslett. [233–5]

Logan, John and Harvey Molotoch.1987. *Urban Fortunes: The Political Economy of Place*. Berkeley: University of California Press. [76]

Lovenduski, Joni and Pippa Norris. 2003. Westminster Women: The Politics of Presence. *Political Studies*, 51: 84–102. [236]

Luke, Timothy. 1997. *Ecocritique: Contesting the Politics of Nature, Economy, and Culture*. Minneapolis: University of Minnesota Press. [292, 305]

Lukes, Steven. 1974. *Power: A Radical View*. London: Macmillan. [65]

Luttwak, Edward N. 1998. *Turbo-Capitalism: Winners and Losers in the Global Economy*. London: Weidenfeld and Nicolson. [315]

Lyotard, Jean-François. 1984. *The Postmodern Condition: A Report on Knowledge*. Minneapolis: University of Minnesota Press. [290]

Macintyre, Stuart and Anna Clark. 2004. *The History Wars*. Melbourne: Melbourne University Press. [200]

Mackie, Gerry. 1994. Success and Failure in an American Workers' Cooperative. *Politics and Society*, 22: 215–36. [212]

Mackie, Gerry. 2004. *Democracy Defended*. Cambridge: Cambridge University Press. [175]

MacKinnon, Catharine A. 1989. *Toward a Feminist Theory of the State*. Cambridge, MA: Harvard University Press. [226, 239, 241]

Madison James. 1787. *The Federalist* 10. [21]

Manin, Bernard. 1987. On Legitimacy and Political Deliberation. *Political Theory*, 15: 338–68. [**217**]

Mansbridge, Jane. 1993. Feminism and Democratic Community. In John W. Chapman and Ian Shapiro, eds, *Democratic Community (Nomos XXXV)*, pp. 339–95. New York: New York University Press. [**240**]

Mansbridge, Jane. 1999. Everyday Talk in the Deliberative System. In Stephen Macedo, ed., *Deliberative Politics: Essays on Democracy and Disagreement*, pp. 211–39. Oxford: Oxford University Press. [**224**]

Marsh, David and Nicola Jo-Anne Smith. 2004. Globalisation, the Discourse of Globalisation and the Hollowing Out of the State. Unpublished paper, University of Birmingham. [**317**]

Marsh, David, Nicola J. Smith and Nicola Hothi. 2006. Globalization and the State. In Colin Hay, Michael Lister and David Marsh, eds, *The State: Theories and Issues*, pp. 172–89. Basingstoke: Palgrave Macmillan. [**317**]

Marshall, T. H. 1950. *Citizenship and Social Class, and Other Essays*. Cambridge: Cambridge University Press. [**41–2**]

Marx, Anthony W. 2003. *Faith in Nation: Exclusionary Origins of Nationalism*. Oxford: Oxford University Press. [**190**]

Marx, Karl. 1867/1976. *Capital: A Critique of Political Economy*. Harmondsworth: Penguin. [**95, 190**]

Marx, Karl and Frierich Engels. *The Communist Manifesto*. [**88, 92**]

Marx, Karl. 1963 [1852]. *The Eighteenth Brumaire of Louis Bonaparte*. New York: International Publishers. [**80, 83, 93**

Mathews, Freya, ed. 1996. *Ecology and Democracy*. London: Frank Cass. [**263–4**]

Mayhew, David. 1974. *Congress: The Electoral Connection*. New Haven, CT: Yale University Press. [**49**]

McGarry, John, and Brendan O'Leary. 1995. *Explaining Northern Ireland: Broken Images*. Oxford: Blackwell. [**188**]

McGarry, John, Brendan O'Leary, and Richard Simeon. 2008. 'Integration or Accommodation? The Enduring Debate in Conflict Regulation.' In S. Choudhry (ed.), *Constitutional Design for Divided Societies: Integration or Accommodation?*. Oxford: Oxford University Press. [**190–1**]

McGinnis, Michael Vincent, ed. 1998. *Bioregionalism*. New York: Routledge. [**266–7**]

Meadows, Donella H., Dennis L. Meadows, Jørgen Randers and William H. Behrens III. 1972. *The Limits to Growth*. New York: Universe Books. [**246**]

Meidinger, Errol E. 2003. Forest Certification as a Global Civil Society Regulatory Institution. In Errol E. Meidinger, Chris Elliott and Gerhard Oesten, eds, *Social and Political Dimensions of Forest Certification*. Remagen-Oberwinter: Forstbuch Verlag, pp. 265–89. [**144, 266**]

Meiners, Roger E. and Bruce Yandle. 1993. *Taking the Environment Seriously*. Lanham, MD: Rowman & Littlefield. [**121**]

Miliband, Ralph. 1969. *The State in Capitalist Society: An Analysis of the Western System of Power*. London: Weidenfeld & Nicolson. [**92**]

Mill, John Stuart. 1859. *On Liberty*. Available at: http://www.utilitarianism.com/ol/one.html. [**23, 40, 296**]

Miller, David. 1995. *On Nationality*. Oxford: Oxford University Press. [**201**]

Millett, Kate. 1970. *Sexual Politics*. Garden City, NY: Doubleday.   [233]

Milliken, Jennifer. 1999. The Study of Discourse in International Relations: A Critique of Research and Methods. *European Journal of International Relations*, 5: 225–54. [299]

Mills, C. Wright. 1956. *The Power Elite*. New York: Oxford University Press.   [64, 72–4, 331]

Minteer, Ben A. and Bob Pepperman Taylor. 2002. *Democracy and the Claims of Nature*. Lanham, MD: Rowman & Littlefield.   [263–4]

Moore, Margaret. 1999. Beyond the Cultural Argument for Liberal Nationalism. *Critical Review of International Social and Political Philosophy*, 2: 26–47.   [187]

Moore, Stanley W. 1957. *The Critique of Capitalist Democracy: An Introduction to the Theory of the State in Marx, Engels and Lenin*. New York: Paine-Whitman.   [91]

Morone, James A. 2003. *Hellfire Nation: The Politics of Sin in American History*. New Haven, CT: Yale University Press.   [281]

Mosca, Gaetano. 1939. *The Ruling Class*. New York: McGraw Hill. (Ed. Arthur Livingston. Trans Hannah D. Kahn.)   [58–9]

Mouffe, Chantal. 1999. Deliberative Democracy or Agonistic Pluralism? *Social Research*, 66: 745–58.   [196]

Mouffe, Chantal. 2000. *The Democratic Paradox*. London: Verso.   [196, 304]

Mumford, Lewis. 1964. *The Myth of the Machine*. New York: Harcourt Brace Jovanovich.   [244]

Muravchik, Joshua. 2006. Operation Comeback. *Foreign Policy*, November/December. [285]

Murray, Charles 1984. *Losing Ground: American Social Policy 1950–1980*. New York: Basic Books.   [280]

Natchez, Peter. 1985. *Images of Voting/Visions of Democracy*. New York: Basic Books.

Ng-Quinn, Michael. 2006. The Normative Justification of Traditional Chinese Authoritarianism. *Critical Review of International Social and Political Philosophy*, 9: 379–98.   [280]

Nimni, Ephraim. 1993. *Marxism and Nationalism: Theoretical Origins of the Present Crisis*. London: Pluto Press.   [187]

Niskanen, William A. 1971. *Bureaucracy and Representative Government*. Chicago: Aldine-Atherton.   [115–7]

Niskanen, William A. 1994. *Bureaucracy and Public Economics*. Aldershot: Edward Elgar.   [117–8]

Noelle-Neumann, Elisabeth. 1984. *The Spiral of Silence: Public Opinion – Our Social Skin*. Chicago: University of Chicago Press.   [157]

Nussbaum, Martha C. 1999. *Sex and Social Justice*. Oxford: Oxford University Press. [241]

O'Connor, James. 1984. *Accumulation Crisis*. New York: Basil Blackwell.   [95]

O'Flynn, Ian. 2006. *Deliberative Democracy and Divided Societies*. Edinburgh; Edinburgh University Press.   [198]

O'Leary, Brendan. 2001b. The Elements of Right-Sizing and Right-Peopling the State. In B. O'Leary, I. S. Lustick and T. Callaghy eds, *Right-Sizing the State: the Politics of Moving Borders*. Oxford: Oxford University Press.   [190–1]

O'Leary, Brendan. 2006. "Consociational Theory, Northern Ireland's Conflict, and its

Agreement. Part One. What Consociationa lists Can Learn from Northern Ireland." *Government and Opposition* 41 (1):43–63; and Part 11, 41 (2):249–77. [193]

O'Leary, Brendan. 2001a. Nationalism and Ethnicity: Research Agendas on Theories of Their Sources and Regulation. In D. Chirot and M. E. P. Seligman (eds), *Ethnopolitical Warfare: Causes, Consequences, and Possible Solutions*. Washington DC: American Psychological Association. [185]

O'Toole, Therese, Michael Lister, David Marsh, Su Jones and Alex McDonough. 2003. Tuning Out or Left Out? Participation and Nonparticipation Among Young People. *Contemporary Politics*, 9: 45–61. [168]

Oakley, Ann. 1972. *Sex, Gender and Society*. London: Temple Smith. [232]

Offe, Claus. 1984. *Contradictions of the Welfare State*. Cambridge, MA: MIT Press. [30, 97–8, 137–8]

Offe, Claus. 1985. New Social Movements: Challenging the Boundaries of Institutional Politics. *Social Research*, 52: 817–68. [139]

Offe, Claus. 1990. Reflections on the Institutional Self-Transformation of Social Movements: A Tentative Stage Model. In Russell J. Dalton and Manfred Kuechler, eds, *Challenging the Political Order: New Social Movements in Western Democracies*, Cambridge: Polity, pp. 232–50. [136]

Offe, Claus and Helmut Wiesenthal. 1980. Two Logics of Collective Action: Theoretical Notes on social Class and Organizational Form. In Maurice Zeitlin, ed., *Political Power and Social Theory*. Greenwich, CT: JAI Press, pp. 67–115. [132–3]

Okin, Susan Moller. 1989. *Justice, Gender, and the Family*. New York: Basic Books. [240]

Okin, Susan Moller. 1999. Is Multiculturalism Bad for Women? In Joshua Cohen, Matthew Howard and Martha C. Nussbaum, eds, *Is Multiculturalism Bad for Women?* Princeton, NJ: Princeton University Press. [241]

Olson, Mancur. 1965. *The Logic of Collective Action*. Cambridge, MA: Harvard University Press. [93–4, 110, 132–3]

Olson, Mancur. 1982. *The Rise and Decline of Nations: Economic Growth, Stagflation, and Social Rigidities*. New Haven, CT: Yale University Press. [111, 125]

Olson, Mancur. 1993. Dictatorship, Democracy, and Development. *American Political Science Review*, 87: 567–76. [9]

Ophuls, William. 1977. *Ecology and the Politics of Scarcity*. San Francisco: W.H. Freeman. [249, 261–3]

O'Rourke, P. J. 1991. *A Parliament of Whores*. New York: Grove Atlantic. [104]

Ortega and Gossett, Jean. 1932. *The Rovolt of the Masses*. New York: Norton. [61]

Orwell, George. 1949. *1984*. London: Secker & Warburg. [39]

Orwell, George. 1990 [1941]. *The Lion and the Unicorn: Socialism and the English Genius*. Harmondsworth: Penguin. [200]

Ostrogorski, Moisy. 1910. *Democracy and the Party System in the United States: A Study in Extra-Constitutional Government*. New York: Macmillan. [69–70]

Ostrom, Elinor. 1990. *Governing the Commons*. Cambridge: Cambridge University Press. [248]

Paehlke, Robert. 1988. Democracy, Bureaucracy, and Environmentalism. *Environmental Ethics*, 10: 291–308. [263]

Page, Benjamin I. and Robert Y. Shapiro. 1992. *The Rational Public: Fifty Years of*

Trends in Americans' Policy Preferences. Chicago: University of Chicago Press. [159]

Paglia, Camille. 1994. *Vamps and Tramps*. New York: Vintage. [231]

Paine, Thomas. 1792. *The Rights of Man*. London: J. S. Jordan. [21]

Pareto, Vilfredo. 1935. *The Mind and Society*. Harcourt Brace and Company. (First published 1916.) [59]

Parkinson, John. 2006. *Deliberating in the Real World: Problems of Legitimacy in Deliberative Democracy*. Oxford: Oxford University Press. [218, 224]

Pateman, Carole. 1970. *Participation and Democratic Theory*. Cambridge: Cambridge University Press. [212]

Pateman, Carole. 1988. *The Sexual Contract*. Cambridge: Polity Press. [233–5, 240]

Pateman, Carole. 1989. *The Disorder of Women*. Cambridge: Polity Press. [247]

Pekkarinen, Jukka, Matti Pohjola and Bob Rowthorn. 1992. *Social Corporatism: A Superior Economic System?* Oxford: Oxford University Press. [138]

Phillips, Anne. 1991. *Engendering Democracy*. Cambridge: Polity Press. [239]

Phillips, Anne. 1995. *The Politics of Presence*. Oxford: Oxford University Press. [239–40]

Pierre, Jon and B. Guy Peters. 2000. *Governance and the State*. Basingstoke: Palgrave Macmillan. [149]

Piven, Frances Fox and Richard A. Cloward. 1971. *Regulating the Poor: The Functions of Public Welfare*. New York: Random House. [219]

Pollitt, Katha. 1999. Whose Culture? In Joshua Cohen, Matthew Howard and Martha C. Nussbaum, eds, *Is Multiculturalism Bad for Women?* Princeton, NJ: Princeton University Press, pp. 27–30. [241]

Popper, Karl R. 1966. *The Open Society and its Enemies*. London: Routledge & Kegan Paul. [39–40, 51]

Poulantzas, Nicos. 1969. The Problem of the Capitalist State. *New Left Review*, 58: 67–78. [94]

Poulantzas, Nicos. 1978. *State, Power, Socialism*. London: New Left Books. [94]

Price, Lance. 2006. *The Spin Doctor's Diary: Inside Number 10 with New Labour*. London: Hodder & Stoughton. [182–3]

Przeworski, Adam. 1985. *Capitalism and Social Democracy*. Cambridge: Cambridge University Press. [83]

Przeworski, Adam, Michael E. Alvarez, José Antonio Cheibub and Fernando Limongi. 2000. *Democracy and Development: Political Institutions and Well-Being in the World, 1950–1990*. Cambridge: Cambridge University Press. [319]

Putnam, Robert D. 2000. *Bowling Alone: The Collapse and Revival of American Community*. New York: Simon & Schuster. [272–3, 277, 281]

Putnam, Robert D. 2007. E Pluribus Unum: Diversity and Community in the Twenty-First Century. *Scandinavian Political Studies*, 30: 137–74. [273, 276]

Putnam, Robert D. with Robert Leonardi and Raffaella Y. Nanetti. 1994. *Making Democracy Work: Civic Traditions in Modern Italy*. Princeton: Princeton University Press. [272–3, 281]

Rae, Heather. 2002. *State Identities and the Homogenisation of Peoples*. Cambridge: Cambridge University Press. [189–90]

Rawls, John. 1993. *Political Liberalism*. New York: Columbia University Press. [218, 222]

Rawls, John. 1997. The Idea of Public Reason Revisited. *University of Chicago Law Review*, 94: 765–807. [216]

Rees, John. 1998. *Algebra of Revolution: Dialectic and the Classical Marxist Tradition.* London: Routledge. [98–9]

Reilly, Benjamin. 2001. *Democracy in Divided Societies: Electoral Engineering for Conflict Management.* Cambridge: Cambridge University Press. [194–5]

Reus-Smit, Christian. 1999. *The Moral Purpose of the State: Culture, Social Identity, and Institutional Rationality in International Relations.* Princeton: Princeton University Press. [7, 190, 296–7]

Reynolds, Andrew. 2000. Majoritarian or Power-Sharing Government. In Markus M. L. Crepaz, Thomas A. Koelbe and David Wilsford, eds, *Democracy and Institutions: The Life Work of Arend Lijphart.* Ann Arbor: University of Michigan Press, pp. 155–96. [194]

Rhodes, R.A.W. 1994. The Hollowing Out of the State. *Political Quarterly*, 65: 138–51. [141]

Rhodes, R.A.W. 1997. *Understanding Governance.* Buckingham: Open University Press. [140]

Rhodes, R.A.W. 2006. Policy Network Analysis. In Michael Moran, Martin Rein and Robert Goodin, eds, *The Oxford Handbook of Public Policy.* Oxford: Oxford University Press, pp. 425–47. [153]

Riker, William H. 1962. *The Theory of Political Coalitions.* New Haven, CT: Yale University Press. [176]

Riker, William H. 1982a. *Liberalism Against Populism: A Confrontation Between the Theory of Democracy and the Theory of Social Choice.* San Francisco: W.H. Freeman. [23, 113, 175]

Riker, William H. 1982b. The Two-Party System and Duverger's Law: An Essay on the History of Political Science. *American Political Science Review*, 76: 753–66. [27, 164]

Riker, William H. 1986. *The Art of Political Manipulation.* New Haven, CT: Yale University Press. [114]

Rorty, Richard. 1983. Post-Modernist Bourgeois Liberalism. *Journal of Philosophy*, 80: 583–9. [290]

Rose, Nikolas. 1999. *Powers of Freedom: Reframing Political Thought.* Cambridge: Cambridge University Press. [295]

Rose, Richard and Ian McAllister. 1986. *Voters Begin to Choose: From Closed Class to Open Elections in Britain.* London: Sage. [159]

Rosenau, Pauline V., ed. 2000. *Public-Private Policy Partnerships.* Cambridge, MA: MIT Press. [144]

Ross, E. A. 1920. *The Principles of Sociology.* New York: Century. [41]

Rothbard, Murray. 1970. *Power and Market.* Menlo Park, CA: Institute for Humane Studies. [107]

Rowbotham, Sheila. 1986. Feminism and Democracy. In David Held and Christopher Pollitt, eds, *New Forms of Democracy.* Beverly Hills, CA: Sage, pp. 78–109. [240]

Ruddick, Sarah. 1980. Maternal Thinking. *Feminist Studies*, 6: 342–67. [231]

Russett, Bruce. 1993. *Grasping the Democratic Peace: Principles for a Post-Cold War World.* Princeton: Princeton University Press. [26]

Sabatier, Paul A. 1988. An Advocacy Coalition Framework of Policy Change and the Role of Policy-Oriented Learning Therein. *Policy Sciences*, 21: 129–68. [**134**]

Sabatier, Paul A. 1993. Policy Change Over a Decade or More. In Paul A. Sabatier and Hank Jenkins-Smith, eds, *Policy Change and Learning: An Advocacy Coalition Approach*. Boulder, CO: Westview. [**134**]

Sagoff, Mark. 1999. The View from Quincy Library: Civic Engagement and Environmental Problem Solving. In Robert Fullwinder, ed., *Democracy and Civic Renewal*. Lanham, MD: Rowman & Littlefield, pp. 151–83. [**142**]

Sandel, Michael J.. 1982. *Liberalism and the Limits of Justice*. Cambridge: Cambridge University Press. [**214, 271**]

Sandel, Michael J. 1996. *Democracy's Discontent: America in Search of a Public Philosophy*. Cambridge, MA: Harvard University Press. [**271**]

Santayana, George. (1922) 'The ironies of liberalism', in his *Soliloquies in England and Later Soliloquies* (New York), pp. 178–89. Reproduced in Russel Kirk (ed.), *The Portable Conservative Reader*. Harmondsworth: Penguin, 1982, pp. 467–80. [**15**]

Sawer, Marian. 1990. *Sisters in Suits: Women and Public Policy in Australia*. Sydney: Allen & Unwin. [**236**]

Schattschneider, E.E. 1942. *Party Government*. New York: Farrar and Rinehart. [**69**]

Schlosberg, David. 1999. *Environmental Justice and the New Pluralism: The Challenge of Difference for Environmentalism*. Oxford: Oxford University Press. [**264, 304–5**]

Schmitter, Philippe C. and Gerhard Lehmbruch. 1979. *Trends Toward Corporatist Intermediation*. Beverly Hills, CA: Sage. [**137**]

Schön, Donald A. and Martin Rein. 1994. *Frame Reflection: Toward the Resolution of Intractable Policy Controversies*. New York: Basic Books. [**297–8**]

Schram, Sanford. 1993. Postmodern Policy Analysis: Discourse and Identity in Welfare Policy. *Policy Sciences*, 26: 249–70. [**299–300**]

Schumacher, E. F. 1973. *Small is Beautiful: Economics as if People Mattered*. New York: Harper and Row. [**248–9**]

Schumpeter, Joseph A. 1943. *Capitalism, Socialism, and Democracy*. New York: Harper. [**43–4**]

Scruggs, Lyle A. 1999. Institutions and Environmental Performance in Seventeen Western Democracies. *British Journal of Political Science*, 29: 1–31. [**138**]

Scruton, Roger. 2006. Conservativism. In Andrew Dobson and Robyn Eckersley, eds, *Political Theory and the Ecological Challenge*, Cambridge: Cambridge University Press, pp. 7–19. [**261**]

Shepsle, Kenneth A. 1979. Institutional Arrangements and Equilibrium in Multidimensional Voting Models. *American Journal of Political Science*, 23: 27–60. [**175**]

Simon, Herbert A. 1981. *The Sciences of the Artificial*, 2nd edn. Cambridge, MA: MIT Press. [**259**]

Simon, Julian. 1981. *The Ultimate Resource*. Princeton, NJ: Princeton University Press. [**248**]

Skocpol, Theda. 1979. *States and Social Revolutions*. Cambridge: Cambridge University Press. [**14, 29, 31**]

Slaughter, Anne-Marie. 1997. The Real New World Order. *Foreign Affairs*, 76(5): 183–97. [**142**]

Smith, Adam. 1791. *An Inquiry into the Nature and Causes of the Wealth of Nations*. Harmondsworth: Penguin, 1970. [101, 106, 246]

Smith, Anthony D. 1971. *Theories of Nationalism*. London: Duckworth. [185]

Soltan, Karol. 1992. A Marriage of Gandhi and Madison. *Newsletter of the Committee on the Political Economy of the Good Society*, 2(1): 1–4. [135]

Sørensen, Eva and Jacob Torfing. 2007. Introduction. In Eva Sørensen and Jacob Torfing, eds., *Theories of Democratic Network Governance*. Basingstoke: Palgrave Macmillan, pp. 1–21. [148, 295]

Spruyt, Hendrik. 1994. *The Sovereign State and its Competitors*. Princeton, NJ: Princeton University Press. [1]

Starhawk. 1987. *Truth or Dare: Encounters with Power, Authority, and Mystery*. San Francisco: Harper and Row. [226]

Steger, Manfred B. 2005. *Globalism: Market Ideology Meets Terrorism*, 2nd edn. Lanham, MD: Rowman and Littlefield. [308, 315, 319, 322]

Steiner, Jürg, André Bächtiger, Markus Spörndli and Marco R. Steenbergen. 2004. *Deliberative Politics in Action: Analyzing Parliamentary Discourse*. Cambridge: Cambridge University Press. [221–2]

Stiglitz, Joseph. 2002. *Globalization and its Discontents*. New York: W.W. Norton. [319–21]

Stiglitz, Joseph. 2006. *Making Globalization Work: The Next Steps to Global Justice*. New York: W.W. Norton. [314–15, 317, 320–1]

Subrahmanyam, Gita. 2004. 'Schizophrenic Governance and Fostering Global Inequalities in the British Empire'. Paper presented at the Annual General Meeting of the American Political Science Association, Chicago, 2–5 September. [15]

Sunstein, Cass R. 1988. Beyond the Republican Revival. *Yale Law Journal*, 97: 1539–90. [214–15]

Sunstein, Cass R. 2007. *Republic.com 2.0*. Princeton, NJ: Princeton University Press. [273]

Susskind, Lawrence, ed. 1999. *The Consensus Building Handbook*. Thousand Oaks, CA: Sage. [222]

Taylor, Bob Pepperman. 1992. *Our Limits Transgressed*. Lawrence: University Press of Kansas. [244]

Taylor, Jonathan H. 2001. Sociological Theory Today. In Jonathan H. Taylor, ed., *Handbook of Sociological Theory*. New York: Springer. [329]

Taylor, Michael. 1982. *Community, Anarchy, and Liberty*. Cambridge: Cambridge University Press. [17]

Taylor, Rupert. 2006. The Belfast Agreement and the Politics of Consociationalism: A Critique. *Political Quarterly*, 77: 217–26. [194]

Tesh, Sylvia N. 1993. New Social Movements and New Ideas. Paper presented at the Annual Meeting of the American Political Science Association, Washington, DC, 2–5 September. [235]

Tiebout, Charles. 1956. A Pure Theory of Local Expenditures. *Journal of Political Economy*, 64: 416–24. [125–6]

Tilly, Charles. 1985. War Making and State Making as Organized Crime. In Peter Evans, Dietrich Rueschemeyer and Theda Skocpol, eds, *Bringing the State Back In*. Cambridge: Cambridge University Press, pp. 169–91. [9]

Torgerson, Douglas. 1995. The Uncertain Quest for Sustainability: Public Discourse and the Politics of Environmentalism. In Frank Fischer and Michael Black, eds, *Greening Environmental Policy: The Politics of a Sustainable Future.* Liverpool: Paul Chapman, pp. 3–20. [293]

Torgerson, Douglas. 1999. *The Promise of Green Politics: Environmentalism and the Public Sphere.* Durham, NC: Duke University Press. [265]

Trotsky, Leon. 1904. *Our Political Tasks.* available at: http://www.marxists.org/archive/trotsky/1904/tasks/index.htm. [84]

Truman, David B. 1951. *The Governmental Process.* New York: Knopf. [45, 51]

Uhr, John. 1998. *Deliberative Democracy in Australia.* Melbourne: Cambridge University Press. [220]

Valadez, Jorge M. 2001. *Deliberative Democracy, Political Legitimacy, and Self-Determination in Multicultural Societies.* Boulder, CO: Westview. [194]

van den Berg, Axel and Thomas Janoski. 2005. Conflict Theories in Political Sociology. In Thomas Janoski, Robert R. Alford, Alexander M. Hicks and Mildred A. Schwartz, eds, *The Handbook of Political Sociology.* Cambridge: Cambridge University Press, pp. 72–95. [132]

van Parijs, Philippe. 1995. *Real Freedom for All: What if Anything Can Justify Capitalism?* Oxford: Oxford University Press. [210–11]

Vanberg, Viktor J. and James M. Buchanan. 1996. Constitutional Choice, Rational Ignorance, and the Limits of Reason. In Karol Edward Soltan and Stephen L. Elkin, eds, *The Constitution of Good Societies.* University Park, PA: Pennsylvania State University Press, pp. 39–56. [124]

Walker, Connor. 1984. *The National Question in Marxist-Leninist Theory and Strategy.* Princeton: Princeton University Press. [187]

Wallerstein, Immanuel. 2005. After Developmentalism and Globalization, What? *Social Forces*, 83: 1263–78. [90–1]

Wallerstein. Immanuel 2003. *The Decline of American Power: The US in a Chaotic World.* New York: New Press [90–1]

Walzer, Michael. 1983. *Spheres of Justice: A Defense of Pluralism and Equality.* New York: Basic Books. [154]

Walzer, Michael. 1991. Constitutional Rights and the Shape of Civil Society. In Robert E. Calvert, ed., *The Constitution of the People: Reflections on Citizens and Civil Society.* Lawrence: University Press of Kansas, pp. 113–26. [151]

Walzer, Michael. 1994. Multiculturalism and Individualism. *Dissent*, 41: 185–91. [151–2, 281]

Walzer, Michael. 1999. Deliberation, and What Else? In Stephen Macedo, ed., *Deliberative Politics: Essays on Democracy and Disagreement.* New York: Oxford University Press, pp. 58–69. [217]

Wapner, Paul. 2003. World Summit on Sustainable Development: Toward a Post-Jo'burg Environmentalism. *Global Environmental Politics*, 3: 1–10. [252]

Weale, Albert. 1992. *The New Politics of Pollution.* Manchester: Manchester University Press. [248]

Weber, Max. 1905. *The Protestant Ethic and the Spirit of Capitalism.* London: Unwin, 1985. [242]

Weber, Max. 1994. *Political Writings*, eds Peter Lassman and Ronald Speirs. Cambridge: Cambridge University Press. [3, 63, 69]

Wennan, Mark. 2008. William E. Connolly: Pluralism without Transcendence. *British Journal of Politics and International Relations*, 10: 156–70. [131]

Wheen, Francis. 2001. *Karl Marx: A Life*. New York: Norton. [79, 86–7]

Wildavsky, Aaron. 1964. *The Politics of the Budgetary Process*. Boston: Little, Brown. [50–1]

Williams, Michael C. 2005. What is the National Interest? The Neoconservative Challenge in IR Theory. *European Journal of International Relations*, 11: 307–37. [252–3]

Wilson, Woodrow. 1887. The Science of Administration. *Political Science Quarterly*, 2: 197–222. [6, 42–3]

Wissenburg, Marcel. 1998. *Green Liberalism: The Free and the Green Society*. London: UCL Press. [261–2]

Wollstoncraft, Mary. 1792. *A Vindication of the Rights of Women*. [227, 239]

Young, Iris Marion. 1989. Polity and Group Difference: A Critique of the Ideal of Universal Citizenship. *Ethics*, 99: 250–74. [152, 239]

Young, Iris Marion. 1990. *Justice and the Politics of Difference*. Princeton, NJ: Princeton University Press. [152, 239]

Young, Iris Marion. 2000. I*nclusion and Democracy*. Oxford: Oxford University Press. [153, 235]

Zakaria, Fareed. 2003. *The Future of Freedom: Illiberal Democracy at Home and Abroad*. New York: W.W.Norton. [25]

Zerilli, Linda. 2006. Feminist Theory and the Canon of Political Thought. In John S. Dryzek, Anne Phillips and Bonnie Honig, eds, *The Oxford Handbook of Political Theory*. Oxford: Oxford University Press, pp. 106–24. [231–2}

Index

This Index contains all references for subjects, along with references to some major theoreticians and authors discussed in the text. For all other author references, please see the bibliography, where the end of each entry shows the pages where that author or work are cited, given in square brackets, e.g [**122, 156**].

Printed by Printforce, the Netherlands